P9-AQA-420

3 2044 049 134 869

GLASS CEILINGS
AND
ASIAN AMERICANS

CRITICAL PERSPECTIVES
ON ASIAN PACIFIC AMERICANS SERIES

Critical Perspectives on Asian Pacific Americans aims to educate and inform readers regarding the Asian Pacific American experience, and to critically examine key social, economic, psychological, cultural, and political issues. The series presents books that are theoretically engaging, comparative, and multidisciplinary, and works that reflect the contemporary concerns that are of critical importance to under-standing and empowering Asian Pacific Americans.

Series Titles Include:

Juanita Tamayo Lott   *Asian Americans: From Racial Category to Multiple Identities* (1997)

Diana Ting Liu Wu   *Asian Pacific Americans in the Workplace* (1997)

Jun Xing   *Asian America Through the Lens: History, Representations and Identity* (1998)

Pyong Gap Min and Rose Kim, editors

    Struggle for Ethnic Identity: Narratives by Asian American Professionals (1999)

Wendy Ho   *In Her Mother's House: The Politics of Asian American Mother Daughter Writing* (1999)

Deborah Woo   *Glass Ceilings and Asian Americans* (2000)

Submission Guidelines

Prospective authors of single or co-authored books and editors of anthologies should submit a letter of introduction, the manuscript or a four to ten page proposal, a book outline, and a curriculum vitae. Please send your book manuscript or proposal packet to:

Critical Perspectives on Asian Pacific Americans Series
AltaMira Press
1630 North Main Street, Suite 367
Walnut Creek, CA 94596

WITHDRAWN

Glass Ceilings and Asian Americans

The New Face of Workplace Barriers

•

DEBORAH WOO

AltaMira
PRESS

A Division of Rowman & Littlefield Publishers, Inc.

Walnut Creek • Lanham • New York • Oxford

BOP 3905 - 5/6

Copyright © 2000 by AltaMira Press
A Division of Rowman & Littlefield Publishers, Inc.

All rights reserved. No part of this book may be reproduced or utilized in any form or by any means, electronic or mechanical, including photocopying, recording, or by any information storage and retrieval system, without permission in writing from the publisher.

For information address:

AltaMira Press
A Division of Rowman & Littlefield Publishers, Inc.
1630 North Main Street, Suite 367
Walnut Creek, California 94596

www.altamirapress.com

Rowman & Littlefield Publishers, Inc.
12 Hid's Copse Road
Cumnor Hill
Oxford OX2 9JJ England

4720 Boston Way
Lanham, Maryland 20706

HD 8081 .A8 W66 2000
Woo, Deborah, 1951-
Glass ceilings and Asian
 Americans

RECEIVED

JUL 2 7 2001

Kennedy School Library

PRINTED IN THE UNITED STATES OF AMERICA

Library of Congress Cataloging-in-Publication Data

Woo, Deborah, 1951-
        Glass ceilings and Asian Americans: the new face of workplace barriers / by
Deborah Woo.
        p. cm. — (Critical perspectives on Asian Pacific Americans series; v. 5)
        Includes bibliographical references and index

        ISBN 0-7425-0334-8 (cloth).—ISBN 0-7425-0335-6 (pbk.).

        1. Asian American—Employment. 2. Discrimination in employment—U.S.
        I. Title. II. Series.
        HD8081.A8 W66   1999
        331.6'395'073—ddc21   99—6106

The paper used in this publication meets the minimum requirements of American National Standard for Information Sciences–Permanence of Paper for Printed Library Materials, ANSI/ NISO z39.48-1992

Production and Editorial Services: Kathy Paparchontis
Cover Design: Raymond Cogan

To Freida and Trish,

and in memory of Howard,

whose insights about the world

I've come to appreciate

CONTENTS

TABLES

ACKNOWLEDGMENTS

The realization of this book has been a long process, and I owe a debt of gratitude to many persons, some of whom are named below.

To Larry Shinigawa, who recruited me for this series and the task of turning my report for the Federal Glass Ceiling Commission into a book, and who persuaded Mitch Allen that this was a good idea. My thanks to all those lent support to that earlier endeavor: the Commission, Sarah Gotbaum, JD Hokoyama, Anny Huang, Susan Lee, Maxine Leeds Craig, David Minkus, Don Nakanishi, Erin Ninh, Paul Ong, David Oppenheimer, Jack Peng, Martha Ramirez, Rose Razaghian, Janice Tanigawa, Bette Woody, Robert Yamashita, and Judy Yung.

The new research undertaken for this book benefited from the assistance of students either at the University of California, Santa Cruz, or the University of California, Berkeley. Michael Truong and Chishan Lin helped jumpstart the interviews that would take place at XYZ Aerospace Technology. Chishan and Roya Razaghian also provided valuable library assistance when I most needed it.

I also want to express my appreciation to all those at XYZ who participated in the interviews. Although they along with the organization must remain nameless, the ideals they share are ones whose realization I hope this book helps to foster.

Several colleagues have indirectly influenced the direction of this book. Some of the research on Asian American faculty was prompted by Elaine Kim, who at an earlier time had suggested I write about the academic lawsuits discussed in chapter 4. Sumi Cho's work on these cases laid the important ground work for my own. Jean Jew, Rosalie Tung, and Marcy Wang permitted me to retrace with them a painful period in their lives to further elucidate issues raised by their lawsuits. Each also carefully reviewed those sections where their cases are discussed. Valerie Simmons, former Affirmative Action Director at the University of California Santa Cruz, could always be counted on as a trustworthy and dependable resource when I found myself bogged down in bureaucratic or legal particulars as I worked on issues of faculty recruitment and retention on campus.

My appreciation to Community Studies for supporting my teaching a course that enabled me to further explore some of the issues in the book, and to those students whose interest was such as to engage me in turn. Other associates and staff at the University of California Santa Cruz also deserve acknowledgment. This includes the Committee on Research and the Social Science Division, for being responsive to late-stage requests for funds to cover transcription and indexing, and Laurie Babka, Cheryl VanDeVeer, and Kimberly Register for facilitating this. Finally, I wish to acknowledge the longstanding support of the Institute for the Study of Social Change, University of California, Berkeley.

Bill Domhoff, Troy Duster, and Shirley Hune provided valuable commentary in their review of select chapters. At various points, the following helped by being responsive to a query, a request, or some need for strategic assistance: Deborah Carter, Sucheng Chan, Kenyon Chan, Harriet Chiang, Gordon Chang, Phil Chang, Sherwood Chang, Melissa Chiu, Diane T. Chin, Henry Der, Ron Edwards, Hardy Frye, Donna Gregory, Thelton Henderson, Allen Kanner, Jerry Karabel, Gillian Khoo, Mimi Kuo, Anna Leong, Lisha Liang, Krista Luker, David Minkus, Herbert Northrup, Paul Ong, Hsinya Shen, Jere Takahashi, Ron Takaki, Janice Tanigawa, My Huynh, Ling-chi Wang, David Wellman, Sao-ling-Wong, Robert Yamashita, and Judy Yung. Bette Woody's collegial support and professional interest in the topic made her an especially helpful resource.

Members of the AltaMira staff—Jennifer Collier, Kathy Paparchrontis, and Pattie Rechtman—were each thorough and conscientious, and their teamwork made it possible to recoup from inevitable as well as unexpected problems during the production stage. Special thanks to Jennifer, for enormously helpful assistance throughout, from her chapter-by-chapter commentaries in the initial reshaping of the manuscript to the more tedious task of proofing at later stages. To Kathy, for her superb copyediting job and later assistance with indexing. To Pattie, who brought her own professionalism to the team, as she took over the final set of page proofs and subjected it to her own meticulous attention to detail. Her aloha spirit and tireless efforts have made the book a better one. My thanks to Mitch Allen, who has waited patiently throughout these improvements.

Finally, thanks to Allen Kanner, Randy Serrurier, Norrie Evans, John Maski and family, Philip Chang, Alison Nagahisa, and four-year old Sammy for reminding me that there are other important things in life besides the completion of this manuscript.

September 1999

INTRODUCTION

THE SIGNIFICANCE
OF GLASS CEILING ISSUES

New York City, symbolized in the popular imagination by the Statue of Liberty, has been a major port of entry to a diverse immigrant population and long the most populous city in the United States. In 1996 many immigrants still intended it as their place of residence.[1] In 1990, more than one of every four persons in New York City had been born outside the United States (U.S. Bureau of the Census July 1993). Other major metropolitan areas, nevertheless, have surpassed New York City with their own sizeable foreign-born populations. Among the top five, Miami, Florida, ranks number one, with three out of five (60%) of its residents foreign born. The four remaining cities with large immigrant populations are in California: Santa Ana (51%), Los Angeles (38.4%), San Francisco (34%), and Anaheim (28.4%) (Gaquin and Littman 1998:lxxxvii).

Racial or ethnic diversity is not a new phenomenon, having its beginning long before the founding of this nation, when diverse indigenous tribes inhabited the North American continent. The Algonquians, for example, who along with the Iroquois resided in the New York Bay area, comprised several hundred tribes, speaking fifty languages. Frenchman Jean de Crèvecoeur settled on a farm in what would become the state of New York, and observed the medley of European nationalities immigrating at the time—the English, Scottish, Irish, French, Dutch, German, and Swedish. His essays and news articles were recognized for their remarkable details of early colonial life, and his forecast for the future was optimistic: "Here individuals of all nations are melted into a new race of men, whose labors and posterity will one day cause great changes in the world" (Spindler and Spindler 1990:42–44). Slaves from West Africa were also a major presence, not only in the southern plantation economy but also in New York and other northern and mid-Atlantic colonies. Their integration into American society would be more problematic, even though they are more likely than all other groups, including *whites*, to be U.S.-born and to have English as their primary language (see tables I.1 and I.2).

As one of the most racially diverse states, and the state with the largest foreign-born population, California presently surpasses New York in diversity and has the daunting task of "assimilating" an immigrant population that is linguistically and culturally unlike any that the United States has ever seen.[2] Specifically, California is home to the largest number of Asian Americans in the country and has been predicted to be so at least until the year 2020 ("Growing Into" 19 January 1997). As the second largest minority population in the

Table I.1. Year of Immigration to the United States by Race/Ethnicity (California).

Race/ Ethnicity	US- born	1987- 1990	1985- 1986	1982- 1984	1980- 1981	1975- 1979	1970- 1974	1965- 1969	1960- 1964	1950- 1959	Before 1950
Chinese	30.2	12.1	7.2	10.0	9.5	12.7	6.3	4.6	2.6	2.2	2.6
Taiwanese	16.3	17.9	11.9	21.4	8.0	14.9	5.2	3.4	0.6	0.6	-
Filipino	30.4	10.7	8.0	9.4	7.5	12.2	10.1	5.8	2.0	2.3	1.7
Japanese	67.5	8.9	2.3	2.0	1.3	2.8	3.0	2.8	3.3	4.6	1.5
Korean	18.6	14.4	8.4	12.9	11.6	17.5	11.3	2.6	1.4	0.8	0.1
Vietnamese	16.8	13.6	6.9	12.9	20.2	26.8	1.9	0.6	0.1	0.1	0.1
Cambodian	22.1	8.5	16.5	21.0	22.1	8.6	1.0	0.1	0.1	-	-
Laotian	24.5	16.5	9.4	9.8	29.1	8.1	0.8	0.2	0.5	0.3	0.1
Hmong	34.6	20.1	6.0	4.9	20.8	13.6	0.1	-	-	-	-
Thai	24.3	11.2	4.6	8.6	7.5	16.0	19.4	8.0	0.5	-	-
Indian	22.1	14.8	11.2	10.8	9.3	14.1	10.7	4.6	1.7	0.5	0.2
Other Asian	37.3	12.8	7.9	8.0	7.8	8.8	5.0	2.7	6.0	3.2	0.5
White	86.4	2.2	1.1	1.1	1.1	1.9	1.3	1.0	1.1	1.4	1.4
Black	94.4	1.0	0.5	0.7	0.8	0.8	0.7	0.5	0.3	0.2	0.1

Source: *Pacific Rim States Asian Demographic Databook* (Oliver et al. 1995:4–10), from 1990 Census (Public Use Microdata).

state, following Chicano/Latinos, the Asian population is highly differentiated in terms of time of arrival to the United States and the relative numbers of those who are foreign born or native (U.S.) born. In 1990, for example, 67.5 percent of Japanese were native-born citizens as opposed to 16.3 percent of Taiwanese (see table I.1).

In 1988, Daniel Rosenheim, city editor of the *San Francisco Chronicle*, observed that the Asian American population, typically associated twenty-five years ago with "nineteen square blocks of San Francisco Chinatown," had long spilled beyond these borders, encompassing immigrants from "sixteen separate nations." Characterizing San Francisco as "the largest single Asian-descended population in the world outside of Asia," Rosenheim labeled this special *Chronicle* report as "the first, comprehensive look at North America's first full-fledged Pacific metropolis" ("Asian Growth" 5 December 1988).[3] By 1994, Asians made up an estimated 29 percent of San Francisco's population, and across the bay in Oakland, about 15 percent of that city's population (U.S. Department of Labor, Bureau of the Census 1997:46–47).

This ethnic diversity is made further complex by language diversity. According to a recent survey, eighty-one languages and dialects are spoken in Sunnyvale, a city of about 128,000 people and one of the few cities in Silicon Valley that has established a municipal "language bank" staffed by volunteer translators ("Labor of Language" 15 July 1998). Among Asians, the ability to speak English varies, with 50 percent of Indians (from the Indian subcontinent) claiming this as their primary language, as compared with 8.6 percent of Taiwanese-born immigrants (see table I.2).

As increasing numbers of Asians have streamed into the United States, their adjustment has been perceived as an affirmation of the ongoing viability of the American Dream—the

Table I.2. Ability to Speak English by Race/Ethnicity (California).

Race/ Ethnicity	As Primary Language	Very Well	Well	Not Well	Not at all
Chinese	20.6	29.8	24.3	18.0	7.3
Taiwanese	8.6	34.8	37.0	14.6	5.1
Filipino	43.5	18.0	4.7	0.4	0.4
Japanese	18.9	13.5	9.4	1.3	1.3
Korean	29.4	23.8	22.4	6.0	6.0
Vietnamese	28.5	33.3	21.3	5.4	5.4
Cambodian	21.2	23.4	28.1	10.7	10.7
Laotian	18.3	26.9	27.3	10.2	10.2
Hmong	18.2	22.0	25.7	14.3	14.3
Thai	34.2	31.8	10.5	1.6	1.6
Indian	50.1	15.1	7.3	2.6	2.6
Other Asian	32.8	15.8	8.1	1.4	1.4
White	82.5	9.6	3.6	2.9	1.4
Black	94.4	4.7	1.1	0.8	0.2

Source: *Pacific Rim States Asian Demographic Databook* (Oliver et al. 1995:4–16), from 1990 Census (Public Use Microdata).

notion that anyone who works hard can be successful. The Horatio Alger genre of success stories first appeared in the nineteenth century and fueled imaginations for several generations. However, during the Great Depression of the 1930s the magnitude of social distress weakened the belief that individual inadequacies, a lack of effort or character, were the primary causes of poverty. This shift in thinking led to the creation of social policies and safety nets consistent with this understanding (Quadagno 1994). Corporate downsizing and its accompanying social dislocation of hundreds of thousands of workers have similarly created fertile soil for more structural explanations of the increasing social inequalities that mark the present (Bluestone and Harrison 1982; *New York Times* 1996). Within this milieu, Asian Americans have surfaced as the new Horatio Algers, thereby reopening the door to *cultural* explanations of racist inequality, while other immigrants, such as Latinos in California and Texas, have been scapegoated for social problems and met with the argument that they "deserve" to be at the bottom of the social and economic order.[4]

Although race and ethnicity are very much a part of our consciousness, a major thesis of this book is that the majority of glass ceiling barriers involve subtle biases, sometimes imperceptible or ineffable, quietly or unconsciously reproduced. Some are embedded into the routines or practices of institutions, others reflected in attitudinal orientations, which over time chisel racially contoured outcomes into the workplace experience, even when there is no discriminatory *intent*. Although forms of prejudice or racial animosity still exist, the threshold of societal tolerance for *explicitly* articulated racial or ethnic discrimination is low, with exposure bringing shame and rather relatively swift punishment.

In 1994, six Texaco employees brought a discrimination suit against their employer on behalf of themselves and at least 1,500 other African American employees (*Roberts v.*

Texaco, Inc.). Settled in March 1997 for $176.1 million, the case represented the largest settlement of a racial discrimination suit in U.S. history to date. It also represents an exceptional case of disclosure, where the racial biases of senior executives had been secretly caught on tape. For any journalist, researcher, or other outsider attempting to uncover and disclose such discriminatory behavior, the generally "locked-door" nature of "closed-door" discrimination inhibits such detective work.[5]

It was such backstage discrimination in the workplace that prompted the first efforts at affirmative action.[6] Yet while tape recorders, hidden cameras, e-mail monitoring, and wiretaps might be the only way to document certain discrimination, and even if their use did not violate other civil rights, only the most blatant of biases would be captured.

For one, biases may inhere not in persons but in institutional practices. One notable example comes from a page in the history of college admissions. As Jews began to enter the nation's universities and colleges in significant numbers at the turn of century, admissions criteria were adjusted to weed out this "undesirable" element. From the 1920s to the 1940s, bureaucratic measures were set in place with the explicit intent to discriminate, and were justified on rational or meritocratic grounds.[7] Institutional biases may produce artificial barriers even when the intent to discriminate is problematic. Thus, Rosener (1995:26–44) explained how American corporations following the idea of the "one best model" have largely organized themselves along the lines of a top-down, "command-and-control model." This implicit gender bias leaves little room for the "interactive leadership model" that women tend to prefer. For such reasons, although affirmative action was originally concerned exclusively with *racial* desegregation, it eventually expanded to encompass gender bias.[8]

Second, though the absence of minorities and women from senior-level management positions is based on individual performance evaluations, there is frequently a level of subjectivity to these assessments that is simply unavailable for review. Furthermore, to ascertain whether discrimination has occurred, one would need to have access to the personnel files of comparable candidates. In the world of academic employment, only recently have individual faculty gained the right to read redacted versions of personnel files. This privilege resulted from a U.S. Supreme Court decision in 1990 (Leap 1993:151–56). Although this decision partially removed certain barriers to disclosure, the tenure review process continues to allow subjective judgment, and thus biases, to play an important role. As attorney Dale Minami (1990:84) notes, adversaries of women and minorities will "simply document their biased opinions better."

Even where gender discrimination has been found (e.g., Chevron Corporation, State Farm, and Home Depot), the prescriptions for change are not clearly defined. As with suits alleging racial discrimination (e.g., Texaco, Denny's, and Freddie Mac), judges have fined corporations and told them to "do something" about the problem so that it will not occur again in the future.[9] But, according to one attorney who attended a meeting on corporate responsibility at the Institute for the Study of Social Change at the University of California, Berkeley, the issue often boils down to deciding which of the adversarial lawyers the judges are going to believe:

> This is heretical what I'm saying, so don't quote me [the individual] but judges "don't know what to do, whereas practitioners have had their own agenda [focused on defending or prosecuting]." Although Title VII was instituted in 1964, it is still

elusive or ill-defined in terms of the information that a judge has available as a guide for making decisions consistent with the statute. (2 April 1997)

Consent-decree fixes have been largely open-ended, leaving it up to corporations to figure out how to correct the problem. Corporations, in turn, have hired diversity consultants. Consulting firms, including some of the nation's leading human resources specialists, have capitalized on this void in knowledge and research. Though consulting strategies and programs run the full gamut, few closely examine how written or unstated institutional practices systematically create or sustain bias. According to a *Wall Street Journal* article by Douglas A. Blackmon (11 March 1997), the solutions proffered by one major consulting firm were formulaic, falling far short of its promise to customize or individually tailor programs for its clients. Founded in 1934, Towers Perrin, with 6,000 professionals worldwide and serving about sixty companies in recent years, has been among the world's largest consulting firms. Its credo ("prescription without diagnosis is malpractice") was echoed in a thirty-five-page proposal, which stated: "No two organizations are identical. . . . They are all as diverse as their workforces and the markets they serve . . . no textbook solutions exist." Recommendations to companies, however, are extremely broad and generic—according to Blackmon, "cookie-cutter advice."[10]

Companies that have retained diversity consultants to ward off lawsuits may create a climate more responsive to diversity. In some cases, a change in corporate culture as a result of affirmative action has made these themselves obsolete. State Farm, for example, was found to be discriminatory in how it lagged the promotion of women as insurance agents and as a result was forced to hire more women. Women have since proven themselves better than men at selling insurance. In short, once the doors were open and women were allowed to prove themselves, the company was motivated to let go of some of its previous biases or prejudices.

Third and finally, our ability to see inequities is masked not simply by hidden biases or deeply embedded assumptions, but also by the explicit assumption of "a level playing field." Because of their high levels of educational and occupational achievement, Asian Americans appear to affirm that assumption. In the workplace, however, we hear a different story.

As one of a series of civil rights legislative acts intended to promote the integration of previously excluded groups into the workforce, the Glass Ceiling Act of 1991 is quintessentially concerned with biases that are systemic—whether attitudinal or organizational—and that bear upon movement into management. Affirmative action initiatives first appeared in the workplace after a long history had shown that the mere prohibition of discrimination, that is, protecting *individuals* against discrimination, was ineffective in significantly altering patterns of exclusion.[11] Despite these developments, and despite affirmative action, minority and female populations remained the most vulnerable persons in the workforce, the last hired and first fired (U.S. Commission on Civil Rights 1977), with higher rates of unemployment; and when employed, occupied lower status jobs with lower pay. Needless to say, their move into the executive suites would be exceedingly slow. This continues to be true even though organizational performance and profitability has been increasingly linked with the ability of employers to fully utilize their human resources (Ouchi 1981; Pacale 1981; Peters and Waterman 1982; Loden and Rosener

1991; Carnevale and Stone 1995; Federal Glass Ceiling Commission 1995; Smith 1995; Catalyst 1999).

Although the Glass Ceiling Act was intended to address the imbalances in the work force, when the term "glass ceiling" was coined in 1986, it applied to white female professionals in a largely male world. Less well known is the fact that slightly more than a decade earlier there was already evidence that Asian Americans had hit such a ceiling.

AN EARLY LOOK AT THE GLASS CEILING: ASIAN AMERICAN WOMEN

My interest in glass ceiling issues goes back to an article I wrote in 1985, "The Socioeconomic Status of Asian American Women in the Labor Force: An Alternative View" (Woo 1985). This interest was piqued by an analysis indicating these women had an "earnings advantage" over white women due to their "superior educational qualifications." Closer inspection, however, revealed they did not even necessarily receive jobs *commensurate* with their education, with some occupying positions far below what one might expect given their educational qualifications. In 1970, a third of native-born Chinese women with four or more years of college were in clerical work. And in 1976, Chinese American women had the dubious distinction of being more likely than any other group of women to be in occupations typically requiring less education than they possessed.

In executive, administrative, and managerial jobs, women in general were underrepresented relative to Anglo men in both 1970 and 1980. For foreign-born Asian women, executive-managerial status meant work primarily as auditors or accountants. Management for Asian Americans in general also meant being owners and managers of small business establishments, a pattern one could interpret as *downward*, not upward, mobility, an indirect indication of their dissatisfaction with or inability to find remunerative mainstream jobs in the field of their expertise or training.

The gender gap was apparent in professional specialties. All women were poorly represented in the most prestigious jobs—as physicians, judges, and lawyers. For Asian American women, education served less as an opportunity for mobility than as a hedge against jobs as service workers, machine operatives, or assembly workers. Occupational segregation affected Asian Americans more than any other group, and Asian American women were the most occupationally segregated of all groups, male and female. According to Catalyst (1999), Asian American women are more likely than other women of color to have a graduate education and yet are the least likely to be at the most senior levels of management (1–3 reporting levels below CEO).

In short, what these different profiles indicate is that educational data taken out of context are often misleading and that cautionary statements should precede any inferential leaps from these data. Although I did not use the term glass ceiling, or attempt to explore "artificial" barriers as such, the recurring patterns of lower returns to education presented a Rorschach which looked very much like a glass ceiling.[12]

Identifying artificial barriers was the central and explicit task of the Federal Glass Ceiling Commission, which contacted me almost a decade later to see what evidence existed for a glass ceiling (Woo 1994). A recurring pattern was of Asian Americans (data mostly on scientists and engineers) being simultaneously overrepresented as professionals and underrepresented as managers. This pattern reflected not simply occupational concentration but clear instances of stagnation. Employment sectors as diverse as industry, government, and academe all exhibited this pattern. The Commission itself found that Asian/Pacific Islander Americans held "less than one-hundredth of one percent of all corporate directorships" (1995:102). Because there have been few *organizational* studies of Asian Americans, I decided to pursue this as a topic of research.

THE PRESENT STUDY

The study site is a highly prestigious government research organization, a diverse workplace employing a large number of scientists and engineers. (To maintain the organization's anonymity, I will refer to it as "XYZ Aerospace.") The director of this organization launched a centerwide study in the early 1970s to prove that the image of Asian Americans as "model minorities" extended to this particular industry. Ironically, systematic compilation of statistical data would document a glass ceiling. Yet, despite documentation, it took many years and a great deal of external pressure before upper management publicly acknowledged a problem, and then only slowly introduced corrective measures.

My own exploration of these issues included reviewing statistical data as well as interviewing Asian American employees and others who had been active in or concerned about monitoring glass ceiling issues. The qualitative data added significant insights into the institutional patterns etched by quantitative data.

Prior to the publication of this book, I presented some of the interview findings to a group of students at the University of California, Berkeley. I had only begun to discuss how corporate cultural values for promotion typically reflected a set of "white male values" when a white male in the audience interrupted and asked rather defensively: "Doesn't a corporation have a right to decide what attitudes or behaviors it wants to reward?" I responded by saying that corporations do have a certain autonomy and control, but they also have goals, which may be thwarted by failure to critically reexamine their own practices. I then referred to a point in the agency's history when the selection of particular white male administrators strongly correlated with organizational crises in functioning and efficiency but which is most likely to be remembered as problems due to the individuals selected rather than to gender and racial bias in the selection procedures themselves.

The insights gained by understanding the influence of culture (corporate, in this case) on individual behavior are often counter-intuitive in American society, which is inclined towards individualistic interpretations. However, there are unique analytic insights that come from *starting at the aggregate level of analysis*. At the top of an organization, circles of acquaintances and friendship easily overlap along racial and gendered lines. Cadres of white males think of themselves as having achieved their positions through normal, meritocratic, and individual achievements. They can not "experience" white-male-corporate-culture any more than they experience the air that they breathe. It is as normal to them as water to fish. These social networks are often racially homogeneous — a social reality of which minority (and women) employees are keenly aware. As organizational subcultures, they are unavailable for review in company organizational charts and thus less evident than the institutional structures that undergird them. Indeed, they are only partially visible to those involved and yet consequential for paving and smoothing the way to promotions.

Presently there are few organizational studies about Asian Americans and the glass ceiling, and if this case study generates more, an appreciation may develop for the different conditions under which a glass ceiling might occur, and for solutions that may be highly variable: "What is best for one organization is not necessarily best for another, even when they are in the same industry. Rarely are two organizations the same" (Rosener 1995:28). Moreover, as Cox and Finley (1995:84) observed from their own research, "the effects of group identity are organization specific and cannot necessarily be generalized across organizations."

ORGANIZATION OF THE BOOK

Chapter 1 examines how the model minority framework diverts attention from the social context of institutional cultures and how this deflection persists because of a number of factors that cloud our vision. Chapter 2 examines the state of research on the glass ceiling and Asian Americans. Beginning with an overview of The Federal Glass Ceiling Commission's research, I then turn to highlighting key conceptual and methodological considerations that have impeded such research among Asian Americans. This chapter concludes with a discussion of internal structural barriers, especially where research has suggested their relevance to Asian Americans. Chapter 3 offers a historical overview of Asians in the United States labor market and early forms of occupational stratification or segmentation, including barriers in the form of a glass ceiling. The chapter also looks at how early Asian immigrants, second-generation Asian Americans, and recent professionals have experienced different artificial barriers to their mobility: the first as a result of laws and ordinances which took advantage of their alien status; the second because of more subtle forms of discrimination at the level of hire; and the third because of alleged language barriers that affect their move into management.

Chapter 4 takes a more critical look at the higher education profile of Asian Americans, focusing on the upper levels of degree attainment and the role that subjective, nonacademic considerations have played in creating a ceiling for not only students but faculty as well. Chapter 5 examines how glass ceiling barriers look from the point of view of Asian American scientists and engineers employed at a federal agency involved in aerospace research. Chapter 6 offers further discussion of these data within a broader context that takes up the following issues: (1) neutral standards and the appearance of a level playing field, (2) "artificial" and "real" barriers, (3) corporate cultural change and the progressive and problematic considerations associated with "diversity management," (3) the global context and new executive core requirements, (4) middleman minority theory, and (5) specific recommendations that might be undertaken by the aerospace center.

NOTES

1. In 1996, of 915,000 total immigrants to the U.S., 133,168 cited New York City as their residence (U.S. Immigration and Naturalization Service 1997:66).

2. In 1990, 69% of California's population was white. Only two other states had a smaller percentage of whites—Hawai'i (33.4%) and Louisiana (67.3%) (Gaquin and Littman

1998:5). In 1997, five states had a larger percentage of foreign-born than that of the entire U.S., of whose total population 9.7 % (or 25.8 million) were foreign born: California (24.8%), New York (19.6%), Florida (16.4%), New Jersey (15.4%), and Texas (11.3%) (U.S. Census Bureau March 1998).

3. Just prior to this report, staff writers at this news agency were commended for another series of articles on Asian Americans ("Special Report" 25–26 July 1988), noted to be "a significant departure for mainstream journalism" in its move away from sensational topics toward more in-depth coverage of a broader scope of issues affecting highly diverse Asian American communities ("The Mainstream" 4 August 1988).

4. In the 1994 gubernatorial race in California, the campaign of Republican candidate Pete Wilson was reinvigorated and ultimately successful because of the strong anti-Latino sentiment generated by Proposition 187, an initiative aimed at restricting the access of illegal immigrants to a range of social services. An analysis of the campaign rhetoric in the literature and electronic media advertising reveals a pattern of innuendo about the burden of supporting a "certain kind of illegal immigrant" with different values. During the same 1994 period, the *New York Times* published figures indicating that illegal immigration from Europe, most especially Irish and Italian, was the major source of "the problem of illegal immigration." At no point did the Wilson campaign raise this issue.

5. A Texaco executive, as part of meeting minutes, had tape recorded racial slurs and insults made by Texaco's executives. After he lost his job because of staff cutbacks, he turned over the tapes to plaintiffs in the civil rights suit.

6. When President Lyndon B. Johnson signed Executive Order 11246 in 1965, it became a government-mandated policy that firms, universities, and all other organizations holding government contracts review their workforce composition to ensure that it reasonably drew upon the available pool of qualified minorities. Because documenting discrimination was beyond the reach of employees, greater accountability was imposed on management. Affirmative action programs of the late 1960s and early 1970s thus made their first appearance in the *workplace,* not in higher education.

7. We can trace many familiar admissions procedures to this period: College Board examinations, psychological or aptitude tests, emphasis on geographical diverse student population, the allocation of scholarships and financial aid, alumni preference, photographs, questionnaires, and personal interviews (Weschler 1977; Synnott 1979; Oren 1985; Levine 1986).

8. Not until the passage of Title IX did Affirmative Action legislation include gender. Moreover, to the extent that Affirmative Action was designed to promote greater racial equality, such policies were aimed at improving the condition of *black Americans.* The inclusion of Hispanic Americans, Native Americans, and Asian Americans, especially those from Southeast Asia, resulted from expanding the category. Affirmative Action has assumed different forms, moreover, ranging from "unspecific" outreach efforts and broader advertising of available positions to more "specific" forms of Affirmative Action, requiring greater accountability and definite goals and timetables (Ezorsky 1991:33–38). See also Barbara Reskin (1998:20–21).

9. See *Butler et al. v. Home Depot, Inc.,* No. C-94-4335 SI, C-95-2182 SI, UNITED STATES DISTRICT COURT FOR THE NORTHERN DISTRICT OF CALIFORNIA, 1997 U.S. Dist. LEXIS 16296, August 28, 1997, Decided, August 29, 1997, Filed; *Morgan v. Federal Home Loan Mortgage Corporation,* No. 1:98CV01397 (PPJ), UNITED STATES

DISTRICT COURT FOR THE DISTRICT OF COLUMBIA; *Dyson et al. v. Denny's, Inc.*, DKC93-1503, UNITED STATES DISTRICT COURT FOR THE DISTRICT OF MARYLAND; *United States v. Flagstar Corporation and Denny's, Inc.*, C9320202JW, C93-20208JW, UNITED STATES DISTRICT COURT FOR THE NORTHERN DISTRICT OF CALIFORNIA; *Vandell v. Chevron*, No,. 945302 SAN FRANCISCO SUPERIOR COURT; *Kraszewski v. State Farm Gen. Ins. Co.*, No. C 79-1261 THE UNITED STATES DISTRICT COURT FOR THE NORTHERN DISTRICT OF CALIFORNIA, 1985 U.S. Dist. LEXIS 20297; 38 Fair Empl. Prac. Cas. (BNA) 197; 36 Empl. Prac. Dec. (CCH) P35,219, April 29, 1985, Decided, Filed and Entered

10. Towers Perrin essentially worked off of a template of 54 basic strategies and tactics, the only difference being the company names. Of the ten diversity clients that Towers Perrin served, nine indicated they did not retain the firm to create an employee training program. One declined to comment. This is not to deny that companies may share general problems. Perhaps similar recommendations reflect that these firms are at the same stage in dealing with diversity issues. As *Wall Street Journal* writer Blackmon noted,

> In some situations, standard solutions provided by consultants have become widely accepted as appropriate and even necessary. In the highly technical world of actuarial, benefits and compensation services, for example, where Towers Perrin built its expertise and reputation, consultants routinely use multicompany survey research to develop pay and pension systems that are then sold repeatedly. Similarly, law firms sometimes provide virtually identical memos to different clients facing similar problems, without disclosing that the work has been recycled. (1997:3–4)

11. Affirmative action initiatives were distinct from previous institutional remedies in recognizing inequality as a "problem of group status, not individual attainment" (Praeger 1982:193). The controversy that has swirled around affirmative action in the 1990s has philosophical roots that go back much earlier in American history. Thus, sociologist Jeffrey Praeger went on to comment that the controversy surrounding the introduction of affirmative action during the 1970s struck a chord which was no means new but part of a larger refrain in which individual liberty and social equality are not always in harmony.

12. I say "very much" (instead of "definitively") because although there was cumulative evidence of inequalities that eventually led to my subtitling the article "An Alternate View," artificial barriers themselves were not apparent.

CHAPTER 1

Inventing and Reinventing "Model Minorities"

> With but a few changes in detail, the same fable can be—and has been—told about the Japanese, Irish, Jews, Italians, Greeks, Swedes and many more. Its form is always the same: a people beset by hardships and oppression in their own country bravely cross the seas to America, a land which promises freedom and opportunity. Once arrived, however, they encounter prejudice, oppression, and difficult times. However, they never lose faith in the dream that originally compelled them. They work hard, refuse to be discouraged by the abuses that harm their lives and hinder their progress, and eventually—usually in the second, or sometime the third generation—succeed. History is, thus, nicely encapsulated within the American Protestant ethic.
>
> Stanford Lyman, in *Review of* The Story of the Chinese in America

Sociologist Stanford Lyman thus indicated how success stories about the Chinese in America were part of "America's perpetual morality tale about its minorities." This imagery has not only been extended to other Asian Americans but also cultivated through reference to statistical data.

During the 1970s, when the Asian American population was composed largely of Japanese Americans and Chinese Americans, gross statistical profiles of these groups pointed to their high educational and occupational achievement (Varon 1967). Conversely, one found relatively low divorce rates (Sanborn 1977; Barringer, Gardner, and Levin 1995:136–44), unemployment (Jaco and Wilber 1975), crime and delinquency (Beach 1932; Strong 1934; Kitano 1969; Takagi and Platt 1978), and mental illness (Jew and Brody 1967).[1] As the fastest growing minority group in the United States (O'Hare and Felt 1991; Gardner et al. 1985; U.S. Census Bureau 1993), Asian Americans are the most highly educated of all groups, including white males, and are projected to make up a disproportionate share of the professional workforce in the next decade (Ong and Hee 1993b; Fullerton 1989).[2] A book about occupational barriers facing Asian Americans thereby flies in the face of a general perception of successful assimilation.

Supporting facts for the morality tale are often based on census data, and media accounts keep the myth alive by aligning these statistics with culturally appealing explanations. Educational achievement and stable family relations are cited among the most influential factors promoting upward mobility, even though educational success may itself depend on other factors, such as social class, background, and the material resources available to pursue an education. Underlying it all is a theme of hard work and determination reminiscent of stories told by Horatio Alger (1832–1899), a Harvard-educated ordained minister who celebrated stories about penniless boys who pulled themselves up by their own "bootstraps." In this tradition, Asian Horatio Algers take the form of the aspiring immigrant who makes good. Yet, these alleged bootstrappers do not always have such humble beginnings, though their stories may appear to fit into this genre.

This chapter discusses how the *cultural* assumptions underlying the model minority thesis ignore certain *structural* or *class* issues. In doing so, it calls into question a fundamental premise of model minority logic—that cultural factors are the primary ingredients for success. Apart from Horatio Alger's legacy, a culturalist approach to understanding social issues has enjoyed great favor in the United States, whereas a long history of class analysis has dominated European thought on social stratification.[3] The controversy between cultural and structural analyses came to a head in the United States during the unrest and agitation of the 1960s, with the emergence of the idea of a "culture of poverty." American leftists saw this idea as "victim-blaming," as the social problems of American blacks were attributed to a "culture of poverty," an "unstable family structure," and way of life that promoted failure or low achievement (Moynihan 1965; Valentine 1968). By the same logic, discriminatory actions on the part of employers and a host of institutions could be dismissed as causes of continuing racial segregation and its consequences for employment (Massey and Denton 1993; Wilson 1997).

As a result, cultural explanations generally became politically suspect among that generation of scholars and activists, particularly as empirical evidence contradicted the tenability of the melting pot ideal and its culturally based mobility assumptions (Glazer and Moynihan 1963; Steinberg 1982). Cultural explanations, however, continued to resurface through a discourse that premised achievement on a cultural repertoire of enabling values associated with Asian Americans.

By the 1980s and 1990s, Asian Americans found themselves in the middle of the debate around affirmative action (Wang 1996). With the publication of *The Bell Curve* in 1994, a genetic twist emerged, with social inequalities reduced to allegedly "natural" differences in inherited intelligence between the races. The inferior economic or educational status of blacks relative to whites and Asians was reframed as one of basic intelligence and, by implication, a problem that government intervention could not remedy (Herrnstein and Murray 1994).

For these reasons, where social inequality intersects with race and ethnicity, Asian Americans occupy a critical place in our thinking about ethnic politics. They are not only a common empirical reference point for evaluating relative progress and achievement among different groups but an ideological one as well. Critics of the ideological agenda have disputed the statistical data, along with the cultural (or genetic) theory purporting to explain the disparities (Jacoby and Glauberman 1995). The concept of "model minority" is itself simplistic, masking extreme inequalities within and between different Asian American groups, as well as deflecting attention from structural issues that might better account for success or failure.[4] Although such critiques have caused a retreat from uncritical use of the term in public discourse, in the larger public arena the image of a successfully assimilating minority continues to be seductive, forming an inescapable backdrop for an array of issues that draw Asian Americans into broader social and political analyses of American society.

The basic argument in this chapter is that model minority theory has withstood counterevidence and counterarguments primarily because subsequent versions of the thesis have been stretched to subsume critical research findings under the core thesis of success (Osajima 1988). In this way, simplistic portrayals became slightly more complex in the 1980s, though the fundamental thesis remained largely unchanged. This chapter reviews some of the major critiques of the thesis and introduces other analyses that deserve attention, thereby explaining how the thesis has survived into the 1990s.

ASIAN AMERICANS AS "MODEL MINORITIES": A LEGACY OF THE 1960S

Until the late 1960s, the Asian population in the United States was a fraction of what it is in the late 1990s, and largely invisible. National immigration quotas introduced in the 1920s had sharply curtailed Asian immigration, reducing it to a trickle. The maximum annual immigration permitted from Asia was 2,990, compared with a total allowance of 149,667 for Europe (Chan 1991a:146). After the abolishment of these quotas in 1965, a surge in immigration brought an increase in the foreign-born and professional population, fundamentally transforming the social composition of Asian American communities (Hing 1993c). The experiences of native-born Chinese and Japanese Americans, the majority of the Asian American population prior to 1965, however, was the original stimulus for media success stories.

There is no question that the United States has absorbed immigrants who have differences in history, religion, race, class, and national origin (Levine 1996). The acculturation of subsequent generations and increasing rates of outmarriage partly occur as a matter of time and increasing social contact, with relations of power setting the terms of that contact. Yet, the persistence of racial inequalities has served as an ongoing challenge to faith in the inevitability of assimilation as well as a catalyst to change.[5]

During the 1960s, the need to reexamine and address issues of racial inequality was pronounced. Racial unrest was one of several sources of societal discontent, which together with the war in Vietnam, led to demands for government reforms not equaled since the Great Depression of the 1930s. Over and against such moves toward fundamental institutional change were competing attempts to recast the causes of social inequality in terms of individual effort and hard work.

Thus, for example, on 26 December 1966, *U.S. News and World Report* printed an article titled "Success Story of One Minority in the United States," which suggested that blacks and other minorities were making unreasonable demands for government assistance. "At a time when it is being proposed that hundreds of billions of dollars be spent to uplift Negroes and other minorities, the nation's 300,000 Chinese-Americans are moving ahead on their own, with no help from anyone else" (p. 73). Earlier in the year, the *New York Times* had published "Success Story, Japanese American Style," emphasizing that self-help was implicitly, if not explicitly, a point of admiration. "By any criterion we choose, the Japanese

Americans, are better off than any other group in our society, including native-born whites. They have established this remarkable record, moreover, by their own almost totally unaided effort" (9 Jan 1966:25).

Such news coverage quickly caught the attention of Asian Americans in the scholarly community, who have sharply criticized such portrayals ever since (Kim 1973; Kitano and Sue 1973;[6] Suzuki 1977; Kim and Hurh 1983; Osajima 1988; Suzuki 1989). The concern was twofold: (1) that there were unwarranted assumptions made about the progress of Asian Americans; and (2) that the comparisons with other racial groups were invidious and insidious, generating ill feelings with the moral injunction that underachievers, particularly "certain" minorities, "re-form" themselves after this "model."

While the 1980s generated research and objective evidence that countered unqualified accounts of Asian American success, the print media continued to promote a picture of extraordinary accomplishment. Thus, for example, in 1982 the *Oakland Tribune* noted that Chinese Americans

> have been inordinately successful on both sides of the Pacific. U.S. Census figures indicate that Asian Americans, including 705,000 of Chinese extraction, now have the nation's highest per capita income, echoing the achievements that have made Hong Kong, Singapore, and Taipei nodal points of booming Asia. (26 May 1982)

With the Immigration Act of 1965, the Asian American population became more diverse, and success stories for other Asian ethnic groups, including Japanese, Koreans, and Southeast Asians, emerged (Caudill and DeVos 1956; Kim and Hurh 1983; Caplan et al.1985, 1992, 1994; Osajima 1988).[7] Even diverging cultural values did not undermine the popular view that had brought this population center stage, namely, Horatio Alger dreams and belief in a "cultural formula for success."

THE PERSISTENCE AND ELASTICITY OF THE MODEL MINORITY THESIS

Insofar as Asian Americans have been seen as representing this cultural formula for success, they have enjoyed a certain status as living, prima facie testimonials to these myths, the model minority thesis persists for several reasons: (1) media celebration of a few dramatic examples of "rags-to-riches" stories; (2) the existence of a sizable and visible group of highly educated professionals; (3) failure to disaggregate census data; (4) unexamined assertions about the relationship between culture and mobility, including a dearth of studies on the relative role of culture and social class background; and (5) the specific political or ideological purposes served by the thesis.

In general, the thesis was never based on careful, systematic analysis but rather on a loose grab-bag of assumptions, where the reasoning has been stretched to accommodate contradictions, both empirical and logical. In the end, the major support for the thesis is ideological—the myth of the American Dream.

Media Celebration of "Rags-to-Riches" Stories

Good journalism minimally implies careful coverage and documentation of the facts about a certain topic. At its very best, journalism goes beyond the mere reporting of facts and brings with it an analysis or critical perspective on the issues. Where Asian Americans have walked onto the stage, their casting as special players has made their appearance "newsworthy." The stories of these individuals are rarely simply about individuals but are about a racial set or cultural mold. This is true whether the subject is an imbroglio as serious as campaign finance contributions with an "Asian Connection" (Wu and Nicholson 1997) or human interest stories told for their popular appeal as morality tales. This section speaks to the latter, and shows how their value derives less from representations that conform with objective reality than from how they support the dominant ideology of the American Dream (Hsu 1996).

In April 1998, the *Washington Post* retold a familiar fable, now rendered in the form of high-tech success. The opening line read: "The classic dream of entrepreneurial American came true in Landover yesterday: Jeong Kim, a Korean-born immigrant who once worked the night shift at 7-Eleven to put himself through school, sold his company—for 1 billion" ("For Immigrant" 28 April 1998). In selecting this news account for special attention, radio commentator Charles Osgood similarly opined: "This is a story that Horatio Alger would love to tell." The impetus for the report was the merger of Jeong Kim's company, Yurie, with Lucent Technology, and Kim's appointment as president of Lucent's Carrier Networks division, making him one of the 100 richest high-tech executives in the country. Such mergers reflect the timbre of our time, though what is considered unmistakably noteworthy and thereby newsworthy was the more personal narrative of bootstrap success.

At fourteen, Kim immigrated to the United States from Seoul with his Korean-born parents, eventually attending Johns Hopkins University, where he studied electrical engineering. Kim went on to the University of Maryland, receiving a Ph.D. in engineering. After serving seven years in the navy, where he was the officer of a nuclear submarine, he worked as a contract engineer at the Naval Research Laboratory. Here he developed the idea for a multimedia technology that would enable reporters to pipe almost instant voice, data, and video feeds from international hotspots, battlefields, or elections. Founded on this technology in 1992, his company, Yurie, made its mark almost immediately, soon marketing to federal agencies and later to worldwide markets.

Although initially framed as a classic story of entrepreneurial success, the *Washington Post* account goes on to reveal that Kim had not pulled himself up entirely by his bootstraps. Yurie had, like other companies, been "born from government contracts," having received $305,000 of Defense Department money through a separate program for small, minority-owned businesses ("For Immigrant," 28 April 1998). This last observation alters the story as a cultural narrative, and it is to the credit of the writers that they explored this issue. This may be 300K to riches, but it is not "rags to riches." Nevertheless, the original framing of the report is what readers will remember.

Over the years, stories about individual dreams that are realized through sheer perseverance have saturated the media. On 16 July 1998, CBS News' *48 Hours* dedicated an entire program, "Making It," to this theme, where the dream now encompasses individual aspirations that surpass even Alger's expectations: "Only in America: a place where you can reach for your dreams and make it big, against all odds, aiming for that million dollar payday." Stories about Asian Americans tailored to mirror the ethos of the American Dream generally attribute this population's resourcefulness and resilience to cultural values (Osajima 1988), and academics legitimate this culturally based perspective (Caudill and DeVos 1956; Petersen 1971; Sowell 1981). Whether because of an unquenched public thirst, or because of particular circumstances surrounding their own condition, ethnic insiders, in turn, have relished success stories where desperate circumstances, and backbreaking or mind-numbing work, are transcended through pluck, ingenuity, and above all, the ability to endure and persevere.

The story of David Tsang is meant to inspire. Now a successful entrepreneur and founder of three high-technology companies in the San Francisco Bay Area, the telling of his life story conforms to the fabled climb from rags to riches. A "shy young man of nineteen," he arrives with only "$300 in his pocket and a shabby suitcase" in a country that "seemed like an intimidating, unfriendly land." Despite being alone (his only contact a "distant friend of his father") and facing obstacles including corporate politics and having "just the barest knowledge of English," Tsang "persevered." In the end, this discipline pays off, and after some thirty years, Tsang is described as someone who continues to work 10- to 12-hour days and 6-day weeks, who "prides himself in never giving up," and now offers himself as a role model to "younger, potential Asian American entrepreneurs" ("Silicon Valley," 8 March 1996).

Another news account describes Chong-Moon Lee, also a Silicon Valley entrepreneur, as one who persisted despite desperate circumstances that forced him to live on "21-cent packages of Ramen noodles," near bankruptcy, and frequenting pawn shops in order to pay a $168 phone bill ("Arts," 3 November 1995). Lee eventually not only recoups but also becomes a major benefactor. Thus, the *San Francisco Chronicle*'s coverage of his story underscored his meteoric rise as follows: "From the depths of longing for a hamburger he couldn't afford and contemplating suicide, this entrepreneur rose to such success he was able to give $15 million to San Francisco's Asian Art Museum. Chong-Moon Lee makes Horatio Alger look like a Slacker" ("Chong-Moon," 5 November 1995).

Although these journalism pieces inspire, they become problematic when elevated to the level of social analyses and their subjects become models for others to emulate, without a commensurate effort to integrate and analyze the role of other factors. These accounts often fail to draw a link between biography, history, and society, which C. Wright Mills saw as necessary for escaping the entrapment created by framing the problems in everyday life as individual "troubles," rather than as public "issues."

> *Troubles* occur within the character of the individual and within the range of his immediate relations with others; they have to do with his self and with those limited areas of social life of which he is directly and personally aware. Accordingly, the statement and the resolution of troubles properly lie within the individual as a biographical entity and within the scope of his immediate milieu—the social setting that is directly open to his personal experience and to some extent his willful activity. A trouble is a private matter.
>
> *Issues* have to do with matters that transcend these local environments of the individual and the range of his inner life. They have to do with the organization of many such milieux into the institutions of an historical society as a whole, with the ways in which various milieux overlap and interpenetrate to form the larger structure of social and historical life. An issue is a public matter. (1959:8)

Individuals who have worked their way up from poverty to wealth are the exception, not the rule (Domhoff 1998). Thus, the celebrated success story of Chong-Moon Lee, on closer examination, can be qualified in important ways. As a first-generation Korean-born immigrant, Lee certainly faced difficulties a native-born American would not have. He also had, however, certain social advantages and connections, including royal descent. Before immigrating and later founding Diamond Multimedia Systems in 1982, Lee had been a university professor as well as a successful pharmaceuticals executive in the family business of manufacturing antibiotics. While his personal success itself is not at issue, his biography deviates significantly from the typical Horatio Alger one of humble beginnings. If this is to be treated as a morality tale, then it seems that the moral of the story is that making it in American society is unlikely, given the formidable odds for someone even from such an elite background as Lee. Conversely, the more poignant social commentary is that many who adhere to an ethic of hard work face insurmountable hurdles. This is not to say that exceptions to this larger pattern cannot be found, but the point is that they *are* exceptions.

Whether details about social origins are omitted or included, narrative as ideology is crafted to suggest that the all-important factors are individual character, high moral standards, and motivation. The contradictions in Chong-Moon Lee's life were bracketed discursively, so that by the end of the narrative, an extraordinary history of privilege, with all of its tangible and intangible resources, recedes into the background. In other biographies, we know little about whether *other* factors were relevant in propelling such individuals out of desperate circumstances. David Tsang's background, for example, is not fully revealed. We are told that his father was a teacher, which one might infer provided at least a certain level of status, security, and economic means, but his beginnings are otherwise sketchy. Even when facts contradict the idea of humble beginnings or of individual "bootstrappers," the main theme of the American Dream is preserved. Those who identify with this dominant ethos generally buy into the model minority assumption that education will bring with it equality and achievement (S. Lee 1996). The life trajectories of those on the bottom, however, are rarely examined for empirically specifying the limits of cultural explanations. An implicit assumption or hope is that it will be simply a matter of time and cultural fortitude before those less fortunate close the gap between themselves and their more successful counterparts.

A. Magazine's cover story a few years ago was similarly opaque about the backgrounds of those individuals identified in the title of the article as "Power Brokers: The 25 Most Influential People in Asian America." Directed toward a young Asian American audience, the magazine did not intend any serious coverage of these personages. As the editors state in the paragraph below, they wanted merely to spotlight those they believed significantly influence not simply "Asian America" but the country as a whole:

> The powerful are artists of the social canvas: agenda-makers, trendsetters, and gate keepers. As a result, the process we followed in choosing these individuals as the nation's 25 most powerful Asian Americans relied less on science than instinct. What we sought was a list of those Asian Americans who had touched more people and done more to alter the cultural fabric than any others. . . . But, like power itself, we know how mutable this list is and how arbitrary. By this time next year, this order will have changed, and some new names will have replaced old. Until then, we'll be

watching these 25 closely. Because they aren't just influencing the direction of Asian America. They're setting the pace for America as a whole. ("Power Brokers" 1993:25)

The omission of a critical information on social background runs the risk that such profiles will be seen as Asian-spun versions of the American Dream. As another article in this same issue points out, the value is in having such individuals as role models, especially where barriers to achieving the American Dream appear. The reference here is to glass ceiling barriers, where the rare few who make it are seen as exemplars for other aspirants: "An Asian who demonstrates talent for leadership at an important American organization sends out the message that Asian Americans *can* do the job, and ultimately empowers the entire community" (Chen 1993:71). Despite the hopefulness behind this conclusion, the viability of role models may be contingent, however, upon other factors not so easily emulated.

In their review of "Asian Americans in the Power Elite," Zweigenhaft and Domhoff (1998) argue that social class is critical to mobility. When looking into the family backgrounds of the Asian Americans in the corporate elite, they found that many did not make the climb from the very bottom of the social ladder but rather from already high rungs:

> Chang-Lin Tien, former Chancellor of the University of California, Berkeley, and a director of Wells Fargo Banks, reports that he arrived in the United States at the age of twenty-one as a penniless immigrant, unable to speak the language. True, but he also was born into a wealthy banking family in Wanchu, and his wife's father was a high-ranking officer in Chiang Kai Shek's army.

> Perhaps the best-known Chinese American is the television personality Connie Chung, daughter of a former intelligence officer in Chiang Kai Shek's army.

> Pei-Yuan Chia, former vice chair of Citibank, was the highest ranking Asian-American executive and corporate director at a world-class U.S. corporation until his unexpected retirement in 1996 at age fifty-six. He also was a prototypical Chinese-American member of the power elite. Born in Hong Kong in 1939, he grew up in a banking family. (1998:140–42, 145–46)

Zweigenhaft and Domhoff's book is replete with such examples for other groups—women, as well as other ethnic minorities—where the biographical details alone contradict Alger's moral message. The true moral behind such life stories seems to be that the American Dream is primarily open to those who come with material advantages and social connections.

A Sizable and Visible Group of Highly Educated Professionals

Pointing to major inroads that Asian Americans have made into both higher education and professional work reveals a rosy portrait of structural assimilation into American society. Though a sizable and visible group of highly educated professionals exists, the conceptual or theoretical leaps from such observations need to be reexamined, especially the view that these professionals are contemporary Horatio Alger heroes.

To remain true to the myth of humble beginnings, one would have to ignore the fact that the 1965 Immigration Act contained special provisions that specifically recruited professionally trained personnel to these shores. As a select group of immigrants, they arrived either already educated and trained, or from sufficiently affluent social class backgrounds to enable them to pursue their education abroad. In fact, the majority of Asian *students* who receive postgraduate degrees from American institutions are foreign born (Escueta and O'Brien 1991; Hune and Chan 1997), with many choosing to remain in the United States after graduation. In their study of diversity in America's "power elite," Zweigenhaft and Domhoff acknowledge that there were few "authentic bootstrappers" among Asian Americans, especially the Chinese who formed the majority of Asian American directors in Fortune 1000 boards: "Unlike most Chinese immigrants to the United States before the 1970s, who came from low-income backgrounds, the great majority of Chinese Americans at the top levels of American society are from well-to-do or well-educated families in China, Taiwan, and Hong Kong" (1998:144, 141).

In general, those in the upper echelons, especially corporate executives, board members, and directors, tended to hail overwhelmingly from the upper strata of society. This generalization was true for Jews, women, blacks, Latinos, Asian Americans, and gays and lesbians. Women and minorities who found their way into the power elite were usually "better educated than the white males already a part of it." For this reason, the authors state that class alone did not explain the composition of the power elite. One had to also have cultural capital in the form of degrees from high-status institutions (Zweigenhaft and Domhoff 1998:179).

Other studies similarly note that those from elite universities and colleges are best groomed or primed for the high-status track (Kingston and Lewis 1990), and that wealth, social connections, and elite educational credentials go far toward explaining disparities in social mobility (Useem and Karabel 1990). Whether education or social class has the greater effect on mobility, the convergence of high educational and social status among Asian professionals in the United States obscures this distinction. The lateral mobility of such immigrants to the United States is premised on their affluence, as is any subsequent rise up the ladder.

Failure to Disaggregate Census Data

Of all the criticisms bearing on the model minority thesis, the most common one is directed toward the glib and facile generalizations that gloss over important internal differences within a population. At one time, German Americans were blanketly viewed as a rapidly assimilating minority, though this was more true of "old immigrants" than "new immigrants"(Kamphoefner 1996).[8]

Like German Americans, Asian Americans include many "old" as well as "new" immigrants,"[9] with segments of this population more accustomed to rural life[10] and more likely than their urban counterparts to resist the pulls of mainstream American society (Knoll 1982; Walker-Moffat 1995). Descendants of older immigrants here are likely to be more culturally assimilated than recent arrivals and more economically adjusted, since length of time in the U.S. bears importantly on not only acculturation but income. Although all U.S.-born Asian Americans, with the exception of Vietnamese, were also less likely to be in poverty than U.S.-born blacks or Hispanics (Barringer et al. 1995: 154–55), culture again may not be the key differentiating factor.

The major point here is that statistical averages obscure the fact that Asian Americans tend to concentrate at the extremes—at both the high and low ends—of social status indicators, reflecting what is called a "bimodal" distribution.[11] Focusing on the aggregate, therefore, perpetuates a picture of high achievement, whether we are talking about educational achievement or occupational mobility. In the case of educational achievement, large clusters of Asian Americans are high achievers and college-bound. There are students, nevertheless, whose high school records are not only less promising but indicative of retention problems, including delinquency (Trueba et al. 1993; Hune and Chan 1997).

Failure to disaggregate statistical data has also resulted in inappropriate conclusions suggesting that Asian Americans are not only doing well but "outdoing whites" (Suzuki 1989). The common belief that Asian Americans earn more than other groups, including majority males, is significantly qualified once other factors are "controlled for." These include region of residence, whether income calculations are based on mean or median income, the number of wage earners per family, and the nature of managerial work.

National comparisons mislead, since Asian Americans tend to reside in metropolitan areas of high-income states, whereas the general population or non-Hispanic whites are more geographically dispersed. In 1990, for example, Asian Pacific Americans (APAs) were reported to have a median home value of $178,300, more than double the median home value of $80,200 for whites (Chen 1995).[12] Yet in 1990, three-fifths of Asian Americans lived in just three states—California, Hawai'i, and New York (Lott 1991:59), which partly explains the discrepancy in property values.[13] Similarly, if we look at the median annual income for Asian Americans nationwide for that year, it was $36,000, whereas that for non-Hispanic whites was $31,100. Disaggregating national income data for this same year reverses this very picture. According to comparisons based on four metropolitan areas, the median annual income for APAs was $37,200, compared with $40,000 for non-Hispanic whites (Ong and Hee 1994:34). Not only are Asian American incomes lower, but when one recalls where they live, their dollars also have lower buying power. (See table 1.1)

Like national income figures, the use of "mean income" can similarly obscure. Given the bimodal character of the Asian American population, median income rather than mean income is the preferred measure (the median being that point above and below which 50% of all cases fall). When calculated, the median incomes of Japanese, Chinese, Filipinos, Koreans, Asian Indians, and Vietnamese are invariably lower than the mean (Barringer et al. 1995:152–53).

The number of wage earners per household tends to be higher for Asian households. The U.S. General Accounting Office explicitly drew attention to this fact when it reported on 1985 incomes. Specifically, it noted that while Asian American households earned $2,973 a month, 28 percent more than the average U.S. household income of $2,325, this difference disappeared once one looked at per capita income (U.S. General Accounting Office 1990:20–21). Therefore, Asian Americans did not necessarily earn more, but household incomes were higher because they were more likely to have more income earners, including unpaid family members.

Finally, where census data are used to gauge glass ceiling barriers, managerial data are seldom disaggregated to distinguish between fundamentally different managerial levels in the corporate hierarchy or between different sectors of the economy.[14] The distinction between managers in mainstream corporate America and those in ethnic enclaves is especially critical for Asian Americans, since these managerial structures are not comparable. As the following chapter will discuss at greater length, managerial status for Asian Americans often takes the form of self-employment, which may indicate not so much an entrepreneurial spirit but downward mobility and disaffection with mainstream employment. Even if this propensity for small business involvement is considered a viable opportunity structure, not all Asian Americans participate.[15]

In sum, these general methodological issues have critical theoretical implications when assessing the relative progress of Asian Americans as compared with other racial or immigrant groups. While there have been some moves to achieve a more accurate picture of the existing demographic diversity among Asian Americans in census data, interpreting these patterns is another matter.

Unexamined Assertions About the Relationship Between Culture and Mobility

Although Asian cultural values are credited for much individual or group success, one cannot assume the operation of certain values, or assuming their existence, predict where they will lead. Despite a frequently presumed relationship between culture and mobility, there has been a dearth of studies in this regard.

For one, census data are not a good source of cultural data, except perhaps for language (Barringer et al. 1995:168). This state of affairs, of course, has not kept people from reading into such data—from inferring or imputing the influence of culture. As noted at the outset of this chapter, statistical data provide a certain profile of successful adjustment among Asian Americans. For each statistic, a cultural value is typically imputed to explain the rate in question: high educational attainment is seen as issuing from a value placed on learning; low unemployment from a strong work ethic; low divorce or delinquency rates from a strong value placed on the family; low rates of psychiatric hospitalization from a philosophical attitude of acceptance, and so on.

Notwithstanding that cultural values may be operating at some level, cultural theorizing and empirical research have not kept pace with demographics. Granted, most critiques of the model minority thesis acknowledge diversity in the Asian American population and repeatedly point out that "not all" Asian Americans have progressed similarly.[16] But how cultural diversity produces differential progress within these populations is not altogether clear. During the 1960s, the Chinese and Japanese were the largest Asian ethnic populations in the United States, and Confucianism was a major part of their cultural orientation, which also included Buddhism, as well as elements of American culture. A comparison of select Asian subgroups in terms of value orientation and objective status even seems to support Confucianism as an enabling body of values. Where the Confucian tradition has been strongest (among the Chinese and Japanese), these individuals cluster at the upper end of the income, educational, and occupational ladders. Conversely, those groups where the historical and cultural trail to Confucianism is moot or absent (among Hmong, Khmer, and Cambodians) are ones where poverty is also higher (Trueba et al. 1993:44).

Table 1.1. Income and Poverty Levels by Ethnicity, 1990.

Income	Non-Hispanic White	Asian Pacific American	African American	Latino
NATIONAL				
Median Income	$31,100	$36,000	$19,000	$24,000
Median per Person	$12,000	$10,500	$6,600	$6,200
% above $75,000	10%	16%	3%	5%
% above $10,000	13%	14%	30%	20%
Poverty Rate	9%	14%	29%	25%
4 METRO AREAS				
Median Income	$40,000	$37,200	$24,100	$25,600
Median per Person	$17,600	$10,800	$8,600	$6,300
% above $75,000	20%	16%	6%	6%
% above $10,000	11%	13%	25%	19%
Poverty Rate	7%	13%	22%	24%

Source: Estimates based on observations drawn from the U.S. Census Bureau, 1990 1% Public Use Microdata Sample. Non-Hispanic whites were sampled at a rate of 1 in 10, and African Americans and Latinos were sampled at a rate of 1 in 2. From Paul Ong, *The State of Asian Pacific America: Economic Diversity, Issues and Policies,* (LEAP Asian Pacific American Policy Institute and UCLA Asian American Studies Center), 1994.

When still other Asian ethnic groups enter the picture, however, it is questionable whether Confucian values can be credited. For example, Korean Americans fall somewhere between Chinese and Japanese in terms of educational attainment. Despite a strong Confucian tradition in Korea, a significant portion of those who immigrated to the United States in the early 1900s and in recent years have been Christian (Kim 1981:87–207; Knoll 1982:116–21; Abelman and Lie 1995:198n7). In the case of both Asian Indians and Filipinos, college completion rates exceed those of other Asian ethnic groups, including the Chinese and Japanese, and yet "neither Filipinos nor Asian Indians can be said to be influenced by Confucianism and they equal or surpass East Asians in educational attainment" (Barringer et al. 1995:164).

The model minority thesis has survived because it has been stretched or reinvented and then merely reasserted to be the case. Thus, where Confucian values do not fit the picture, the picture of success has been repainted with broader brush strokes positing values related to "hard work" as the key differentiating factor between the poor and the successful. Such broad cultural generalizations are insufficient, however, for explaining why those who strongly adhere to the same values are not similarly positioned in life.[17]

Some of the relatively greater educational progress of Asian Americans over blacks or others can be linked not simply to cultural values but to preexisting experiences or structures of support. These include preimmigration work experiences, either prior professional training or commercial involvement, as well as access to investment capital (Carnoy 1995). Money for educational pursuits or business adventures came through family borrowing, rotating credit associations, and more recently, for a select group of entrepreneurs, through large-scale venture capital firms (Park 1996). For those with little education or English fluency, entrepreneurialism establishes an economic *floor* for pursuing educational ambitions. First-generation immigrant parents might be uneducated and illiterate, but their ability to set up small shops offers a possible escape from poverty.

Factors other than culture, however, often influence the ability to take advantage of entrepreneurial opportunities. In the case of Korean Americans, for example, it has been suggested that the relative contribution to mobility played by Confucian or Christian cultural traditions may be less important than situational or structural factors (Min 1996). If cultural aspirations were the determining factor, Koreans would avoid commercial pursuits altogether, in favor of government or academic jobs.[18] As Abelmann and Lie have written about Korean immigrants to the United States, small businesses confer comparable lower social status.

> Commercial pursuits, especially shopkeeping, were less prestigious, if not frowned upon. . . .
>
> Many 1970s immigrants had graduated from college, including extremely prestigious universities such as Seoul National University (SNU). . . . For an SNU graduate to "make it" as a greengrocer or a dry cleaner in the United States is akin to an elite U.S. university graduate succeeding as a convenience store owner in opulent Japan. . . .
>
> The incongruous image of a college-educated European American opening up a shop in a poor inner-city neighborhood should make us question the idea that Korean Americans are somehow naturally inclined toward opening and running small businesses. . . .
>
> Korean immigrant entrepreneurship should thus . . . be seen as a concatenation of conscious decisions, albeit made under strong structural constraints.
> (Abelman and Lie 1995:123–25, 129)

Self-employment was taken up because of language barriers, the nontransferability of professional credentials or college degrees, and other structural constraints to white-collar and professional employment, including racial discrimination (ibid.:126–47).

As long as culture is viewed simply as a property of individuals rather than of structures, cultural explanations will give short shrift to structural explanations. The relative absence of small business activity among American descendants of slaves can be linked partly to the disappearance of such structures as the *esusu,* an African form of the rotating credit association.[19] As a result, blacks have depended upon white employers and government policies to establish an economic floor from which they can make educational gains. The educational progress of black children, in turn, has been most rapid when public policy measures are directed toward improving schools and alleviating poverty (Carnoy 1995).

The presumption of entrepreneurial values among Asian Americans in general is a recurring one of no small consequence. Moreover, the problem with cultural explanations has to do with the conditions under which they are invoked. As Portes and Rumbaut (1990:77) point out, they are "always *post-factum.*" In addition, the numerous "unique entrepreneurial values" invoked for different ethnic groups are not only theoretically untidy but cannot explain the numerous empirical exceptions to the theory.[20]

Finally, though education is now almost a prerequisite for mobility, culture need not be. In their book *Inequality by Design,* University of California, Berkeley sociology professors drew upon a cumulative body of research to show how social class background as well as social or national policy arrangements significantly affect social inequalities. Social status was shown to have direct implications for IQ. For example, though Koreans have achieved high levels of education in the United States, their lower, minority status in Japan is manifested in lower IQ scores. In the United States, however, IQ differences between Koreans and Japanese fade (Fischer et al. 1996:172, 191–93, 199). Rather than being a direct measure of innate intelligence, IQ test results reflect access to resources that affect performance on these very tests. As we saw earlier, social class background might better explain important differences among Asian Americans, as well as between Asian Americans and other racial-ethnic groups.

To return to the point raised at the beginning of this section, census data are not designed to address cultural theories. Despite this limitation, we might make the best of this situation were we to approach such statistics as a basis for *generating* theories. Besides cultural explanations, one might posit a range of structural explanations for the rates in question. For example, even when student achievement can be traced to parental pressures to perform, the motivation need not be culturally based. Parental exhortations to "work hard," for example, may be derived from the realization that discrimination makes it necessary for a minority to work "twice as hard" in order to succeed. This alternative, structural perspective has yet to garner the attention it deserves even in the educational context where the model minority thesis prevails. In the occupational sphere, research has noted that the motivation behind ongoing education among Asian Americans is not cultural but "structural"—a response to blocked mobility (Sue and Okazaki 1990).

Political or Ideological Purposes Served by the Thesis

Cultural explanations like the model minority thesis ignore structural conditions, institutional policies, and social class privileges that have assisted the large majority of those who "make it." In doing so, they have served to maintain the status quo, persisting because of their ideological appeal.[21] Were there not blacks and other minorities who form a prominent part of the picture of sustained economic disadvantage, the thesis would not exist.

Because of the value placed on social equality in the United States, gross inequities are a source of national embarrassment, ill ease, and social if not *ideological* crisis. In this context, model minorities serve as a sign of the ongoing viability of the American Dream. Where inequities exist, these are largely reduced to matters of individual will or choice: "If Asian Americans can apparently make it, then why not blacks, other minorities, or other groups?" As noted at the outset of this chapter, model minorities have been invented and reinvented throughout America's history. Success on the part of individual Jews at the turn of the nineteenth century similarly occasioned some to wonder aloud why blacks do not imitate or emulate those strategies.

> Jews have moved up in American life by utilizing middle-class skills—reason, orderliness, conservation of capital, and a high valuation and use of education. . . . Finding that playing by the "rules of the game"—reward based on merit, training and seniority—has worked for them, many Jews wonder why Negroes do not utilize the same methods for getting ahead. (Friedman, cited in Steinberg 1982:88)

The Jewish Horatio Alger story has been critiqued in ways that parallel some of the analysis in the previous pages. Sociologist Stephen Steinberg made several pointed criticisms in this regard: (1) that success was not uniformly distributed throughout the Jewish population, (2) that even those who managed to climb the occupational hierarchy still found their mobility limited, (3) that Jewish cultural values have limited explanatory power, and (4) that structural considerations have a vital bearing on the degree to which preimmigration skills interfaced well with the needs of the American economy. For these reasons, he said, "The popular image of Jews as a middle-class monolith tends to be overdrawn," and even those who entered the professions were far from being an "economic elite" (Steinberg 1982:90-91).[22] Zweigenhaft and Domhoff's more recent study supports this last point. As late as the 1970s,

> Jews were well represented in the corporate elite but were more likely to be in small Fortune-level companies rather than large ones. We also found that they had traveled different pathways in getting to the corporate elite than had their Gentile counterparts. Whereas Gentile executives were most likely to have advanced through the managerial ranks of the corporation, the Jewish directors were more likely to have joined the boards as outsiders with expertise in such areas as investment banking, corporate law, or public relations—unless they had risen through the ranks of companies owned or founded by Jews. (1998:20)

Since the 1970s, however, Jews have made such significant inroads into the largest Fortune-level boards that the authors conclude they are now "most certainly overrepresented in the corporate elite" (ibid:23). These same authors saw four factors as critical to the assimilation of Jews (as well as to the assimilation of other minorities and women): identity management, class, education, and light skin (176–281).

In those contexts where Asian Americans have supplanted the standard reference point for assimilation (white Americans), model minority logic has acquired its appeal from the fact that it is couched in values consistent with middle-class American values and taps into familiar cultural beliefs and myths (e.g., Horatio Alger and the American Dream). One might even argue that it has persisted largely because it serves an ideological or political purpose. Attitudes toward Asian Americans have shifted depending on whether they represent a greater or lesser threat than other groups to the existing hierarchy. While dubbed a model minority, Asian Americans have rarely, if ever, been seriously elevated as a model for majority whites, especially in the presence of direct competition between the two. It is precisely in these situations where the thesis is no longer considered tenable and where ideology and politics become most apparent, particularly to those who run up against these new or unexpected barriers.

Thus, where Asian American admissions to colleges and universities have been associated with declining white enrollments, praise is at best faint and more often accompanied by concerns about Asian American overrepresentation and by unflattering characterizations of them as academically narrow or lacking in socially desirable qualities ("East-West," 23 February 1998; Takagi 1992:58, 60–61; Woo 1990, 1996`). In work spheres where Asian Americans professionals have appeared in significant numbers, glass ceilings and negative assessments of their allegedly poor managerial potential have impeded mobility. Whatever the justifications for their exclusion, the idea of them as "model" no longer surfaces.

THE LIMITS OF CULTURAL IDEOLOGIES

The social soil in which the idea of a model minority germinated may say more about the politics of power than it does about the cultural factors underlying achievement. The questions concerning us here are of a different order than those that motivated the original formulation of the thesis. Instead of asking, "What are the cultural factors behind success?", the appearance of a glass ceiling prompts one instead to ask: "What are the rationales or justifications offered to explain differential progress? If cultural factors are inadequate, to what extent are structural factors at issue? What place, if any, do cultural explanations occupy within this structure or scheme of things?" These questions can be seen as a product of a social, historical context that breathes life into them.

Historically specific, the model minority thesis is premised on the fundamental assumption that educational achievement is the *sine qua non* of success. For this reason, it is unlike its Horatio Alger counterpart, which was born at a time when institutions of higher education served as finishing schools for the elite, while the masses or ordinary people in agrarian and newly emerging industrial sectors could still find decent work without so much as a high school diploma. Only in the postwar decades has the nation firmly embraced an ideology that links educational achievement with occupational mobility. The postwar economy was an expanding one, and the GI bill made it possible for education to be widely pursued. In this way, opportunities were created for educational achievement to become a form of social or cultural capital that could be converted into job security, greater socioeconomic benefits, and professional autonomy or authority. In this new ideological formulation, education would substantially counter and overcome the effects of racial discrimination and entrenched racial privilege.

However, as the following chapter indicates, the prerequisites for mobility go beyond education. Glass ceilings, specifically, exemplify the artificial barriers that limit this ideology of education as a doorway to mobility and success.

NOTES

1. Between the years 1870–1890 Chinese were incarcerated in California State Prisons at a rate higher than their proportion of the population, particularly for crimes involving economic gain (e.g. burglary and larceny). For example, while only 8% of the California population in 1870, they were 14% of those imprisoned. By 1890, the Exclusion Act of 1882 had clearly had its effect: not only did the Chinese population drop to 5% but the prison rate fell to 2% (Shimabukuro 1980).

2. While the Census Bureau has published different population estimates for Asian and Pacific Islanders, there is little question that their rate of growth has surpassed other groups, including blacks, Hispanics, and non-Hispanic whites. Now the third largest minority, after blacks and Hispanics, they are expected to approximate 9.9 million, or 4% of the U.S. population, by the year 2000. In 1970, the Asian American population numbered 1.4 million. By 1980, that population was 3.5 million, or 1.5% of the total U.S. population of 226.5 million. The 1980 figures represent a doubling of the population since 1970. And by 1990, they numbered 7.3 million, having doubled their size since 1980.

3. Part of this difference can be attributed to the relative diversity—or lack thereof—in these respective countries or continents. Given the racial homogeneity of Great Britain during Marx's time, inequality was largely reflected in social class differences.

4. Reference to the term "model minority thesis" is most commonly made in Asian American

academic circles where the construct survives as a shorthand way of referring to the hidden cultural assumptions which continue to underlie social or political debates where Asian Americans figure as a successful minority.

5. Insofar as interracial marriage with the white, mainstream majority of Americans is the result not only of greater contact in both business and social affairs but also of greater social acceptance, such rates have been treated as an important indicator of assimilation (Kitano and Sue 1973). More recent interpretations, however, suggest that trends toward interracial marriages among Asian Americans point to an alternative view of acculturation, namely, the assimilation of ideas in the context of social and economic experiences associated with the experience of "race" in America (Shinigawa and Pang 1996).

6. This volume was a special issue devoted to "Asian Americans: A Success Story?"

7. While the 1970 Census included designated categories for four Asian groups (Chinese, Japanese, Filipino, and Koreans) and one Pacific group (Hawaiians), by the 1980 Census, the number of Asian American groups had increased to twelve, with as many as six Pacific groups (Lott 1991:58). The 1990 Census includes nine major subcategories of "Asian or Pacific Islanders," and at least twenty "other" Asian ethnic groups.

8. Germans had arrived as early as the eighteenth century, and their mass migration to the U.S. during the 1840s and 1850s was such that by World War I German Americans already included many second-generation descendants. Descendants of older immigrants could be expected to be completely assimilated and invisible by the 1970s simply because they had arrived so much earlier. One reason offered for the overall perception of complete assimilation was "Anglo-Saxon race ideology at the turn of the century," which, according to Kamphoefner, "caused people to see what they wanted to see." The allusion here was to the "anti-German hysteria of World War I" and the psychological need to counter negative attitudes toward Germany as an enemy nation with positive attitudes toward German Americans as "easily Americanized." No explanation, however, was offered for why Japan's enemy status did not prompt a similar attitude toward Japanese Americans, who were instead subject to internment.

9. The German American population, however, suffered few curbs on its numbers through restricted immigration. Unlike Asian immigration, national immigration quotas in the 1920s had little effect on German immigration because aliens from the western hemisphere were exempted from such quotas and specifically classified as "nonquota" immigrants.

10. According to Kamphoefner, those German Americans who were less assimilated were geographically isolated in rural areas. Patterns of cultural survival were most evident here. These included use of the German language, social resistance to prohibition and anti-alcohol legislation, and other signs of cultural preservation, including a "locational persistence" associated with peasant attitudes toward landownership as a major form of security. Attitudes in this regard were so tenacious that sacrifices on behalf of landholding might well be pursued at the expense of children's education.

11. The "modal" tendency simply refers to the frequency of an occurrence on any given measure or indicator.

12. The report from which these figures were drawn was a May 1995 study by the U.S. Department of Commerce, *Housing in Metropolitan Areas.*

13. Nina Chen (1995) made two additional observations relevant to interpreting the housing situation of Asian Americans: (1) that the value of homes was based on owners' estimates

regarding what their home might sell for on the open market rather than on computations by an impartial appraiser, and (2) that APAs were eight times more likely than whites to live in "crowded" households, defined by the Census Bureau as having more than one person per room.

14. Dual labor or split labor market theorists have referred to these respective sectors as "primary" and "secondary," or as "core" and "periphery."

15. Filipinos, for example, have been underrepresented in small business, whereas Koreans are heavily concentrated here, more so than other Asian Americans and or other immigrant groups. According to Min, "The Korean group shows the highest rate of self-employment among seventeen recent immigrant groups classified in the 1980 Census, while the Filipino group ranks fifteenth, ahead only of the Portuguese and Haitian groups." Min theorized about distinctions between Filipino and Korean immigrants that might explain their differential distribution. For one, there is a higher representation of Filipino immigrants as professional or white-collar workers in non-Filipino firms, which itself might be traced to the fact that the Philippines is an English-speaking country. In contrast, Koreans had greater language barriers to entering the U.S. general labor market. In addition, as immigrants they have some previous history of working in an industrial business economy, which can be seen as giving them an "advantage" when it came to starting up small businesses (Min 1986–87:56).

16. Even among Japanese and Chinese Americans, who were the original inspiration for the model minority thesis, one can find high poverty levels among recent immigrants (Barringer et al. 1995:155).

17. Values alone—seen as wants, preferences, or subjective inclinations—are inadequate for understanding action or conduct. Culture of poverty theories notwithstanding, blacks themselves have highly valued education as a path to mobility, leading some researchers to explore the gap between these abstract and concrete attitudes, and their different implications for predicting achievement or mobility outcomes (Zweigenhaft and Domhoff 1998:186, 190). For this same reason, sociologist Ann Swidler argued against this conventional view of culture in favor of defining culture as a repertoire of skills, habits, or styles that organize action (Swidler 1986).

18. Kwoh (1947:86–87, 114) has similarly explained the paucity of business persons among American-born Chinese graduates to the low prestige and lack of opportunity for mobility afforded by such work, along with the expectations associated with their college training.

19. The disappearance of the *esusu* has been attributed to the patriarchal relationship between the American plantation owners and their slaves. In contrast to West Indian slaves, whose absentee owners permitted them to develop their own subsistence economy (if only out of necessity, because the slave population here was much larger relative to slaveowners), American slaveowners discouraged their slaves from independently cultivating their own plots of land or else devoting themselves to trades and crafts. Moreover, slaves in the United States were legally denied the right to maintain their own traditions, customs, and language, and otherwise positioned to "absorb the culture of the slaveowner" (Light 1987). In his study of the Mississippi Chinese, James Loewen further underscores the importance of situational factors by explaining how a variety of situational and structural factors positioned the Chinese so that they were able to become prosperous in the grocery business, a "ready-made niche" unavailable to blacks. Mississippi Chinese, in fact, were more concentrated in the grocery business than other Chinese immigrants ("with identical

geographic and class origins") elsewhere in the United States (Loewen, 1988: 32–57).

20. As Portes and Rumbaut explain:

> A first problem with culturalistic theories . . . is that they are always post-factum (that is, they are invoked once a group has achieved a notable level of business success, but they seldom anticipate which ones will do so). A second problem is the diversity of national and religious backgrounds of entrepreneurially oriented groups. Among minorities with high rates of business ownership, we find Jews and Arabs, southern and northern Europeans, Asians, and Latin Americans. They practice Protestantism, Catholicism, Greek Orthodoxy, Buddhism, Confucianism, Shintoism, and Islam. If a set of unique entrepreneurial "values" must be associated with each of these distinct religiocultural backgrounds, it is difficult to see what is left out as a point of comparison. This theoretical untidiness is compounded by the presence of other groups of similar cultural and religious origins that are not significantly represented among minority business owners. Why, for example, are Chinese Buddhists prone to entrepreneurship, but not Buddhist Cambodians; why Catholic Cubans and not Catholic Dominicans? A theory that must invent a unique explanations for each positive instance or for each exception ends up by explaining nothing. (1990:77–78)

21. According to Karl Manheim, dominant groups, given that the existing order supports their own group interests, will be particularly invested in an ideology that supports the status quo.

> The concept "ideology" reflects the one discovery which emerged from political conflict, namely, that ruling groups in their thinking become so intensively interest-bound to a situation that they are simply no longer able to see certain facts which would undermine their sense of domination. There is implicit in the word "ideology" the insight that in certain situations the collective unconscious of certain groups obscures the real condition of society both to itself and to others and thereby stabilizes it. (1936:40)

22. While acknowledging that cultural values certainly played an important role in promoting literacy, study, and intellectual achievement, Steinberg directly questioned the viability of the Jewish Horatio Alger myth as *cultural* ideology. Preimmigration skills were also critical, and it happened that the industrial skills of Eastern European Jews intersected well with the needs of the burgeoning American industrial economy. Their decision to become merchants, shopkeepers, money lenders, and liquor traders, on the other hand, cannot simply be attributed to cultural traits since these were occupations they might not otherwise have engaged in were it not for discriminatory laws that restricted their ability to own land (Schwarz 1956:296; Steinberg 1982:94; Cowan and Cowan 1989:14, 21–27).

CHAPTER 2

THE STATE OF RESEARCH
ON THE GLASS CEILING

> The glass ceiling is most clearly defined as those artificial barriers based on
> attitudinal or organizational bias that prevent qualified individuals from
> advancing upward in their organization into management level positions.
> *U.S. Department of Labor 1991*

> Many Americans are unwilling to accept the reality that Asian Americans,
> despite their reasonably good record of achievement, face a real, hard,
> shatter-proof glass ceiling when it comes to moving up to managerial
> positions.
> *Joy Cherian, EEOC Commissioner 1993*

> Whatever one makes of "model minorities," there is abundant evidence
> that the high levels of education of Asian Americans are not always translated
> into other measures of success.
> *Herbert Barringer, Robert W. Gardner, and Michael J. Levin*
> Asians and Pacific Islanders in the United States

"Is there or isn't there a glass ceiling?" This is a normal, perhaps even inevitable, question. A
colleague who reviewed an earlier draft of this manuscript wrote that a binary yes-no
response would be misleading, indeed, "dangerously naive." Naive because there are many
kinds of ceilings (and floors), and they change with circumstances, type of firm, sector of
the economy, and scale and diversity of employees involved. Dangerous because any singular
policy is too formulaic. Instead, much depends on context, conditions, and unit of analysis
(e.g., are we talking about individuals or aggregations?).

A 1986 *Wall Street Journal* article about barriers faced by white women attempting to
penetrate corporate management first popularized the concept of a glass ceiling. As minorities
began to enter the professional workforce, the phenomenon disproportionately affected
them as well. The main purpose of this chapter is to review the state of research on the glass
ceiling and in particular to present relevant empirical data, especially where this pertains to
the relative absence of Asian Americans in administrative or managerial work. Although I
begin with research conducted for the Federal Glass Ceiling Commission, I also refer to
other research published during the last two decades.

REPORT OF THE
FEDERAL GLASS CEILING COMMISSION

In 1991, Congress passed the Glass Ceiling Act, a result of its own findings that:

1. despite a dramatically growing presence in the workplace, women and minorities remain underrepresented in management and decision-making positions in business;

2. artificial barriers exist to the advancement of women and minorities in the workplace;

3. U.S. corporations are increasingly relying on women and minorities to meet employment requirements and are increasingly aware of the advantages derived from a diverse work force.[1]

A bipartisan federal commission was created with the broad mandate to study and prepare recommendations. Specifically, such legislation had two goals: "(1) eliminating artificial barriers to the advancement of women and minorities; and (2) increasing the opportunities and developmental experiences of women and minorities to foster advancement of women and minorities to management and decision-making positions in business." To explore barriers, the Federal Glass Ceiling Commission did several things. In addition to commissioning eighteen research papers, it conducted five public hearings in different parts of the country, surveyed twenty-five chief executive officers (CEOs) from white and minority-owned businesses, facilitated group interviews of six racially homogeneous focus groups, elicited the views of two focus panel groups comprised of American Indians, and initiated special runs of U.S. Census Bureau data.

In March 1995, the twenty-one-member Commission released the results of its research, finding that despite inroads that both minorities and women have made into executive, administrative, and managerial positions over the past two decades, non-Hispanic white males hold 95 to 97 percent of all management positions in the private sector. Women held only 3–5 percent of senior positions and Asian/Pacific Islander Americans "less than one one-hundredth of one percent of all corporate directorships" (1995:60, 102, 143).

Despite these findings, it is often believed that *college-educated* women and minorities face few barriers. The majority of CEOs surveyed admit that biased attitudes on the part of middle-level managers might impede advancement, or that parity between women and white non-Hispanic men had not yet been achieved in terms of compensation or equal access to senior levels of decision-making. But women were seen as having made relatively greater progress, compared with minority males, for two reasons: (1) they had been in corporate management longer (20–25 years being the length of time estimated to pass through the glass ceiling); and (2) in sheer numbers, women represent more than half the total population, thereby costituting a larger pool of candidates. Women, however, testified to barriers in the form of stereotypes which did not pass "the reality check" (Federal Glass Ceiling Commission 1995:146–51). Such disparities in perception can themselves impede further progress.

Asian American professionals, too, are surrounded by the general perception that they experience few occupational barriers. In the Commission's focus group interviews,

Asian Americans saw barriers even when outperforming whites. As documented elsewhere, whites are less likely than any other racial-ethnic group to perceive race discrimination as a barrier for minorities. When they acknowledge barriers, they are more likely to agree that minorities are "excluded from informal networks by whites" (36%) than that minorities have to be "better performers than whites to get ahead" (32%). In contrast, Asian American employees were most likely to feel that people of color have to meet higher standards for promotion (58%). They have a "harder time finding a sponsor, or mentor, than whites" (57%), and are likely to be excluded from informal networks by whites (42%) (Fernandez and Barr 1995:257, 260–61).

Similarly, in a study specifically focusing on scientists and engineers, whites were again less aware of either barriers or job dissatisfaction that their Asian counterparts experienced. Not only did they see race relations as "excellent" or "good," but more than 80 percent indicated no special effort was needed to explore opportunities for Asian Americans to enter administrative positions (Wong and Nagasawa 1991). Because they rated their own opportunities for advancement as "excellent" or "good," white employees seem devoid of any fears of encroachment or "interest-group conflict." The anonymity that the surveys provided would have minimized any need for face-saving postures such as optimistic forecasting about one's own career. Both assumptions suggest that ignorance about the subjective experiences of their Asian American colleagues is because of social or cultural walls that prevent dialogue about problems in the workplace.

In its own fact-finding report, the Federal Glass Ceiling Commission identified three broad levels of artificial barriers: (1) societal barriers which may be outside the control of business, (2) internal structural barriers within the direct control of business, and (3) governmental barriers (table 2.1). Governmental barriers in the form of inadequate reporting categories and other weaknesses in nature of employment-related data will be reviewed later in this chapter.

Artificial Barriers

The concept of "artificial" barriers needs to be addressed at the outset because it has consequences for our very orientation, attitude, or approach to occupational barriers, in particular how we interpret and address them. Strictly speaking, glass ceiling barriers are those that have little to do with individual qualifications as such, except as they impede qualified individuals from advancing. Educational qualification and other formal credentials are not in question. Instead, failure to make inroads into management is linked to *artificial* constraints that have little to do with competence or potential.

In general, the concept of artificial barriers is significant because it strikes directly at the heart of the powerful ideological view that the American Dream is available to all who would simply "work hard." The Commission noted that attitudinal and behavioral biases on the part of coworkers and bosses (e.g., counter-productive behavior and harassment by colleagues) represented internal structural barriers. In addition, it reopened the door to analyses of "institutionalized racism" or "institutionalized discrimination," which have shown how even in the absence of prejudice, organizational practices can effectively create a glass ceiling for certain segments of the workforce. While the concept of "institutionalized

Table 2.1. Glass Ceiling Barriers.

Societal Barriers that may be outside the direct control of business

The Supply Barrier related to educational opportunity and attainment

The Difference Barrier as manifested in conscious and unconscious stereotyping, prejudice and bias related to gender, race, and ethnicity

Internal Structural Barriers within the direct control of business

Outreach and recruitment practices that do not seek out or reach or recruit minorities and women

Corporate climates that alienate and isolate minorities and women

Pipeline Barriers that directly affect opportunity for advancement
- Initial placement and clustering in staff jobs or in highly technical and professional jobs that are not on the career track to the top
- Lack of mentoring
- Lack of opportunities for career development, tailored training, and rotational job assignment that are on the revenue-producing side of the business
- Little or no access to critical developmental assignments such as memberships on highly visible task forces and committees
- Special or different standards evaluation
- Biased rating and testing systems
- Little or no access to informal networks of communication
- Counterproductive behavior and harassment by colleagues

Governmental Barriers

Lack of vigorous, consistent monitoring and law enforcement

Weaknesses in the formulation and collection of employment-related data which makes it difficult to ascertain the status of groups at the managerial level and to disaggregate the data

Inadequate reporting and dissemination of information relevant to glass ceiling issues

Source: The Federal Glass Ceiling Commission, *Good for Business: Making Full Use of the Nation's Human Capital* (Washington, D.C.: U.S. Government Printing Office), March 1995, pp. 7–8.

discrimination" is not new, the Commission's work focused on concretely identifying the barriers themselves.

Apart from discerning what some of these corporate barriers look like, the Commission implicitly surfaced another issue, namely, that some of these barriers bear directly upon managerial preparedness: specifically, lack of mentoring, lack of management training, and lack of opportunities for career development. Unlike the formal definition of a glass ceiling as artificial bias impeding "qualified individuals," the issue of preparedness implies "real" barriers (i.e., underqualifications). Where the responsibility lies, however, ultimately turns on the question of whether montoring/training/career development opportunities is viewed as essential to advancement.

The problem of the glass ceiling—as a methodological one—is to capture what occurs at the interface of relationships, whether it is the relationship between employee and employer, between individual attitudes and organizational ones, or between socialization at home and social treatment on the job. A shared belief among the groups the Commission surveyed was that their respective skills and talents were not appreciated, valued, or recognized. There were also distinctively different contours and configurations of experiences that were particular to each racial-ethnic group.

The Glass Ceiling: Variable Contours and Perceptions for Different Groups

Although the glass ceiling has an official definition, other metaphors have arisen in reference to these mobility barriers. Thus, the Federal Glass Ceiling Commission found that African American men prefer to speak of a "brick wall," whereas American Indians describe the glass ceiling as "more than glass." And Hispanic Americans talk of an "opaque" barrier and a "two-way mirror" from which "they feel that they are always being watched and judged" (1995:69, 86, 122)—an "adobe ceiling," if not a glass ceiling. Elsewhere, Asian Americans have spoken variously of the "broken ladder" (Chinese for Affirmative Action 1992) or the "bamboo ceiling" ("Battling," 31 May 1993). The metaphor captures barriers experienced as well as possibilities for change:

> [Researchers] Bell and Nkomo explain that white women feel that they are held down by a glass ceiling. Glass is dangerous and it can injure those who break it, but it can be broken. Furthermore, glass is clear—those below a glass ceiling can see through it and learn by observation. They can see those above and they, in turn, are visible to those who are above the glass ceiling. Visibility, sometimes known as "face time," is a critical factor in breaking through the glass ceiling.
>
> African American women, on the other hand, feel that they face a concrete wall. It is almost impossible for one person alone to poke a hole in a concrete wall. Furthermore, those closed in behind the wall cannot learn about the organization because they are isolated from the mainstream of organizational life and, worse, they are invisible to the decision makers on the other side. (Federal Glass Ceiling Commission 1995:58)

Many factors converge to situate racial-ethnic and gender groups differently within the occupational world, despite equivalent education. Cultural stereotypes were mentioned by all groups. Sector of the economy, job positions occupied therein, and mentoring opportunities also affect upward mobility.

Thus, the Federal Glass Commission reported: "A black business class has grown and flourished outside the corporate culture. The glass ceiling question is whether Black Americans are prepared to grow and flourish within the mainstream corporate culture." Specifically, African Americans are disproportionately employed in government and nonprofit sectors. Where they appear in private, for-profit mainstream corporations, they are "concentrated in staff functions rather than line positions," and if in management, more likely to be "clustered in the areas of community relations, public relations, personnel and labor relations, and affirmative action/equal employment opportunity areas." According to the CEOs interviewed, the supply of such candidates was limited despite a high demand for their services; moreover, those recruited into positions that would "normally lead to top management positions" often leave, if not for better offers, then for reasons that remain unknown to the CEOs (1995:64, 66, 77–78).

American Indians were largely invisible within corporate America partly because only 9 percent of them in the workforce have college degrees but also because of conflicts between traditional values and corporate values. An estimated half of those with MBAs were employed in their communities or elsewhere, while those who enter the corporate world encounter stereotypes that they are *"most deficient in the appearance and assertiveness deemed necessary for management . . . more physical than mental—given to risky behavior that is not consistent with the presence and control needed for managerial positions"* (Federal Glass Ceiling Commission, 1995: 93). Culture conflict did not simply refer to differences in interactional skills or behavioral styles relevant to climbing the corporate ladder but to conflict with values represented by corporate America in general. Specifically, the emphasis that American Indians placed on spiritual education and on conservation of natural resources ran counter to the corporate drive to exploit resources for material profit.

Like African Americans, Hispanic Americans were reported to be "relatively invisible in corporate decision-making positions. . . more frequently employed in government and the nonprofit sector than in the for-profit sector." Similarly, "when they enter the private sector they are clustered in staff jobs that lack career mobility. . . . " The corporate motivation for promoting Hispanics into management is the Spanish-speaking market, and CEOs in states with high concentrations of Hispanics were "especially concerned that they could not find many U.S.-born Hispanics who are literate in English and Spanish." While such news may be welcomed by those fluent in Spanish who have been criticized or held back for speaking English with an accent, the language requirement may be double-edged. Two-thirds of Hispanics born in the United States (those who speak limited or no Spanish) may find their options circumscribed because they are *not* bilingual (1995:121, 126, 131).

For Asian Americans, complaints about the glass ceiling are most audible in those fields where we might reasonably expect their professional concentration to lead to greater managerial representation, that is, in the sciences, engineering, and other technical professions. Education facilitates entry into the professional ranks but brings lower returns in terms of high-ranking executive jobs. While underrepresentation is most apparent in corporate work arenas, evidence of blocked mobility in other areas, such as law, journalism, government, and academia is emerging (Duster et al. 1988; Lan 1988; Asian Americans at Berkeley 1989; Tan 1990; Chinese for Affirmative Action 1992; Nakanishi 1993a; "Bad News" 13 August 1998).

RELEVANT RESEARCH ON THE GLASS CEILING AND ASIAN AMERICANS (1970s–1990s)

The Federal Glass Ceiling Commission's research provides a broad overview and profile of women and minority group representation in corporate management. Its effort to identify glass ceiling barriers was unprecedented, and the relevance of these barriers for Asian Americans will be drawn later in this chapter. There has been relatively little research, however, on the glass ceiling in general, and little on mobility issues among Asian Americans, even though this group's presence in the United States goes back to 1587, when approximately 400 Filipino seamen settled in the bayous of southeastern present-day Louisiana.

During the 1970s, historians and social science researchers began to scrutinize the literature on Asian/Pacific Islanders. According to historian Chris Friday (1994a), writings in the area of labor history largely neglected Asian Americans. Until 1970, the *Journal of Labor History* contained not a single article on this group of workers, and it would take another ten years before four more articles appeared. The substantive focus of most writing, moreover, centered on anti-Asian activities rather than on the contributions of Asian labor. Academic interpretations were also more concerned with how European Americans perceived and acted toward Asian Americans than with the perceptions and actions of Asian Americans themselves. While this focus eventually shifted with a new generation of scholars, the writings revolved around agricultural labor, labor contracting, and organizing activities, with garment workers becoming a major area of contemporary research interest.

> In the 1993 listing of literature relating to Asian American Studies, Glenn Omatsu and the staff at *Amerasia Journal* compiled and published a list of 1,850 entries from a database of 2,776 works. Of those in the "Labor, Business, and Economy" section, 43 of 130 were clearly related to labor issues with contemporary garment workers getting the most attention. (1994:546)

Friday attributed the dearth of labor history about Asian Americans partly to the "tendency for those in Asian American studies to publish in ethnohistory and sociological journals" (Friday 1994a:525). Research on the glass ceiling and Asian Americans in the contemporary workplace is essentially nonexistent. This is true even amongst sociologists, who for disciplinary reasons have been interested in both social inequality and comparative occupational mobility.[2]

In a 1980 review of the four oldest American sociological journals, Lucie Cheng Hirata (1980) reported a paucity of research on Asian Americans in general. In an eighty-year period (1895–1975), she found 137 articles on Asian Pacific Americans (APAs), less than 1 percent of the total number of articles.[3] Of these 137, eight focused on mobility.

A survey of these same journals from 1976 through 1997 turned up an additional thirty-six articles on Asian Americans. Less than one-third of these publications addressed mobility issues. However, a number of books and articles the status of Asian Americans appeared.[4] Ethnic small businesses provided the major empirical focus for a theoretical discussion of occupational mobility.[5]

Existing studies that explicitly address the glass ceiling in large-scale corporate or bureaucratic settings have largely been initiated by nonacademic groups, including civil rights organizations, community groups, or employees. In 1987, Asian American professionals and managers conducted a survey of Asian Americans in the San Francisco Bay Area (Cabezas et al. 1989). The *San Francisco Chronicle* (16 July 1988) subsequently included a segment on the glass ceiling in a special series on Asian Americans. It would fall, however, largely upon Asian American community organizations to produce their own comprehensive reports.

Beginning in 1986, Chinese for Affirmative Action (CAA), a San Francisco-based civil rights organization published a series of detailed reports on the glass ceiling in city civil service (Chinese for Affirmative Action 1986, 1989, 1992). The Organization of Chinese Americans (OCA), a national educational and civil rights organization headquartered in Washington, D.C., issued a brief report, *Shattering the Glass Ceiling: Entering the "Pipeline of Progress,"* in 1992. In November 1993, Chinese for Affirmative Action collaborated with the Council of Asian American Employee Associations to develop a survey to identify glass ceiling barriers. The participating Asian employee associations came from eight major employers in the Northern California region: Lawrence Livermore National Laboratory, Levi Strauss & Company, NASA Ames, Pacific Bell, PG&E, Port of Oakland, Stanford University, and University of California, Berkeley. The resulting product was a resource manual for both emerging and established employee groups (Chinese for Affirmative Action 1994).

In 1993 as well, Asian Americans for Community Involvement (AACI), the largest Asian American community agency in Santa Clara County, conducted the first broad survey of Asian Americans in Silicon Valley: *Qualified But . . .: A Report on Glass Ceiling Issues Facing Asian Americans in Silicon Valley.* Among the study participants were the following groups: Asian American Association of City Employees, Chinese Institute of Engineers, Indo-American Business League, Indo-American Chamber of Commerce, Japanese American Citizens League, Korean American Professionals, and Northern California National Taiwan University Alumni Association.

Several observations can be made about the state of the research on Asian Americans and the glass ceiling. First, data are more available on the *aggregate* status of Asian Americans or Asian/Pacific Islanders than on ethnic subgroups within this population.[6] Second, the majority of these studies are quantitative and statistical. Some specifically call attention to inadequacies of census data and government reporting categories, including problems created by the aggregation of population data or managerial data. Almost two decades ago, Asian American professors, researchers, attorneys, community leaders, directors of social service agencies, and direct service providers brought these serious problems with federal data before the U.S. Commission on Civil Rights. In doing so, they countered the myths surrounding conditions in the community, including employment conditions. The two-day meeting is believed to be the first consultation with Asian Americans ever sponsored by a federal agency, and some of the testimony will be reported when I discuss methodological issues.[7]

Third, although few researchers initiated studies with the glass ceiling in mind, those who sought to critically assess occupational status used one or two kinds of measures: professional-managerial representation and returns on education. The first measure simply refers to the ratio of Asian Americans in managerial positions to their numbers in the professional pool, as compared with the ratio of whites (or other groups) in these corresponding categories. The second looks at the relationship between education and occupational mobility, in particular returns on education in terms of income or occupational status. When racial-specific patterns are factored in, a recurring pattern of managerial underrepresentation and lower returns on education is typical for Asian Americans. As snapshots of a given moment, however, such strategies do not capture the dynamics of "discrimination," "choice," or larger factors relating to organizational culture, industry dynamics, or an economy that shapes opportunity structures.

Although the Federal Glass Ceiling Commission was concerned primarily with corporate employment in mainstream sectors of the economy, ethnic small business activity is indirectly relevant to the topic of a glass ceiling for two reasons. One reason is that the statistical aggregation of managerial categories from different sectors of employment includes many Asian American managers who are self-employed, as opposed to salaried managers in large-scale bureaucratic organizations. The other reason is that disaffection with mainstream employment can lead to self-employment. Both factors conceal disparities and problems related to upward mobility, and both have special significance for Asian Americans because of a tendency toward small business management (see section below, "Aggregation of Managerial Categories").

Finally, few studies—whether they are social science studies, government reports, or independently initiated surveys on the part of Asian American interest groups—are organizational analyses. Some studies at the master's or dissertation level, however, have situated their research in a local or regional context (McLeod 1986; Lau 1988; Mark 1990; Park 1992).

Despite limited information, this chapter draws upon a range of research data—statistics, surveys, interview data, individual testimonies, academic research, and government reports—to paint a composite picture of how Asian Americans have fared, especially in science and engineering. In the process, I will discuss the importance of certain methodological issues necessary for our understanding. Some of the internal structural barriers that the Federal Glass Ceiling Commission identified will be discussed at the end of this chapter in the context of data available on Asian Americans.

Conceptual and Methodological Considerations

Although official studies of the glass ceiling are a recent phenomenon, some early critiques of the model minority thesis refer to a ceiling on mobility. Based on their findings, Charles Hirschman and Morrison Wong (1984:603) concluded: "What did prove to be a fairly important mechanism across all ethnic minorities. . . was the unequal participation in the occupational hierarchy. If minorities with the same resources and opportunities . . . as whites were able to reach the same mark on the occupational ladder, earnings inequality would be reduced substantially."

In a review of social science analyses using 1970 census data, Sucheng Chan distinguished between "studies that depict continual improvement since the 1960s" and those "studies that paint a far less rosy picture of Asian American socio-economic status" (Chan 1991b: 219–20, n4). Upon closer examination, even research depicting "continual improvement since the 1960s" qualified their overall findings that Asian Americans were approaching occupational parity with whites. Thus, in an analysis of immigrant and native-born Asian Americans (Chinese, Japanese, and Filipinos) between 1960 and 1976, Hirschman and Wong (1981) found that the educational levels of immigrant and U.S.-born Asians in general "equaled or exceeded those of whites in recent years," and that with certain exceptions, they were "more likely to be found in professional occupations than whites" (Hirschman and Wong 1981:495).[8] At the same time, these same authors noted a "ceiling on advancement into positions of authority or institutional power," invoking "middlemen minority" as a possible explanation.[9]

> [M]iddlemen minorities are permitted to occupy certain "occupational niches" which are noncompetitive with the dominant group. These positions allow for somewhat higher socioeconomic status than other minority groups, but there remains a ceiling on advancement into positions of authority or institutional power. This perspective has been applied by several authors to account for the relatively high socioeconomic position of the Asians in America. . . . The positions which these middleman minorities occupy are precarious and dependent upon the goodwill of the dominant group. They are allowed to achieve, but only so high. (Hirschman and Wong 1981:496)

Panelists at the 1979 consultation with the U.S. Commission on Civil Rights pointed to problems hidden by statistical indicators. The nature of federal data continues to frustrate researchers. Where researchers could disaggregate these data, they uncovered a pattern of lower returns on education, occupational segregation, and exclusion from policy-making positions. For these early spokespersons and representatives, such indicators strongly qualified the view that the institutionalization of legal protections, if not the passage of time, had ameliorated historical discrimination.

Census Data, Government Reporting Categories, and Indicators Relevant to the Glass Ceiling

The aggregation of Asian and Pacific Americans as "Asian Americans" has always been a prime concern. When only this aggregate census category existed, it was particularly troublesome since there were vital social, economic, and historical differences among Asian American subgroups which had implications for service needs.[10] By 1980, the census better reflected the ethnic diversity of this population. How Asians are enumerated in the census continues to be a controversial, ongoing concern, because of practical implications for funding service needs and for a population's constitutional right to equal protection under the law ("Professors Blast," 11 December 1987; "Asians Fear," 20 December 1987).

Related to this problem of aggregation is the frequent failure to control for the geographical diversity of Asian Americans, particularly when income data for this aggregate is being compared with those of others groups. As explained at greater length in chapter 1, their concentration in certain regions of the country has important implications for assessing the state of their well-being. In 1979, the majority of Asian Americans resided in two states—California and Hawai'i. This meant that the use of *national* median income created misleading comparative differences. Specifically, Asian Americans often appeared as if they were not only on parity with other groups but were excelling, when in reality their incomes were largely artificially inflated because they lived in high-income states where the high cost of living cut deeply into earnings.[11] Disaggregated data, such as metropolitan area statistics, by contrast, produce more meaningful comparisons than national averages. Unfortunately, even the Federal Glass Ceiling Commission (1995:119) overlooked this problem when providing only national income data for Asian Americans.

Participants in the 1979 consultation emphasized that this poor state of research was in large part due to Asian Americans being underrepresented in key decision-making bodies, especially in federal agencies. Professor Ling-chi Wang (University of California, Berkeley) pointed out the absence of any comprehensive federal study on Asian Americans, together with the "conspicuous absence of Asian Americans on Federal commissions, boards, councils, advisory committees, and task forces," including the staffs of the Commission before which he spoke (U.S. Commission on Civil Rights 1979:24–25).

Asian Americans continue to be strikingly absent from high-level government administration. Bill Lann's appointment in December 1997 to the post of Acting Assistant Attorney General is significant because he is the first Asian Pacific American to hold that position (*Asian Pacific American Institute for Congressional Studies* 1998:3). According to Zweigenhaft and Domhoff (1998:152–53), other "firsts" include Patsy Takemoto Mink's appointment in 1977 as Assistant Secretary of State for Oceans and International Environmental and Scientific Affairs, "the first Asian American whose executive-branch appointment required Senate confirmation," and Julia Chang Bloch's appointment in 1981 as Assistant Administrator in the Agency for International Development, "the first Asian American to head a major agency," and in 1989 as head of the United States Embassy in Nepal, "the first Asian American to serve as an ambassador." Nevertheless, no Asian American has ever served in a president's cabinet. Where Senior Executive Service (SES) positions in the federal government are concerned, Asian Americans hold less than 1 percent of these positions.

In 1988, almost ten years after the 1979 consultation, the U.S. Commission on Civil Rights produced a report devoted to assessing the economic status of Asian Americans. Ironically this report, *The Economic Status of Americans of Asian Descent: An Exploratory Investigation,* is more likely to be remembered among Asian Americans for the controversy over the interpretation of the data and the failure to conduct certain analyses than for the data which it had on Asian Americans and management (see below). Its critics referred specifically to the failure to consider "structural issues [such as] race and gender discrimination and labor market segmentation which ultimately limit the economic well-being of Asian Americans despite their heavy investments in human capital such as education and work experience" (1988:119).[12]

From its own findings, the Federal Glass Ceiling Commission concluded that government data collection continues to be inadequate and ill-suited to the task of ascertaining the precise nature of the glass ceiling and recommended that the public sector commit more resources to provide and disseminate accurate information. CEOs themselves voiced a critical view of reporting categories that the government requires of companies. As the Commission noted:

> It is significant that a number of the CEOs volunteered the information that the reporting categories required by government agencies do not yield accurate profiles of their staffs in terms of race and ethnicity, gender, and level of management responsibility. One CEO scoffed at "the absurdity of the categories—they don't get at what they should want to know—it's criminal what people of ill will can get away with using those categories.
>
> The issue raised by the CEOs regarding the collection and disaggregation of compliance data affects all data related to the glass ceiling. It is not readily available in contexts and forms that clearly reveal whether minorities and women are advancing in management positions in the private, public, and nonprofit sectors. What is available is broad brush, and in many cases has to be arrived at by working backwards from statistics—for example, compensation levels that hint at status or levels of

responsibility. In other cases, the datasets that contain the needed information are not large enough to permit detailed disaggregated analyses. (1995:30)

While patterned differences in managerial representation are pronounced, what is not readily available is data that shows how specific Asian subgroups are distributed across various managerial categories. This breakdown is necessary because there are critical qualitative differences associated with the title of "manager."

Aggregation of Managerial Categories

Despite the criticisms leveled at the 1988 report by the U.S. Commission on Civil Rights, the report did discuss how certain difficulties in assessing the reasons behind managerial underrepresentation lay in the shortcomings of census data. Census data were said to contribute to this problem in three ways: (1) although the census category "manager" details "a diversity of occupational positions ranging from high corporate positions to managers of small retail stores," it does not enable these positions to be qualitatively differentiated so that high-status managerial positions can be systematically distinguished from managerial titles which are less consequential; (2) census data do not enable one to determine whether the presence of Asian Americans in professional but nonmanagerial positions is a matter of "discrimination or choice"; and (3) census data do not indicate whether a person's self-identification as "manager" derives from specific job responsibilities or training, or conversely, a more amorphous or broadly defined set of duties. About this third ambiguity, the Commission explained, "Managers whose work reflects specific fields of training may be more likely to list the occupations pertaining to their specific fields of work than to list manager as their occupation, whereas managers whose work is less tied to a specific field of training may be more inclined to list manager as their occupation" (1988:72, 74).

In short, a number of qualitative distinctions would be important in evaluating management data, including managerial type (office manager, research and development [R&D] supervisor vs. high-level corporate executives), employment sector (public administration vs. corporate management), individual choice or interest in managerial work, and factors behind self-identification as manager. Although technical distinctions between managerial levels can *theoretically* be accessed by statistically trained analysts, this information is not readily available in more general studies and reports. Instead, managerial information is "collapsed," without there being clear distinctions between high-status managerial positions and less rewarding types. Differences in mainstream and ethnic economies are also glossed over this way.

Although occupational mobility and managerial representation were otherwise hardly touched upon, the 1988 report noted that education had failed to reward Asian Americans with the same opportunities for career advancement as it did non-Hispanic white males. Among the few facts cited in this regard was that U.S.-born Asian men in professional jobs were less likely to be in managerial positions, even with "comparable skills and characteristics" (U.S. Commission on Civil Rights 1988:4, 7–8, 72–76). Specifically, 6.5 percent of U.S.-born Filipinos and 10.5 percent of U.S.-born Japanese were identified as managers in 1980, compared with 12 percent of whites (1988:74). Even after controlling for education, work experience, English ability, urban residence, and industry of employment, along with other variables, such as marital and disability status, "Asian descent" continued to have a negative effect on one's chances of moving into management (1988:74–75). Some of the commissioners who had come under criticism underscored the importance of this finding in terms of a glass ceiling:

> [T]he report presents, for the first time, an analysis of the likelihood that American-born Asian men become managers, taking into account education and other background variables. It also examines the relative earnings of Asian men with high levels of schooling, adjusting for occupation and industry. The results of these two analyses suggest that Asian men face a "glass ceiling": their relatively high levels of education enable them to enter high paying occupations and industries, but within these occupations and industries, Asian men may face obstacles to their career advancement. (1988:117)

Compared with white males, Asian Americans were more likely to have jobs as managers in areas such as research and development (Wong and Nagasawa 1991; Ong and Blumenberg 1994) or food management (U.S. Commission on Civil Rights 1979:390; Ong and Azores 1994, 112). According to William Marumoto, managing director of Boyden Global Executive Search in Washington, D.C., there is some break with this trend as Asian Americans move into sales and marketing fields, which have typically been the route into executive suites ("Asian Americans Finding" 15 July 1998).

Their representation in government jobs is also changing very slowly. In San Francisco's sixty-one city departments, Asian Americans were absent even in "second-in-command" positions (Chinese for Affirmative Action 1986). For this reason, Pan Kim concluded after presenting the following data that "Asian American participation in American politics and national political attention to Asians lags far behind other minority groups."

> Of 8,136 SES positions, only 73 (0.9%) were held by Asian Americans in 1990. At the local level as of 1990, only 15 Asian Americans were elected mayor/chairman in municipal governments among a total of 7,065 positions; only eight Asians were chief appointed administrative officer (CAO) [or chief managers] among 5,056 positions; six Asian Americans were assistant manager or assistant CAO among 1,524 positions. Overall, less than 1 percent of municipal officials are of Asian descent. (Kim 1994:98)

Again, given such data, analyses that do not consider different spheres and levels of managerial employment are liable to *overestimate* the significance of managerial representation among Asian Americans. In 1998, Robert Naksone gained the distinction of being "the sole Asian American CEO of a Fortune 500 company that he or she did not found" ("Asian Americans Finding" 15 July 1998). Among Exxon Production Research's 600 scientists and engineers in Houston, 75 are Asian. Few, if any, of these even reach first-level management. In California's Silicon Valley, Asian Americans are approximately "one-fifth of the total population and 10 percent to 30 percent of the employees of white-owned companies," yet a survey of this white-collar workforce suggest increasing underrepresentation the higher the managerial position (see "Battling" 13 May 1993). The following percentages reflected agreement with the sentiment that Asian Americans are underrepresented at a particular managerial level: lower-level management positions (49%), middle-management (64%), and upper-management (80%) (Asian Americans for Community Involvement 1993:6, 11).

Though the majority of Asians in the United States are employed as private wage and salary workers, Asian Americans are more likely to be involved in small business activities than other groups.[13] In California, the high self-employment rate among Asian American workers (more than 11%) is exceeded only by the white self-employment rate (17%) ("Asian Americans Finding" 15 July 1998).

Because minority-owned firms tend to be concentrated in the retail and service sectors, rather than in the manufacturing or finance-insurance-real estate sector (Waldinger et al. 1990:56–57), Asian Americans experience a form of disguised underemployment (U.S. Commission on Civil Rights 1979:372–73ff). As high-risk operations, these firms have been associated with lower than average sales, with profits depending on long hours, unpaid family members, and overall fewer workers per firm. Moreover, these businesses are more likely to be concentrated in highly competitive, low-wage industries.

> Asian entrepreneurs are more likely to be concentrated in less desirable and highly competitive niches. Of self-employed Asian immigrants, 42 percent are in the wholesale and retailing sector, compared to only 16 percent of self-employed Anglos. Although the two groups have nearly identical percentages in manufacturing (9%), four-tenths of Asian manufacturers are in apparel compared to only one-tenth of Anglo manufacturers. As a consequence of this maldistribution, average self-employment income for Asians is about only four-fifths that for Anglos. Self-employment may be a better option than the limited opportunities in the labor market, but it is not a guarantee of economic success on a part with Anglos. (Ong and Azores 1994:114–15)

Lateral Mobility Across Employment Sectors

As reactions to blocked mobility, underemployment, or exclusion from mainstream occupations (Li 1977; Chung 1979; Lau 1988; Bonacich 1988; Park 1996:169–70), small business start-ups are identified with foreign-born and non-native English speakers, who cannot take jobs in the mainstream because of language barriers or inadequate education. But it is also true for those with professional or college backgrounds, who have started their own subcontracting firms in Silicon Valley because of disaffection with mainstream employment.

The meaning of job stability or lateral mobility among Asian Americans is relevant to the glass ceiling, though there are differing interpretations here. In her study, Joyce Tang (1993a) not only pointed to greater job stability among foreign-born Asian engineers than whites but also arrived at a positive, optimistic interpretation of this pattern. Noting they were far less likely to change jobs, and therefore much more likely to have a longer tenure in engineering than whites, she concluded that an important factor explaining the long-term retention of Asian Americans was the operation of universalistic criteria in technical fields (ibid.:242).

Job stability, in other words, was seen as a sign not only of satisfaction but of the personnel review process more objectively in engineering than in other fields. Moreover where Tang discusses the greater tendency for *native-born* (i.e., U.S.-born), over foreign-born, Asians to change jobs, she similarly interprets this as reflective of greater options rather than as a negative reaction to barriers to upward mobility: "Native-born Asians are as likely as Caucasians to venture outside engineering. Contrary to the prevailing view that Asian professionals in general are in a closed job market . . . native-born Asian engineers do not seem to be confined to specific jobs because of their training" (ibid:240). Despite these optimistic conclusions, Tang acknowledges that in the case of Asian immigrant engineers, structural constraints, including discrimination and language barriers, may inhibit access to other jobs, a more pessimistic view consistent with other research of hers (1993b), which notes a glass ceiling for both foreign- and U.S.-born Asians.

According to J. D. Hokoyama, President and Executive Director of Leadership Education for American Pacifics (LEAP), when the aerospace industry was at its height more than five years ago, discontent among Asian American professionals took the form of lateral transfers to other companies. One could easily move, say, from TRW to Hughes Aircraft or to McDonnell Douglas. In this way, "high-tech coolies" became transformed into "electronic migrant workers." During periods of economic restructuring and downsizing, it is not only the glass ceiling at issue but job security itself—the "floor" below which individuals hope not to fall during this organizational reshuffling. In the case of mergers, middle-and upper-level management positions themselves are being pared back.

Although the loss of talent incurred because of glass ceiling issues is seldom systematically recorded, the available evidence is nevertheless striking. A 1987 survey of 308 Asian American employees in a wide range of industries in the San Francisco Bay Area (Cabezas et al. 1989) found career advancement and greater monetary rewards to be some of the primary reasons for job changes. Among Chinese Americans, where the median number of job changes was three, 75 percent of Chinese Americans mentioned "career advancement" as an important reason, whereas 56 percent left for "better wages." Filipino and Japanese American employees, although a smaller part of this sample, cited the same barriers to upward mobility as Chinese Americans: "about three-fourths reported company-related barriers, such as corporate culture, management insensitivity, and lack of informal networking. Lack of mentors and role models were cited by more than one-half of the respondents" (ibid.:92). According to estimates by the Asian American Manufacturers Association (Menlo Park, California), there are more than 500 Asian American high-tech companies in the Bay Area (Park, 1996:165). It remains for future study to determine the extent to which glass ceilings spur entrepreneurship as well as how venture capital combines with social or cultural capital to make this possible. For engineers changing careers, computer science has been the most popular field of choice (Tang 1993a).

In addition to firms losing employees to job change and to start-up companies, talent was lost to overseas enterprises, particularly among foreign-born professionals returning to their country of origin. According to one estimate, this reverse migration was reported to be at an all-time high since World War I, estimated at 195,000 a year ("Skilled Asians," 21 February 1995). Hsinchu Science Park, a high-tech enclave in Taiwan, is a major receiving facility ("A 'Reverse,'" 19 July 1993). Yaw-Nan Chen, director of Taiwan's science division at its Los Angeles diplomatic mission, estimated that approximately 6,000 to 7,000 Taiwanese scientists and engineers have repatriated ("Aerospace Careers," 16 November 1992). U.S. policies that have led to downsizing and research cutbacks have been the "push" factor behind some of this brain drain. Recruiting firms have been the "pull" factor, having actively searched for managerial talent (Ong and Hee 1993a; "Reverse Brain," 8 July 1994; "Chinese American Establishes," 30 September 1994; "High Tech Firm," 30 June 1995).

Similarly, attractive salaries, state-of-the-art research facilities in places such as Singapore, Taiwan, Hong Kong, and South Korea (the so-called tigers of Asia), and a general atmosphere supportive of basic research ("Tigers," 21 November 1994) are also draws.

In short, focusing solely on vertical mobility *underestimates* the amount of dissatisfaction expressed through job changes. While it is in these new, start-up firms that Asian engineers and scientists truly are afforded the opportunity and experience of being CEOs, especially Chinese Americans (Zweigenhaft and Domhoff 1998:149), this employment situation is considerably more high risk. According to Edward Park (1996:163), "large, mainstream firms . . . provide a sense of employment stability rarely found in subcontracting firms where nearly all Asian Pacific American firms are concentrated." In terms of power to set major agendas in the corporate world, these small entrepreneurs are not seated at the table with executives of major companies. For these reasons, another perspective must be taken toward Asian entrepreneurship, besides that of success through enabling values. As outlets for frustrated ambitions in the mainstream, these enterprises may also better illustrate how cultural or ethnic ties act as safety nets rather than ensuring success in the mainstream.[14] Research is presently inconclusive, and even conflicting, regarding the role of small business employment in mobility.[15]

Occupational/Industry Concentration

The distribution of Asian Americans across occupations and across industries is uneven. In terms of occupational concentration, they are predominantly in the sciences and engineering. Moreover, according to National Science Foundation data, since 1978, the percent of Asians employed as scientists and engineers has been growing at a much faster rate than that of whites.[16] In 1982, they were three times more likely to be scientists and engineers than their percentage in the population would predict (Wong and Nagasawa 1991:3). As Ph.D.s, they clustered in the fields of engineering (25.7%), physical sciences (21.4%), and the life sciences (21.1%) (Ries and Thurgood 1993:54).[17] As scientists and engineers, they are also, however, a group for whom the issue of the glass ceiling has surfaced repeatedly.

In industries, Asian Pacific Americans were concentrated at the lower end of the occupational scale or in less than desirable sectors.

> In the transportation, communication, and public utility industries, and in finance, insurance, and real estate, Asian Pacific Americans predominantly are clerical workers; and in the service industries, Asian employment is high in hotels, restaurants, and health services, however, they are mostly food and cleaning service workers. In hospitals they are mostly nurses rather than physicians, and even in the ranks of nurses, discrimination apparently exists. (U.S. Commission on Civil Rights 1979:390)

The first systematic study to analyze how industry concentration affected employment for Asian Americans reported that low wages could be attributed to a combination of "low-employment in high-wage industries" and "high employment in low-wage industries" (Cabezas and Yee 1977:9–10).[18] Even in retail trade, where they are known to concentrate more than other groups, they were most likely to be in low-wage rather than high-wage sectors.[19] Summarizing these findings for the U.S. Commission on Civil Rights two years later, in 1979, Amado Cabezas remarked that Asian Americans were "below parity as managers even in industries where they are above parity as professionals and technicians."[20] Lower pay and lower occupational status among college-educated Asian Americans has been attributed to industry or occupational segregation, not lower qualifications.[21]

This occupational and industry concentration along racial and ethnic lines continues today (Barringer 1995:207, 209; Oliver et al. 1995:3–16 to 3–23; Reskin 1998:19–43). On the lower incomes accruing to Asian Americans because of underrepresentation in certain industries, Barringer and his associates (1995:207) explicitly commented: "Asian Americans were less heavily concentrated in insurance, real estate, and finance than were whites, by about half. This is an important category, because high incomes are generated here." According to other data (see table 2.2), Asian Americans were more underrepresented than other racial groups as executives, managers, and administrators in major industries.

Some have posited the "crowding hypothesis" to explain the depressing effect numbers have on income: Simply put, a high number of individuals concentrated in a particular occupational field is said to negatively effect wages. This idea has been used in the past to explain the lower wages of Asian females, including the college educated, who are concentrated in the lower-tier, primarily clerical occupations in generally high-wage industries (Cabezas and Yee 1977; U.S. Commission on Civil Rights 1979:9–10, 28; Fong and Cabezas 1980:293).

What the crowding hypothesis fails to address is why the doors to high-ranking executive jobs should be closed more often to some groups than others, and particularly why Asian Americans should have such difficulties when they have a larger pool of candidates from which to choose. In 1979, research indicated that the occupational segmentation among highly educated Asian Americans was not simply a benign development: "those well-educated and considered to have successfully entered the primary sector of the labor market are found to be in only certain jobs that are . . . segregated consistently by racial prejudice, lower salary schedules, restricted upward mobility, and inferior employment status and benefits" (U.S. Commission on Civil Rights 1979:45).

Table 2.2. Executives, Managers, and Administrators in Major U.S. Industries, by Ethnicity.

Industry	Hispanic		Asian/ Pacific Islander		African American		White	
	M %	F %	M %	F %	M %	F %	M %	F %
Business Services	5.2	3.2	1.7	1.2	3.5	0.5	51.6	32.8
Finance	3.4	5.0	1.8	2.6	2.6	2.6	44.8	37.6
Communications	6.1	3.4	1.7	0.3	2.4	1.0	58.4	25.6
Insurance	2.0	4.2	0.5	1.7	3.2	3.0	44.0	40.7
Retail Trade	2.8	2.0	3.5	1.7	2.3	2.6	41.7	39.1
Utilities	3.1	0.7	0.0	0.8	3.1	0.8	71.9	17.2
Transportation	6.1	3.4	1.7	0.3	2.4	1.0	58.4	25.6
Wholesale Trade	2.7	2.1	2.4	1.8	1.2	0.3	53.4	36.2

Source: Chinese for Affirmative Action, 1995 Asian American Civil Rights Symposium: Summary Report of Proceedings (San Francisco 1995, 15).

The corporate sector is viewed as having the worst promotional opportunities for Asian Americans in California's Silicon Valley: Fifty-three percent of respondents from the corporate sector said promotional opportunities for Asian Americans were inadequate, as compared with 44 percent of respondents who worked in government. Of all industries, the electronics industry evoked the most dissatisfaction: Fifty-four percent said promotional opportunities were inadequate, compared with 39 percent in all other industries. In general, 66 percent of those in the private sector felt that race limited their chances. Foreign-born (56%) and technical personnel (62%) were more likely to say their promotion opportunities to management were limited in this way, as opposed to those who were U.S.-born (33%) or in nontechnical jobs (48%) (Asian Americans for Community Involvement 1993:15–16, 21).

Increasing seniority was associated with increasing perceptions of a glass ceiling. Fifty-three percent of those with eleven to fifteen years of tenure with their current employer felt their promotional chances were worse than their non-Asian American coworkers. Only 24 percent of those with fewer than five years with their current employer held this view (ibid.:2, 18–19).

In short, while the above study was spurred by complaints of a glass ceiling from a wide range of sectors—high technology, government, education and others—certain occupational or industry concentrations were more problematic than others for Asian Americans.

Ratio of Managers to Professionals

A low ratio of actual managers to those in the eligible pool of professionals suggests distinct thresholds to mobility for both Asian Pacific American men and women. A strong presence in the professional workforce (23%), Asian Pacific American males find their numbers shrink in the executive ranks (14%). Similarly, Asian Pacific American females in professional jobs (17%) form an even smaller percentage of managers (12%). Non-Hispanic white males, by contrast, make up a smaller share of professional workers (14%) but are more likely to advance into executive-managerial levels (17%) (Ong, and Hee 1993:147).

Before leaving office, former EEOC member Joy Cherian presented a cumulative picture of limited mobility and managerial underrepresentation for Asian Americans across a number of occupational sectors, including private employment, all levels of government, and both public and private institutions of higher education. In a speech given in June 1993, he pointed to the following constellation.

> Virtually across the board, in private employment; in employment with state, local, and federal government agencies; in employment with public and private institutions of higher education, Asian Americans enjoy the distinction of being represented very highly as professionals. But, for some strange reason, the same data show that when it comes to being part of the management team, those same professionals—a category of workers from which most managers come—do a disappearing act. . . .
>
> In public employment at all levels of government, Asian Americans are employed as officials and administrators at the rate of only one-third of their representation in professional jobs with the same employers. . . .
>
> When it comes to employment in the ranks of executives, administrators and managers at our private and public institutions of higher learning—colleges and universities—the situation seems to be worse for Asian Americans than in any other

employment sector. Here, Asian American managers are only one-fourth of their participation in professional and faculty positions. (Cherian 1993:7, 8, 10)

According to EEOC data, Asians were more statistically underrepresented as managers than all other minority groups. Cherian thus summarized:

> Among the minority groups for which we collect these data, Asian Americans are the only ones that are disproportionately underrepresented in the management positions by comparison to their participation rates in professional jobs. All other minority groups are employed as managers and officials in numbers very roughly equal to their representation in the professional fields, but Asian American managers and officials make up fewer than half of their representation in professional jobs. (ibid.:7)

In California's Silicon Valley, where Asian Americans have started a quarter to a third of all new electronic companies ("It's 'Asians,'" 14 January 1992), and 23.6 percent[22] of the high-tech manufacturing workforce in 1990 (*Global Electronics*, October 1992), this pattern of professional concentration and managerial underrepresentation is repeated. While 21.5 percent of Asians were professionals, only 12.5 percent were officials or managers (*Global Electronics*, February 1990, October 1992, September 1993).[23] White males, in contrast, were more likely to be managers (62.8%) than professionals (50.9%). Education alone did not explain this differential mobility into management. According to the Pacific Studies Center (Mountain View, California) which conducted this research, since most of these "high-level employees" have one or more college degrees, "discrimination and other cultural factors appear to reduce the management opportunities for qualified Asian professionals" (*Global Electronics*, October 1992:1). As late as 1992, not a single Asian Pacific executive could be found as head of any of the large computer or semiconductor companies in Silicon Valley ("It's 'Asians,'" 14 January 1992).

Data from specific Southern California corporations echo this pattern. For example, in 1992, Asian Americans made up 24 percent of the technical staff at Hughes Aircraft, 15.7 percent at Rockwell International, 13.8 percent at Aerospace Corporation; 20 percent of the science and engineering staff at TRW's space and defense sector, and 10 percent at Northrop. At the same time, their percentage in management was relatively small: they were 5 percent of the managers (in technical areas) at Hughes Aircraft, 11 percent at TRW, and 3 percent of managers companywide at Northrop. Rockwell and Aerospace declined giving further information, and McDonnell Douglas and Lockheed declined to provide any data.[24] In general, high-level administrative appointments for Asian Americans are practically unheard of. A rare exception was the appointment in 1992 of Don Tang as "chief of Lockheed's top secret military spacecraft unit in Sunnyvale—one of the most sensitive jobs in the United States defense industry" ("Aerospace Careers," 16 November 1992).

Although the managerial-professional ratio presents an objective profile of how groups are variously distributed between these two broad tiers, there are any number of reasons— some benign, others not so benign—which might explain the differences in these occupational distributions across racial groups. Lack of managerial interest among Asian Americans is one of the more benign interpretations. Yet, Asian Americans have increasingly given voice to differential treatment. The following remarks cited in a 1992 report by the U.S. Commission on Civil Rights are typical.

> Within my company there are about 800 to 1,000 research and engineering professional staff members. About 60 of them are of Asian origin. We think that there are altogether about 200 management and management track positions in the company. There are no Asians in management positions and only one Asian in a management track position. [W]e usually have to prove that we are better in order to be equal. (U.S. Commission on Civil Rights1992:133)

The next section refers to research which looks more closely at the relationship between formal education and managerial attainment.

Returns on Education

A recurring theme in different studies of Asian Americans in the workplace is not only their simultaneous overrepresentation as professionals in science and technical fields and their underrepresentation as managers but lower returns on their education. When Asian Americans first met with the U.S. Commission on Civil Rights in 1979, they pointed to underemployment among both longtime residents and recent immigrants, who for different reasons were denied access to jobs and promotional opportunities commensurate with their education and training.[25] What this suggests is that inferences based on educational data alone can be misleading. While education facilitates mobility in general, there is cumulative evidence that education brings lower returns for Asian Pacific Americans than for other groups.[26] A glass ceiling into management is but the extreme, upper end of this dynamic.

In a review of the career histories of Caucasian and Asian engineers, Joyce Tang (1993c) found that Asian engineers compared poorly in terms of relative earnings, occupational status, and promotions. The earnings differential was particularly noticeable between foreign-born Asians and whites, with Asians earning 18 percent less and taking six to eleven years before reaching parity. Though Tang suggests that recency of arrival may partially explain this income difference, she found no evidence of such income loss among white immigrant engineers (Tang 1993c:474). Where occupational status is concerned: "Asians regardless of nativity status, are heavily underrepresented in authority positions compared to Caucasians. They also have a lower tendency than their Caucasian counterparts to move into management from technical positions" (ibid.:472).

The relative absence of U.S.-born Asians in upper echelon positions is the most striking finding, since they did less well than foreign-born, immigrant whites. This difference is explained not by educational qualifications but by "a fairly large mismatch between career status and qualifications in the native-born Asian workforce" (ibid.:479). This racial difference in managerial presence persisted even when certain factors that might account for this pattern were introduced and controlled for.

> A low tendency for native-born Asians to be managers cannot be attributed to their lack of human resources, placement in undesirable sectors, or uneven field distribution. . . . the underrepresentation of native-born Asians in management suggests that neither mastery of English nor familiarity with American labor market practices is the key to achieving higher occupational status. (ibid.)

The impact of immigrant status is practically nonexistent for their white counterparts:

> In contrast, the negative impact of nativity status for Caucasian immigrants is attenuated and becomes insignificant, when everything else is held constant. These

results are in line with the "glass ceiling" hypothesis of Asians' absence in management. (ibid.)

Similarly, other research has indicated that even with English skills, U.S. citizenship, comparable or superior levels of education, Asian Americans continue to earn less than their white counterparts in the same occupations, and the cost of being an immigrant is greater if one is Asian than white (Hsia 1988: 186–89, 192). The fact that foreign-born whites faced no such blocked mobility suggests racial barriers or the possibility that European employees with English-language difficulties are treated differently than Asians with such problems.[27] A *Times* analysis of 1993–1997 census data found that college-educated Asian Americans who were in management earned $46,706 on average— 38 percent less than white college graduates. Moreover, separate reviews of 1994–1997 and 1990 census data found that this pay differential persisted for native-born Asian American males, despite English fluency ("Asian Americans Finding" 15 July 1998).

In a multiyear national study, Paul Wong and Richard Nagasawa analyzed a National Science Foundation survey of 88,000 scientists and engineers in both the private and public sectors, the largest survey of this type conducted in the United States. Not only were Asian American scientists and engineers "grossly" underrepresented in management, but inequities in income persisted even when they were situated in the same occupations as their colleagues. Managerial appointments were circumscribed to areas such as "research administration, particularly as supervisory project leaders in technical projects which are composed of small groups of scientists and engineers" (Wong and Nagasawa 1991:4). In Wong and Nagasawa's own in-depth sample survey of 235 Asian American scientists and engineers in the Phoenix and Tucson metropolitan areas, two of several field sites under study, the inequities in management were such that whites earned *twice* the income of Asian Americans similarly situated.

> The disturbing results from the National Science Foundation survey . . . are also supported by our own in-depth sample survey. . . . Even when Asians rise to middle or top level manager positions, they do not receive economic returns comparable to whites in similar positions. In fact, the income returns for whites for holding these positions are twice that for Asian Americans occupying similar positions. (ibid.)

Although lower returns on education are thus strongly suggestive of artificial barriers, and there are volumes of statistics on educational attainment and occupation status, these data are available in a form making it impossible to assess racial parity in terms of the *relationship* between education and occupational progress. The *Statistical Record of Asian Americans* suggests that education improves one's managerial chances: 22.9 percent of Asian Pacific American men with four or more years of college were executive, administrative, and managerial workers, as opposed to 16.6 percent of those with only one to three years of college.[28] A similar pattern held for women: 19.3 percent of Asian American women with four or more years of college were listed as executive, administrative, and managerial workers as compared to 9.8 percent of their counterparts with only one to three years of college (Gall and Gall 1993:281). This information source, however, offers no comparative data for white males.

The last time that statistical measures were devised with such comparative measures in mind was in a 1978 report by the U.S. Commission on Civil Rights, *Social Indicators of Equality for Minorities and Women*. The Commission noted then that, with the initiation of this publication in 1973, the United States had joined other nations in the world (including Canada, France, Germany, Great Britain, Japan, the Netherlands, the Philippines, and Malaysia) in developing social indicators for its population. This report was ground breaking in that it not only systematically addressed issues of relative progress between groups but also attended to many of the methodological problems which previously stood in the way of meaningful comparative data. Thus, while the *Statistical Record of Asian Americans* contained no comparable figures for white males, the *Social Indicators* report created indices with "majority males" as the benchmark for comparison. The latter report, however, was discontinued in 1978, when responsibility for monitoring agency compliance was transferred from the U.S. Commission on Civil Rights to the EEOC (Reskin, 1998:12). Weaknesses and problems which formerly beset such data, including the aggregation of data at the national level, reemerged. Where researchers have undertaken their own research to recreate certain indices of inequality (e.g., indices of occupational segregation) 1990 data indicated unwarranted levels of race and gender inequality (ibid.:22, 53–54).

Glass Ceiling Barriers

The conceptual and methodological considerations in the preceding pages revealed some key barriers to researching the glass ceiling. Where relevant analyses exist, there is strong evidence of inequities in occupational status. A major challenge is to capture what occurs at the interface of various relationships. Statistical data on managerial representation may suggest racially disparate outcomes, but they tend not to be "process-sensitive."[29] Glass ceiling barriers will not be evident without some consideration of those social dynamics that impinge on work relations job assignments, and ultimately managerial appointments. These include those factors, *apart from employees' skill-related attributes*, that affect recruitment, career development, and promotional decisions.

The remainder of this chapter turns to glass ceiling barriers that the Federal Glass Ceiling Commission found to be important "internal structural barriers within the direct control of business." The relevance of such factors will be drawn for Asian Americans by including other, independent research. In addition, reference will be made to barriers not mentioned in the Commission's report.

Outreach and Recruitment Practices that Bypass Minorities and Women

Among the early pipeline barriers that the Federal Glass Ceiling Commission listed as adversely affecting minority and female recruitment were outreach efforts that bypassed individuals in these groups. Because career paths begin to take form early on, employer recruitment efforts are critical, especially in firms that have strong growth potential and thus offer a real opportunity to escape work in unattractive job sectors. CEOs reported few problems locating Asian American men and women at the level of initial recruitment and hiring (Federal Glass Ceiling Commission 1995: 32).

Sustained outreach efforts at the worksite itself, however, were notably lacking. Nonminority CEOs said Asian Americans rarely came to their minds as prospective managerial candidates: "The overwhelming majority of the CEOs interviewed in the survey commissioned by the Glass Ceiling Commission think of the glass ceiling in terms of women. When reminded that it also affects minority men, almost all interpreted 'minority' as African American" (ibid.:102).

Institutional Tracking

Among the first pipeline barriers that have long-term implications for one's career trajectory is initial job placement, specifically placement in staff jobs or in highly technical and professional jobs that are not on the career track to the top. In San Francisco City government, for example, Asian Americans were found clustered in "dead-end technical positions," such as finance or operations (Chinese for Affirmative Action 1992). The city's civil service had, in fact, been described as a "giant white-collar sweatshop—one that is increasingly reliant on Asian labor and Asian expertise but offers little promise for advancement" (Chinese for Affirmative Action 1989:7). The Department of Public Works, in particular, epitomized the endemic problem of the "ghettoization of Asian American professionals" (ibid.:1, 11–13).

The types of upper-level jobs in which minorities and women cluster reveal how this early tracking crucially affects later prospects for entering management: "the relatively few women and minorities found at the highest levels tend to be in staff positions, such as human resources, or research, or administration, rather than line positions, such as marketing, or sales, or production" (Federal Glass Ceiling Commission 1995:iv).

Such barriers have been explicitly noted for Asian Americans who are often channeled "into staff, not line positions" or otherwise "pressured into accepting positions in the relatively unfavorable specialties," such as R&D positions where promotions seem to follow a slower pace (Lau 1988:24–28). Managerial positions tend to be restricted to "research administration, particularly as supervisory project leaders in technical projects which are composed of small groups of scientists and engineers" (Wong and Nagasawa 1991:4). This form of segregation might explain either social marginalization or ignorance of insider knowledge that facilitates mobility into the senior executive ranks.

Little or No Access to Critical Informal Networks

To the extent that recruitment patterns follow certain informal networks within the organization, Asian Americans are also at a disadvantage because they frequently are not part of "old boy networks" which involve mentoring and the exchange of varied and important career information. At the workplace investigated in chapter 5, it was suggested that even when information about positions is widely circulated, those outside this network are reviewed less favorably than friends or acquaintances within the inner circle.

Differences in language and cultural socialization clearly inhibit social interaction and thereby the ability of some to network in unfamiliar circles. The following employee explained how cultural differences made it uncomfortable to intermingle in certain social circles:

> Even though I'm a U.S. citizen, in some ways I was still a "foreigner" in America because of language and culture. . . . It's not just because I can't speak English

well. . . . In Taiwan, I can mix in much easier. I can tell or understand jokes, or politics. In America, we had no common background [with white male executives]. ("A 'Reverse,'" 19 September 1993)

Although the ability to network may be impaired by language or cultural barriers, these networks also seemed closed. In the Silicon Valley survey, 36 percent of Asian Americans said that they felt excluded or unwelcome when they sought entry to networks outside their own circles (Asian Americans for Community Involvement 1993:26–27). This is true for even U.S.-born Asian Americans, who reported a "lack of full participation in an English-speaking network" (Tang 1993c:489), despite being more acculturated or assimilated. The case of Japanese Americans is instructive because although they have assimilated along a number of dimensions, they receive lower returns on their education relative to whites of equivalent qualifications. Thus, for the decades from 1950 to 1970, Eric Woodrum reported that minority disadvantage was a persistent feature.

> An irony substantiated by these findings is that precisely those college-educated, professional Japanese Americans celebrated as exemplifying an "assimilation success story" systematically receive less prestigious, authoritative employment and less financial compensation than similarly qualified whites. (Woodrun 1981:166)

In short, given barriers for the most assimilated and acculturated among Asian Americans, cultural stereotypes and discriminatory preferences may be a large part of the problem.

An Imputed Lack of Managerial Interest

Assessing the pool of not only eligible but also "interested" candidates is an important first step in gauging the extent of any glass ceiling. In the most sanguine of interpretations, the relative absence of Asian Americans from executive-managerial positions is said to be due to their lack of interest in managerial positions. Where erroneous, such perceptions constitute artificial barriers, perpetuated by cultural stereotypes of Asians as better equipped and inclined toward technical rather than people-oriented work.

There is some empirical basis or reason for this general perception. A high proportion of Ph.D.s among Asian Americans prepares them for research activities. In some organizations, dual career ladders have been created for the very purpose of retaining and accommodating highly talented researchers who have no interest in the managerial track but nevertheless desire opportunities for advancement. Were one interested in management, a detour into the administration side of the ladder might also introduce the risk of being derailed from one's research. The saliency of such issues would depend on the organizational context in question and provisions made to assist the candidate in staying current or abreast of new developments in his or her specific field of expertise.

On the other hand, the absence of Asian managers cannot be attributed entirely to lack of managerial interest. A survey of Asian American scientists and engineers in the Phoenix and Tucson metropolitan areas indicated that 56 percent expressed an interest in administrative work (Wong and Nagasawa 1991:5). Similarly, in the Silicon Valley survey, a large majority of Asians (75%) expressed an "interest in being a manager." Opinion, however, was fairly evenly divided over whether promotional opportunities were the same as that of their non-Asian coworkers. Of those expressing an interest in managerial work, 46 percent felt their promotional chances were worse than non-Asian workers, while 43 percent thought their chances were the same (Asian Americans for Community Involvement 1993).

Therefore, if the perception of managerial disinterest among Asian Americans is widespread, there are clear, empirically documented instances showing that it is also misinformed. Employers, supervisors, or bosses acting upon this stereotype will likely ignore potentially good candidates. Rumors of an old boy network and a glass ceiling are further reinforced by an impersonal review process that discourages all but the most ambitious; a vicious circle is set up, which at its worse squelches all expressions of managerial interest. Like unemployed and "discouraged" workers who cease applying for jobs and therefore do not show up in the official unemployment statistics, managerial aspirants may, after several repeated unsuccessful efforts at applying for managerial vacancies, simply "give up." It thereby becomes the "chicken-and-egg" question of which came first: Do Asian Americans fail to apply for opening positions in management because they are "uninterested" and thereby neglect to develop the necessary skills? Or do employers fail to seriously consider them as candidates because they are not perceived as "management material" and thereby do not invest in these employees? According to Wong and Nagasawa (1991:4), the presence of both tendencies creates a cycle of expectations which is "self-fulfilling."

Alleged Deficiencies in Language or Communication Skills and Leadership Qualities

Were objective qualifications (as measured by years of education, degree attainment, training or work experience) the sole considerations in promotion, Asian American candidates would probably be overselected into management. Yet, a recurring explanation for their under-representation has not only been their alleged lack of managerial interest but their deficiency in certain qualifications, specifically, language abilities, communication skills, and leadership qualities. Cultural stereotypes aside, organizational culture itself privileges certain cultural styles of interaction over others (chap. 5). Where Asian Americans have been appointed managers precisely because of certain imputed linguistic or cultural abilities, these appointments have largely been limited to supervising all-Asian groups or to overseas job assignments. Even with high levels of formal education, foreign-born Asians are particularly vulnerable to being perceived as having language and cultural barriers that make them unsuitable as management material. An Asian American, speaking on these issues states,

> Even though I'm a U.S. citizen, in some ways I was still a "foreigner" in America because of language and culture. It was tough on our careers. We did well in the technical world, but after you reach 40 years old, what are you going to do? I wanted to explore different areas, but I didn't feel I had many opportunities to explore management options in America. . . . In the technical field in America, there's a ceiling on chances for Chinese-American engineers to rise to senior management positions. There's "unfound talent" among Chinese engineers in America. They don't have a chance to show their talent. ("A 'Reverse'" 19 July 1993)

Even Asian Americans acknowledge that their own communication skills might be further developed;[30] they also saw a great deal of arbitrariness surrounding the review process. Among the *company* characteristics seen as creating career obstacles, "arbitrary and subjective promotional processes" was the single most frequently mentioned barrier to career advancement (40%), followed by lack of encouragement from supervisors (30%), and racial prejudice and stereotypes (25%) (Asian Americans for Community Involvement 1993:26–27).

In another study, Asian employees commonly talked about discrimination in terms of issues related to "style, culture, and language" (Fernandez and Barr 1993:259–261). Reference was made to greater tolerance of poor English spoken by a non-native "European" speaker than by an Asian speaker. The relative silence of Asians at meetings, in turn, was interpreted by management as their having little to contribute substantively, a perception reinforced by their own tendency to undersell themselves and to more readily acknowledge the contributions of others.

In other words, while English-language ability may seem to be a straightforward issue, there is a great deal of uncertainty over whether required competence levels are intrinsically the problem or merely a convenient basis for exclusion. Asian Americans have simultaneously acknowledged both views—that communication skills, including language proficiency, are important to set standards for, but that allegations of poor English facility may rest on standards that are set artificially high. Commenting before the U.S. Commission on Civil Rights, one person testified that standards were "unreasonably high" and "prejudicial" against foreign-born Asians:

> Many of us feel that our Asian accent is a major stumbling block in our career path. . . . There is no doubt that communication skills are very important. However, adopting a standard that is unreasonably high may be tantamount to allowing an employment practice that is prejudicial against foreign-born Asian American employees. (U.S. Commission on Civil Rights 1992:132)

The overall conclusion from these findings is that while specific language and leadership skills are highly desirable in managerial work that involves motivating, supervising, or leading others, there were also strong perceptions of discrimination and unequal treatment.

Special or Different Standards for Performance Evaluation and Biased Rating and Testing Systems

Among the pipeline barriers the Federal Glass Ceiling Commission identified as affecting the evaluation process, two called attention to the issue of standards: (1) special or different standards for performance evaluation and (2) biased rating and testing systems. The former refers to the fact that candidates are not truly evaluated in accordance with the same objective standards but that subjectivity, bias, preference, and arbitrariness compromise the way in which these standards are adhered to. The latter refers to biases inherent in the standards themselves.

Employment discrimination has been generally pursued on these two legal grounds under Title VII of the Civil Rights Act of 1964: namely, disparate treatment and disparate impact. In the case of *disparate treatment*, persons similarly situated but treated differently can claim unlawful discrimination on the grounds they were intentionally not accorded the same treatment as members of another group (e.g., because of race, color, religion, sex, or national origin).

Thus, former EEOC member Joy Cherian underscored clearly that Asian Americans who were similarly situated as whites were treated differently. Criteria for managerial promotion were said to be differentially applied. The following case represents a common grievance among Asian Americans—that the emphasis on educational credentials is set aside for white males. The position in question is a high-level position in the federal government.

> If it is not the glass ceiling then I don't know what it is when an Asian American with extensive supervisory experience, with two masters degrees, with highly successful performance in the same position on an acting basis, is denied a permanent position as Division Chief at the GS-14 level in a federal government agency by the same selecting official who had rated him highly successful. That Asian American was passed over in favor of a White male with a high school education and little managerial experience. . . . The evidence showed that the same selecting official had earlier passed over another Asian American with almost identical qualifications, in favor of . . . another white male with a high school education. (Cherian 1993:11)

While the legal meaning of "disparate treatment" implies intent to discriminate, *disparate impact* can occur whether or not there is any individual intent to discriminate. What is at issue is the disproportionate and adverse impact of apparently neutral institutional practices on some groups more than other groups.

An example is the height requirement of 5 feet 8 inches, which was at one time essential for joining a police force until it was found discriminatory in 1973. According to Henry Der, "no more than five Chinese police officers were members of the 1900-strong police force, accounting for less than 1 percent of all patrol officers. Based on preliminary arguments presented to him, the federal judge struck down the requirement which had an adverse impact against Asians, Hispanics, and women" (U.S. Commission on Civil Rights 1979:407).

In a series of studies of artificial barriers in San Francisco city government, civil service exams, along with loopholes in the appointment process, were identified as a source of bias.[31] In the case of written exams, failure to allow sufficient reading time was found to disqualify otherwise eligible candidates. The oral interview as well was fraught with subjective bias, which could be traced to interviewers having narrowly conceived notions of leadership qualities or otherwise prejudging certain candidates according to stereotypes about accents, ability, or other criteria which have little to do with job performance.

Other artificial barriers inhered in the latitude permitted to department heads where appointments are concerned. In appointment situations where civil service exams are waived, Asian Americans have fared worse than in situations where civil service exams are required of all candidates. "Temporary" appointments, for example, bypass civil service exams, and in turn can be extended indefinitely. In 1989, 69.7 percent of these non-civil service/limited tenure jobs in San Francisco went to whites, whereas 15.5 percent went to Asians, 16.5 percent to blacks, and 5.5 percent to Hispanics. The "Rule of Three," similarly, had enabled departments to choose from the top three candidates on a civil service list, a situation which has generally worked against minorities, even though it had held out the hope of encouraging affirmative action appointments (Chinese for Affirmative Action 1989:16, 24–25). Although the "Rule of Three" was subsequently replaced by the "Rule of the Lists," which gave even greater latitude to civil service managers, the change was described as a "double-edged sword," since managers could thereby use the flexibility either toward "promoting underrepresented minorities" or "to discriminate further." Finally, the category of "exempt appointments" has been a major source of Asian American underrepresentation at the highest levels of decision-making. As political appointees of elected officials, these top administrative appointments are exempt from having to sit for civil service examinations. In 1986, there were reported to be approximately 1,900-plus exempt appointments under the San Francisco City Charter, 131 of which were in high-level administration, and only four of these held by Asian Americans. In 1992, Chinese for Affirmative Action described Asian Americans as "the least likely group to gain an exempt administrative appointment" (Chinese for Affirmative Action 1992:8, 10). In fact, whites were increasingly likely to be appointed to these positions, with transparently negative consequences for diversifying civil service leadership.

Language requirements and selection by personal connections or by seniority might be similarly included among those facially bias-free requirements that nevertheless produce a disparate outcome (Ezorsky 1991:9–27). According to Matsuda, accent discrimination is pervasive yet rarely a product of malice, "conscious pretext or discriminatory intent." Rather it occurs "because of unconscious bias, careless evaluation, false assumptions about speech and intelligibility, mistaken overvaluing of the role of speech on the job, or concessions to customer prejudice" (Matsuda 1991:1383). The following case shows how evaluators frequently bring an unconscious bias about accents, judging some more harshly than others. In a lawsuit by Manuel Fragante, the plaintiff had been rejected for a civil service job at the Department of Motor Vehicles because of his Filipino accent, despite the fact that he scored highest on an exam taken by over 700 other applicants. In the courtroom proceedings described below, however, comprehension was never an issue, according to the objective evidence. Fragante's English was, if anything, better than many of the other participants.

> The linguist sat through the trial and noted the proceedings with interest. Attorneys for both sides suffered lapses in grammar and sentence structure, as did the judge. Mr. Fragante's English, a review of the transcript confirmed, was more nearly perfect in standard grammar and syntax than any other speaker in the courtroom. Mr. Fragante testified for two days, under the stress of both direct and cross-examination. The judge and the examiners spoke to Fragante in English and understood his answer. A court reporter understood and took down his words verbatim. In the functional context of the trial, everyone understood Manuel Fragante's speech. Yet, the defendant's interviewers continued to claim Fragante could not be understood well enough to serve as a DMV clerk. (ibid.:1338)

Given such examples as the above, Matsuda has argued that in cases of accent discrimination, judges themselves would be better informed and aided by guidelines that enable them to distill and isolate elements deeply embedded in cultural prejudices and those directly related to business necessity (ibid.:1357–84). While the Equal Employment Opportunity Commission has published guidelines regarding "national origins discrimination," which includes language discrimination (EEOC "Facts about National Origin Discrimination" [FS/E-1], 1992), controversy still attends whether language requirements are an essential screening device for certain job tasks, a legitimate "business necessity," or whether they reflect undue prejudice toward certain accents, as in the case of

English-only rules in the workplace (Chen 1994) or hiring decisions based on accent (Matsuda 1991; Nguyen 1994).[32]

English-only rules are, under certain conditions, justifiably applied across the board when unimpeded communication between workers is proven to be essential. Workplace conditions where an accent might be dysfunctional might exist in those jobs where teamwork, time pressures, quick response, and high stress are involved, and where the consequences of miscommunication are serious. Even in these situations, however, the uniform requirement of standard English may not be the most efficient option. According to Matsuda (1991:1348), every reported case of accent discrimination under Title VII has run up against the following "doctrinal puzzle" in determining whether accent discrimination is acceptable.

1. Title VII absolutely disallows discrimination on the basis of race and national origin.
2. A fortiori, Title VII absolutely disallows discrimination on the basis of traits, like accent, when they are stand-ins for race and national origin.
3. Title VII absolutely allows employers to discriminate on the basis of job ability.
4. Communication, and therefore accent, employers will insist, are elements of job ability.

Despite the statutory protection afforded by Title VII against language discrimination and proposals for more objective guidelines (Nyugen 1994), employers' job-related justifications appear as the single major factor responsible for differential treatment. Cases brought before the recent Federal Glass Ceiling Commission indicated that even demonstrated language ability can be misrepresented by superiors. Allegations of language problems are but one of several ways in which an applicant's file can be misrepresented. In the following case, the person in question was alleged not only to have "communication problems" but to have generated cost overruns. The contrary, in fact, turned out to be true.

> An Asian American was denied a promotion to a GS-15 position in spite of enviable academic qualifications and a distinguished career inside and outside the government on the pretexts of communication problems and cost overruns under his command. The true facts were otherwise. He had been rated outstanding in written communications six times by five different supervisors, and above average another four times. And the cost overruns had occurred not under him, but under others—all of whom were White Americans—who had been promoted ahead of him. Even more [sic], the evidence was that he had in fact brought the costs under control during his command. (Cherian 1993:12)

Successful legal action against misrepresentation is not without precedent, yet the closed door nature of decision making and the de facto exclusion of underrepresented groups from the very ranks of these decision-makers places an inordinate burden of proof on employees.[33]

CONCLUDING REMARKS

A review of relevant research on the glass ceiling and Asian Americans underscores the poor quality of the governmental databases upon which studies must frequently rely. Where studies have circumvented the methodological problems associated with aggregate managerial data, they have typically found Asian Americans concentrated at the lower levels of mainstream management, notably absent in supervisory positions wielding significant authority or power.

Relevant studies of Asian American professionals note relative stagnation in terms of one or more of the following patterns: (1) a low ratio of administrators or managers, as compared with their representation in the professional pool; (2) lower returns on education; (3) longer lengths of time to achieve managerial promotion, especially into top executive-managerial positions; and (4) strong employee perceptions of being bypassed for promotion because of discrimination, stereotyping, or a less than objective review process.

Theories about managerial underrepresentation range from "cultural" or "human capital" models to "structural" explanations. The former suggests the absence of eligible candidates with requisite qualifications or skills and thus a problem with the "supply" side to recruitment. Structurally oriented perspectives, on the other hand, have noted how occupational structures themselves, industry characteristics, or features of the general economy influence mobility in these sectors. Although the aggregation of data from different organizational contexts or settings obscures the dynamic processes at work in any single context, the Federal Glass Ceiling Commission identified several typical *internal* structural barriers, which include outreach and recruitment practices, initial placement in the occupational hierarchy, and other specific pipeline barriers.

As an empirical problem, the glass ceiling has remained invisible for many reasons. The scale on which large-scale corporations operate can itself contribute to the invisibility of barriers. Frustrations related to managerial aspirations can result in these problems being suppressed or internalized as "personal deficits" or, alternatively, being expressed through job transfers and departures leading to alternative career pursuits. More benign interpretations for Asian American underrepresentation include personal choice, lack of managerial interest, the availability of dual career ladders, or company incentives that reward Asians for remaining on the technical track.

Where a glass ceiling is suspected, explanations have included exclusion from informal networks critical for career advancement or instrumental for dispelling myths about managerial disinterest. Standards themselves are vulnerable to subjective or cultural biases. Although educational institutions have generously rewarded and reaffirmed Asian Americans for their academic achievements, the workplace not only introduces new and unexpected standards but a strong sense that fair play or claims to objectivity are subverted by arbitrary processes.

Chapter 3 takes a historical look at how the structure of the economy at large has played a role in the occupational segmentation or virtual segregation of Asian Americans in the labor force. Depressed patterns of mobility were the norm for the illiterate laborers who immigrated during the late nineteenth and early twentieth centuries. College-trained Asians, either educated in the United States or abroad, also found their career paths blocked by artificial barriers.

NOTES

1. Title II-Glass Ceiling Act, Section 203a. Public Law 102-66, 21 Nov. 1991.

2. While other disciplines such as political science and economics have also been interested in these dynamics, the present review limited itself to the sociological literature where research on racial mobility could be expected to include discussions of social and cultural as well as structural considerations.

3. The four journals were *American Journal of Sociology, Sociology and Social Research, Social Forces,* and *American Sociological Review.* The review centered on articles which focused on Asians, excluding others that made only very brief passing mention of Asians. In addition, Mely Tan, *The Chinese in the United* States (1973) and James W. Loewen, *The Mississippi Chinese* (1971) were two monographs noted by Hirata (1980).

4. Of the four major sociological journals reviewed here, the *American Journal of Sociology, American Sociological Review,* and *Social Forces* included book reviews. A total of at least twenty-five books on Asian Americans were reviewed. Nine focused on socioeconomic adjustment, of which eight centered on ethnic small businesses or work in enclave economies. Articles include Boswell (1986); Jiobu (1988); Min and Jaret (1985); Nee and Saunders (1985); Portes and Nee (1996) and Zhou and Logan (1989).

5. Bonacich and Modell (1980), Light and Bonacich (1988), Min (1988), and Sui (1953). This last book, based on extensive fieldwork in the 1930s and 1940s, was written more than thirty-five years ago, to be rediscovered in 1980 by John Tschen, when researching New York Chinese laundry workers.)

    Among the three exceptions to this focus on the enclave economy were Caplan and Whitmore (1990), Kim (1983), and Montero (1983). Chapter four of Kim's book focuses on "Small Business as an Entry Point for Korean Immigrants." However, the overall book is concerned with the implications for community.

6. While the term "Asian Americans" was coined early on in the 1960s, Pacific Islanders were not enumerated in government databases until much later. The terms "Asian American Pacific Islander" (AAPI) and "Asian Pacific American" (APA) are synonymous and reflect the inclusion of Pacific Islanders as a distinct part of the Asian American Aggregate. See also chapter 4 *n*5, this volume.

7. The collective testimony encompassed civil rights, the census, women's issues, immigration, inclusion of Pacific Americans, education, employment, housing, and health. Individual Asian Americans have previously testified before Congress, as in the case of Stephen Thom's grandfather who spoke against the Chinese Exclusion Act of 1882 (U.S. Commission on Civil Rights 1979:367).

8. Chinese and Filipinos showed more of a bimodal distribution, with concentrations also at low-level service occupations and retail trade.

9. For a fuller discussion of the middleman minority concept, see pp. 13–36 of Bonacich and Modell (1980).

10. U.S. Commission on Civil Rights 1979: 27–28, 55–59, 389–93, 402–3, 434–44, 500–502.

11. Median household income, for example, was considered less accurate that median household per capita income.

12. A draft of this report had been viewed so egregious in its analysis and omission of certain facts about Asian Americans that it prompted a written critique, which eventually became part of the final report (U.S. Commission on Civil Rights, 1988:119–131).

13. Although such activity was not as prevalent among some groups, such as Filipinos, Vietnamese, and Cambodians (Min, 1986-87; Huynh 1996; G. Lee, 1996), small business participation for other Asian subgroups exceeded that of the general population. Whereas 6.4% of the total population were self-employed, 9% of Koreans reported that they owned their own businesses, followed by 7.1% of Asian Indians, 7% of Japanese, and 6.6% of Chinese. Only 1.3% of blacks, by contrast, were so listed (Waldinger et al. 1990:56). Similarly, among the case Spanish-speaking populations, the percentage of business ownership was smaller 4.7% of Cubans, 1.7% of Hispanics, 1.6% of Mexicans, and 0.7% of Puerto Ricans owned their own businesses.

14. Koreans seem to be an exception to the general pattern for immigrants to employ primarily family members or ethnic workers (Kim and Hurh, 1983:10–11; Min and Jaret, 1985:423–29).

15. Bonacich (1988, 1989), Min (1989), U.S. Department of Labor (1992), Wadinger et al. (1990:49–78).

16. "Since 1978, the employment rate of Asian American scientists and engineers has been growing 9% per year, or 146% through 1988, which is much faster than the 7% per year growth (or 97% overall) in scientific and engineering employment for whites over the same period" (Rawls 1991:24).

17. By 1987, Asian doctoral scientists or engineers made up 9% (or 36,400) of the total number of doctoral scientists and engineers in the U.S. even though they were only 3% of the professional work force, and only about 2% of the total U.S. work force. Asian Ph.D.s also concentrated in engineering. Compared to 16% of all other races, Asians represented 35% of all engineers with Ph.D.s (Rawls 1991:24).

   As scientists, Asian Americans are more likely to be chemists. Thirteen percent of all Asians who were scientists were chemists, compared with only 8% of whites and other minorities combined. Similarly, of those scientists with Ph.D.s, 20% of Asians were chemists, compared with 13% of Ph.D. scientists representing other racial groups. (Rawls, 1991:21).

18. High-wage industries included construction, wholesale trade, and manufacturing industries such as food products, paper, printing and publishing, petroleum refining, primary metals, and fabricated metal products (Cabezas and Yee 1977:9).

19. These retail businesses included "Eating and Drinking Places, General Merchandise Stores (mostly department stores), Apparel Stores, and Miscellaneous Retail Stores (mostly drug stores)—versus Building Material Stores, Food Stores (mostly the supermarkets), and Furniture and Home Furnishings Stores, which are all higher wage retailers" (Asians employed in Commercial Banking and Insurance were mostly clerical workers) (Cabezas and Yee 1977).

20. These industries were identified as "Chemical Products, Electric and Electronic Equipment, and Commercial Banks" (Cabezas and Yee 1977:10).

21. Cabezas and Kawaguchi (1988, 1990); Cabezas, Shinagawa, and Kawaguchi (1987); Fong and Cabezas (1980); and Kim and Hurh (1983).

22. In terms of their overall representation in high-tech manufacturing, this figure is high, not only because Asians represent only 16.8% of the area's population but because this

represents a doubling of their size between 1980 and 1990 from one-tenth to one-fifth of the high-tech workforce.

23. Asian Americans also worked as technicians (30.8%), craft workers (30.3%), semiskilled operatives (47%) and unskilled laborers (41.2%) (*Global Electronics,* October 1992).

24. An internal study of the above companies was conducted by UCLA professor William Ouchi ("Aerospace Careers" 16 November1992).

25. See the first three presentations by Minoru Yasui (Executive Director of the Commission on Community Relations in Denver), Canta Pian (Acting Director, Division of Asian American Affairs, U.S. Department of Health, Education, and Welfare), and Professor Ling-chi Wang (University of California, Berkeley).

26. Lan 1976; Woodrum 1981; Hirschman and Wong 1984; Nee and Sanders 1985; Li 1987; Tienda and Lii 1987; Cabezas and Kawaguchi 1988; Woo 1989; Wong and Nagasawa 1991; O'Hare and Felt 1991; Orcutt and Sanders 1992; Tang 1993b, 1993c; Ong and Blumenberg 1994

27. Another study similarly found that foreign-born white males were more likely to be on a par with U.S.-born white males than Asian American males, for whom foreign-born status brought lower returns on their human capital investments (Cabezas and Kawaguchi 1988).

28. This source compiles information from published reports from government and private associations.

29. According to Judy Rosener, while there is general agreement that employee "under-utilization" refers to untapped potential, there is far less agreement on how to measure or quantify it. Figures on unemployment, underemployment, underrepresentation, occupational segregation, and pay equity have been the most common indicators used (Rosener 1995:45–66). As such, statistical data on managerial representation by race are basically outcome data. They tell us little how managerial positions are filled as a process. As was evident from a review of the research in chapter 2, studies which have included data on Asian Americans have been overwhelmingly quantitative and of this nature, that is, reflective of outcomes. The conventional method under such circumstances is to "control for" certain factors which might account for occupational differences. Thus, for example, if education is thought to explain differences in occupational mobility, then the analyst would seek to compare Asian Americans and whites with the same education, say, those with a postgraduate degree, to see if these inequalities "disappear" after education is "controlled for." If racial differences persist, other explanations might surface. Perhaps the differences, one might theorize, are due to greater seniority on the part of whites? The analyst would then look to compare those with the same years of work experience. In short, this manner of controlling for variables would continue until either all possible explanations or means of exploring them had been exhausted. Any residual differences are often attributed to "discrimination."

30. About their own personal or professional abilities, they noted the following *employee* characteristics as barriers: written and verbal communication skills (25%), interpersonal interaction styles (17%), and leadership ability (11%). While these responses give some credence to the view that certain management requirements were lacking, there was also a strong perception of unequal treatment (Asian Americans for Community Involvement 1993:25).

31.   Chinese for Affirmative Action 1986:3, 11–12; 1989:8–9, 16; 1992:6, 10–11, 13.

32.   The case of *Griggs v. Duke Power Co.* (1971) is considered a singularly important Supreme Court decision in terms of equal opportunity employment because it ruled illegal those practices that systematically exclude on the basis of criteria which are unrelated to job performance or "business necessity," and placed the burden of demonstrating job-performance relevance upon employers, rather than employees (Ezorsky 1991:111–21).

33.   A federal court judge, for example, ruled that Vincent Maximilian-Yee, an administrator for Hughes Aircraft who had been fired in 1985, be reinstated; the grounds: his employment history had been misrepresented by his supervisor (*Los Angeles Times,* 16 September 1992).

CHAPTER 3

A HISTORY OF VIRTUAL SEGREGATION

> It would be erroneous to perceive the new job opportunities afforded these well-educated Asian Americans in war-related industries during the war and throughout the Cold War as the definitive removal of the racial barrier and final acceptance or assimilation of Asians in the American mainstream, as many, including Asian Americans, have come to believe. . . . In the case of the well-educated Asian Americans, it was by necessity that they were drawn or drafted into the war industries, clearly not due to such politically charged notions of "success" and "assimilation." In other words, Asian Americans were recruited . . . in very much the same manner as their ancestors or parents when they were first brought over from Asia to meet the demand for a particular type of labor in the rapidly developing economy of the West.
>
> *Professor Ling-chi Wang, University of California, Berkeley, testifying before the* U.S. Commission on Civil Rights, 1979

The present-day rhetoric that motivates corporations to diversify their workforce is that it is "good for business." Yet, U.S. corporations have always been aware of the "value of diversity," and whenever possible have manipulated it in favor of profitability. It is the restricted use of minorities and women in the *upper* reaches of the occupational hierarchy which prompted the Federal Glass Ceiling Commission to title its own report *Good For Business: Making Full Use of the Nation's Human Capital* (1995). Insofar as the glass ceiling reflects depressed mobility, most Asian American labor history can be so characterized.

While a general history of Asians in the United States typically unfolds as a linear account of each ethnic group's chronological arrival, their history is essentially an economic history, with ethnic succession determined by the role that the U.S. economy played in the immigration of each group. Each wave would be initially welcomed as hard laborers, low-level service workers, or as a skilled and controllable workforce, with this welcome withdrawn as soon as aspirations clashed with the interests of either white workers or white employers. The degree of hostility that Asians in general faced during any historical period depended on their relationship to the general economy, to other workers, as well as to particular employers (Takaki 1990a). Sentiments toward this labor force were thus swayed not simply by "free-floating" racial prejudice but by specific interests. Even liberal tolerance, where it could be found, was influenced by industry characteristics, though it might be articulated in terms of democratic principles or ideals.

In rewriting the labor history of Asian Americans in the United States, scholars have countered previous research rendering these workers passive victims in the face of either impersonal market forces or active racial discrimination. In the process, they have underscored the contributions of Asian Americans to the economy as well as their grassroots organizing efforts to transform their work conditions (Friday 1994b). The present chapter is less concerned with this issue of human agency than with how industry and occupational patterns reflect "virtual" segregation over the past century and longer.[1] This has been true for early Asian immigrants, second-generation Asian Americans, and recent professionals who, respectively, experienced different artificial barriers: the first as a result of laws and ordinances directed at their "alien" status; the second because of discrimination at the hiring level; and the third because of barriers to entering the ranks of management. Major issues overarching this entire history were immigration exclusion, the denial of citizenship rights, and occupational subordination. When *economically* expedient, Asian immigration was regularly and predictably restricted, and justified based on either Asians' perceived "unassimilability" or the depressing effect they had on overall wages.

As U.S.-born citizens, the "second generation" of Asian Americans also faced employment barriers, especially Chinese and Japanese Americans, who not only formed the majority of Asian Americans prior to World War II but who also were more likely to be college educated. Beginning in 1929 and through most of the 1930s, the Great Depression severely curtailed opportunities for individual advancement. College-educated, American-born Asians retreated to ethnic enclaves in Chinatowns and Little Tokyos for work. While it can be argued that the barriers they faced were not "artificial" and that they were also "overqualified" for the times (since it would not be until after the end of World War II that higher education became more widespread with the assistance of the GI bill), they suffered more than their share of unemployment when compared with their white counterparts. Only when the wartime economy drew heavily on the untapped potential of all Americans did their situation improve. As Wang noted at the outset of this chapter, the entry of technically trained Asian American professionals into the war effort was motivated not so much by egalitarian, democratic considerations as by the economic needs of the war effort.

Highly trained and educated Asian professionals recruited from overseas after 1965 make up a different social category. While on the surface they appear to have escaped the longstanding depressed mobility patterns of their earlier counterparts, it is with this group that glass ceiling barriers into management have been linked with more subtle forms of discrimination, an issue to be taken up in subsequent chapters.

Though not formally enslaved like blacks, Asians were subordinated to white workers through formal legislation and informal practices.[2] After the Civil War and the freeing of slaves in 1868, blacks formally had many of the same rights as whites and apparently could not be enticed by agricultural capitalists to leave the South for California's low field wages (Cheng and Bonacich 1984:157).[3] To the extent that Asian workers made themselves available as cheap laborers, they were blamed for depressing wages, even though there is some evidence that they resisted those agents or impersonal market forces that depressed labor costs.[4]

Apart from racism in the form of individual or collective acts of violence, politicians passed numerous laws or ordinances during periods of tension and social conflict, directly injuring or crippling the livelihood of Asian workers. As forms of government discrimination, these laws played a critical role in shaping some of the earlier barriers to occupational mobility.[5] Denied the right to citizenship through naturalization, the majority of these early Asian immigrants were thereby denied other civil and political rights considered "inalienable" by most Americans, including certain political, legal, or economic rights, such as the right to vote, own land, or form a corporation.[6] According to attorney Angelo Ancheta (1998:35): "Using 1965 as a watershed year, the history of legal discrimination against Asian Americans can be divided into two distinct eras: a pre-1965 era of explicit discrimination based on race, and a post-1965 era of implicit discrimination based on citizenship and immigration status." Although the history of such laws, he says, is generally omitted in civil rights studies, the court decisions here have their contemporary significance as legal precedents. It was especially in their quest for citizenship that Chinese, Japanese, Indian, Filipino, and Korean immigrants challenged both state and federal discrimination and in the process gave rise to landmark cases (McClain 1995).

Early nineteenth-century immigrants, their second-generation descendants, and later post-1965 immigrants fall, respectively, into three historical periods that roughly parallel the U.S. economy's steady shift over the past century from agriculture ("primary") to industrial ("secondary") and finally to post-industrial service ("tertiary") work (table 3.1).[7] Early immigrants were concentrated either in agriculture or in the tertiary sector as low-level service workers, and were largely excluded from the growing industrial sector that employed 34 percent of Californians in 1870 (see table 3.2). California, in fact, developed its agricultural backbone by promoting racial or ethnic diversity within its labor force. With the freeing of black slaves, successive waves of Asian immigrants were actively recruited to meet the needs of large-scale agriculture. Unlike farming in other parts of the country, California never really shared America's tradition of small family farms (Chan 1986:272–301). Growers diversified not only their crops, but their labor force whenever economically feasible. In addition to Chinese, Japanese, Asian Indians, and Filipinos, the state's agricultural workers have also included Mexicans, Portuguese, Koreans, and Puerto Ricans (Takaki 1990a:30, 270–93). Although Asian workers migrated to other parts of the United States, including Hawai'i, the Pacific Northwest, the East Coast, and the South, they are heavily concentrated in California, and therefore the history in the following pages focuses on this state.

The geographical concentration of Asians on the West Coast also explains some of their early exclusion from industrial work. Although England's industrial revolution began around 1760, thereby giving rise to the idea of the "melting pot" in its original and literal sense, America's own industrial revolution would not occur until the late 1880s. While Chinese entered a wide range of light manufacturing jobs in San Francisco, industrialization largely took place in the northeastern and midwestern states, bypassing the majority of Asians who resided outside these regions (Bonacich 1984b; Liu 1984). Then, as today, Asians have been concentrated on the Pacific Coast, blacks in the South, and those of Mexican ancestry in the Southwest (Lieberson 1980; Portes and Rumbaut 1990).

While the exclusion of minorities from the industrial sector might be viewed as an unfortunate coincidence of circumstances, "social engineering" has been very much a part of American history, as profit-oriented owners or capitalists sought specific forms of labor.

Table 3.1. U.S. Labor Force Employment by Sector: 1870–1993 (in thousands).

Year	Total Employed	Agriculture	Total Primary Sector	Secondary Sector	Tertiary Sector
1993	119,306	2.6%	3.1%	22.4%	74.4%
1950	65,470	12.0%	13.5%	29.9%	25.8%
1870	12,930	52.5%	54.1%	26.8%	21.5%

Source: U.S. Census of Population, Statistical Abstract of the United States 1994. Census data of 1870 combine manufacturing and mining into one category.

Table 3.2. California Labor Force Employment by Sector: 1870–1990 (in thousands).

Year	Total Employed	Agriculture	Total Primary Sector	Secondary Sector	Tertiary Sector
1990	13,996	3.0%	3.4%	23.7%	72.9%
1950	2,754	7.3%	8.4%	27.2%	63.2%
1870	239	20.1%	NA	34.2%	45.8%

Source: U.S. Census of Population, Statistical Abstract of the United States 1994. Census data of 1870 combine manufacturing and mining into one category.

Thus Stephen Steinberg (1995:80–183) attributes the exclusion of blacks from manufacturing work to "Northern racism," which preferred to rely on Southeast European immigrant labor. Only later, during World War II were blacks brought up from the South to work the East Bay shipyards in the San Francisco Bay area. After the war, most of these approximately 10,000 black shipyard workers lost their jobs (Brown 1998:268–71).

Elbridge Sibley (1953) explained how the burgeoning population of southeastern Europeans entering manual work at the turn of the century created the floor upon which other white workers could ascend. Even though technological change created opportunities for mobility by replacing blue-collar jobs with white-collar jobs, these blue-collar jobs would be filled by Europeans, thereby setting up a dynamic that allowed their successors to rise up the ladder.

> Of the 642,724 immigrant workers admitted during the year ending 30 June 1914, 603,378 stated that they were engaged in manual occupations. This means that the immigrants included about 105,000 more blue-collar workers than would be found among an equal number of workers taken at random from the American population. An equal number of persons must therefore have shifted from blue-collar to white-collar jobs during that one year in order to maintain the same broad occupational distribution in the population. Most of those who ascended were in all probability native Americans. (Sibley 1953:382–83)

After the 1960s, a post-industrial economy surged. Education and professional training became a *necessary* prerequisite for mobility, especially in the tertiary sector. The most populous state in the union, California epitomized this move from an industrial to a service economy. While agriculture remains an important source of production, it accounts for only 3 percent of California's workers (table 3.2). Workers in the service sector face a two-tiered structure: (1) low-tech, labor-intensive service jobs at the bottom; or (2) high-tech, labor-expensive managerial jobs in the upper echelons. The high-tech industry offers an especially glaring instance of an increasingly two-tiered economy, which is also racially stratified (Burris 1993; Colcough and Tolbert 1992; Walters 1992).

EARLY IMMIGRANT STATUS: MIDDLE TO LATE NINETEENTH CENTURY

From the mid-nineteenth to the early twentieth century, Asians who immigrated to the United States aspired to improve their economic lot. Their overall occupational options were restricted not simply because the large majority were unable to speak or write English, but also because their move up the ladder was artificially constrained. As the last frontier, California was largely rural and agrarian, as was the rest of the United States, and Asians were recruited to develop a fundamentally agricultural economy. Although their total numbers in the United States prior to World War II (between 1860 and 1940) never reached .25 percent of the total U.S. population (Chavez and Bonacich 1984:61–62), active attempts to exclude them from the country tended to follow their entry into direct competition with white workers. Typically, this occurred when they were called upon as strikebreakers or, alternatively, when they resituated themselves as independent entrepreneurs in direct competition with their former employers. Restrictive immigration laws were then passed to control the size and nature of this foreign labor pool. The Exclusion Act of 1882, the first in a series of such laws aimed at the "Oriental problem," made the Chinese the first national group to be excluded by law on the basis of ethnicity and race (U.S. Commission on Civil Rights 1980:8).

Naturalization laws narrowly circumscribed the range of jobs available to Asians (Ancheta 1998:82–103). As early as 1790, the first federal naturalization statute reserved the right to apply for U.S. citizenship to "any alien, being a free white." Although these rights were extended to former slaves following the Civil War, Asians were essentially "aliens ineligible for citizenship."[8] As the mainland state with historically the largest concentration of Asian immigrants, California classified "Orientals" as nonwhites. Admitted into the Union in 1850 as a free state (i.e., nonslaveholding), California nevertheless inscribed into its early state constitution terms that restricted naturalization to "white, male citizens of the United States and Mexico" (Nee and Nee 1974:31–32). The "white person" prerequisite was included in every subsequent naturalization act until 1952, when racial restrictions on naturalization were finally lifted (Lopez 1996:31–32).

Economic factors, driven by racial-group interests, not only consigned Asians to the lowest levels of those work spheres they were allowed to enter but also skewed the gender balance among Asian immigrants. The shortage of women was a general phenomenon as men pioneered the West in search of gold, and was exacerbated by employers who sought to exploit the labor of the men without incurring the responsibility and costs of supporting their families. Detaching the male worker from his household increased profit margins because it shifted the cost of reproduction from the state and the employer to the kin group left behind in Asia (Espiritu 1997:17).

Some employers, such as plantation owners in Hawai'i, allowed women to immigrate because they thought this would have a stabilizing effect on workers, but even in Hawai'i female immigration was eventually limited. Of all immigrants, Chinese were most adversely affected in terms of family formation. Being the first Asians to immigrate in large numbers and the first to have their numbers restricted, they endured the stranglehold of exclusionary laws longer than any other group.[9] In general, the growth of Asian American families and communities would not come about until the passage of the 1965 Immigration Act, which actively encouraged family reunification.

In the context of an unbalanced sex ratio and the general absence of female workers in the American West, Asian men performed not only hard labor but domestic work as well. Chinese, Japanese, and Filipinos took up domestic service more often than Koreans and Asian Indians. Commenting on the latter's relative absence from such work, Sucheng Chan (1991:40) wrote: "Few Koreans or Asian Indians, however, relied on domestic service for their livelihood, for reasons that have not yet been studied."

Chinese Immigrants

Like whites who flooded into California during the 1850s, the Chinese, too, had been lured by the 1848 discovery of gold. The availability—or unavailability—of mining jobs shaped their occupational distribution (Chiu 1963).[10] From their first arrivals in the 1850s until their formal exclusion in 1882, conflict characterized the relationship of these Chinese newcomers with "native" whites.

Twenty thousand Chinese came to "Old Gold Mountain" in 1852 alone, prompting the passage of a Foreign Miners' License Tax that same year.[11] Compared with other legislative proposals barring Chinese outright from working California mines, confiscatory taxes were subtler and less offensive to state legislators, who eventually voted to increase the fee "each succeeding year ad infinitum" (McClain 1994:12–13, 16–19). Race-neutral on the surface, the tax had a disproportionate impact on Chinese, though it would not afford them the representation that normally comes with taxation (Ancheta 1998:28).

Chinese who competed with white miners in the more productive or lucrative mining sites were beaten, shot, and otherwise forcibly removed, their campsites burned. A conservative estimate of Chinese deaths, based on a committee investigation in 1862 by the state, produced a list of eighty-eight known murders (Nee and Nee 1974:35–38). Legislation denying Chinese the right to testify in court or "be witnesses against whites" had long ruled out recourse in the courts.[12] Chinese miners eventually turned to working abandoned mines or providing needed services as cooks and launderers (Chan 1991c:33–34). Whenever they found mining jobs, however, they were less likely to be laborers or service providers, though the decline of mining from the 1860s on decreased this likelihood (Chan 1986:56).

These former miners subsequently moved into railroad construction (Mei 1984) and agriculture (Lydon 1985; Chan 1986). As railroad workers, they were not only tolerated but also seen as indispensable. When the dangerous work of laying the mountainous western half of the Transcontinental Railroad (Nee and Nee 1973:38–43) was finished and the railroad finally completed in 1869, almost 10,000 Chinese were discharged (Chan 1991c:32). Many eventually found work as migrant laborers, harvesters, truck gardeners, or tenant farmers. As tenant farmers, they did the back-breaking work of reclaiming swamplands, digging ditches, and building dykes—developments that became the basis for the irrigation system that would enable California agribusiness to flourish. White small farmers thereby saw their "dignity" as free and independent producers threatened by corporate growth, including mergers that allowed food to be produced cheaply and profitably for national and international markets. Despite their significant role in agriculture, the Chinese were not as concentrated here as subsequent Asian laborers would be.

Restricted as it was, Chinese employment was nevertheless more wide-ranging than that of other Asian immigrants before 1965. Their engagement in various occupational pursuits, however, narrowed over time. Chan (1986:52) describes their shifts in employment as falling into four periods: (1) mining and trading (1850-1865); (2) agriculture, light manufacturing, and common labor (1865–late 1870s); (3) a period of consolidation (late 1870s and 1880s); and (4) decline and abandonment of many occupations (late 1880s to the turn of the century).

The economic stagnation and depression of the 1870s made the presence of working Chinese galling, and the drive for exclusion accelerated. By 1876, California's economic troubles included severe drought, cattle deaths numbering in the thousands, a one-third decline in mining output, speculation, and a stock crash. The swell of unemployed white drifters in San Francisco was matched only by the large population of foreign-born immigrants, who made up half of the city's population (Nee and Nee 1973:46–47). Petitions for an anti-Chinese immigration law included the argument that thousands of whites were leaving California because of the Chinese presence, although the occupational structure reflected their virtual segregation in jobs that offered little mobility.[13] Boycotts, employer sanctions, and the pressure to fire Chinese eventually confined them to manufacturing ethnic foodstuffs and to low-level service work traditionally done by women, for example, laundry and cooking (Takaki 1990a:28–29; 80–112; Chan 1991c:33, 40).[14]

Significantly, even though relegated to operating these marginal operations, Chinese laundry workers were penalized by a series of restrictive ordinances, neutral on the surface but implicitly biased (McClain 1994:48, 52–54, 100–102). These differential actions toward the Chinese culminated in *Yick Wo v. Hopkins* (1886), a class action suit that resulted in landmark civil rights legislation, where the U.S. Supreme Court ruled for the first time against arbitrary economic discrimination affecting a class of people.[15] Equal protection under the law thus entered into the area of employment discrimination long before Title VII of the 1964 Civil Rights Act outlawed employment discrimination. Centered on *economic* discrimination against nonwhite minorities rather than other kinds of racial discrimination, the case was precedent-setting (Cruse 1987:99-100ff.; McClain and McClain 1991:12–16; McClain 1994:115–26).

Japanese Immigrants

With the exclusion of Chinese from the country in 1882, the demand for fieldhands led to the introduction of Japanese workers. Although early Japanese immigrants, like the Chinese before them, would seek jobs in the general economy (e.g., shoe manufacturing), they were eventually forced to confine themselves to occupations that did not compete with white workers (e.g., shoe repairing) (Takaki 1990a:197–98). Insofar as they became a sizeable population within less than two decades, they were specifically recruited into agricultural economies in California and Hawai'i.

When Hawai'i formally became a U.S. territory in 1900, contract labor became illegal, and free immigrants, such as the Japanese, were actively recruited. The mainland also desired Japanese workers for railroad work, lumber mills, and farming. But before 1908 few Japanese lived on the mainland (only 55,000) as compared with Hawai'i (150,000). Beginning in 1902, almost 34,000 Japanese were lured from Hawai'i to the mainland, until an executive order from President Theodore Roosevelt in 1907 prohibited such remigration.[16] Nevertheless, the production of specialty crops so depended upon such labor that between 1908 and 1924 more than 120,000 arrived on the Pacific Coast, with two-thirds of Japanese in California earning their living as farm laborers (Chan 1991c:38).

As with the Chinese, the Japanese would have their numbers later restricted when their social presence seemed more threatening than their economic utility. The above immigration figures, in fact, represent a general decline in Japanese immigration from 1900–1910, as a result of the "Gentlemen's Agreement" (1907) whereby Japan agreed to stop issuing passports to laborers seeking to emigrate to the United States. Because of a loophole enabling wives (and relatives) to enter, between 1909 and 1923, more than 33,000 Japanese women came as wives or "picture brides" (Nakano Glenn 1984:472). Any loopholes to Japanese immigration were dealt with by the 1924 National Origins Act, which permitted immigration only to those emigrating from the Western Hemisphere (U.S. Commission on Civil Rights 1980:92–10). On the surface neutral, it created a ceiling of 150,000 per year on the total number of alien immigrants to be based on 2 percent of the total numbers of a nationality group residing in the United States according to the 1890 census. Since the number of Asians in the 1890 census was relatively small, their exclusion was ensured. Aliens from the Western Hemisphere, on the other hand, were exempted and specifically classified as "nonquota" immigrants (ibid.:9–10, 13).

With Japanese families creating permanent settlements, California passed the first Alien Land Law in 1913 (McClain 1995:43–44) preventing such immigrants from owning or leasing land for more than three years.[17] In 1920, the law was extended to prevent their American-born children from holding title to land with their parents as guardians. Not until 1948, in *Oyama v. California*, would the U.S. Supreme Court rule such laws unconstitutional (Ancheta 1998:29–30, 33, 84). That same year, the Court in *Takahashi v. Fish and Game Commission* also struck down another California law that had forbidden Japanese as aliens ineligible for citizenship from acquiring commercial fishing licenses (Ancheta 1998:33; McClain 1994:81–82, 93–95).

As agricultural laborers, the Japanese, like the Chinese, were excluded from advanced sectors of the economy. Reporting on occupational data for 1910, Bonacich found that:

> When we combine the occupational structure of the Chinese and Japanese in California and Hawaii, we find the Asian workers occupying a few economic niches: agricultural labor, domestic and personal service, some retailing, and heavy labor in a few manufacturing lines. They were more or less absent from the more advanced sectors of the economy, including most of manufacturing, the professions, and public service. To some extent their skewed occupational distribution can be accounted for by the economic character of the territories in which they resided,

which was probably not fortuitous. But allowing for this, we find that even within California and Hawaii they were more likely than other workers to concentrate in the same few occupations. (1984a:72)

Like their male counterparts, Japanese women were concentrated in labor-intensive, low-wage work that was not directly competitive with white women, namely, domestic service (Nakano Glenn 1984:477–80). Japanese male labor would eventually, however, become increasingly expensive and thus undesirable, especially as they organized and demanded higher wages (Takaki 1990a:198–201).

Asian Indian Immigrants

Since Japanese immigration in the late 1880s had basically satisfied planters' needs for cheap labor, it was not until this immigration was restricted by the 1924 National Origins Act that Asian Indians—specifically, Sikh laborers from the Punjab region of northwest India—began in the 1920s to enter California agriculture in significant numbers (Takaki 1990a:294–314). In the early 1900s workers from India were employed largely in lumber mills in Washington and Oregon or in railroad construction on the Pacific Coast (Mazumdar 1984:560–61; Takaki 1990a:297, 302). The organizing activities of white workers, however, eventually forced most of them out of the lumber industry, so that they, along with former railroad workers, ended up in California's agricultural fields (Mazumdar 1984:555).

By 1910, at least three-quarters of all Asian Indian immigrants in the United States were unskilled workers and agricultural laborers. Following the passage of the Gentlemen's Agreement just a few years before, they found employment in every area once monopolized by Japanese, especially cultivating labor-intensive crops in fruit orchards and vegetable fields (Mazumdar 1984:562–63). Given the need for such tractable, cheap workers, it had even been proposed that their entry into the United States might be facilitated if they became naturalized British subjects, thereby escaping the immigration restrictions imposed on other Asians (Mazumdar 1984:553).

Exclusionist pressures, however, would eventually surface. By the 1920s, Indian workers were "demanding, and receiving, the same wages as white workers" (Mazumdar 1984:565). As leaseholders, many shifted to becoming employers, hiring not only Mexicans, blacks, and even whites as laborers but their own countrymen at higher wages (1984:568, 575). Legal immigration from India was curtailed in 1917, when India was listed among those countries in the "Asiatic barred zone" (U.S. Commission on Civil Rights 1980:8–9), which also meant men could no longer bring their wives to the United States (Takaki 1990a:309–12). Citizenship, too, became problematic in terms of their eligibility for naturalization. Originally, the courts had granted them citizenship by their racial eligibility. Based on two court rulings (*Unites States v. Balsara* in 1910 and *In Re Ajkoy Kumar Mazumdar* in 1913), Asian Indians were initially treated as "high caste Hindus of the Aryan race" and by extension "Caucasian," which in turn was equated with their being considered "whites" eligible for citizenship. In 1923, however, the Supreme Court case of the *United States v. Bhagat Singh Thind* reversed this judgment and declared that despite the common ancestry that Asian Indians might claim as Caucasians, this view violated the racial sensibilities of the common person, who understood the term "white person" to refer to those from northern or western Europe (Takaki 1990a:298–300; Lopez 1996:204–5, 221–25, 243 *n*54; McClain 1995:47–50). The Asian Indian, in other words, was thereafter to be viewed as "Caucasian" but not "white," thereby allowing the annulment of previously granted citizenship.

Denial of citizenship meant that they were subject to the Alien Land Law (Mazumdar 1984:558). The revised 1920 Alien Land Law forced those Indians who were farm owners either to become laborers again or to find some other way to register their land (Takaki 1990a:307–8). Thus, again, the denial of citizenship made certain avenues of employment no longer viable.

Korean Immigrants

The first official record of Koreans in the United States was in 1899. Their numbers were, prior to World War II, relatively small compared with the Chinese and Japanese (and later Filipino) immigrant populations. (The same might be said of Asian Indians.) Until 1902, Korean emigrants totaled 168, averaging 42 per year, until 1905, the peak year of Korean immigration (4,929), when the Korean government decided to restrict emigration. Additionally, a large number of Koreans left the United States for Korea between 1905 and 1910. Japan's annexation of Korea in 1910, in turn, sharply reduced emigration from Korea, such that over the next decade, the total emigration from Korea would approximate the earlier rate of forty-two persons per year (Yim 1984).

Like Asian Indian immigrants, who were actively involved in the struggle for India's independence from Great Britain, Koreans derived their strong sense of ethnic identity from their nationalistic movement for independence (Takaki 199a:277–86). Nevertheless, some served in the U.S. Army during World War I, which became the basis upon which at least two of these veterans petitioned for citzenship. The court, however, refused to grant naturalization because this would contravene earlier statutes which all contained the "white" person prequisite (McClain 1995:56-56).

The vast majority—98 percent—of these immigrants were farm laborers. California's Alien Land Law, again, prevented farm ownership. The few who managed to purchase in the names of their American-born wives and children met with high failure rates (Yim 1984:537–38), especially when farm prices collapsed after World War I. With an unstable work situation, they remained largely concentrated in agriculture as migratory wage laborers. Those who sought to escape such work were "never too far from this class and would easily rejoin it in the face of economic adversity" (Yim 1984:530–38, 543–44).

Much of the scattered evidence suggests that those who found employment outside agriculture became maintenance workers for railroad companies, miners, or domestic workers. In terms of entrepreneurial activities, hotel operations, inns, or boardinghouses were apparently the most extensive and, along with barbershops and laundries, were by one account apparently quite profitable (Takaki 1990a:276–77). Other evidence suggests that such Korean small businesses operated marginally with a high turnover rate (Sharma 1984:533, 543). Generally, Koreans did not develop an ethnic economy comparable to that of the Chinese and Japanese, though like the latter they were locked out of jobs in white-owned establishments and experienced the overall hostility that white workers directed toward Asian immigrant workers in general (Yim 1984:529–30).

Filipino Immigrants

During the 1920s Filipino workers were imported in larger numbers than many immigrant groups (Takaki 1990a:315–54). While this period also saw the recruitment of Mexican workers, the latter were vulnerable to the national origins immigration quota (Portes and Rumbaut 1990:9, 13, 30). In contrast, since the Philippines was U.S. territory, Filipinos were U.S. nationals and therefore entered the United States more freely than other Asian immigrants. Their right to become naturalized citizens, on the other hand, was unclear, precisely because they were not aliens and therefore could not avail themselves of naturalization laws which applied only to aliens (McClain 1995:50–53). With the passage of the Tydings–McDuffie Act in 1934, Filipino immigration itself was severely curbed: by making the Philippines independent, the act reclassified Filipinos as aliens, and thereby put an end to their unrestricted entry.

Like other Asian immigrants, Filipinos were overrepresented in agriculture as unskilled, illiterate wage laborers. Yet, unlike their predecessors, Filipinos found opportunity structures even more restricted because of their late entry. Arriving in Hawai'i as early as 1906, they were the last important wave of immigrants recruited to meet plantation demands for cheap labor, and were invariably at the bottom of the pay scale. At its peak in 1931, the Filipino population in Hawaiian territory was more than 63,000, or 17.1 percent of the population of the islands (Sharma 1984:586). By the 1920s, they constituted the largest group of Asian agricultural workers on the mainland, with their overall numbers growing by leaps and bounds thereafter. In 1910, the Filipinos on the mainland numbered 406. But by 1920, they had multiplied their numbers almost fourteen-fold (5,603), and by 1930, almost another nine-fold (45,208) (Takaki 1990a:314).

Ambivalence toward this new element in California's diverse population developed into intolerance when Filipino men intermarried with white women. Yet it was the restrictions the Tydings-McDuffie Act placed on the immigration of Filipino women that encouraged this pattern of outmarriage: "The Tydings-McDuffie Act did not have a provision allowing Filipino 'merchants' to bring wives here as the 1888 law did for the Chinese, and it did not exempt family members and wives as the 1908 Gentlemen's Agreement did for Japanese" (Takaki 1990:337).

The agricultural economy following World War I saw falling farm prices and therefore substantially reduced possibilities for making a livelihood as tenant farmers or landowners (Chan 1991c:39). In 1930, 80 percent of Filipinos were still on the plantations, and few had become independent planters or farmers (Sharma 1984:591–92). While there may have been cultural reasons for this failure to move into landownership, the only jobs really open to them in the post-World War I decade were jobs as low-level service workers, whether as private domestic household servants, as janitors in office buildings, or as waiters and cooks in food establishments.[18]

The salmon cannery industry, running from Alaska down to Central California, offered Filipinos somewhat better employment as cannery hands (Friday 1994a:125–48). Given that Chinese and Japanese already dominated the industry as labor contractors, Filipinos could at best aspire to be foremen. They therefore supplemented their income with seasonal jobs as field laborers, traveling a wide circuit that included California, Oregon,

Washington, Idaho, Montana, Arizona, and Texas (ibid.:127–28). The Great Depression and mechanized farming, combined with their own dissatisfaction as agricultural wage laborers, propelled many off the plantation altogether. Between 1929 and 1933, their wages as unskilled cannery workers dropped as much as 40 percent (Friday 1994a:134). White mob violence became particularly virulent as the Depression deepened (Takaki 1990a:326–27). Like other Asian immigrants, Filipinos found greater acceptance as workers in the service sector, where in 1930, 25 percent (11,400) were so employed (ibid.:316–17).

In general, the shift from rural to urban work was slow, as was the move toward greater occupational differentiation. In 1930, four-fifths of unskilled Filipinos were still plantation workers. With the move away from agriculture, there was a slight shift to small retail businesses. In 1939, there were thirty-nine Filipino business establishments in Honolulu. However, these businesses suffered a high failure rate (Sharma 1984:602). Unlike the Chinese and Japanese, Filipinos did not enter the retail trade for a number of reasons (Takaki 1990a:336; Chan 1991c:41), including the fact that their Asian predecessors in the retail business apparently accommodated Filipino needs. In the Philippines, moreover, Spanish colonialism had also inhibited native capitalist development and entrepreneurial tradition. The indigenous population that acquired such experience were Filipinas, not Filipinos (Chan 1991c:41). The Great Depression made it hard to start up such ventures in general. By 1935, 58,281 workers had left Hawai'i for the Philippines; another 18,574 migrated to the U.S. mainland (Sharma 1984:585–86).

Finally, though Filipinos may have had educational aspirations, long hours at wage labor did not permit these hopes to come to fruition, especially during the Great Depression.[19] Consequently, occupational segregation also meant underrepresentation as professionals (Sharma, 1984:602). The presence of Filipino professionals in the United States has come about largely as a result of their recruitment for a postwar, post-industrial economy.

In summary, Asian immigrants were vulnerable to restrictive immigration laws, and as aliens ineligible for citizenship, could not vote, own land, or pursue careers that required citizenship status, such as the legal profession. Japanese law graduates in Southern California, for example, generally worked as "court reporters and go-betweens for the Japanese in business dealings with Americans and as advisers to the Japanese" (Mears 1928:320). Other kinds of public service work also required citizenship status, such as public office holders, public schools teachers, or public works labor. While freely employed in the construction and maintenance of public utilities (steam and electric railways, electric light, gas, and water), Asians as aliens confronted numerous state statutes limiting their right to engage in other public works (Mears 1928:330–38).[20]

UNDEREMPLOYMENT AND UNEMPLOYMENT BEFORE WORLD WAR II

American-born Asians had somewhat greater options for pursuing careers than their largely uneducated and non-English-speaking parents (Takaki 1990a:33, 423). They were, moreover, immune to the naturalization laws that continued to deny citizenship to the foreign-born. World War II (1939–1945) was an important turning point in the nation's attitude toward naturalization. Except for Hitler's Germany, the United States in 1935 was the only country in the world that was racially restrictive on the issue of naturalization; that it should continue such policies when many of its wartime allies were Asian nationals was a particular embarrassment. For this reason, Chinese along with Filipinos were naturalized en masse (Chan 1991c:122). By contrast, Japanese in the United States, including their American-born offspring, were identified with Japan as the enemy and consequently suffered the loss of property and liberty through their internment during the war. It was not until 1952 that the McCarran-Walter Act overhauled the notion of naturalization based on race (Lopez 1966:44–46; U.S. Commission on Civil Rights 1980:11).

Although American-born Asians automatically had citizenship and hence other legal rights as a matter of their birthright, this second generation nonetheless faced their own set of obstacles in the form of prejudice and discrimination, barriers insurmountable even with a college education. Some of the earliest data on the employment problems of college-educated Asians in the United States were collected prior to World War II and bear the hallmarks of what we presently describe as "glass ceilings."

Between 1910 and 1930, the percentage of Chinese and Japanese enrolled in U.S. schools steadily increased, so that by 1930 they had already surpassed white school attendance (Hirschman and Wong 1986). Despite educational parity, Asian Americans nevertheless found their job opportunities circumscribed and were unable to secure positions, whether in union jobs, white-collar employment, or jobs as highly trained professionals. In short, although the Great Depression produced widespread unemployment, its impact was nevertheless differentially distributed.

Data on the underemployment and unemployment of first- and second-generation Chinese and Japanese were among the major findings that Robert E. Park gathered in his 1925 Survey of Race Relations. Eliot Grinnell Mears (professor of geography and international trade) used occupational data from this 1925 survey for his own study, *Resident Orientals on the American Pacific Coast: Their Legal and Economic Status* (1928). Sociologist William Carlson Smith, in turn, authored another study based on this database, *Americans in Process: A Study of Our Citizens of Oriental Ancestry* (1937).

College and university officials in eight western colleges were among those surveyed in Park's 1925 study.[21] In the collective opinion of these officials, Chinese and Japanese graduates had a much harder time finding employment than white graduates did. There was a distinct prejudice against hiring such individuals in engineering, public utilities, manufacturing, and business (Mears 1928:100–200). A Stanford University official further noted that "many firms have general regulation against employing them" even when fluent in English and culturally assimilated.

> Just recently, a Chinese graduate of Stanford University, who was brought up on the Stanford campus with the children of the professors, who speaks English perfectly, and who is thoroughly Americanized was refused consideration by a prominent California corporation because they do not employ Orientals in their offices. (Mears 1928:200)

Some were thus forced, as a last resort, to seek employment as foreigners in their parents' homeland.

Reviewing the period from 1920 to 1942, Beulah Kwoh noted that the occupational status of American-born Chinese college graduates was not uniformly poor. Two-thirds of her respondents stated that being Chinese was not a factor in their choice of occupation, and only a small percent (8.1%) said that race had strongly influenced their occupational choice. Similarly, almost half said that race was not an obstacle to career advancement. More than a third, on the other hand, did point to being occupationally hindered, especially with respect to managerial positions. Kwoh did not break down these attitudinal findings by sphere of employment (e.g. civil service jobs vs. private employment), but in the few instances where government employment was mentioned, opportunities were evaluated more positively (Kwoh 1947:103, 105, 108).

Although Kwoh described her American-born graduates as "highly successful" when compared with other U.S. college graduates, with their fellow minority graduates, as well as with their family members, this rosy picture is due largely to their privileged backgrounds. As "the most highly educated in their families," they came from "select families in the Chinese population": "Two-thirds of their fathers are business or professional men, very few of whom are in the traditional restaurant or laundry work." Although World War II broke down barriers of discrimination that even these well-to-do and highly privileged individuals faced (ibid.:106–7, 113–14), the experiences of this second generation foreshadow later experiences of the glass ceiling.

The problem of employment for second-generation American-born Asians was chronic in that they lacked the language facility for jobs in their own communities (Mears 1928:321–22, 328–29); ethnic enclaves which most desperately wanted to escape, as jobs there were lower-paying, of lower occupational status, and unable to absorb all these college graduates. According to the available evidence, while Asians were officially enumerated in professional service work, there were many barriers to their actually practicing as professionals (ibid.).[22] Doctors, dentists, chemists, and engineers also found their career options severely limited. Explaining their vocational problems, Mears noted, "it is difficult to arrange an internship in medicine, laboratory research opportunities in science and engineering, or positions in engineering works for an Oriental graduate" (ibid.:319–21).

The only job options Mears saw available to them were in those undesirable sectors of the economy to which their parents had been relegated, namely, agricultural labor, domestic and personal service, or small ethnic enterprises. The managerial occupations, too, were in these enclaves; for example, as managers of tea rooms. Venturing outside these segregated communities and directly competing with whites meant that Asian Americans either had to have higher qualifications for the same job or accept positions at lower rungs of the ladder. Mears summarized these two options as follows:

> The second-generation youth are facing the future with the prejudice toward the first generation continued, without that command of language. . . necessary for employment in city Japtowns or Chinatowns or in the land of their fathers, and, most of all, without leadership among themselves. There would be no difficulty at all for employment in domestic and personal service or entering agricultural pursuits; but American schools have educated them to the social caste of a white-collar job. In time they can capitalize [sic] their physical difference in the movies, as stewards of country clubs, as managers of tearooms, as artists and handicraft workers; also, they can work for each other and do business with each other. American business houses will utilize them more and more as intermediaries in reaching the local community, and foreign trade houses will pay high for Americans if they can speak the languages of both America and Eastern Asia. (ibid.:208)

Mears (ibid.) essentially acknowledged a glass ceiling on mobility, concluding: "In the meantime they must exhibit unusual qualifications to compete successfully against Americans in the same line of work; therefore it is not surprising that well-educated persons of Oriental parentage are forced to a lower step on the occupational ladder, because they cannot get a hold on the upper rungs."

Reporting on research conducted between 1929 and 1933 by Stanford social scientists Edward K. Strong, Jr., Reginald Bell, and their associates, Sucheng Chan (1991) noted similar sentiments expressed about the career aspirations of second-generation Japanese Americans (Nisei). Like Mears, Strong and his colleagues advised the Nisei to steer away from professional jobs, such as medicine, dentistry, engineering and geology, teaching, and law, even though many polled had indicated a preference for such occupations over agricultural work.[23]

In general, the work considered suitable for Asians and Asian Americans during this period was in areas where racial prejudice was said to be less pronounced—work that did not compete directly with white workers, was certainly subordinate, and did not require close physical contact or social interaction. Indeed, as Chan points out, one area of professional employment which Strong and his associates considered plausible for Nisei (U.S.-born) was "as accountants and actuaries, because such work was 'an inside activity in which there is little need to contact the general public' " (Chan 1991c:114). The few who managed to gain entry into the same line of work as whites were frequently passed over for promotion.[24] An even less fortunate scenario was that of professional graduates facing downward mobility into low-level service work.[25]

It would take World War II to bring many Asian professionals into the mainstream by facilitating naturalization and hence recruitment into the war industry. Previously underemployed college-educated Americans of Asian ancestry were among the first beneficiaries. Reporting on the few figures available shows how important the war was in facilitating this transition, Sucheng Chan stated:

> In 1940 only about 1,000 Chinese—a fifth of them women—held professional and technical jobs out of a gainfully employed population of 36,000. Ten years later, some 3,500—a third of them women—did so among 48,000 gainfully employed. Most of the professionals worked as engineers and technicians in war industries, which experienced an extraordinary boom and were desperately short of manpower. Among Chinese American women, the rise in the number of white-collar clerical workers was also noticeable—from 750 in 1940 to 3,200 in 1950. Like women of other ethnic backgrounds, Chinese American women entered the labor force in significant numbers in the 1940s: working women numbered 2,800 in 1940 and 8,300 ten years later. (Chan 1991:121–22)

The camp experience also enabled Japanese who were college educated and U.S.-born to finally find work in their professional fields as doctors, dentists, and teachers. Thus, Yen le Espiritu (1997:47) observed the irony of incarceration for Japanese Americans: "College-educated Nisei who had been trained as doctors, dentists, or teachers found work in their professions for the first time behind barbed wire."

In sum, despite their professional training, American-born Asians found it hard, if not impossible, to find jobs commensurate with their education or outside the racial-ethnic enclaves of their own segregated communities.[26] The period immediately preceding World War II was one of widespread economic depression, stagnation, and unemployment. The engineering profession, then largely white, was especially "overcrowded," and other scientific fields suffered from an oversupply of trained professionals (Northrop and Malin 1985:9– 10). Nevertheless, racial and cultural prejudice seems to have made the prospects of educated minorities much bleaker than that of the majority population. The move toward addressing formal discriminatory practices emerged from a political context that made it imperative for the nation to seek out and use a wider band of its human resources, including its untapped supply of technical reserve labor. Postwar economic needs, in their turn, brought about the end of exclusionary immigration laws and the introduction of statutes that encouraged Asian immigration, especially that of the professionally trained.

THE POST-WAR PERIOD: PROFESSIONALIZATION AND RECENT ASIAN IMMIGRATION

The postwar period witnessed an unprecedented number of Asian professionals being rapidly absorbed into the U.S. labor force. The Soviet Union's launching of the Sputnik satellite in 1957 drew the United States into a technological race in space exploration, and as the nation moved from a manufacturing economy toward one increasingly dominated by the service sector, the rate of education of its own citizenry was insufficient to meet these new labor demands.[27] Consequently, there was a need to actively recruit new entrants into the workforce who were largely foreign born and foreign educated.

Historically, there have been relatively few restrictions on the immigration of students to the United States. Small in number, they, along with travelers and businessmen, have been listed among those exempted from earlier exclusionary laws. Because of the global inequality in standard of living, wages, and career opportunities that exists between developing and developed nations, international students increasingly sought jobs in the United States after graduation. In this international labor market, the United States after World War II surpassed other advanced countries by having the largest number of foreign students. Even so, a more significant departure from previous historical patterns has been the recruitment of foreign-trained professionals (Ong, Cheng, and Evans 1992:551, 556–58).

The major impetus for this dramatic change was the 1965 Immigration Act, which opened the door to new waves of immigration on a scale unprecedented since the arrival of Southern, Central, and Eastern Europeans prior to the Great Depression (Lieberson 1980:20). As a remedy to years of past exclusionary policy, the 1965 Act marked a turning point in U. S. immigration policy by abolishing the Asiatic barred zone and repealing the 1924 National Origins Act, which had imposed a quota on Asian immigration for almost half a century. This historical bias was rectified by raising the annual admission for immigrants from the Eastern Hemisphere to 170,000, over and against 120,000 for those from the Western Hemisphere (U.S. Commission on Civil Rights 1980:11). In this way, Asians from developing nations in the Pacific Rim constituted a majority of these new immigrants. Less than one-tenth of the total immigration into the United States before 1965, they made up more than half after 1971 (Ong, Cheng, and Evans 1992).

Apart from encouraging immigration from the Eastern Hemisphere, the 1965 Immigration Act contained provisions that facilitated the entry of a select group of workers. Just as early immigration laws responded to the labor needs of an agricultural or industrializing society, the 1965 law sought, among other things, to attract a professional work force. Its seven-category preference system gave priority not only to relatives of U.S. residents and to refugees, but to immigrants with special abilities, talents, or skills (U.S. Commission on Civil Rights 1980:11; Hing 1993b:38–41). The effect of these amendments was to produce an eight-fold increase in Asian scientists and engineers between 1964 and 1970. Whereas only 14 percent of 5,762 immigrant scientists and engineers had come from Asia in 1964, by 1970 Asians made up 62 percent of the absolute total of 13,227 (Ong and Liu 1994:58). Asians became a dominant minority in the scientific, engineering, and technical fields, especially during the latter half of the 1970s, when the growth of high-technology industries, including aerospace and defense, outpaced that of more mature, old mass-production industries that traditionally employed blue-collar workers (Northrup and Malin 1985:26–30). Underscoring this demographic change in the science and engineering (S&E) labor force, Ong and Blumenberg (1994) pointed out:

> No other minority group has contributed more to the technological capacity of this nation than Asian Pacific Americans. Although the S&E labor force is still largely non-Hispanic white, Asian Americans have become an increasing presence. They account for less than 2% in 1970 but nearly 7% by 1990. . . . During the two decades, the number jumped from about 21,000 to 150,000, an increase of 603%. Extrapolating from recent trends, it is likely that there are now over a quarter-million Asian Pacific scientists and engineers. Like the larger Asian Pacific population, the S&Es come from ethnically diverse groups. Chinese comprise the largest ethnic group (34%), followed by Asian Indians (23%), Japanese (12%), and Filipinos (10%).

The medical field also benefited from this dramatic shift in immigration between 1965 and 1972. In 1965, only 10 percent of the total number (2,012) of foreign medical graduates (FMGs) came from Asia, falling below the 28 percent from Europe and 42 percent from North and Central America. By 1972, however, Asian FMGs had jumped to 70 percent of the total FMG population (7,144) (Ong and Liu 1994:58). Asian immigrant professionals tended to come from four major sending countries. Between 1972 and 1988, as many as 200,000 Asians with science-based professions entered the United States from India, South Korea, the Philippines, and China (Ong, Cheng, and Evans 1992:544).[28]

The 1990 Immigration Act reaffirmed and expanded the occupational preference category for foreign-trained professionals. According to Ong and Liu, "the act more than doubled the allocated visas for occupational immigrants and their families, from 54,000 to 120,000, with 80,000 for high-level professionals and their families. Members of professions with advanced degrees or aliens of exceptional ability received 40,000 visas, as did skilled and unskilled workers (with a cap of 10,000 for the latter)." While the intent was to increase the proportion of employment-based immigrants, especially skilled labor, it also included provisions for capitalist investors, allocating 10,000 visas to employment-creating immigrants (Ong and Liu 1994:64–65).[29]

While the end of the Cold War in the 1990s led to major defense plant closings, other kinds of technological growth have continued to feed the demand for highly trained scientific personnel. The most publicly visible examples are the microelectronics industry, biogenetic engineering, and communications technology related to the "information superhighway." Manufacturing in Southern California has included not only jobs in high-tech electronics, such as defense-related jobs in the aerospace industry, but an "explosively expanding service base—particularly in finance, retail trade, medical and professional services and information technologies" (Walters 1986:26). For these reasons, the country's technological needs continue to outpace the production of trained personnel.

Approximately two out of every ten Asian immigrants, however, are estimated to be semiskilled and unskilled (Liu and Cheng 1994:90). Although the family reunification provision of the 1965 Immigration Act was intended to facilitate the entry of southern or eastern Europeans, poor segments of the Asian population also benefited.[30] The nation's shift from a manufacturing economy to one increasingly dominated by the service sector has meant their relegation to those jobs with the least mobility in either of these sectors. In the manufacturing industry, they are in garment factories (Bonacich 1994) or the electronics industry (Hossfeld 1994, 1990). Involvement in the service sector has meant low-skill, clerical white-collar jobs (e.g., cashiering, bookkeeping, accounting, accounting clerk positions as opposed to full accountants, or restaurant jobs as waiters and cooks) (Ong and Azores 1994:114).

Post-1965 immigration has also increased the internal ethnic diversity of the Asian population in the United States. Table 3.3 shows their disproportionate concentration in manufacturing and retail jobs, while table 3.4 shows their occupational distribution in terms of gross census categories, with Southeast Asians (Vietnamese, Cambodians, Laotians, and Hmong) in particular concentrated in semiskilled work.

When total earnings are compared, systematic racial disparities emerge. In the West, Asian males (age 25 and over) with four or more years of education earned less than their white male counterparts: $38,519 compared with $41,416 (U.S. Census Bureau, Current Population Reports, 1992a:58–59, 61). The following annual incomes for Californians further underscore the stratifying effects of race and ethnicity as well as citizenship status and age.

> College-educated, 45-year-old white males average $60,776 annually, 33% more than the average for all college-educated 45-year-olds. But this narrows sharply among 30-year-olds. White males in that age group lead at $39,279, 19% more than the overall average of $32,861. Then come Asian male citizens ($35,361), Hispanic male citizens ($34,554), black males ($30,843), white females ($28,938), Asian female citizens ($28,046), black females ($26,588), Hispanic female citizens ($25,488), Asian male immigrants ($24,713), Hispanic male immigrants ($21,191), Hispanic female immigrants ($19,392) and Asian female immigrants ($19,202). ("Young Minorities," 6 September 1993:A7)

In the context of an economy where professional and technical knowledge is highly in demand, the question perhaps more than ever revolves around skills and qualifications as the basis for upward mobility. For this reason, some theorists have emphasized that racially neutral, meritocratic criteria are at work, given the industry's search for talent regardless of one's skin color, gender, or other ascribed attributes (Wilson 1987; Northrup and Malin 1985). Education—or lack of it—might explain a great deal of the stratification, especially when one considers the disadvantages of limited English-speaking ability, low education, and poor job skills.[31] Other researchers who have pointed to "downward" mobility and the appearance of a "glass ceiling" (Ong and Azores 1994:111–14) suggest barriers of a different nature.

Table 3.3. Industry Employment by Race/Ethnicity, California.

Ethnicity	Mining	Construc- tion	Manu- facturing	Trans- portation	Wholesale Trade	Retail Trade	Other Service
Entire Population	2.9	6.5	15.4	6.5	4.2	17.2	45.0
Chinese	0.8	2.6	20.9	6.0	5.2	22.4	42.0
Taiwanese	0.7	2.8	19.0	4.3	10.2	15.9	40.0
Filipino	2.1	2.5	18.1	7.0	3.3	15.1	49.0
Japanese	5.2	2.4	15.8	6.9	6.1	17.2	46.0
Korean	0.9	4.4	16.5	3.4	5.1	30.9	37.0
Vietnamese	1.4	1.8	37.8	3.8	3.5	17.4	32.0
Cambodian	1.4	2.2	32.4	4.7	5.3	23.9	27.0
Laotian	2.8	3.4	39.0	2.7	3.7	22.7	28.0
Hmong	8.3	2.6	20.1	2.0	3.3	18.3	46.0
Thai	0.9	2.1	21.0	4.4	5.4	31.5	34.0
Indian	3.2	2.9	23.4	5.3	4.0	18.5	43.0
Other Asian	2.4	3.1	17.3	5.9	4.4	22.3	44.0
Pacific Islander	2.7	5.2	16.2	8.1	4.4	18.2	
White	3.1	7.2	15.0	6.2	4.3	17.1	45.0
Black	1.3	4.4	11.9	10.5	2.8	14.0	51.0

Source: Oliver et al., *Pacific Rim States Asian Demographic Databook* (1995:3–20), from 1990 Census (Public Use Microdata Sample, table 3-5).

Table 3.4. Occupational Employment by Race/Ethnicity, California.

Ethnicity	Professionals	Technical/ Sales	Service	Agriculture/ Mining	Semi- Skilled Work	Skilled Work
Entire Population	28.7	34.1	12.6	2.2	10.7	11.7
Chinese	31.8	35.4	14.3	0.5	6.8	11.1
Taiwanese	44.8	39.7	6.8	0.4	4.3	4.0
Filipino	22.0	40.5	15.3	1.9	8.5	11.8
Japanese	36.3	36.1	9.9	4.2	6.5	7.1
Korean	25.7	43.3	11.7	0.7	9.9	10.7
Vietnamese	16.9	34.0	13.6	1.5	14.9	19.1
Cambodian	11.1	32.4	15.0	1.3	16.5	23.6
Laotian	7.0	22.0	19.3	2.4	19.9	29.5
Hmong	11.4	22.2	24.0	6.9	11.7	23.8
Thai	23.8	32.3	20.8	0.7	9.3	13.1
Indian	36.0	34.6	9.0	2.6	6.3	11.5
Other Asian	28.5	37.8	13.0	2.2	7.9	10.7
Pacific Islander	16.1	34.4	17.2	2.6	12.5	17.2
White	29.7	33.5	11.9	2.4	11.1	11.4
Black	20.3	35.5	19.2	1.2	8.9	14.8

Source: Oliver et al., *Pacific Rim States Asian Demographic Databook* (1995:3–16), from 1990 Census (Public Use Microdata Sample, table 3-1).

One sign of possible career stagnation has been occupational concentration in certain limited areas of professional endeavor. In the recent past, the appearance of Asian American males in "professional and technical" jobs has meant their narrow concentration into two or three areas, namely, engineering, accounting, and health technology (U.S. Commission on Civil Rights 1979:28). In 1990, they continued to cluster here: 31 percent of Asian Pacific Islander (API) males in professional specialties were engineers, as compared with 20 percent of white males.[32] As "accountants and auditors," API males, again, clustered here more than white males: 15 percent, compared with only 9 percent of white males in such management-related occupations. Racial differences were greater than gender differences, except where health management was concerned. Like Asian males, however, API women were overrepresented in food management. Asian females (22%) and males (20%), in fact, were two and a half times as likely to be in these less remunerative operations than were white males (8%). Their concentration here was second only to their being salaried managers, where they were, respectively, less well represented (37% of females and 46% of males) than their white male counterparts (54%), who likely held higher level positions here. As self-employed managers, 5 percent of white males earn their livelihood this way, as compared with 3 percent of API males and 4 percent of API females. When APIs are disaggredated by ethnicity, Koreans and Asian Indians in particular have been overrepresented as small business managers (Oliver et al 1995:6).

THE NEW FACE OF WORKPLACE BARRIERS

The contemporary workplace is decidedly different from that of the past. First, the United States is now predominantly a service economy, dependent on a professionally qualified workforce. Second, language and communication skills, in turn, have become paramount in the professional part of the service sector. As the workplace has become much more racially and ethnically integrated in the last three decades, however, national origin or accent discrimination have become more prevalent. At the same time the overall climate regarding diversity creates a societal context less tolerant of overt racial prejudice. Whether diversity is regarded as a "compelling interest" for any particular organization, it has certainly emerged as a new value with egalitarian implications. This development, alongside the legacy of the Civil Rights movement and the passage of Title VII, has made it almost unthinkable to argue openly in favor of employment discrimination or inequality. (Instead, "business necessity," "national security," or some other competing value might be invoked.).[33]

With prejudicial attitudes muted or sublimated, workplace discrimination has become much more difficult to prove. This is especially true as civil rights enforcement has hinged increasingly on discriminatory intent, conscious bias or bad motives. According to attorney Angela Ancheta (1998:50, 52–61), court interpretations have generally required discriminatory intent as the requisite level of proof in equal opportunity claims. They have, in turn, demonstrated an aversion to disparate impact, and otherwise applied higher judicial standards of review (i.e., "strict scrutiny" standards) that have made it harder for racial minorities to prove violations of the equal protection clause.[34] Discriminatory intent places a heavier burden of proof on plaintiffs largely because it requires knowledge about aspects of the decision-making process that may be hidden and unavailable for review. Thus, Ancheta explains:

In many situations, such as applying for a job or seeking housing, it is often impossible to determine whether discrimination has occurred, given the applicant's lack of knowledge about the decision-making process. Without obvious evidence of discrimination—such as an interviewer's saying "I don't know if our clients will want to work with an Oriental"—there is typically insufficient information to raise a claim of discrimination. The use of "testers," individuals of different race who submit the same application, offers one solution to this problem, but the process is rare because of limited government resources. (ibid.:58)

Finally, an underlying point of contention has been over the nature of universalistic criteria and their applicability across the board. This is illustrated by accent discrimination. It is also illustrated in the schools by admissions controversies which have revolved around abilities measured by test scores and grades. It also implies a shared investment in the standard itself. A linguistically diverse group of employees will have different investments in the English-only standard, and the very standard of language comprehensibility is a shifting one. About this, Ancheta points out the issue of comprehending another's spoken word is not race neutral but highly dependent upon the listener. By proposing that the courts consider an objective "reasonable listener" standard, he suggests that this basis for evaluating language skills might offer some protection to language minorities from employer bias (1998:121–26). While legal solutions can lend themselves toward promoting greater equality, there are limits to legislating equality. The following chapter suggests that the solutions must be multifaceted, embracing a range of social issues which arise from the construction of standards to their implementation.

NOTES

1. In a statistical review of these patterns, Bonacich (1984a, 1984b) documented a disproportionate amount of occupational segregation among Asian workers in the pre-World War I period.

2. Segregation in the Mississippi Delta region had created a certain "profitable niche" for Chinese to exploit as grocers, an area of employment which neither blacks nor whites could easily move into. According to sociologist James Loewen, the formal system of social segregation, especially status considerations, had a profound influence on occupational "choice" or occupational avoidance, since this had direct implications for how these respective racial groups interacted daily with one another. For example, since these early Chinese were sojourners, they (unlike upwardly striving whites) did not derive their self-esteem from how the white upper classes viewed them and so were impervious to social judgments regarding work that involved serving others in a trade, especially blacks. As foreigners, they also benefited from having few social ties with the local community and thus were able to carry on their business decisions rather impersonally, whereas blacks were more likely to be burdened in this way, such as, by customer claims to credit extensions (Loewen 1988:32–55). In other respects, however, the Chinese were, prior to 1940, the status equals of blacks, segregated and largely excluded from white institutions (Loewen 1988:58–72).

3. Despite certain freedoms and rights acquired by blacks, there were certain similarities between Chinese and blacks in their legal status in that various state statutes denied both groups certain privileges or rights (e.g., the right to testify in court, either for or against a

white person, or the right to attend schools with white children). Racial characterizations previously attributed to blacks ("as heathen, morally inferior, savage, childlike, and lustful") were later applied to the Chinese (Takaki 1990b:217).

4. Addressing how Chinese agricultural workers affected the development or shift to intensive agriculture in California, Sucheng Chan (1986:272–340) looked at how different theorists viewed the question of "cheap labor" and the Chinese. While some views grant greater agency to growers in terms of their ability to monopolize land and deliberately encourage an oversupply of labor (especially at harvest time) so as to depress labor costs, others have argued that the Chinese are largely to blame for being treated as cheap laborers because of their allegedly low aspirations and willingness to work for low pay. Government agencies were seen as playing a critical role in terms of how they situated themselves with respect to growers and laborers. Still others downplayed human agency, pointing to larger impersonal, structural, or fortuitous circumstances. Growers, according to one view, did not intentionally seek out cheap labor but merely took advantage of the fortuitously available Chinese who had formerly been miners and railroad workers. Impersonal market forces, on the other hand, included factors such as the labor requirements of intensive crops, the high cost of land, consumer preferences, freight rates, and distance from markets. Chan's own view is that the Chinese did not simply offer themselves as "cheap" farm hands. She bases this view on the relatively small proportion of the farm labor force that is Chinese as well as on instances where Chinese had protested against their wages falling below a certain "floor," particularly after the 1882 Exclusion Act, which placed their labor in greater demand. Moreover, although they were not able to control the larger structural factors that shaped their lives, they brought a variety of skills to tenant farming and ingeniously carved out niches for themselves as truck gardeners by adapting their agricultural knowledge to the California landscape. In that sense, cheap labor did not imply the de-skilling of the workforce. Cheap labor meant several things: (1) that workers could be hired at lower wages than white workers; (2) that they spared employers certain overhead costs, such as the cost of food and shelter by boarding themselves out; (3) that they could be counted on to be available as seasonal labor, thereby defraying any year-long overhead an employer might otherwise bear; and (4) that if skilled, they reduced waste or losses due to inefficient or careless work and thereby increased profit.

5. Among the largest groups of early Asian immigrants to be denied the right to naturalization were the Chinese, Japanese, and Filipinos. Historian Sucheng Chan notes that while there were instances in which individuals might petition to become naturalized, such cases were the exception, not the rule. Chinese would not be granted the right of naturalization until 1943; Filipinos would not obtain these rights until 1946. One major exception was during World War II, when mass naturalization of Chinese and Filipino men made possible their participation in the war effort. Japanese in the U.S. were denied these rights unequivocally beginning in 1922 and until 1952 (Chan 1991c: 47, 122). American-born women, however, could risk losing their citizenship upon marrying aliens ineligible for citizenship (Lopez 1996:46–47; Ancheta 1998:24).

In 1913, California passed its first alien land law, denying those ineligible for citizenship the right to either buy land or to lease it for more than three years. This and subsequent alien land laws passed by the state were not repealed until 1956. In the interim, other states followed California's lead in the passage of alien land laws. These states included

Arizona (1917), Washington and Louisiana (1921), New Mexico (1922), Idaho, Montana, and Oregon (1923), Kansas (1925), and during World War II, Utah, Wyoming, and Arkansas (Chan 1991c:47, 142).

6. As a result of the Ozawa decision, Takuji Yamashita and Charles Hio Kono, naturalized as a result of a superior court decision, lost their citizenship. In addition, they also lost their right to form a corporation, since citizenship was a prerequisite for doing so in the state of Washington. At the time of Ozawa, Yamashita and Kono were litigants contesting the Washington Land Act, which claimed that they had been "illegally naturalized." Their case turned on the outcome of Ozawa (Yamashita and Park 1985).

7. Total primary sector includes not only agriculture but mining, fishing, and hunting.

8. Racial categories at this time were rather fluid. Skin color alone was an inadequate indicator of one's race. The issue of whether citizenship rights embraced other nonwhites, such as "Asiatics," "Mongolians," or "Orientals," was problematic because they were not explicitly included as eligible candidates for citizenship. A few Chinese, Japanese, and Asian Indians successfully petitioned their local courts for citizenship during the 1870s (Chan 1991c:47, 92; McClain1994: 70–73). However, the majority of all racial prerequisite decisions in the early twentieth century disqualified people of mixed or Asian ancestry (Lopez 1996:49–109).

9. Although many early Chinese came to the U.S. as "sojourners," intending eventually to return to China, they were no less likely to be sojourners than many other Europeans, such as Greeks, Italians, Poles, Danes, Germans, and Slovaks. Others struggled to make America their home. Furthermore, though these early Chinese communities have been typically described as "bachelor" societies, more than half of them were married men who had left their wives in China (Yung 1995:18, incl. n6). While merchants, more often than not, brought their wives because they could afford to, laborers were inhibited by the costs of passage. There were exceptions here. Sucheng Chan (1986:103) found that in Sacramento County in 1860 the profitable livelihood provided by truck gardening enabled Chinese men to support wives. Only launderers had higher rates of marriage. In both cases she speculates that sedentary circumstances and the benefits of unpaid family labor may have been the common elements enabling family life to develop. When unmarried women were shipped from China, they were generally prostitutes, laundresses, or seamstresses; women who were considered valuable in terms of their "economic return." The numbers of married Chinese women, however, did not become significant until around 1880, and relatively few were wives of farmers, even when farmers were economically well off. The reason had to do with a lifestyle that required moving when leases expired, and the roughness of rural life, which could mean sharing homes with single men (Chan 1986:103, 386–402). Finally, contrary to the common belief that it was the 1882 Chinese Exclusion Act that made laborers and their wives the target of exclusion, Chan argues that government legislation in the early 1870s had already begun to target Chinese women (Chan, 1991:94–146).

10. There are certain regional variations. The Chinese who came directly to the Monterey Bay area were fishing pioneers not gold seekers. Portuguese whalers were extremely competitive with these relatively few Chinese fishermen and resorted to such tactics as cutting their fishing nets. Monopolizing the waters by day, they forced the Chinese to cultivate squid fishing at night. In other respects, too, Lydon shows how the Chinese of Monterey Bay helped diversify California's agricultural economy by seeing opportunities in materials

that others rejected (e.g., abalone shells, fish waste products, mustard, and apple culls) and turning these into profitable resources (Lydon 1985).

11. Australia was the "New Gold Mountain" (Chan 1986:37). In 1853, Chinese immigration to California dropped to less than 5,000. Chan ascribed this drop also to the discovery of gold in Australia. Chinese immigration in 1854 eventually climbed back up to 16,000, and then oscillated for the next ten years between 2,000 and 9,000 immigrants a year (Chan 1991c:28). Despite the large numbers of Chinese, by the time the U.S. had acquired California from Mexico, the state was officially 99% white (Thornton 1986:107). Gold miners by the end of 1849 had pushed the state's population beyond 100,000.

12. *The People v. Hall* (1854).

13. Edna Bonacich (1984a) found Chinese overrepresented in the service industries (44.6%) and mining (26.9%). Although only one-third of California's population worked in service industries, the Chinese, who were only 14% of the labor force, were overly concentrated here, representing 70% of laundry workers. They were underrepresented, on the other hand, in agriculture (10.3%), manufacturing (10.3%), and in trade and transportation (5%). Within these occupational fields, moreover, they were again narrowly distributed, such that in manufacturing, they worked primarily as cigar makers and tobacco workers, boot and shoemakers, brick and tile makers, and cotton and wool mill operatives. Almost half (49.11%) were employed as cigar makers and tobacco workers, making up 90% of the total workers here. They were notably absent, by contrast, from construction (5%), where a large percentage of manufacturing workers (30%) found jobs. Summarizing these data, Bonacich noted how this occupational segregation implicitly amounted to exclusion from growing sectors of the economy that offered better job opportunities.

14. In the South, the Chinese were unlikely to be found in domestic service partly because blacks dominated this area of work at competitively low wage levels and partly because they were able to carve out somewhat better opportunities for themselves as grocers (Loewen 1988:32).

15. Yick Wo was the Chinese owner of Yick Wo Laundry. Following his application for a license in June 1885, he was denied a license to operate. Arrested and fined though his present license would not expire until October, he filed a class action suit, raising issues of due process and equal protection of the law under the Fourteenth Amendment.

16. This order specifically prohibited those with passports to Hawai'i, Mexico, or Canada from remigrating to the continental U.S. (Chan 1991c:37).

17. Some managed to circumvent the Alien Land Law by registering land in the name of their American-born children (as the Japanese did). Alternatively, since few had families, many more placed these holdings in the name of white bankers, lawyers, or farmers who served as "silent partners" (Takaki 1990a:307–8).

18. Individual landownership was unnecessary in the Philippines since the system of tenant farming and family teamwork entailed certain implicit obligations and responsibilities on the part of the landlord toward the security and well-being of these dependent workers. The wage system in Hawai'i undercut such traditional relationships, and thereby made the situation for Filipinos one of greater hardship (Sharma, 1984: 594–95).

19. In 1928 alone, an estimated 1,000 Filipinos attended school, but those who matriculated declined steadily in the succeeding years: 800 in 1932, 500 in 1935, and 300 in 1939 (Friday 1994a:135).

20. A distinction was apparently made between "public works" and "public construction works" (Mears 1928:337).

21. The colleges and universities surveyed included the following: In California, the State Teachers and Junior College in Fresno; Pomona College in Claremont; UCLA; USC; the University of California, Berkeley; and Stanford University. The State College of Washington in Pullman, and the University of Washington, Seattle were also included.

22. Mears included tabulations from the 1920 census, which listed Japanese and Chinese men and women in various professions. No figures, however, were included from which to assess their representation in the professions relative to other occupations. Nor were comparable figures made available for the general population.

23. Twenty-two percent aspired to become doctors, dentists, and pharmacists, and 15% engineers; compared with 9% who mentioned agricultural work (Chan 1991c:114).

24. Thus, it was reported that a Japanese draftsman working for the Southern California Telephone Company for ten years found he could not advance despite his recognized ability. He eventually left for Japan where he became vice-president of a small steamship company (Mears 1928:320).

25. An example is given of a Harvard graduate who had no choice but to work as a janitor in Los Angeles (Mears 1928:322).

26. After World War II, Asians, like blacks, would also find it impossible to buy homes outside their segregated communities. The National Housing Act (1934) had laid the groundwork for perpetuating such racial segregation. Specifically, the Federal Housing Authority's Underwriting Manual's guidelines for granting housing loans explicitly used race as the single most important criterion: "If a neighborhood is to retain stability, it is necessary that properties shall be continued to be occupied by the same social and racial classes." Continuing in this vein, the National Association of Real Estate Boards barred its members from selling houses across the racial divide and expelled those who violated race-based sales. This was part of their official "Code of Ethics." A 1943 brochure entitled "Fundamentals of Real Estate Process" outlined the grounds for expulsion of real estate agents who violated race-based rules (Duster 1996:46–47).

27. See Paul Ong and John Liu (1994:53–59) for a detailed discussion of how immigration policy around occupational preferences has been continually redefined, from 1924 until the present, to address labor shortages produced by the changing needs of the economy.

28. Depending on the field of expertise, there can be slight shifts in these major sending countries. By 1990, for example, 71% of all foreign-born Asian Pacific scientists and engineers came from one of the following four countries: China (20%), Taiwan (20%), Korea (19%), and India (14%) (Ong and Blumenberg 1994:174).

29. Bill Hing (1993b:135) specifically lists these employment preference categories as follows: "First preference is for immigrants with extraordinary ability (such as in the sciences, arts, education, business or athletics), outstanding professors and researchers, and certain executives and managers of multinational companies. Second preference is for members of the professions holding advanced degrees or for those of exceptional ability. Third preference is for skilled workers, professionals, and other workers. Fourth preference is for special immigrants (except returning lawful permanent residents and former citizens). Fifth preference is a category for investors whose investments are to each create at least ten new jobs."

30.   Although family-based visas have been a major avenue by which many Asians have entered the U.S. since 1965, it is unfortunate that Asian Americans have narrowly viewed immigration issues in terms of this one-dimensional interest in family reunification, a concern which has undermined other immigrant rights issues, such as those related to undocumented aliens, and more broadly, the general civil rights implications raised by legislation that is multifaceted (Tamayo 1991).

31.   Following a year of research focusing on low-income Asians in inner-city communities, a 1993 study outlined a number of strategies at the community, state, and national levels that would improve the workplace opportunities for this impoverished segment (Ong 1993). For an overview of that part of the Asian labor force in the U.S. who are wage workers or part of the "working poor," see articles included in the special volume Asian Pacific American Workers: Contemporary Issues in the Labor Movement, *Amerasia Journal* 18 (1), 1992.

32.   These and the statistics that follow were calculated from the raw data provided by the U.S. Census Bureau (1992). Managerial percentages were calculated from "executive, administrative, and managerial" totals after excluding "management-related occupations" (e.g., accountants and auditors, underwriters, other financial officers, management analysts, personnel, training, and labor relations specialists, etc.) from these totals.

33.   During the late 1980s, for example, the U.S. Coast Guard raised "national security" objections to prevent about 400 Vietnamese fisherman as noncitizens from operating their boats in Northern California's coastal waters (Ancheta 1998:72–73). The case recalls earlier attempts aimed at curbing the rights of Japanese as well as Chinese fishermen.

34.   The Civil Rights Act of 1991 recognized there may be excessive burdens of proof on plaintiffs in disparate impact cases and therefore shifted the burden of proof back to the employer, thereby reversing seven earlier Supreme Court decisions on these grounds. Plaintiffs in the *Wards Cove Packing Co. v. Atonio* case, Filipino and Native Alaskan cannery workers, did not benefit, however, because of an obscure clause involving the time frame of a suit that made this case the one exception (Ancheta, 1998:57, 60–61).
        Ancheta (1998:53), states that strict scrutiny standards, intermediate scrutiny, and rational-basis scrutiny have been, respectively, applied to (1) "suspect classifications" (race, ancestry, national origin, and in state legislation, alienage); (2) gender concerns and illegitimacy; and (3) economic class, sexual orientation, and in federal legislation, alienage. The case of *Adarand Constructors, Inc. v. Pena* was a court decision which changed federal reviews of affirmative action programs so that they conformed with the strict scrutiny standards established for state and local laws (Ancheta, 1998:54, 108, 181 *n*34).

CHAPTER 4

THE EDUCATIONAL PIPELINE

In general, American society, at least within the realm of higher education, values a person who is not only excellent in academic areas but also well-rounded. Leadership, social skills, self-confidence and self-awareness are all important aspects of American cultural tradition. The hidden curriculum is something that Asians are just beginning to discover.

Trueba, Cheng, and Ima, Myth or Reality: Adaptive Strategies of Asian Americans in California

Thousands of blacks and women have been passed over for promotion when they held positions or possessed attributes that would have merited promotion by the use of universalistic criteria. The grounds and the rationale have often been the same as that used in professional sports; namely, whites don't want to take orders from blacks; or men don't want to take orders from women; or it destroys the "team" or *esprit de corps.* And if that has been true in sports, where the desire to win is enormous and where the situation is public, imagine how many more times it is true in private business and "craft" unionism, where decisions are hidden and comparative outcomes are often obscured, where millions are not watching "the playing field" with passionate interest in the outcome.

Troy Duster, The Structure of Privilege and Its Universe of Discourse

For Asian Americans, higher education has been the pathway to advancement in American society. Indeed, their high rates of eligibility, enrollment, and retention (Hsia and Hirano-Nakanishi 1995:254–55) have greatly contributed to their image as "model minorities." Yet despite their tremendous investments in education, Asian Americans are not only likely to receive lower returns compared with other groups, but *increasingly* lower returns for more years of education (Fong and Cabezas 1980:270–72; Li 1987; Tienda and Lii 1987; Duleep and Sanders 1992; Barringer et al. 1995:256, 266).[1] In terms of income, table 4.1 indicates that having a bachelor's degree or higher brings lower median annual earnings for Asian Pacific Americans than for whites—while a college degree offers whites seven times more protection from poverty.[2] In terms of job mobility, the glass ceiling data presented in the previous chapters should also force a reconsideration of what we know about their relative occupational success.

Table 4.1a. Median Annual Earnings in Dollars of Full-Time Workers 25 Years Old and Over by Educational Attainment: 1993.

Median Income (in dollars)	U.S.	APA	White
Not High School Graduate	17,020	14,459	19,022
High School Graduate	22,719	21,076	24,124
Some College or Associate Degree	27,003	29,481	27,932
Bachelor's Degree or more	40,240	36,844	41,094

Table 4.1b. Family Poverty Rate by Educational Attainment: 1993.

Family Poverty Rate (percentage)	U.S.	APA	White
Not a High School Graduate	27.5	41.0	18.0
High School Graduate	12.7	13.4	8.0
Bachelor's Degree or more	2.4	7.0	1.9

Source: Hune and Chan 1997:106, after U.S. Department of Commerce, Bureau of the Census, 1994 Current Population Survey, The Asian and Pacific Islander Population in the United States, March 1994.

The quotations at the beginning of this chapter bring two very different perspectives to the issue of achievement and have radically different policy implications. It is because of their relevance to workplace mobility barriers that they are cited here. The first observation, made by Henry Trueba and his associates, notes that there are hidden dimensions to the American educational curriculum that Asian American students are only beginning to appreciate; that is, the importance of developing and displaying "leadership," "social skills," and other personal qualities that are not strictly academic. However sterling their academic records, perceived deficiencies in these qualities have been their Achilles' heel in the work world, the grounds for employers or bosses alleging underqualification for jobs in management.

An alternate perspective is that the often ineffable social or cultural qualities associated with leadership traits have served also as exclusionary rationales linked more with the willingness of others to "follow" than with a candidate's abilities. These biases, more transparent in the sports arena, are still relatively hidden even in academia.[3] Although student performance has become an increasingly public issue, hiring and promotional decisions involving faculty are notoriously secretive.

The academic context is both a pipeline into professional jobs and itself an important employment sector, especially for those with higher degrees. As noted toward the end of chapter 2, technological needs in the past decade have so outpaced the supply of trained technical expertise and the ability of American universities to fill this need that immigrants from other countries have been recruited.[4] The immigration of Asians to the United States as either professionals or students has enabled corporations to meet some of their labor needs. The present chapter provides a general profile of Asian Americans in higher education, acknowledging the increasing importance of nonacademic criteria. Such considerations have influenced not only student access but faculty tenure rates and other forms of the glass ceiling.

Between 1980 and 1990, the Asian Pacific American population grew from 1.5 percent (or 3.5 million) of the total U.S. population to 3 percent (or 7.3 million) in 1990 (Gardner et al. 1985:3; Escueta and O'Brien 1991:1). As of July 1996, they made up an estimated 3.6 percent of the U.S. population, numbering 9,638,000 (Hune and Chan 1997:46). According to Hune and Chan, moreover, there is a larger foreign-born element in the Asian Pacific American (APA) population than in the Hispanic population: "Over the past three decades, the APA population has shifted from being largely American-born to being one in which the majority of its members are first-generation Americans. Their places of birth . . . reflect the predominance of recent immigrants and war refugees (see table 4.2). Only 7.9 percent of the total U.S. population is foreign born, yet 63.1 percent of APAs were born in a country other than the United States. In contrast, 36 percent of Hispanics and 3.3 percent of whites are foreign born" (1997:46–47).

Table 4.2. Foreign-born APAs by Year of Entry (to 1990) by Percent.

Ethnicity	1990	Before 1975	1975–1979	1980–1990
Total Asian	65.60	15.60	12.30	37.80
Vietnamese	79.90	3.50	27.10	49.40
Laotian	79.40	0.90	15.40	63.10
Cambodian	79.10	1.30	8.10	69.70
Thai	75.50	27.10	1.20	32.30
Asian Indian	75.40	17.90	13.60	43.90
Korean	72.70	16.40	15.30	41.00
Chinese	69.30	18.50	11.40	39.40
Hmong	65.20	0.04	15.30	59.50
Filipino	64.40	21.70	11.10	31.60
Japanese	32.40	12.00	2.30	17.70
Other Asian	58.20	11.90	8.00	38.40

Source: Hune and Chan 1997:47, figure 23, after U.S. Department of Commerce, Bureau of the Census, 1994 Current Population Survey, The Asian and Pacific Islander Population in the United States, March 1994.

Doubling their college enrollment since 1984 (from 390,000 to 797,000), Asian Americans in 1995 were 5.6 percent of all college students. In terms of degrees awarded, they received 8.2 percent of bachelor's degrees and 14.2 percent of first professional degrees (Carter and Wilson 1997:20, 25). In the five-year period from 1990–1995, they were the fastest growing group in professional schools (ibid.:78). According to the Office of Minorities in Higher Education (1993:9–10, 12–13), rapid growth in degrees awarded was directly tied to population growth, with the sharp increases of the 1980s having "leveled off" in the 1990s.

Competition for graduates from the top schools is so keen that the larger firms, which can afford to do so, recruit as early as the freshman year, and high-tech firms are particularly likely to desire degree attainments at the Ph.D. level. CEOs interviewed by the Federal Glass Ceiling Commission indicated that campus recruitment was a major area where companies competed for future executive talent. Companies reported no difficulty recruiting Asian Americans, men or women.

Asian and Pacific Islander American men presented no recruitment challenges, according to the CEOs who were interviewed. They said that they know where to find them; they go after them and place them in professional positions. They also reported no problem in recruiting Asian and Pacific Islander American women. (Federal Glass Ceiling Commission 1995:32)

Since those at high educational levels often face glass ceiling barriers, the data in the following pages focus primarily on those with higher degrees. The information on doctorates includes foreign nationals; that is, Asian students who are *not* American citizens. In general, where the term Asian American or Asian Pacific American is used, international students are not included in these educational data. Asian American includes Pacific Islanders.[5]

EDUCATIONAL ATTAINMENT

In 1995, the educational attainment of Asian/Pacific Islanders, twenty-five years and older, continued to reflect the college completion rates of earlier years, rates higher than those of any other racial/ethnic group, including whites. Specifically, 38.2 percent of Asian/Pacific Islanders (APIs) held a bachelor's degree or higher, compared with 24 percent of whites, 35 percent of Arab Americans, 13.2 percent of African Americans, and 9.3 percent of Hispanics (American Council on Education Fact Sheet, August 1997).[6]

Despite these high levels of educational attainment, a large percentage of this Asian Pacific population is "at risk" for not completing high school, let alone college, and therefore not likely to achieve the degree levels that would funnel them into professional jobs. Thus, in the *Fifteenth Annual Status Report on Minorities in Higher Education*, Shirley Hune and Kenyon Chan (1997:105) noted that Southeast Asian and Pacific Island populations are "at-risk." A breakdown of college enrollment by ethnic group indicates how they are moving more slowly through higher education than other Asian ethnic groups (see table 4.3; see also Hune and Chan 1997). At the college level enrollments are relatively lower: Vietnamese (49.3%), Cambodians (36.3%), Hmong (31.7%), Laotians (26.3%); and the following Pacific Islander populations: Hawaiians (28.9%), Samoans (29.7%), and Guamanians (30.6).

Not surprisingly, of all Asian Americans, those at risk such as Southeast Asians (Vietnamese, Cambodians, Laotians, and the Hmong) have graduated at rates well below the national average (Trueba et al. 1993).

The high matriculation of *other* Asian Americans, however, was such that the overall aggregate here exceeded the national average in 1994: 24 percent of the general population had graduated with a bachelor's degree or higher, whereas 41 percent of APAs had B.A.s (almost twice the rate of the general population) (Hune and Chan 1997:105). The relatively large increases in APA enrollment were reflected in degrees awarded by gender and by citizen ship status as well.

Women contributed significantly to the increase in the overall representation of Asian Americans in higher education. As a proportion of the Asian American student body, the percent of females remained fairly stable, at approximately 50 percent of Asian undergraduates, and slightly more than 40 percent of Asian graduate students. Their actual numbers, however, had doubled at the undergraduate level, increasing by 75 percent at the graduate level and quadrupling in terms of "first-professional" degrees, which include medicine, law, dentistry, and divinity among the eleven subfields here. Consistent with this trend, Asian American

Table 4.3. College Enrollment of APA Persons Aged 18–14, by Ethnicity.

Ethnicity	%
All U.S.	34.4
All APA	55.1
Chinese	66.5
Japanese	63.5
Asian Indian	61.9
Korean	60.3
Thai	53.1
Vietnamese	49.3
Filipino	47.1
Cambodian	36.3
Hmong	31.7
Guamanian	30.6
Samoan	29.7
Hawaiian	28.9
Laotian	26.3

Source: Hune and Chan 1997:53, after U.S. Department of Commerce, Bureau of the Census. *1990 Census of Population, Social and Economic Characteristics* (CP-2-1), 1993.

women earned a significant portion of bachelor's, master's, and even doctorate degrees, although their share declined with each degree earned. Specifically, in 1994 these women earned about half of all bachelor's degrees awarded to Asian Americans (28,722 out of 55,660), slightly more than a third of master's degrees (7,042 out of 15,267) and of all doctorates (358 out of 949) (Carter and Wilson 1997:81, 82, 94). In general, the last decade has seen a dramatic increase in college enrollment among Asian Americans, both men and women, although women still lag.

In terms of doctoral conferrals relative to their male counterparts, Asian American women did not fare as well as white females, and both groups of women lagged behind men. At the same time, Asian women have made striking progress since 1989, the lowest point for these women in the past decade. Thus, among all U.S. citizens, white women in 1989 accounted for 43 percent of all doctorates, and 45 percent of them in 1995 (10,808 out of 23,811). Asian women who were U.S. citizens represented only 29 percent (187 out of 633) of Asian Ph.D.s in 1989 but by 1995 were earning 41 percent of these degrees, or 468 out of 1,138 (Carter and Wilson 1997:94). Hune and Chan interpret these gains as "modest," maintaining that although the period from 1985 to 1995 represented an impressive (149%) increase in doctorates awarded to APA women, the absolute number of doctorates remained small relative to the total number of doctorates conferred on all recipients. Accordingly, academic employment reflects these gender disparities: "The implications for women in the higher education employment pipeline are profound. The disparity partially explains women's increasing, but still limited, presence as faculty members" (Hune and Chan 1997:55).

Among Asians who were U.S. citizens earning bachelor's, master's, and doctoral degrees, the most impressive gains were at the bachelor's and master's levels, where the number of degrees awarded more than doubled between 1979 and 1989.[7] While the figure for doctorates is less impressive, the 46 percent increase in doctorates earned by Asian

Americans put them ahead of other groups, including whites: "This was the biggest increase in earned doctorates of any ethnic group from 1979 to 1989. The number of African Americans and whites earning Ph.D.s actually declined by 23 percent and 6 percent, respectively, while Hispanics and American Indians increased their number of doctorates by 23 percent and 15 percent, respectively" (Escueta and O'Brien 1991:6).

Despite their overall gain in doctorates, Asian Americans earned slightly fewer Ph.D.s than might be expected given their numbers in the population at large (Rawls 1991:24). In 1995, Asian Pacific Americans were awarded only 2.7 percent (1,138) of all doctorates (41,610), compared with the 21 percent (or 8,558) that went to Asians who were international students from Asia on temporary or permanent visas (Carter and Wilson 1997:95).[8] If one looks at the relative share that Asian citizens and noncitizens receive of all doctorates awarded to Asians alone, the trend has been for a lion's share of these doctorates—at least 88 percent—to be granted to those with temporary or permanent visas (Escueta and O'Brien 1991:6–7).[9] This pattern is true for Asian women as well. In 1977, Asian women who held temporary or permanent visas earned 72 percent (246) of all doctorates earned by Asian women, steadily increasing their share to 83 percent (1,524) in 1992 (Ries and Thurgood 1993:74).

Among noncitizens in general, Asian students would have been the largest contingent of foreign students were it not for whites, who formed by far the largest group of doctoral recipients who were noncitizens. In 1995, Asians of foreign-born status received 23 percent (9,696) of all doctoral degrees, whereas foreign-born whites received 65 percent (26,993) (Carter and Wilson 1997:95). Again, compared to Asian *Americans*, these noncitizens from Asia took the lion's share of doctorates in all fields, including the social sciences (table 4.4).

Commenting on the current situation, Hune and Chan emphasize that this distinction between international and American students is critical to keep in mind when evaluating the status of Asian American students, their enrollment, and educational attainment.

> International students from Asia earned eight times the number of doctorates in 1995 as Asian Pacific Americans. . . . Most APA doctorate recipients have received all or most of their education in the United States and should not be confused with Asian doctorate recipients, most of whom are educated first in Asia, arrive in the United States as graduate students, and most often return to their countries of origin for employment. Some foreign students do remain in the United States, become permanent residents and citizens, and find employment in industry and higher education. They often are included within the APA framework. Observers of American colleges and universities frequently confuse Asian foreign students with APA students; they thereby bolster the perception that Asian Pacific Americans are overrepresented in higher education, which they are not. Separating APAs from Asian foreign students results in a modest representation of APAs at the doctoral level. (Hune and Chan 1997:55)

NON-ACADEMIC CRITERIA, NARROW FIELDS OF SPECIALTY, AND PROBLEMATIC LANGUAGE SKILLS

College enrollment of Asian Americans has increased dramatically since the mid-1970s and into the 1980s, providing the appearance of an unmitigated success story. On closer inspection, the actual rate of acceptance declined (Takagi 1992:21–56). During this period,

Table 4.4. Doctoral Degree by Field and Citizenship Status, Asians (1995).

| | Citizenship Status | | | | |
| | Non–citizen | | U. S. citizen | | Total |
Doctoral Field	n	%	n	%	N/field[10]
Physical Sciences	2,293	34	223	3	6,806
Engineering	2,833	47	255	4	6,007
Life Sciences	2,141	27	266	3	7,913
Social Sciences	980	14	168	2	6,623
Humanities	454	8	91	2	5,061
Education	456	7	80	1	6,546
Professional/Other	539	2	55	3	2,654
Total Doctorates	9,696	23	1,138	2.7	41,610

Source: Excerpted and adapted from Carter and Wilson (1997:95, National Research Council, Doctorate Records File, various years.

their admittance rates was described as "the lowest among all groups of applicants," with less than an average chance of being accepted to all institutions, both public and private, with slightly better chances at the most selective public institutions than at the most selective private institutions (Hsia 1988:93). As pointed out in the previous section, the rapid growth in the Asian student population during the 1980s was linked to the overall growth in the Asian American population because of increased immigration. This demographic change alone meant more student applicants. Their rate of acceptance, however, was lower than might be expected.

One explanation for below-average acceptance rates has been the use of nonacademic criteria: intended major, extracurricular activities, the quality and originality of recommendation letters, personal essays or written statements, interviews or other assessments of personal qualities or ascribed characteristics, and alumni preferences (Hsia 1988:89–120; Wang 1988:10–18; Tsuang 1989:663–65). At various elite universities, these criteria have had a disproportionate effect on Asian admissions, as compared with white applicants (Takagi 1992:37, 65–70, 107, 132, 164, 166).

In the case of medical school admissions, their acceptance rates have been consistently below that of whites and other applicants. Again, their overrepresentation in the applicant pool is likely a major reason for their facing more stringent standards, especially as Asian American applicants doubled, while total applications declined (Hsia 1988:139–45). Thus, the *Washington Post* reported that Garrett Yam, the son of a Washington state doctor, "had been rejected by more than 20 medical schools without so much as an interview, despite a 3.5 grade point average and above-medical board scores." His rejection has been linked with the overrepresentation of Asian Americans in medical schools—Asian Americans form "a fifth of the nation's 67,000 medical students, but only 4 percent of the overall population" ("For Asian Americans," 20 June 1998:A09). It would be a mistake, however, to assume that the rejection of applicants like Yam is due to professional and other highly selective schools having taken a mechanistic approach to admissions or having sacrificed "meritocratic" ideals. Grades and test scores, for one, are inadequate predictors of future potential. "Taken together, grades and test scores predict only about 15 to 20 percent of the variance among all students in academic performance" (Bowen and Bok 1998:277).

The notion of merit, moreover, can legitimately encompass other social, institutional considerations. These have included the creation of a diverse entering class or the recruitment of those who show high potential for making special contributions to particular professions or to society at large (ibid.:23–26). The admissions process is thus a necessarily complex one, especially at highly selective institutions, because the goal is to admit both *qualified individuals* and an *entering class* that meets larger social goals that correspond to an institution's mandate.

Insofar as universities have sought to recruit within an overall framework of diversity, the narrow areas of subject interest where Asian students tend to concentrate (e.g., math, science, engineering, premedical programs or health sciences) have contributed to lower than expected acceptance rates (Hsia 1988:93–148). Thus, the ironic observation was made that while Asian Americans are "more likely than all other college applicants to plan majors in science and technology fields, they are more likely to be denied on account of their interests and abilities in mathematics, science, engineering, and medicine." While immigrants are likely to be rejected because of language problems, even English-proficiency, together with excellent grades and test scores, does not ensure admission if student interests are confined to these career tracks (ibid.:1–2,146).

In general, if we compare the distribution of Asian American students in terms of the degrees that they earn at the bachelor's, master's, and doctoral levels, we see certain similarities to the general student population along with some important differences. At the bachelor's and master's levels, they are similar to other students, more likely to choose business as a major than any other field. At the same time, they are much more likely to be concentrated in engineering and sciences (tables 4.5–7)

There was very little difference in this regard between Asian students who were U.S. citizens and those who were not.[11] Among Asian doctorates with permanent visas, 25.9 percent were in engineering and 23.4 percent the physical sciences. Similarly, 25.7 percent of Asian U.S. citizens who had doctorates were in the field of engineering, and 21.4 percent were in the physical sciences. By contrast, only 7.7 percent of U.S.-born whites with doctorates had engineering degrees. The figures for U.S.-born Mexican Americans and U.S.-born blacks with Ph.D.s in engineering were lower still, 4.9 percent and 3.3 percent, respectively.[12]

The concentration of Asian Americans in quantitative and scientific fields of study can be traced to many factors—language barriers as non-native English speakers, parental pressures, and perceived job opportunities, to name a few (Hsia 1988:131). Their presence and persistence in these fields of specialization partly reflect underlying academic problems.[13] Asian Americans have routinely performed more poorly on tests of verbal or written skills than on quantitative tests (Escueta and O'Brien 1991:4–5). It has even been suggested that standardized tests and grades probably *overestimate* English proficiency levels, whereas math scores likely *underestimate* their quantitative skills. The nature of the test items administered plays an important role in accurately measuring true abilities. Asian Americans, for example, did less well on "usage items" than "sentence-correction items." Test items in quantitative areas, conversely, underestimated math skills because such items inevitably contained verbal content making such tests more difficult for those with limited English skills (Hsia 1988:70–78).

Table 4.5. Bachelor's Degree by Selected Field: APAs vs.
All Degree Earners: 1994.

Degree Field	All Degree Earners (%)	APAs (%)
Business	21.2	22.4
Engineering	8.8	17.4
Social Sciences	17.4	16.6
Sciences	7.2	14.6
Humanities	14.2	9.3
Health	6.4	5.5
Arts	4.2	4.1
Education	9.2	2.0
Other	11.4	8.1

Table 4.6. Master's Degree by Selected Field: APAs vs.
All Degree Earners: 1995.

Degree Field	All Degree Earners (%)	APAs (%)
Business	24.2	30.3
Engineering	6.7	5.0
Social Sciences	6.5	5.1
Sciences	25.7	10.1
Humanities	10.4	25.9
Health	3.9	5.9
Arts	7.3	6.6
Education	4.2	4.1
Other	12.4	8.6

Table 4.7. Doctoral Degrees by Selected Field: APAs vs.
All Degree Earners: 1995.

Degree Field	All Degree Earners (%)	APAs (%)
Life Sciences	18.1	23.4
Engineering	8.6	22.5
Physical Sciences	13.2	19.6
Social Sciences	18.2	14.8
Education	20.6	8.0
Humanities	14.4	7.0
Other	6.8	4.8

Source: Hune and Chan 1997:53–54, figures 26, 27, and 28; after U.S. Department of Education, National Center for Education Statistics, Integrated Postsecondary Education Data System (IPEDS), "Completions" Survey.

Unlike whites and other minority groups, Asian Americans showed a greater propensity to excel in quantitative subjects despite their social class background (as measured in terms of parental education) (ibid.:153). Because their educational achievement has largely been unquestioned, students here have often been looked to as "models" for educational strategies that might be applied to other groups. Professor Uri Treisman and his colleagues, for example, found that the reason for the underperformance of black students as compared with Chinese students was study habits: Black students usually worked alone, whereas a majority of Chinese students worked collectively in informal study groups, where they reviewed, critiqued, and edited one another's homework, as well as freely shared information (Treisman 1989, 1992; Fullilove and Treisman 1990). To counter the isolation that led to failure among many middle-class black and Latino students, Treisman created an intensive workshop in 1978. The program emphasized collaborative learning and a community life around math interests, with problem sets as the core focus of group interaction. The results of this early experiment were dramatic: "Black and Latino participants outperformed not only their minority peers, but their White and Asian classmates as well" (Treisman 1992:369).

The educational needs of Asian Americans, on the other hand, are quite different. Against an overall record of high test scores and grades based on mathematical competence, strategies to develop their verbal, writing, and critical thinking abilities are needed. Not surprisingly, deficiencies here are concentrated among immigrants.

The most clearly documented factor affecting the decision to major in science, especially the applied sciences (e.g., engineering or computer science) has been recency of arrival in the United States. As Hsia notes, "Being male, Chinese, Korean or Vietnamese, and recent immigrants were related to the choice of an applied science major field in college. Being native born, acculturated to American values, of high socioeconomic status, female, and Japanese were related to a pure (as opposed to applied) science or nonscience major field choice" (Hsia 1988:129).[14]

Choice of major, moreover, has typically meant career tracks that preclude opportunities for improving English language skills. Many have avoided the humanities, the arts, the social sciences, and (until recently) professions such as law (ibid.:85–148). This imbalance was also observed at the doctoral level: "Almost 70 percent of the doctorates awarded to Asian Americans were in the areas of engineering, life sciences and physical sciences, yet less than half of all doctorates was awarded in these fields. Asian Americans earned the least number of Ph.D.s in professional fields and the humanities" (Escueta and O'Brien 1991:7).

Strategies for promoting language skills have implications for performance, affecting early career decisions, progress through the educational pipeline, as well as later employment opportunities.[15] According to Hsia, teachers who reward students despite poor English-language skills may unwittingly be doing them a disservice. This is especially true, Hsia says, if students manage to maintain high grades by avoiding courses that are demanding of English communication skills.

> The failure to take high-level English courses may mean opportunities foregone to master verbal reasoning abilities important to subsequent performance in higher education and on the job. . . . Immigrant Asian students may be using a strategy that could enhance short-term rewards, high grades, but exact long-term costs in inability to communicate adequately for a fast-track career path. (Hsia 1988:75)

The discrepancy between objectively scored indirect and direct tests of writing and teacher-assigned grades is disquieting. By perceiving their Asian students relatively favorably, and awarding them above-average grades in language-related subjects, teachers may unintentionally be doing them a disservice. If teachers fail to hold Asian American students to the same standards of achievement in language-related subjects as other students, Asian Americans will never master the fundamental communication skills necessary to participate broadly and effectively in all aspects of American society. (Hsia 1988:84)

Teaching practices, however, cannot change without resources that would also support better access to quality English language instruction.

The dramatic growth in the undergraduate Asian population at the University of California has recently brought these language deficiencies to broader public attention. In a story that focused specifically on this topic, *The San Jose Mercury News* noted how these linguistic difficulties were apparent in writing problems that called for creative, imaginative, or analytical abilities. While an inability to write articulately might be traced to problems with English, other problems were seen as cultural; specifically, associated with a certain scholarly tradition that encouraged rote memorization and an intellectual reliance on authoritative sources. In general, the clash between student performance and teacher expectations was framed as a broad one between two different educational traditions, namely, "the intellectual independence expected in a Western university" and "a centuries-old Asian tradition of valuing authoritative classics over individual analysis" ("East, West," 23 February 1998:12A).

As early as the 1980s, faculty at the University of California were polarized over the presence of Asian immigrant students and the level of language competency expected among students who are admitted. An abrupt change in admissions criteria at the Berkeley campus became the lightning rod for controversy because it explicitly raised the minimum verbal score on the SAT, did so *covertly*, with evidence of racial bias and discriminatory intent (Wang 1988; Tsuang 1989; Takagi 1992:25–26, 42–56). A major outcome of this policy decision was the redirection of Educational Opportunity Program (EOP) applicants "who were not Blacks, Hispanic or Native Americans" to the University of California, Santa Cruz. Asian EOP applicants were disproportionately affected by this decision, compared with white applicants (Wang 1988:8; Takagi 1992:48). The controversy led to major changes in admissions policy, which, beginning in 1989, represented a retreat from race-based *guaranteed* admission, by increasing the proportion of students admitted competitively and ending the automatic admission of UC-eligible racial minorities (Takagi 1992:149–52). A ban on affirmative action would occur with the passage of Proposition 209 by the California electorate on 5 November 1996. According to systemwide data on admissions since Proposition 209 went into effect (August 1997), African Americans experienced the greatest decline. The following percentages represent the *percentage change* (from 1997 to 1998) in representation (i.e., a *drop* in admissions) for underrepresented groups: African American (17.6%), Latinos (12.9%), Chicanos (4.7%), and American Indians (5.4%). Whites, who were 42.3 percent of the total admits for 1998, also experienced a decline (8.9%). At 37.9 percent of the admitted students, Asian Americans were the only group that did not experience any percentage change in their representation during this period

(University of California, 2 April 1998). At UC Berkeley, they made up 39 percent of the freshman class (Office of Student Research, July 1998a) and 38.9 percent of all new EOP undergraduates in 1997 (Office of Student Research, 9 January 1998b).

In commenting on the criteria for admission to the entering class at the University of California at Berkeley for 1998–1999, the chair of the Academic Senate Admissions Committee at UC Berkeley indicated to the Regents of the University of California that in placing additional emphasis on the essay as a demonstration of writing skills, they might consider a proctored essay as a supplement to the student's application (Excerpts from the Board of Regents Meeting, 14 May 1998). Whether the task of language instruction falls increasingly upon secondary schools or on colleges and universities, language skills have long-term developmental and career implications quite apart from their role in college admissions. In the early 1980s, the Asian American studies department at the Berkeley campus had begun to frame and approach language instruction in terms of this much broader context. The reading and composition class was the site of this effort and a specific response to the growing number of Asian American students already on the campus.

In an experimental course offered in the Winter Quarter of 1982 ("The Meaning of Verbal Communication Skills"), Professor Sucheng Chan took a holistic approach to linguistic competency that linked communication skills with modes of intellectual inquiry and discourse expected of undergraduates in academia. Cognitive skills were taught in conjunction with substantive issues related to language use, to social adjustment at the university, and to contemporary American society. The following six goals thus appeared in the course description:

1. Strengthening students' knowledge of English vocabulary, grammar and modes of rhetorical organization;

2. Increasing their mastering of college-level study skills, which are needed for the conduct of academic inquiry;

3. Providing lots of practice to engage in particular styles of verbal discourse which are expected of college students and college graduates;

4. Increasing the immigrant students' familiarity with certain aspects of American history and contemporary society;

5. Imparting to all students a familiarity with the structure of knowledge in American higher education, and in American information storage and retrieval systems; and

6. Preparing students to cope with racism, particularly "linguistic racism," which manifests itself in subtle and not-so-subtle forms of discrimination against persons who do not speak English well. (*Asian American Report* January 1981)

The problem of instruction was seen as more than a matter of remedial education and one which had important implications for undergraduates as a whole and their ability to do university-level work. Because the majority of these students are in their first year of college and uncertain about their majors, it was ultimately hoped that this course would simultaneously improve the quality of students' overall educational experience as well as further broaden Asian students' choice of majors to include the social sciences, humanities, and other "verbally dependent fields" (Chan 1982:2). Because students in the Asian American composition class are freshmen (too early for them to have declared a major), there is no student information on the course evaluations that indicate choice of major, though a question might have been included to explore the possible effect which exposure to this course might possibly have had on choice of major. It is clear, however, that the availability of such writing courses as a standard part of the curriculum plays a critical role in socializing students to intellectual inquiry and analysis and developing their confidence and voice as writers.

According to Anna Leong, a full-time lecturer in Ethnic Studies who has been responsible for coordinating the reading and composition series in the Asian American Studies department since 1990, the composition class continues to emphasize critical thinking and communication skills that challenge students to articulate their own ideas and analytically grapple with issues and problems from their own perspective. Anything but rote memorization is suggested by the goals listed below:

1. Help students develop a keen sense of self by developing insight and sensitivity to his own experiences, ideas and feelings, and help students to see the value and the joy of sharing themselves with others.

2. Develop each student's ability to critically analyze situations of immediate concern to himself; help him to identify and understand the problems of his society and to formulate ways of acting constructively to solve them.

3. Help students to discover enduring themes and fundamental ideas that will provide direction for both learning and living challenge him to work out his own sense of values that will giving meaning and integrity to his life.

4. Develop an understanding of language's role in perception, thinking, and communication and of course, develop each student's speaking and writing abilities. (Leong 1996)

The freshmen English program in Asian American Studies is oversubscribed, in such high demand that waiting lists can only be filled during the summer session. This is true, even though reading and composition classes are also available in other departments, including Composition and Literature, English, Women's Studies, Drama, Rhetoric, and the School of Education (Interview, Anna Leong, 30 October 1998).

We are concerned here, however, with the long-term implications of language skills for any course of study. As late as fall 1997, undergraduates of Asian ancestry were more likely than whites to be found in the College of Engineering than in the School of Letters and Sciences (Office of Student Research 1998a). If choice of major occurs at the expense of developing linguistic skills, this pattern has dubious implications for subsequent moves through the occupational pipeline. Only some kind of comparative, longitudinal investigation will determine whether students who opt for scientific and engineering fields have sufficient opportunities for developing the communication skills these fields require. Given an economy dependent upon highly technical research and development projects, *and* a professional service sector that has increasingly called upon communication and writing skills, industry and other employment sectors will experience the consequences perhaps more keenly than the academic institutions charged with the task of education.

Despite a precedence for studies that evaluate how colleges and universities have shaped the subsequent lives and careers of their graduates (Bowen and Bok 1998), undertaking such an effort is no small matter and would require a major change in the way institutions of higher education presently view their commitment to both students and society.

FACULTY AND ADMINISTRATIVE REPRESENTATION

Despite their significant numbers in the undergraduate and graduate student body, the presence of Asian Americans becomes increasingly problematic as one moves up the academic hierarchy. Overall, fewer Asian American doctorates are entering higher education compared with industry. In 1992 only 38.9 percent of Asian Ph.D.s had postgraduate commitments in academia, compared with the majority of all Ph.D.s in the United States (52.2%).[16] Other minorities, such as blacks (54.5%) and Hispanics (59.4%) were more likely to concentrate in institutions of higher learning than in other employment sectors (Ries and Thurgood 1993:32). For Asian Americans, however, the period from 1972 to 1989 indicated an overall trend away from academic careers. In 1973, 45 percent of Asian American Ph.D.s planned careers in academe, with this figure dropping to 39 percent in 1989 (Escueta and O'Brien 1991).[17]

Despite industry's claim on a large proportion of Asian Ph.D.s, the percent of Asian faculty has steadily increased. In 1980, Asian Americans were 3.4 percent of all 60,000 postsecondary level faculty (Asian Americans at Berkeley 1989:38), more than *double* their overall percentage in the total U.S. population (1.5%) (Gardner et al. 1985:3). By 1990, the APA population had increased to 3 percent of the total U.S. population and in 1994 still hovered at this mark (Bureau of the Census 1995a). Yet, in 1993 they were already 4.7 percent of faculty in higher education (Carter and Wilson 1997:97).

A racial group's numbers in the population at large are, admittedly, less meaningful as a practical baseline for realistic hiring than the number of doctorates theoretically eligible for hire.[18] In 1993, for example, Asians (U.S.-born and noncitizens combined) who earned doctorates in American institutions received 24 percent of all doctorates (10,834 out of 39,755) awarded that year (Carter and Wilson 1997:95). Were this 24 percent figure used as the baseline, the fact that Asian Americans are 4.7 percent of faculty in higher education suggests underutilization. The government's formula for assessing "underutilization," however, is much more specific, calculating the "availability pool" from the number of graduates with Ph.D.s in particular fields.[19] In 1992, Asians (both U.S. citizens and those on permanent visas) received 1,731 doctorates from all fields, but were overwhelmingly concentrated in engineering (447), the physical sciences (388), and life sciences (351), as compared with the social sciences (171), humanities (110), education (139), and professional/other fields (125) (Ries and Thurgood 1993:44–47).

The matter of what should be the appropriate "mix" of considerations where diversity is concerned is ultimately a social policy question, not a statistical matter. Government statistics on underutilization are nevertheless an important part of official policy governing hiring in public institutions. Any number of other considerations might be entertained if statistics were to lend themselves as a yardstick for measuring change. If race and ethnicity, for example, are seen as pedagogically relevant in terms of role modeling and mentoring, as well as for the kinds of Ph.D.s that will be produced, then it would be crucial to consider how Asian American faculty appear in the student/faculty ratio, in the range of specialties taught, and what can be done to enhance their representation in certain fields. On certain campuses, they are proportionally underrepresented in relation to their counterparts within the student body, and lack critical mass in a range of disciplines or fields.[20]

Academic Employment and Nativity Status

The Immigration Act of 1965, combined with the college matriculation of the baby boom generation, led to the first Asian American faculty in American universities: "By 1980, over 21,000 Asian American faculty were teaching at U.S. institutions making up 3.3 percent of all American university professors" (Yun 1989:135). There has been a slight growth in the percent who are full-time faculty, from 2 percent in 1975 to 5 percent in 1989 (Escueta and O'Brien 1991:7).[21] Data on "Asian American" faculty, however, are here inflated by the inclusion of foreign nationals. Since international students and other foreign-educated scholars from Asia tend to come from more privileged socioeconomic backgrounds, their economic and cultural resources may provide them with a certain edge over their American-born counterparts.

This problem was noted as early as 1980. Looking at statistics for California State University, Long Beach, Nancy Wey (1980:40) found that Asian Americans were under-represented among the faculty, with the percent of foreign-born and foreign-educated Asians more than *double* that of American-born Asian faculty: "only 1.8 percent of the total faculty consist of Asian Americans born and educated in the United States, while 3.9 percent are Asians born and educated for the most part in Asia." By 1989, the ratio seems to have tipped slightly more in favor of American-born Asians, though a still large percentage of Asian faculty—40 percent—continued to be foreign nationals (Escueta and O'Brien 1991:7). In fact, it has been suggested that a decline in the overall number of Asian Pacific *American* faculty between 1991 and 1993 may be an artifact of a methodological change in statistical procedures, specifically, the adoption in 1993 of the practice of enumerating "non-resident aliens" as a separate category (Hune and Chan 1997:57).[22]

The Glass Ceiling

The problems that APA faculty face as colleagues or instructors are wide-ranging, not least of which is how the routine workday experience can negatively affect their career development.

> APA faculty report little support or mentoring from their departments and a lack of respect for issues of importance to them. They are consulted when diversity issues arise, but rarely as colleagues with academic expertise. On those occasions when their specialization and skills *are* sought, they are expected to be "superstars." APAs generally carry a heavier workload than white male counterparts because of additional responsibilities for student advisement, committee service, and the preparation of new courses in response to student demands. (Hune and Chan 1997:58)

While the above observation points to factors that undermine the productivity of Asian American faculty, studies have also indicated that Asian American faculty receive lower returns than other faculty despite their greater productivity. Several have found slower overall advancement and a concentration in the lower ranks despite a stronger commitment and interest in research, manifested by an overall record of research publications higher than that of their colleagues (Freeman 1978:196–99; Minami 1988:99; Sowell 1976:47–65; Wey 1980:44; Yun 1989:139–41).[23] In fact, they were "invariably the lowest paid," regardless of field, degree level, or articles published. More recently, Hune and Chan report:

> Their salaries generally are lower than those of their white counterparts, even when rank and college affiliation are taken into consideration. The low promotion and tenure rates of APA faculty raise serious questions about their "equal" treatment in higher education. APA faculty at one institution were asked by their respective chairs to delay their requests for promotion to enable non-APA colleagues to be put up before them. The fact that APAs from several ethnic groups and disciplines and in a range of higher education institutions, large and small, public and private, have charged bias in their tenure review indicates that the problem is widespread. (Hune and Chan 1997:59)

Asian American faculty are virtually absent in high-level administration positions. According to former EEOC member Joy Cherian, Asian Americans were administrators at a rate only one-fourth of their representation in professional and faculty positions. In his opinion, the situation in academia was "worse for Asian Americans than in any other employment sector" (1993:10). Other statistics underscored their absence in the executive ranks of academic employment in terms of their share of the total number of academic administrative jobs (as opposed to the proportion one might expect as administrators given their numbers as faculty). In 1996, Asian Americans at four-year institutions occupied less than 1 percent of these executive positions, whereas 62 percent of all CEOs were white males. In absolute numbers, thirteen Asian American males (no Asian American females) were college and university chief executive officers, as compared with 1,160 white males in such positions (Hune and Chan 1997:102).[24] (See table 4.8.)

One plausible reason for the small numbers of Asian American faculty in management is a greater interest in research. According to a survey by the National Research Council, in 1985 "41 percent of Asian American faculty listed research as their primary activity in contrast to only 21 percent of all full-time faculty" (Miller 1992:1225). However, a confinement to research priorities may be an indirect reflection of perceived artificial barriers, including concerns that promotional evaluations at the administrative level may be even more subjective. Thus, University of California Berkeley chancellor Chang-Lin Tien explained, "The people who are doing the evaluating for these positions are mostly members of the majority, and so minorities don't get totally equal evaluation. So rather than fighting for equal judgment, they find that it is not worth it to fight" (ibid.:1227–28). It is noteworthy that these barriers were acknowledged by someone such as Tien, whose own social class background, as noted in chapter 1, offered advantages other Asian Americans may not have had.

There is little research on the lack of Asian academic administrators, though Professor Sucheng Chan has theorized that Asian American faculty remove themselves from participation in certain committee work and other "quasi-administrative" activities because of "old boy" networks.

Table 4.8. College and University Chief Executive Officers by Institutional Type, Race/Ethnicity and Gender, 1996.

CEOs	All Institutions	4-Year Institutions	2-Year Institutions
Total CEOs	2939	1865	1074
White CEOS			
Female	384	248	136
Male	1791	1160	631
TOTAL	2175	1408	767
African American CEOs			
Female	45	22	23
Male	147	109	38
TOTAL	192	131	61
HISPANIC CEOs			
Female	31	14	17
Male	68	34	34
TOTAL	99	48	51
AMERICAN INDIAN CEOs			
Female	9	1	8
Male	19	7	12
TOTAL	28	8	20
ASIAN CEOs			
Female	2	0	2
Male	18	13	5
TOTAL	20	13	7
UNKNOWN ETHNICITY CEOs			
Female	17	7	10
Male	408	250	158
TOTAL	425	257	168

Note: CEO of a regionally accredited, degree-granting institution in the U.S. and outlying areas (e.g., Puerto Rico). The term CEO is defined with the American Council of Education's Corporate Database as the president, Chancellor, Superintendent, Executive Director, Campus Dean, etc., including interim/acting CEOs heading regionally accredited institutions, branches, and affiliates.

Source: American Council on Education Corporate Database. Numbers compiled February 1996. Reproduced from Deborah J. Carter and Reginald Wilson, *Minorities in Higher Education: Fifteenth Annual Status Report, 1996–97* (Washington, D.C.: American Council on Education), April 1997, p. 102.

> In major research universities where shared governance exists, administrators interact routinely with a fairly stable corps of senior faculty who participate in committee work and perform quasi-administrative functions. These, of course are the very individuals who maintain old-boy networks among themselves, the collegial power-brokers; among other things, they are the people who sit on search committees, where they tend to look for one of their own. Sensing this, many Asian Americans hesitate to participate.
>
> Thus, very few Asian Americans have attained high administrative positions in American universities. The handful who have done so tend to become deans of engineering or the natural sciences—fields in which their reputational power is sufficiently great to overcome the barriers in their path. (Chan 1989:50)

Despite the range of authority or power that faculty can theoretically exercise, Asian Americans are also vulnerable to cultural stereotypes about their leadership abilities: "In campus hallways, one hears learned reasons for the dearth of Asian American administrators.[25] One is that Asian Americans lack 'leadership' qualities, American style. If foreign-born, the Asian candidate is said to be either insufficiently assertive or too rigidly authoritarian. If American-born, the candidate supposedly lacks self-esteem or is too militant" (ibid.). Asian American women in educational administration have noted social and cultural barriers such as male "chauvinism," institutional pressures to assume "assertive" roles, contradictions stemming from their own cultural socialization, as well as resistance from those expecting more traditional role behavior (Washington Association for Asian and Pacific American Education 1980).

More visible on college campuses as staff and faculty, Asian Americans find their influence as administrators has largely been confined to student-oriented services. Like other minority administrators, their participation here is more acceptable to whites because existing racial lines of authority are not disturbed.

> They head units such as EOP, student affirmative-action programs, student learning centers, and offices overseeing multicultural activities. There the issue of non-whites supervising whites will not arise to the same degree as elsewhere in the university's bureaucracy.

> The small number of minority administrators in the academic sector of the university tend to hold staff, not line, positions—carrying out decisions made by others rather than exercising independent decision-making power of their own. (Chan 1989:50)

Tenure Rates

Although tenured faculty status theoretically grants access to administrative lines of authority closed to staff, the tenure process in and of itself marks an important threshold and critical turning point in a faculty person's academic career because of the job security entailed. There are divergent interpretations, however, regarding how Asian American faculty have fared with regard to tenure.

Some accounts have suggested few problems with reappointment. A study sponsored by the Graduate Records Examinations Board and Educational Testing Service (Brown 1988) concluded that "Asian Americans had the highest rates of post-doctoral appointments and positive promotion and tenure decisions" (Sands, Parson, and Duane 1992:125).

Moreover, when compared to other minorities, Asian faculty appear to have less difficulty with the tenure process. Escueta and O'Brien (1991:2), on the other hand, noted under-representation at several levels of the academic hierarchy and advised: "Colleges and universities should examine their tenure and promotion practices to determine the causes for the low tenure rate of Asian faculty, their concentration in non-tenure track positions, and their underrepresentation among higher education administrators."

One reason for these apparent divergences in facts and interpretations has to do with whether one is looking at "cross-sectional" data or "process-sensitive" data. The former is a snapshot at a particular moment in time of who is tenured, regardless of age or years of service. In 1993, for example, the tenure rate of Asian Americans (64%) compared less favorably with that of non-Hispanic white males (78%) and was more like that of other minorities: American Indian (63%), Hispanics (63%), and non-Hispanic African Americans (61%) (Carter and Wilson 1997:98). Process-sensitive data, on the other hand, pertains to success rates as individuals come up for tenure promotion. Brown's study, cited above by Sands, Parson, and Duane, looked at tenure decisions in 1981 and 1985 of minority faculty in four-year colleges and universities who were not tenured in 1977 (Brown 1989:24). Based on this method, Asian Americans had higher promotion and tenure rates relative both to other minorities and to the national average. The fact that Brown's data are not current could also perhaps explain the contradictory interpretations surrounding Asian American tenure rates. But more important, a critical problem with Brown's data is the absence of comparative data for white males. Where such information is available, as in table 4.9, we can see that a smaller percentage of Asian American faculty is tenured than their white counterparts. Moreover, while these racial differences decreased somewhat over the 1983–1993 period, the gender differences tended to become larger—not only for Asian American women but for women of other racial groups as well.

Finally, whether one looks at tenure rates by following a particular cohort or by examining a cross-section of faculty who have tenure at a particular point in time—neither approach speaks to factors that influence these rates. These include a variety of circumstances shaping departure or job change (apart from tenure denial). Also included are factors that may have a more direct bearing upon tenure, including career development efforts, the departmental culture, and nature of the institution itself (Woo 1995). It is the way in which the subjectivity of reviewers enters the *tenure review process* that is the single most important factor, however, underlying glass ceiling complaints in academia.

Subjectivity in Tenure Reviews

"A primary difficulty in dealing with wrongful discharge or employment discrimination cases in academia is that such cases almost always hinge on *personal* attributes that must be evaluated *subjectively*" (Leap 1993:62). Terry Leap's observation was intended to underscore the idea that despite procedural guidelines to reduce bias and to increase the chances of a fair review, subjectivity is an unavoidable feature of the evaluative process. Indeed, subjective judgments are a necessary and expected part of decision making. At the same time, subjectivity was also acknowledged to be the avenue by which unfairness is typically introduced into personnel reviews. The congressional decision to subsume academics under

Table 4.9. Tenure Rates of Tenure-Track Faculty by Race/Ethnicity and Gender, 1983, 1991, and 1993 (Percentages with tenure).

	1983			1991			1993		
	Total	Men	Women	Total	Men	Women	Total	Men	Women
Total	71	75	60	70	75	58	71	76	60
White (non-Hispanic)	72	76	60	72	76	59	73	78	61
Total Minority	63	65	59	59	61	54	62	66	56
African American (non-Hispanic)	62	65	58	58	60	56	61	63	58
Hispanic	67	69	62	61	64	54	63	66	57
Asian American	61	62	55	58	60	49	64	67	52
American Indian	65	66	61	61	68	49	63	72	49

Source: From Deborah J. Carter and Reginald Wilson, *Minorities in Higher Education: Fifteenth Annual Status Report*, 1996–97 (Washington, D.C.: American Council on Education), April 1997, p. 98, after U.S. Equal Employment Opportunity Commission. "EEO-6 Higher Education Staff Information" surveys, 1983 and 1993. U.S. Department of Education, National Center for Education Statistics.

Note: Details may not add to totals due to rounding. Employment counts are based on the following number of higher education institutions for each year: 3,011 in 1983; 3,285 in 1991; and 3,385 in 1993. Data for 1983 and 1991 are based on reported counts and are not imputed for non-reporting institutions, while 1993 data were imputed for non-reporting institutions. These tenure rates only include full-time faculty that are on tenure track.

Title VII was in large measure a result of the increasing understanding that neutral procedures can camouflage covert forms of bias.

When Congress decided in 1972 to include academic institutions under Title VII, there was extensive discussion of the fact that the central problem of employment discrimination was not overt discrimination but covert bias and the systematic exclusion of women and minorities from certain jobs because of facially neutral hiring and promotion criteria. . . . Faculty who have challenged negative promotion or tenure decisions have not focused on the legitimacy of the teaching, research, and service requirements per se. Instead, they have primarily attacked the fairness with which colleges and universities have administered these criteria. (ibid.:65–67)

According to attorney Dale Minami, who has handled several tenure cases for Asian American faculty, procedural errors are but a small part of problematic tenure reviews. In his legal defense of UCLA professor Don Nakanishi, he detailed how subjective interpretations of a candidate's file were a major source of "artificial barriers to a favorable recommendation" (Minami 1990:83).

The secrecy and confidentiality that typically surround the academic decision-making process have been chief barriers to investigating cases where differential or discriminatory treatment has occurred (Leap 1993:136–56). Universities argued that opening their personnel files would jeopardize the First Amendment privilege of "academic freedom," and that loss of confidentiality would make for less candid peer review evaluations, thereby eroding tenure standards. In 1990, however, the U.S. Supreme Court dismissed the university's right to categorically keep all such documents confidential (see *University of Pennsylvania v. Equal Employment Opportunity Commission* in Leap 1993:151–56). The long-term implications of this decision for minority and women faculty, however, are still undetermined. For although the Court effectively challenged the university's claim that tenure documents were protected from being handed over in litigation involving employment discrimination, justifications for discrimination are simply better documented, says attorney Minami:

> The Court ruled that no special privilege existed for such documents in common law and that the costs of disclosure were outweighed by the need to determine whether illegal discrimination has taken place.
>
> This decision will probably not alter the *result* of tenure reviews, only the *manner* in which information is presented. Rather than alter their opinions, opponents of a minority or female candidate will simply document their biased opinions better. The decision will significantly change, however, the chances of winning complaints and lawsuits based on sex and race discrimination, because dismantling the confidentiality shield will expose biased decisions. (Minami 1990:83–84)

Even without malice or discriminatory intent, the tenure review process is still vulnerable to biases against those who engaged in research that departs radically from the conventional. Although an important criterion for reappointment, moreover, is whether the candidate's research is "pioneering" or "pathbreaking," a delicate balance must be maintained between the pressure to forge new ground and yet to stay within the realm of known and familiar territory. Where minority and women faculty have sought to carve out new areas of research, especially where particular issues have been historically and systematically neglected, the significance of this work may not necessarily appreciated by colleagues: "APA faculty with interests in 'new' scholarship, such as ethnic studies and women's studies, find their research is given less value in tenure, promotion, and merit decisions. Most are 'solo' in their departments and frequently are viewed as tokens" (Hune and Chan 1997:59).

Since tenured faculty, the majority of whom are white males, will judge these junior faculty, it is highly probable that certain biases will be present, including those created by different areas of research interest. Even where departments routinely solicit the opinions of external reviewers to offset such bias, there may still not be a critical mass of faculty who have the appropriate or overlapping areas of expertise to evaluate the files of such candidates who work in different or competing paradigms, or with different methods of investigation. Thus, Ling-chi Wang (1990) pointed out that the influence of "non-specialist outsiders" in such reviews frequently inserts "extraneous standards of scholarly excellence."

Tenure outcomes, furthermore, depend not only on issues of academic merit but on how socially ensconced a candidate is within the department. As Leap (1993: 61) noted, "Subjective measures . . . are open to varying degrees of interpretation by peer review committees, department heads, faculty member's ability to work in harmony with colleagues." Minorities and women are at greater risk of being marginal members for two reasons. For one, cultivating collegial relations implies a certain mutuality. Despite their hire, there is no guarantee of a warm reception. Apart from differences in social experiences and background that marginalize, departmental recruitment is often highly specialized, such that faculty may have few overlapping interests with one another. Conversely, where overlap occurs, competition and rivalry can also undermine collegiality. Given this situation, the social isolation of minority and women faculty is not surprising. The following minority faculty, which included both men and women, illustrates how their support derived from just a few individuals.

1. " 'X' and 'Y' (faculty colleagues) were the only ones, the few individuals who cared. They gave me a reception and were the only ones who really looked out for me. No one in my department ever invited me to dinner or gave an orientation to the town."

2. "I was lucky because I have good minority faculty (as mentors). In general, I felt more welcomed at 'X' (my old university). I feel half-welcomed here. The retention of these senior faculty would be really helpful. They are really important. A shield of protection. They listen. Show concern."

3. " 'X' (nonminority faculty) is the only person who has really listened to me, read my material, given me feedback. Other than he, no one has supported me. I had no real mentor even as a graduate student. In other ways, the faculty have ignored and actively excluded me from activities."

4. "You have to help minority faculty to be professionally connected. Personal contacts matter even more than ever even with connections with the Internet." (Woo 1995:37, 39, 44)

A second reason why minority faculty are more socially isolated is that their different research interests and needs, the particular ties that they have with their own communities, are often at odds with the campus culture and its values. With varying degrees of estrangement from their department, the following faculty described how their university obligations divorced them from the population that they saw as their constituency.

1. "There is no large ethnic community here. No class diversity. It's basically a wealthy, resort community."

2. "My basic values are in conflict with the elitist values of the institution . . . we're serving a very tiny fishbowl . . . the privileged, elite. After two weeks, I asked myself, 'What am I doing here?'. . . It's a class issue, not race."

3. "The campus does not seem to appreciate that research occurs in other parts of the world."

4. "Being very busy, everyone has their own life. There's a disappointment. If you have a family, that may be different. The life of an academic is having to be productive. There is also teaching and other things to do. But these will never replace family."

5. "I chose not to move here initially because there was no ethnic community. As liberal or nice as people are, I still have a sense of being alien, of feeling like the token person of color in many situations, committees."

6. "I'm isolated on campus both personally and professionally . . . I'm in a department that is strongly supportive. . . . However, whenever I see a job that's in (certain regions of the country), I put in an application." (ibid.: 39–42, 44)

Summing up the predicament of Asian American clients whom he represented in tenure suits, Minami emphasized how their isolation from important informal social networks—whether by choice or default—made them vulnerable to "racism and fierce politicking":

> Although we tend to idealize universities as centers of enlightenment, the level of racism and fierce politicking is numbing. Thus, candidates who do not socialize with other professors, who have many interests outside the university, who study subjects not considered significant or not well understood by their colleagues, and who do not play the game of courting favor with those in power in their department may find themselves out of a job at tenure time. (Minami 1990:85–86)

Three high-profile legal cases involving Asian American women—Marcy Wang, Rosalie Tung, and Jean Jew—capture how arbitrariness in the review process is affected by factors which have little to do with the merits of their cases. Jean Jew had been denied promotion to full professor. Rosalie Tung and Marcy Wang had been denied tenure, the quintessential glass ceiling in academia. Their cases have been discussed elsewhere in their legal particulars, as well as in terms of the race and gender politics and political mobilization that occurred around them (Chamallas 1994; Cho 1997; Cho, 1992; Leap 1993). In interviews with Marcy Wang (17 February 1996; 29 October 1998), Rosalie Tung (19 February 1996; 20 September 1998) and Jean Jew (21 and 30 October 1998 and 22 November 1998), I was interested in further exploring their perceptions of glass ceiling barriers and how they perceived these barriers in a context where procedures and standards are designed to be neutral. These procedures ensure that a certain objectivity governs the review process itself. At the same time, all three cases demonstrate how procedures are vulnerable to abuse, while their purported use acts as a shield for discriminatory behavior, thereby contributing to the perception of a level playing field. In each instance, the university was itself a formidable Goliath, invested as it was in self-protection. Precisely because the internal grievance procedures were grossly inadequate, each woman was forced to seek legal recourse outside the university.

Artificial barriers in the three cases originated at the departmental level and spanned a continuum from procedural irregularities to abuse of power. In each case, a single disgruntled colleague, powerfully positioned within the department, acted variously to discredit or diminish the faculty person's research or teaching record, to sway departmental opinion against a candidate, and to actively construct a negative personnel file (Cho 1992:25–27, 41–47, 129–31, 138; 1997:206–7). Once introduced, bias was well concealed from public scrutiny, though racial or gender bias was also manifested with highly variable degrees of overtness.

In the case of Jean Jew, expressions of prejudice were blatant and crude. The hostile environment which enveloped her over a decade took the form of graffiti, gossip, and anonymous written communications, all intended to impugn her professional reputation in the eyes of faculty, staff, administrators, or students. This included references to her as a "stupid slut," "bitch," "whore," "chink," "hatchet woman," and "Chinese pussy" (Cho 1997:208–9), as well as false and malicious gossip about her having a salacious affair with her mentor (ibid:25–28). The only thing more shocking was that these characterizations, along with the locker-room language that colored them, were initiated and promulgated by a senior faculty person, intent on undermining her credibility as a scholar.

Race and gender bias were more muted and less publicly visible in Tung's and Wang's cases. Rosalie Tung's suit included the charge of being "sexually harassed" by her department head (Leap 1993:151), and although the incident was somewhat isolated and contained compared with Jew's experience of harassment, her rejection of these overtures had direct consequences for her tenure review the following year (Cho 1997:206–7). Like Jew, Tung found that people in the university at large were more likely to trust the system, and thus the opinions of their detractors, than were those who questioned its fairness.

For Marcy Wang, sexual harassment complaints in her department were common and even students had brought public attention to the unhealthy atmosphere of sexism and favoritism that prevailed ("Discord," 19 October 1992; "Architecture," 11 November 1992; "Students Urge," 17 November 1992; "Tales of Sex," 17 November 1992). Sexist or racist opinions regarding the acceptability of pregnant faculty or the appropriate demeanor of Asian women, along with behavioral challenges to her authority as an instructor, were biases that Wang's legal defense team cited as part of the general atmosphere that polluted her tenure review. The chair who would oversee her tenure review, moreover, was identified as the key actor who undermined the notion of fair play (Gwillliam et al. 1995:7, 9–10).

One can, given the above, look at discrimination in terms of disparate treatment that takes the form of conscious, individual acts of bias. Yet as noted in chapter 3, whether or not there is any individual intent to discriminate, certain policies or procedures can exert a *disparate impact*. A university environment, particularly one where there is a lack of diversity, can itself serve to marginalize faculty who are not part of the dominant culture. As faculty, Asian Americans have "the largest gender gap of any racial/ethnic group," with women here making up only 25 percent of all full-time APA faculty (largely foreign nationals) and more likely to be found at the junior, untenured levels (Hune and Chan 1997:57; Hune 1998:17). In terms of academic expertise, APA women were overrepresented in the health sciences (especially nursing) but underrepresented in all other areas (Hune 1998:17).

As professors, Jew, Tung, and Wang had been working in disciplines or departments where minorities or women were a very small percentage of the academic appointments. As an associate professor at the University of Iowa School of Medicine, Jean Jew had been the only woman in the anatomy department among some twenty other faculty (Cho 1992:42), and the only Asian faculty member for many years.[26] Rosalie Tung had been an associate professor at the University of Pennsylvania Wharton School of Business, where she had been the only Asian (male or female) in a management department with more than sixty faculty members. Only two of the faculty here were tenured minority faculty (both male), and only one was a tenured woman (ibid.:207). In 1979, the time when Marcy Wang was appointed assistant professor in the School of Architecture at the University of California, Berkeley, there had never been a tenured Asian faculty, male or female. In the entire College of Environmental Design, of which the School of Architecture was one of three departments, only two out of sixty-nine faculty were Asian from 1986 to 1989 (Asian Americans at Berkeley 1989:42).[27] In short, the departments in which Jew, Tung, and Wang were situated were anything but diverse, and their presence as minority women became lightning rods that brought attention to existing problems in their departments or universities. Until they were finally vindicated by the courts, none of these women felt she could effectively counter the negativity set in motion by her departments. The rumor mill was damaging in all three cases.

Although Jean Jew had arrived at the University of Iowa School of Medicine in 1973 and was successfully tenured in 1978, she was from the time of her arrival a target of animosity in an already factionalized department (Chamallas 1994:74–75; *U.S. District Court*, Southern District of Iowa 28 August 1990:3–4, 9–11). Gossip, initiated and promulgated by Robert Tomanek, served as an occasion for socializing new faculty, a kind of collegiality that Sumi Cho has described as approaching "male bonding."

> New faculty members were initiated into the department with sordid gossip about Dr. Jew by Dr. Tomanek. Crude graffiti adorned the men's restroom in the anatomy department. The rumored sexual activities of Jean Jew was (sic) the cohesive glue used to forge a collective identity for an often warring faculty with widely divergent interests.
>
> Few faculty members within the department found the courage to support Jew and to resist the male bonding tactics out of fear of retribution. When one professor did challenge the outrageous departmental behavior toward Jew, a department administrator intimated that he was mentally disturbed. (Cho 1992:44–45)

The Department of Architecture, where Marcy Wang had arrived to work in 1979, was not only factionalized but, as already noted, fraught with unsettled complaints regarding favoritism and discrimination. According to the Academic Senate's five-year departmental review, "influential members of the faculty may have been too busy 'defending their own turf,' at the expense of the broader well-being of the department" (ibid.:127–28). These departmental problems became public after Wang decided to sue in 1992 ("Cal Architectural," 28 October 1992; "Review Rocks," 13 November 1992; "$1 Million Deal," 9 January 1996). Her stated goal was not reinstatement because, in her words, "it was the most horrible place, the worst work environment I had ever experienced." Rather it was to take a stand against the group culture and mentality that socially ostracized and sought to "eliminate" from membership those who were non-white and female (Cho 1992:109). Before her suit, there were two separate occasions where she had dissented on matters in the area of teaching and hiring.

> Wang asserted that her refusal to "play ball" with the departmental power brokers led to retaliation against her. In particular, she refused to give a pet student an "A" who had failed to attend class or submit the required homework. She was asked by Chair Protzen to give the student an "A." She later discovered that the department had given the student an "A." After complaining to the ombudsperson for faculty, he prophetically told her that her refusal to grant the chair's wishes may obstruct her tenure bid. In another episode, Wang participated in a hiring committee in which the top candidate in Wang's opinion was a woman. When she objected to the suggestion to offer the position to a lesser-qualified male candidate who was friends with the chair, she again ruffled feathers. . . . Her steadfast refusal to assimilate to the departmental culture of favoritism and cronyism made her a target for retaliatory treatment. (Cho 1992:130–31)

As she spoke further about the significance of the above instances, Wang explained that they represented some of the many obstacles that racial minorities and women face simply in the everyday routines of their work experience. Elaborating on the chair's subversion of her own teaching authority, Wang described this interference as an "outrageous, illegal demand" that was outside the bounds of academic norms, and therefore an act that would have been "inconceivable" if imposed on any other faculty member (Interview, 23 November 1998).

Unlike Jew and Wang, Rosalie Tung was not situated in a departmental culture that was rife with overt or ongoing displays of racism or sexism. The sudden negative turn of events in her case, moreover, cannot simply be attributed to the isolated actions of a rebuffed male. As apparent in the matter of how her tenure file was handled, the voting faculty voiced little objection to adopting procedures that made her review a far more arduous one than was normal. This is true even though the University of Pennsylvania, like Harvard, is different from most other universities in requiring that faculty in general meet special standards in order to be tenured. As an associate professor, Tung was not tenured and was about to be reviewed for tenure.[28] Although acceding that her overall experience at Wharton was fairly positive before the tenure review, upon reflection Tung indicated that race and gender had "something to do with" the amount of arbitrary bias that was allowed to be introduced. Calling attention to the profile of the school's faculty, she characterized the school as having a reputation not only as the oldest business school in the country but also as an "exclusive" one which was "not hospitable" to minorities or women (Interview, 20 September 1998). When she left the campus in 1986, the entire school of more than 300 faculty still did not have a single tenured Asian faculty person. Cho thus notes the school's disinterest in Asian faculty:

> Although a majority of her department faculty recommended tenure, the personnel committee denied Professor Tung's promotion. . . . Tung later learned through a respected and well-placed member of the faculty that the justification given by the decision makers was that "the Wharton School is not interested in China-related research." Tung understood this to mean that the Business School "did not want a Chinese American, an Oriental [on their faculty]." (Cho 1997:206–7)

Misrepresentation, Disparate Treatment, and Higher Standards

Whatever may have been the exact role of race and gender in the disposition of these cases at the departmental level, in the intellectualized discourse that framed the personnel reviews of these three women, arguments about "qualifications" took the foreground.

When Jean Jew petitioned in 1983 to be reviewed for full professor, she had little objective reason for concern about her progress since she was aware of the standards by which previous colleagues had been promoted. She had a research record that included numerous peer-reviewed articles and book chapters, authored or coauthored, some published and some in press, twenty-four based on research carried out at the University of Iowa. She was a manuscript reviewer for three major national journals, *Archives of Neurology*, *Experimental Neurology*, and *Physiology and Behavior*. She was also principal investigator on three grants, two from the National Institutes of Health and one from the National Science Foundation. Doubts, nevertheless, would be raised concerning her intellectual independence and credibility (*U.S. District Court*, Southern District of Iowa, 28 August 1990:14).

The prism, in fact, through which Jew's merits were largely evaluated, was that based on her collaborative research involvement with her mentor, Terry Williams. Jew, along with one other person on his research team at Tulane University, had joined him when he was recruited to head Iowa's department of anatomy. In an already factionalized department,

Williams' presence did little to diminish existing tensions.[29] By virtue of her ongoing research involvement with him, Jew encountered resistance to the idea that she could have been an intellectual force in her own right or could have played more than a secondary role.

> They thought because I was working with the chair, I was his handmaiden. Many faculty testified that in intercollaborative work, I was doing work that led to publication but that he was the intellectual, with Jean Jew as his lackey. The term used was that I was the collaborative force, but not independent. (Cho 1997:209)

As noted earlier, there was also gossip suggesting the two were engaged in an affair, which was used to bring further skepticism about her contributions to this research enterprise.

By the time of her promotion, a new acting chair had been appointed, and in this position moderated the discussion around her case and was entitled to a vote in case of a tie. Departmental opinion among the voting faculty, however, was divided three in favor, and five against, and the department's written summary of its deliberations reflected only the more negative views. Signed by those senior faculty who voted negatively, the report stipulated that in order to be considered for review for full professor in the future, she would need to establish her independent status by seeking new collaborators and concentrate on a single research theme that would bring national and international recognition, issues never raised in her previous developmental evaluation only one year before (*U.S. District Court,* Southern District of Iowa, 28 August 1990:12–13, 15; Interview, 22 November 1998). The requirement to dissociate herself from collaborators essentially meant she would need to undertake research in an entirely different area, to "start all over again," to "build a new reputation," which also meant bringing external funding to this new area as well. These expectations were, according to Jew, unprecedented in the department's history, and in her words, introduced criteria that were "new, never before used—standards set just for me" (Interview, 21 October 1998).

The motives behind this disparate treatment have been linked to intra-departmental rivalry and "competition among men" (Chamallis 1994:87) and jealousy on the part of "underachieving colleagues" (Cho 1992:23–25). Even if there were no trace of ill intent toward Jew herself, the court would later find that she had been held to different standards than other candidates in her department. The issue of shifting standards, moreover, Jew noted to be one that changed with the gender of the candidates rather than one that reflected a fundamental change in departmental policy. As she learned through her advocacy work on behalf of other women faculty on campus, where ambiguity shrouds collaborative endeavors, "The question of independence is often fallaciously raised in the case of women." Although the most straightforward and common way of determining the relative contributions of collaborators would be simply "to ask" the candidates themselves, she said, it is too frequently *assumed* that the contributions of female collaborators are inferior (Interview, 21 October 1998).

As with Jew, Marcy Wang's intellectual contributions were also trivialized by characterizations that questioned her capacities as an independent researcher. She was, moreover, labeled "aloof, uncollegial" and lacking in "leadership and presence." While her attorneys noted these to be stereotypical characterizations applied to Asians, especially Asian women (Gwilliam et al. 1995:10), Wang incisively dispelled these very characterizations as mere rationalizations for exclusion. Collegiality was noted to be a "two-way," reciprocal matter, and if she were singled out as "cool and aloof," it was as much a response to the cold reception she received from the majority of her colleagues. The allegation that she lacked "presence" or "leadership abilities" was contradicted by the professional activities in which she was engaged.

> I was described as cool and aloof, lacking in presence, having no leadership abilities—this despite the fact that I was running conferences, leading a major grant research project, and conducting experiments. They said, "It is not clear what her involvement is"—the implication is that someone is ghosting my work for me. (Interview, 17 February 1996)

Collegiality is thus a delicate, double-edged tightrope walk. Where it invites collaboration, it can be a mutually fruitful endeavor that benefits the university at large. The establishment of organized research units at major universities frequently presumes that the professional activities conducted here will be fundamentally collaborative. As an implicit expectation, however, the requirement for collegiality can also place faculty in awkward, untenable situations. As an associate professor, Rosalie Tung indicated she already had a well-established research profile and national reputation quite early in her career, a major reason why it was eventually a "shock to a lot of people" when her credentials were called into question. An incident she recalled in the course of our interview, moreover, clearly captured how collegiality and collaborative work are not in the career interests of junior faculty for other reasons, namely, because they have relatively little status or power and are thus more easily exploitable. Tung had been asked by two senior faculty if they might jointly author a paper using her data. Although she complied with this request, it is also clear she could not have actively refused without jeopardizing collegiality itself (Interview, 20 September 1998).

Apart from the cloud cast over collaborative work, review of a faculty person's independent publications can be subjected to artificial bias introduced by those with little expertise on a subject matter. Although departments are ostensibly the unit on campus most well informed about a faculty member's contributions, academic institutions frequently depend upon an external review process, whereby the opinions of experts outside the campus are sought. This is especially true for large research universities with highly specialized areas of research (Leap 1993:78–79). Jean Jew's case for full professor did not reach this stage of review since her department did not support her request to be considered for advancement. Rosalie Tung and Marcy Wang, on the other hand, did receive such external evaluations for their tenure reviews. The parallel with Jew's case lies in the elevated expectations brought to bear on their files. The solicitation of expert reviewers was "routine" only in the sense that such letters were solicited. In other respects, not only procedural rules but also spirit of fairness were violated by the manner in which the review was conducted and how the file was summarized.

In Wang's case, the procedural violations were numerous and included augmenting her file, without her knowledge, with late letters solicited after the departmental vote. In Tung's case, numerous letters were solicited far beyond what would normally be required. In both their cases, the opinions of these external experts were overwhelmingly favorable in their assessment. What was unusual was that the respective departments went to great lengths to suppress these views, to seek damaging evidence, and to construct a negative summary that belied the actual content of these files. As in the case of Jew, these summaries even contradicted the departments' own favorable assessments of these candidates in the short period prior.

Since her initial hire in 1981, Rosalie Tung reported that she had been "consistently praised for research, teaching, and service." The Dean had, in fact, selected her to represent the Wharton Business School at the Harvard Business School's 75th anniversary in 1983. This situation changed dramatically in the fall of 1984, when she came up for tenure and after she rejected the romantic advances of her chair. The evaluation from her department now included remarks that represented, in Tung's words, "a complete about-face from the evaluation six months earlier," with this particular chair going to extraordinary lengths to solicit damaging evidence in the form of outside review letters. While five to six outside letters was the norm for most faculty, in her case anywhere from thirty to forty-two letters were solicited, the exact count being unclear because they came in different "waves" (Interview, 20 September 1998). Of these, only three letters were negative, two of which were written by the chair himself, one of them based on a conversation with a faculty member who was not even tenure-track within the school and, therefore, an inappropriate person to comment. The third negative letter, received after the deadline, was from a person who had applied for a position within the department but had been rejected. The external letters in general, however, were overwhelmingly positive and a wide margin of the voting faculty were in Tung's favor. The chair, however, wrote a completely negative three-page summary of her work that did not reflect the majority sentiment (Interview, 19 February 1996).

The fact that none of the voting faculty themselves formally protested the unusual number of external letters requested or questioned the chair's negative summary is telling of the extraordinary degree to which subjective bias can be insinuated. The negative summary belied her objective record of accomplishments.

> Professor Tung's file constituted an impressive list of achievement with letters . . . consistently praising her as one of the best and brightest young scholars in her field, including one from a Nobel Prize laureate. Her contributions had been acknowledged by her peers through election to the board of governors of the Academy of Management, a professional association of over seven thousand management faculty. Tung was the first person of color ever elected to the board. (Cho 1997:207)

Tung was offered no reason at the time for the tenure denial and given no information about her actual file. It was routine, she explained, for the University of Pennsylvania Wharton School of Business to simply let faculty go without so much as an explanation. She later learned, when she eventually gained access to her files through her EEOC suit that the negative summary had criticized her teaching, claimed she didn't publish, and that she "didn't get along with other people" (Interview, 20 September 1998).

Like Tung, Marcy Wang had felt no reason, based on her objective record of accomplishments, to be concerned about her tenure review in the fall of 1985. A licensed architect and civil engineer, who also had a structural engineering degree from Stanford, Wang had been "the recipient of many grants, the prestigious *Progressive Architecture* award and the author of well-received studies in her field," and the department had assured her at the time of her midcareer review in 1982, that her chances for tenure were very good (Gwilliam et al. 1995:1–2, 5). Her attorneys commented on the significance of the midcareer review as follows:

> The positive comments regarding her work makes the denial of tenure particularly suspect. The ad hoc committee appointed to conduct the midcareer review noted that Professor Wang was the Director on a project which developed and organized a research workshop on the Seismic Upgrading of Existing Buildings which was "well received by its participants" and "attracted leading authorities in earthquake engineering located in Northern California and others from out of state." . . . The committee also noted a "second research project that received funding from NSF (National Science Foundation) is more impressive, involving a grant of about $87,000 over a two-year period. "With respect to this project . . . the committee commented: "it is a landmark project for the testing of building components at the international level. . . . Her writings are receiving recognition at the national level and have had a decided impact among representative design professionals. . . . we think she is making good progress, and that she definitely has a future here." (ibid.:5–6)

As in Jew and Tung's case, the surprise for Wang would be a 180-degree reversal of departmental opinion at the time of her tenure review.

As noted earlier, highly irregular procedures included the solicitation of additional letters *after* the department had already reviewed and voted on Wang's tenure file (Cho 1992:110–17, 120–24). Although the pretext was to seek "clarification" on the letters submitted by the external reviewers, the most obvious avenue for this purpose—contacting the original reviewers—was never taken (Gwilliam et al. 1995:4). About these additional letters, Wang says that these reviewers were all "intramural," from the campus' own Civil Engineering Department, none of whom were in her field of expertise, and none of whom saw the file itself. Thus, one person apparently indicated he or she did not know her work well enough to even comment. Another pointed out that the criteria that they were being asked to evaluate her on were unrealistically high: "From your description, no one could fit that description on this planet, and therefore Marcy Wang clearly doesn't" (Interview, 17 February 1996). Finally, among these additional letters was a confidential letter from the chair, which raised new substantive issues. Since Wang was unaware of any of these letters, she was never allowed to respond before her file was forwarded for campus-wide review.

The outcome of the first departmental vote was close—with seven votes in favor of tenure, eight against, and three abstentions among those faculty who were voting members. Alleging her case to be a weak one, the chair strongly advised her to withdraw her application for tenure. As she recounts below, his summary of the departmental review was damning and later proved not simply to be in conflict with the evidence in her file, but in her words, an egregious "lie":

> I asked him, "Why? What's in my file? Just characterize the external review letters for me." He said, "I don't know. They're not very clear. There's a lot of criticism, though. You're terrible in everything. In fact, you're the worst professor they've ever seen."
>
> His successor, who had been in the department for decades, later took me aside and told me it was, in fact, one of the best cases that he had seen, that there was an attack on me by certain factions in the department that was completely personal and not based on the merits of my case (Interview, 17 February 1996).

Instead of withdrawing her tenure application, Wang submitted a written rebuttal to the arguments against tenure laid out in the written departmental summary. Shortly thereafter, the first Privilege and Tenure committee that would be convened in her case ruled that the high number of voting faculty who chose to abstain was unusual and that this warranted a second departmental vote. Wang's written rebuttal, however, was never provided to the departmental faculty for their consideration this second time around (Cho 1992:106–7), and the second departmental vote occurred with only superficial deliberation, ending in a second denial (ibid.:112–14; Gwilliam et al. 1995:17–19).

Like Tung, Wang did not know the exact contents of her file until her attorneys proceeded with the legal process of discovery. In addition to learning that some of her written submissions had been deleted from her file without her knowledge (Cho 1992:105–6), yet even with these deletions, external reviewers had unanimously recommended tenure.

> My file contained nothing but publications in top-rate journals in architecture and engineering. My external reviewers were all positive, not one negative. But my department chair's summary of these letters was so negative that a member of the campus ad hoc committee (who later waived her own right to privacy) was surprised when actually seeing the file because that person expected something negative after reading the chair's summary. My chair had no negative information. (Interview, 17 February 1996)

A member of the campus-wide ad hoc committee who reviewed her file concurred, indicating that the chair's summary of her external review letters was a gross distortion of their content: "I expected her outside peers to be disparaging based on the departmental letter—to the contrary, they were wildly enthusiastic" (Gwilliam et al. 1995:11). This person thus stated in her legal deposition that the

> report does not reflect the excellent outside assessment of her [Wang's] work. Protzen ignores the research evaluation done by his committee and goes with his own evaluation and the two most negative letters *out of 20* and many indications that his evaluation is ungenerous. (ibid.:13)

A subsequent acting chair also acknowledged that Wang's record compared favorably to that of other tenured faculty in the Department of Architecture: "In certain respects, this is true, for example Professor Wang's academic credentials do in fact 'equal or exceed' those of (some) males and non-Asians granted tenure within the Architecture Department"(ibid.:22).

Limited Avenues of Recourse and Redress

The corrective mechanisms within university apparatus were ponderously slow and powerless to implement changes that would truly rectify biases originating at the departmental level. Lawsuits were therefore the last or only resort for these plaintiffs. This was true even when administrative investigative committees detected procedural irregularities or substantively ruled in favor of the plaintiff.

Upon being denied tenure, Marcy Wang filed a grievance with the campus' Privilege and Tenure Committee in 1986. The ultimate arbiter at this stage in her case, this committee agreed that procedural errors had been committed and ordered the department to "deliberate anew." Opinion, however, had already jelled and set according to factions within the department, so that the injunction to do a "normal review" was a hollow one. At least two departmental colleagues went on record expressing their dismay over the degree of prejudice surrounding Wang's case. Thus one faculty person wrote that the failure to objectively assess the merits of her record was a problem from the very beginning.

> I feel that from the first discussions the faculty and administration have been biased by arguments that have nothing to do with the merits of the person and indicated grievances and personal whims which have gone unexamined. The discussions have been fraught with hearsay and prejudices which should have been ironed out. (Gwilliam et al. 1995:21)

Another wrote that the second departmental vote would unlikely be "more than a hanging."

> I don't believe that the coming vote will be more than a hanging. I see no other outcome and it sickens me that someone's academic career is ruined because we have been so entirely negligent. Such injustices will sit heavily and contribute to the lack of morale and disengagement already rampant among us.(ibid.)

Wang, in turn, stated that the departmental atmosphere had already been so contaminated with negative hearsay that the second vote was unlikely to rescue the situation, even though at least five Privilege and Tenure Committees would review her case: "By this time, people in the department had heard so much poison about me in the university that there was no real deliberation." The last committee saw no serious harm created by the procedural violations, reaffirmed the denial of tenure, offering some compensation for legal fees, not to exceed $30,000 (Cho 1992:124).

Over the course of twelve years, Jean Jew patiently registered her complaints with various internal bodies in the university (the university affirmative action office, the anatomy review and search committee, and the academic affairs vice-president), resorting to legal action only after she had exhausted these channels. Not until she hired her own attorney, Carolyn Chalmers, a proven successful litigator on behalf of women, did a university panel even convene. Its own findings of discrimination and recommendations calling for immediate action to repair the situation were ignored by the university and never implemented. Another six years would pass before the case finally came to trial (Chamallas 1994: 75–76, 83–84). In Tung's case, the internal grievance commission also found the university guilty of discrimination but again no action was forthcoming (Cho 1997:207). Filing a formal complaint with the EEOC brought the attention of the Dean, whose gesture was to offer money to assist in her departure. The implied message was that unless she dropped her case with the EEOC, she would be jeopardizing her career: "Deans talk and no one wants a trouble maker," she explained (Interview, 19 February 1996).

Given the principle of the matter and their own convictions about the injustice surrounding their cases, Jew, Tung, and Wang all waged long, hard-fought battles against their respective universities, and in the end successfully countered negative interpretations of their professional record. For Jew and Tung, these were court victories; for Wang, a $1 million out-of-court settlement.

Jean Jew filed two lawsuits, one in federal district court aimed at correcting her hostile work environment and the other in state court for defamation and sexual harassment. As others have noted, the legal significance of her case lay in the fact that there are so few where an academic department has been successfully demonstrated to present hostile work conditions (Chamallas 1994:73; Cho 1997:210). Indeed, the University sought to cast further doubt on her character, arguing not only that certain alleged behavior provoked the sexual and racial slurs against her but that this language was itself justifiable as academic free speech (Chamallas 1994:77–78; Cho 1997:211–13). Academic institutions aside, sexual harassment and hostile environment claims were relatively ill-defined matters which the courts in general were only beginning to grapple with from the time of her arrival at Iowa to the point of her suit.[30]

In considering the hostile work environment sexual harassment claim, the federal district court judge, Judge Harold Vietor, also ruled on the matter of disparate treatment. While the University did not believe Jew's harassment was due to her status as a woman but rather to the political turmoil in the department and her alignment with Williams (Chamallas 1994:80, 87), Vietor's judgment pointed out that Jew had, indeed, suffered unduly as a woman since Williams and his male allies were not slandered to the same degree, or in ways that affected their professional reputation (*U.S. District Court*, Southern District of Iowa, 28 August 1990:24).

In the matter relating to the department's failure to promote her, the judge concluded on the basis of evidence that Jew had in fact been qualified for promotion to full professor and therefore ordered retroactive promotion, an unusual decision given the court's traditional deference to universities where personnel decisions are concerned (*U.S. District Court*, Southern District of Iowa 28, August 1990:27–29, 31–33). Jew received $50,000 in back pay and benefits in her federal suit, and as a result of her state defamation suit, a unanimous jury decision awarded her $5,000 in actual damages and $30,000 in punitive damages (Cho 1997:210–11). Finally, in a separate court decision, the court motioned to award $895,000 attorney's fees. She retains, moreover, the right to disclose the details of her settlement (Chamallas 1994:82–83). Jean Jew was thus victorious in litigating issues specific to her own case and in the process set a precedent for state employees to use the Civil Rights law.[31] Other analysts of Jew's case have appropriately cautioned on the limited nature of legal remedies, Martha Chamallas (ibid.) thus wrote: "[Sometimes] I regard Jew's case as a warning that legal claims of sexual harassment offer only very limited prospects for social transformation. . . . Beyond the specific litigation demands [it was] considerably less clear what Jew had won from the University." Sumi Cho pointed out how the disciplinary effect of punitive damages was essentially erased by the fact that the University paid the $35,000 defamation judgment against the defendant, Robert Tomanek, along with a total of $171,094 toward his legal defense expenses. After months of delay, moreover, it relocated the defendant's research lab away from Jew's in newly constructed quarters that cost $46,790, meanwhile fighting the $11,417 legal fees Jew's attorney accrued for monitoring compliance (Cho 1992:47, 52–56). Jew thus recounted the University's resistance to compliance and its efforts to appeal the verdict itself:

> The University threatened to appeal the civil rights case and the personal defamation case but withdrew on both accounts because campus sentiment had been generated on my behalf. Had the University implemented the recommendations of its own faculty panel in 1984, the attorney fees would have been only $4000, instead of $895,000. With respect to the hostile environment, two years after the judge's ruling was handed down, the University hired consultants from all over the country in order to demonstrate that the problem had been corrected. These experts would not give the University a clean bill of health. (Interview, 30 October 1998; 22 November 1998)

To date, the university must still comply with the court injunction, which involves meeting with Jew annually about her work situation. While her own situation was thus remedied in important ways, Jew also pointed out that the university has found ways to retaliate against her research associate, Terry Williams, who had also testified and provided evidence that the department had given her a good job rating prior to the promotion denial. Blamed for poor performance as department chair, especially with respect to handling Jew's own discrimination complaints, he was subsequently denied salary increases. According to Jew, "This and other actions against him send the message that if you challenge the university, they can continue to harass you (Interview, 30 October 1998). The university arbitrator who investigated this matter acknowledges it was "both unfair and unrealistic" to expect him to resolve Jew's problems, especially since he himself was under attack because of rumors that implicated them both in an affair. In her conclusion, she wrote that he should be appropriately compensated for losses in his salary and for humiliation suffered (Greenbaum 1995, 1997). To date, however, the university has not complied. As Jew explained, "There is a heavy price to pay for challenging the system or for helping those who challenge the system. . . . I think they want to drag this on until he becomes too ill to fight them anymore or until he dies" (Jean Jew, personal communication, July 1999).

Jean Jew remains a permanent member of the faculty in the Anatomy Department at the University of Iowa. Her expressed reasons for staying were both a commentary on the significant change that nevertheless has taken place and a testimony to the fact that change is still needed. Among the positive things that transpired with the court judgment in her favor was the immediate cessation of hostile graffiti and the restoration of her character in the public's eye.

> Just being able to go into work and not having to face graffiti and to know that people can't say things with impunity is such a big difference. I'm still relatively isolated but I can collaborate with people outside the department. There are people of good will. When they heard these things [the original gossip], they thought it was true. I wouldn't have received this public exoneration had I merely settled with the university and not gone to trial. (Interview, 30 October 1998)

Speaking of the political role she has come to play as a social change agent, she pointed to her work with various advocacy groups on campus and the establishment of a special award in her name that serves as an ongoing reminder of these issues:

> To the extent that one can, there is a value in staying and trying to advocate for change. I've gotten involved with different advocacy groups on campus. The Council on the Status of Women created the Jean Jew Justice Award, which recognizes the efforts of any university faculty, staff, or student in terms of his or her contributions toward the rights of women. It's an annual award with a monetary sum attached. This grassroots committee emerged when the University committee tried to appeal the injunction. The downside is that the University is reminded every year that I am a thorn in their side. For this reason things have not returned to normal. Not that I have any illusions of that things will return to normal once the injunction is lifted. (Interview, 30 October 1998)

When Rosalie Tung filed her complaint with the EEOC, this investigating body was initially impeded in forming its own independent judgment about the relative merits of her case because the University of Pennsylvania denied the EEOC's request for access to the files of other tenured faculty. As noted earlier, the university lost its countersuit to retain the right not to release such information, thereby resulting in a major U.S. Supreme Court decision (*University of Pennsylvania v. Equal Employment Opportunity Commission*). Though

Tung was terminated and forced to leave the University in 1986, her strong academic record was recognized elsewhere. "Hired immediately" by the University of Wisconsin, she was made Wisconsin Distinguished Professor in 1988. The University of Pennsylvania's Grievance Commission, however, would continue its slow deliberations for the next several years, requiring her to fly back to Pennsylvania almost every other weekend to address issues raised by her case. In addition to the financial drain incurred from the cost of airfare and legal fees during the five years she contested the tenure decision, the process took an emotional toll.

On 9 January 1990, the U.S. Supreme Court ruled that the university could not claim immunity from disclosure based on First Amendment rights. Consequently, Tung gained access to files enabling the EEOC to compare her own record with that of five white male faculty who had gained tenure in the same department during the time she was denied. The Court also affirmed the finding of the university's own grievance commission, after which the university offered to settle for an undisclosed sum of money and to publicize the findings of its grievance commission. By then, Tung, already full professor at the University of Wisconsin, had become program chair of her department (Interview, 20 September 1998). She subsequently moved to Canada, where she is an endowed chaired professor (The Ming & Stella Wong Professor of International Business) in Business Administration at Simon Fraser University, and presently resides with her family in Burnaby, British Columbia. At the time I met her for a second interview, she was being honored at a reception at the Women's Faculty Club, where she had been elected the 1998 Vancouver YWCA's Woman of Distinction in the Management, Professions, and the Trades Category.

About her own experience, Marcy Wang remarked "I had no idea how entrenched the university was in protecting itself or extensions of itself no matter how reprehensible the behavior was" (Interview, 17 February 1996). In retrospect, what "surprised" her was not so much the fact that many of her former colleagues were capable of undermining her, but that the University of California would, in her words, "do everything to discredit, destroy, and spread negative reports" about her lack of qualification, while failing to abide by its own rules and standards. About the absence of fair play, she remarked: "I'll play by your rules but you have to play by your rules, too." In a legal deposition for the plaintiff, UC Berkeley's Title IX officer during the 1987–1989 period underscored a fact which her attorneys noted in boldface: **"Women tenure candidates were being held to a higher standard then their male counterparts"** (Gwilliam et al. 1995:16). Marcy Wang's legal trek would involve seven years of grievance procedures, and three years of court proceedings. Now working independently as an architect in Berkeley, Wang recalled how the very fact that "I fought back" surprised a former departmental colleague, who found her to be "quiet, shy, and hard-working" (Interview, 17 February 1996).

In their struggle for a fair review of their respective cases, Professors Jean Jew, Rosalie Tung, and Marcy Wang sought recourse in the university's appeals process, only to discover that the procedures in place were inadequate to address the substantive concerns for redress. Despite strong evidence that the "rules of the game" were differentially applied, their respective universities have maintained that there was no bias based on "race" or "sex." Indeed, one might agree that many of the subjective judgments and organizational dynamics were not expressly racist or sexist, except in glaring instances, such as Jew's case.

Though these women came from different institutions and disciplines, important aspects of their experiences are shared and generalizable. Because of their race and sex, they experienced a certain marginality, having to navigate an organizational or departmental culture that was alien, if not actively hostile. As evident in the decision-making process over their promotions, subjectivity entailed great liberty in interpreting their personnel files, which both trivialized their accomplishments and erected higher standards. Departmental bias, in other words, did not have to manifest itself in any overtly racist or sexist manner. Rather, their cases illustrate how race and gender bias can assume subtler forms that are no less damaging to the reputations of individuals, if not to the reputations of institutions themselves.

Given the enormous energy, stamina, and resources it would take·to challenge a negative departmental decision, it is likely that these discrimination suits filed by Asian American women faculty are but the "tip of the iceberg" (Hune and Chan 1997:59).

CONCLUDING REMARKS

This chapter has taken a critical view of Asian American educational achievement and their progress through the educational pipeline, particularly as this pertains to higher education. The focus has been on aspects of this profile that have implications for career mobility.

For students, a configuration of considerations, including not only grades and test scores but also proposed major and nonacademic criteria, affects one's chances for process. Lower than expected acceptance rates have been found in elite universities, which are more likely to use nonacademic criteria. The narrow areas of subject interest where Asian students tend to concentrate (e.g., math, science, engineering, premedical programs or health sciences) have also contributed to a "ceiling." Although Asian Americans place a great faith in objective performance, major barriers before them now include assessments related to leadership and language skills.

The pipeline into faculty positions, not to mention the top of the professoriate, is also problematic. Beginning with the training and recruitment of graduate students, up through the administrative ranks, fewer and fewer Asian Americans are noticeable at each subsequent juncture in the pipeline. While it is clear that untenured faculty are particularly vulnerable, tenure itself is no protection against marginalization or exclusion. Indeed, in a study of 487 campuses in eight Midwestern states, Caroline Turner and her co-researchers came to just this conclusion for minority faculty who otherwise appeared objectively well-positioned within the academic hierarchy. Their ongoing exclusion and isolation suggest that surmounting the glass ceiling is but one of many hurdles.

> The fact is that this elite and successful group of scholars, even among those who are not only tenured but who also hold high-level, high-profile academic appointments, still experience continued exclusion and isolation. This sobering fact must check any premature optimism about the distance yet to travel toward equality in American higher education. (Turner et al. 1999:29)

Notes

1. Barringer and his associates noted that while whites receive a higher income from their college education than do Asian Americans (from any of the subgroups), Asian Americans are more likely to earn more than whites in the professions. Thus, they concluded, "The upshot seemed to be that whites gained more from education directly than Asian Americans, and that Asian Americans must translate their superior education to appropriate occupations to gain commensurate incomes" (Barringer et al. 1995:256).

2. In 1993, the family poverty rate for Asian Pacific Americans (APAs) with a bachelor's or higher was 7%, as compared with 1.9% for their white counterparts.

3. Writing about specific factors that adversely and disproportionately affect the admission of Asian students to the University of California Berkeley, Professor Ling-chi Wang (1988:11) pointed out that nonacademic criteria, such as "leadership potential," as demonstrated through extracurricular activities,

   > appear designed precisely to make a large number of Asian Americans less competitive than white applicants . . . (Based on publicly announced admissions criteria, most Asian immigrant parents had discouraged, if not prohibited, their children from participation in extracurricular activities because most of them had assumed such activities to be worthless for gaining access into the most academically selective universities).

4. Some of the largest growth in the future, according to politically conservative projections, is expected to be in jobs requiring increasing education and skill levels. Whereas a college education is required for only 22% of today's jobs, one-third of all new jobs created between 1984 and 2000 are estimated to require a college degree (Hudson Institute 1987:20–32, 96–101.)

5. Since the 1960s, the government has compiled more systematic statistics on Asian Americans as a racial aggregate. The term "Asian American" eventually came to encompass Pacific Islanders as part of this aggregate. In the 1996–1997 Annual Status Report on Minorities in Higher Education, the information in the tables on "Asian Americans" actually includes "Pacific Islanders," even though these are not generally interchangeable categories since the subgroups within are very different. Elsewhere in this same report, the term Asian Pacific American is used to make clear the fact that statistical information is included for Pacific Islanders or Pacific Americans as well as for those groups officially designated as Asian American.

   In general, the umbrella category Asian American has been mainly troublesome when separate listings for specific Asian ethnic groups are not available. As a result of lobbying by Asian Pacific American groups, the 1980 census was broadened to include nine separate Asian ethnic groups (Japanese, Chinese, Filipinos, Koreans, Vietnamese, Asian Indian, Hawaiians, Samoan, and Guamanians), plus an "other" category for other possible Asian responses. More recently, there have been pressures to add a "multiracial" category, which captures a different kind of problem associated with collecting data on race or ethnicity, and that is that racial identification is based on individual self-identification, which is itself subject to changing attitudes about race and shaped by the politics associated with certain designations. Hawaiians, for example, have indicated they do not want to be lumped with "Asian or Pacific Islanders" but with "American Indians and Alaska natives," reflecting concern that they might be misperceived as immigrants. American Indians, on the other hand, disagree with the Hawaiian proposal, seeing themselves as distinctly different in terms of their history, culture, status, and relationships with the government. According to Kenyon Chan (California State University, Northridge), certain Department of Education data stretch the definition of Asian Americans even further to encompass populations in the Near East and Middle East (such as Iraq, Iran, and Israel) (personal communication). Given such inconsistencies in statistical sources, it is advisable to be alert to these issues when making inferences from these data.

6. Whether Arab Americans were included here because they resisted being classified as either "Asian" (see previous footnote) or "whites" is not clear.

7. This amounted to a 148% increase at the bachelor's level and 95% at the master's, and 46% at the doctorate level, whereas corresponding increases for the total population were, respectively, 11%, 3%, and 10% (Escueta and O'Brien 1993:5).

8. For a discussion of the increasing presence in the U.S. of foreign graduate students from Asian countries, see Ling-chi Wang (1993:50, 55–56).

9. Between 1979 and 1989, Asians who were U.S. and non-U.S. citizens significantly increased their number of total doctorates. Asians who were noncitizens doubled their number of doctorates (from 2137 to 4508), while the number for the Asian U.S. citizens almost doubled (from 427 to 624) (Escueta and O'Brien 1991:6–7).

10. Includes all persons who did not report their citizenship at time of doctorate and those who did not report their racial/ethnic background.

11. U.S.-born Asians, however, have shown a lesser tendency to choose careers in math and the sciences. Hsia (1988:161) thus made this observation a decade ago: "The 'over-representation' of Asians among science and engineering doctorates had never been due to high rates of participation on the part of native-born Asian Americans."

12. An extensive report on the demographic makeup of doctoral degree recipients for 1992 can be found in Paula Reis and Delores Thurgood, *Summary Report 1992: Doctorate Recipients from U.S. Universities,* Washington: National Academy Press (1993:54–55).

13. Not surprisingly, this pattern in science concentration is also reflected in employment data. The occupations in which Asian Pacific Americans concentrate reveal they are far more likely than other racial-ethnic groups to be overrepresented in the sciences. Even though blacks, Hispanics, American Indians, and Alaskan natives together make up 22% of the total U.S. population, they are less likely to be scientists or engineers than the other 78%. These fields have become increasingly less attractive for white males as well (Rawls 1991:20).

14. Contrary to the conventional view that Asian Americans are naturally gifted in the science and math fields, some research has noted that American-born Asians, specifically English-proficient, middle-class students have academic difficulties here.

> These middle-class, English-proficient, Asian American students, with mean SAT Verbal scores of 550 and SAT Mathematical scores of 620, used the following strategies more frequently than non-Asian comparison group members: dropping science and mathematics courses, completing freshman year with less than the normal course load, taking more courses in summer school, taking nine semesters to graduate instead of the normal eight, and withdrawing from college. Lack of congruence between parents' aspirations and students' interests or abilities was one possible explanation for the Asian American students' behavior. (Hsia 1988:154)

It has been suggested that their representation in the sciences and engineering is maintained primarily because they continue to enter these careers more frequently than other racial-ethnic groups: "U.S.-born Asians earn Ph.D.s in all fields at a rate that is slightly below their representation in the population . . . but because they are more likely to earn those degrees in science and engineering than other groups are, they end up equitably represented among Ph.D. scientists and engineers." Chemistry, for example, is a field where Asians are more likely than other racial groups (including whites) to concentrate. In a study of 6,653 students taking general chemistry courses at the University of Wisconsin, Madison, covering the period from 1988 through 1990, Agnes Sec found that American-born Asians were about "5% more likely to get Ds, fail, or drop out of these courses" (Rawls 1991:24, 25).

15. The acquisition of English language skills will need to be somehow balanced against the maintenance of the mother tongue, which is itself critical for maintaining high career aspirations for some students (Azores 1986–87).

16. Academe included two- and four-year colleges, universities, and medical schools. The data on "all Ph.D.s" included not only U.S. citizens but those who were temporary or permanent residents.

17. A similar and somewhat larger decline was also noted for white Ph.D.s. In 1973, 64% of white Ph.D.s. planned careers here; in 1989, this figure had dropped to 52%.

18. The issue of whether one uses national or regional baselines for recruitment, however, has consequences for recruiting minorities, who are more likely to be geographically concentrated in some regions rather than nationally dispersed. As with blacks and Chicano/ Latinos, who are most likely to receive their Ph.D.s in the South and Southwest, respectively, recruitment policies at the University of California tend to bypass those institutions in which Asian Americans are most likely to be concentrated.

According to a 1989 report issued by UC Berkeley's Asian American advisory subcommittee, the recruitment of Asian American faculty in general, and more diverse Asian American faculty in particular, was made difficult by how the campus has interpreted affirmative action guidelines related to the way recruitment goals must be tied to some designated availability pool (Asian Americans at Berkeley 1989:43–45). According to federal regulations, minorities and women are considered to be underutilized when their current employment levels are lower than their availability. The relevant availability pool, however, might be determined on the basis of the "minority population, minority unemployment force, minority workforce, and minority workforce with requisite skills in the immediate labor." The committee authoring this report argued that the immediate labor area for UC Berkeley was the San Francisco Bay Area, where Asian Americans were 10% of the population, double that of the Asian faculty at UC Berkeley, who then numbered eighty-one, or 5% of the 1,587 ladder-rank faculty. The University, however, casts its net much more widely in the sense that it not only advertises nationwide, but hires from a pool that lies largely outside the "immediate labor area." Specifically, this hiring tended to flow from a select few institutions: "nearly one-half come from only five universities: Berkeley, Harvard, Stanford, MIT, and Columbia." These institutional pools were not ones where the diversity among Asian Americans was reflected. Since Asian Americans were "more likely to earn their doctorates from institutions on the West Coast," certain Asian ethnic groups at UC Berkeley—Filipinos, Koreans, and Southeast Asians—were strikingly underrepresented in the faculty. In terms of gender distribution,

Asian American women were less than 1% of the ladder-rank faculty.
Among the eighty-one Asian American ladder-rank faculty members at Berkeley, 51% (40) are Chinese Americans; 21% (17) are East Indians; 21% (17) are Japanese Americans; 2% (2) are Filipinos; 2% (2) are Koreans; and the remaining 3% (3) are other Asians—showing a clear need also for affirmative action for Filipino, Korean, and other Asian American faculty. Nine Asian American women comprise less than 1% of the faculty. (Asian Americans at Berkeley 1989: 42–43)

19. According to Valerie Simmons, Director of the Affirmative Action Office at the University of California Santa Cruz (23 November 1998), "availability" is calculated according to many factors. Where faculty hiring is concerned, many institutions will use National Research Council (NRC) data, though there may be variations in how they use this database. For assistant professor hires, they might use the most recent NRC data, such as the most recent year, while other campuses might combine several years (e.g., the last five years). For higher level positions, even older NRC figures might be used (e.g., data from five to ten years ago). This potential pool, however, must be narrowed down even further, because technically only those Ph.D.s who succeed in getting tenure at major universities are really in the pool of potential candidates for higher positions. Presently, however, data are not available on employed tenured faculty by subdiscipline.

20. Looking at the status of Asian American faculty at the University of California, Los Angeles, Nancy Wey (1980:46) thus pointed to the fact that while Asian Americans were 4.7% of the total faculty, this figure was "less than the Asian-American student enrollment at UCLA which is 8.9%; less than the Asian American Ph.D. recipients nationwide, which are 6.5%; and less than the 15% Asian Americans in the Greater Los Angeles population." More recently, Don Nakanishi noted this to be true at UCLA. Beginning with the training and recruitment of Asian Americans as graduate students, up through the administrative ranks, fewer and fewer Asian Americans are noticeable at each subsequent juncture in the pipeline.

At UCLA, for example, in 1987, the representation of Asian Pacific Americans followed a common downward pattern of declining representation (found at practically all major colleges and universities): 20% of the entering freshman class were Asian Pacific Americans, but they constituted only 10% of all entering graduate students, 6% of the nontenured faculty, and 4 percent of the tenured faculty. . . . On the other hand, at practically every major university in America, Whites reflect the opposite, upward pattern of increasing representation in the academic pyramid. For example, in 1987 at UCLA, Whites constituted 48 percent of the entering freshman class, 67% of all entering graduate students, 81% of all nontenured faculty, and 90% of all tenured faculty. . . . Furthermore, Asian Pacific Americans in top administrative posts at UCLA and most major universities are practically nonexistent. . . . Currently, only 2 of the top 75 administrators at UCLA are Asian Pacific American. (Nakanishi 1993b:52–53)

The relative absence of Asian American faculty in certain disciplines, schools, or fields of study was the major issue in a report issued at the University of California, Berkeley in 1989. Specifically, Asian Americans, who comprised 5.1% of UC Berkeley's ladder-rank faculty (81 out of 1,587) during the 1986–1989 period, were concentrated in just three of the campus's ten organizational units.

Asian Americans are underrepresented in all but three (Ethnic Studies, Engineering, and the Physical Sciences) of the ten organizational units. Nearly one-half of Asian American faculty are concentrated in Engineering and the Physical Sciences; only 43 Asian Americans, or 3.6% of the 1,195 ladder-rank faculty are in the remaining eight organizational units. (Asian Americans at Berkeley 1989:42)

These imbalances are reinforced by the university's hiring practices. For example, the College of Engineering, which has the "highest representation" of Asian faculty on the Berkeley campus (11.6%), is more likely to be targeted for a faculty appointment than other units. One reason is that recruitment efforts have been defined by the availability pool, that is, "availability of minorities having requisite skills in an area in which the contractor can reasonably recruit."

21.   EEOC numbers cited were 24,252 out of a total of 514, 552 (or 5%) of full-time faculty.

22.   Thus in 1991, "Asian American" faculty were 5.1% (26,545) of all full-time faculty in higher education, dropping to 4.7% (25,369) in 1993 (Carter and Wilson 1997:97).

23.   Wey (1980: 43–44), for example, reported that at California State University, Long Beach, a larger percentage of Asian American faculty in the lower ranks had Ph.D.s compared to non-Asian faculty: "Of the Asian American faculty, 87.3% have Ph.D. degrees, 12.7% have Master's degrees. Of the non-Asian American faculty, 73.7% have Ph.D. degrees, 23.8% have Master's degrees and 2.4% have less than a Master's degree." Some of this difference (especially among the highest ranking faculty), Wey suggests, might be explained by the relatively recent hiring of Asian Americans so that they have in total fewer years of service, and therefore fewer opportunities for promotion since hiring. However, among faculty lower on the ladder, Asian Americans were found to take a longer time to be promoted from associate professor to full professor.

24.   If we include two-year institutions, in 1996, there were seventeen APA males and three APA females, with the majority of the APA male presidents heading four-year institutions (Hune 1998:18).

25.   Chan (1989) has identified six forms by which influence or power might be wielded: *collegial, reputational, administrative, bureaucratic, personal, and agitational.* Asian-American faculty in engineering and the sciences are seen as having achieved considerable reputational power, due to their achievements in these fields, without, however, this being translated into collegial or administrative power.

26.   Jew arrived as a postdoctoral candidate in 1973 and was appointed to an assistant professor position the next year. As she recounted, she was the only woman and the only Asian faculty person in a tenure-track position until 1978. In 1978, the department hired three assistant professors. One was a white woman on the tenure track. Another was an Asian woman who was not on the tenure track. The third was an Asian male, who was hired on tenure track. The first woman was denied tenure and the second was not reappointed; her husband, who was the third candidate, consequently decided to leave as well.

27.   Marcy Wang was one of the two faculty here enumerated since the 1986–1989 Academic Affirmative Action Plan for Berkeley was based on 31 October 1985 data, and Wang would come up for tenure that same fall.

28.   The University of Pennsylvania, like Harvard, has associate professors who are either tenured or non-tenured. If one is in the latter category, one must be reviewed for tenure. In sharp contrast, typically in most American universities, the title "associate professor" implies one has already undergone such a review and is already tenured.

29.   According to Jew's account, Terry Williams was recruited to "boost research" and thereby bring life to the graduate program. The department had been without a chair for years and was run by a committee chaired by the only faculty person in the department with a grant. What Williams did not realize until much later was that many in the department had opposed his hire and that the department was as factionalized as it was. He may have been rather naïve, she said, since he had no prior administrative experience and believed he could change the departmental culture without approaching the problem more strategically, as by recruiting more senior faculty. "Terry didn't want people to feel threatened. He didn't want to eliminate anyone. He made the mistake of believing people could change" (Interview, 22 November 1998).

30.   "When Jew first complained to the central administration at Iowa in 1979, there were no federal guidelines defining harassment and no national policy condemning the practice. When Jew first filed suit in 1985, there was no Supreme Court opinion recognizing hostile environment claims. Only the cumulative efforts of many plaintiffs like Jew made it possible for Jew to articulate her harm as a legal injury and to secure a legal judgment. The irony of Jew's long ordeal is that it took almost that long for the law to catch up with her injury" (Chamallas 1994: 86).

31.   Once Jew filed her law suit at the state level, the University petitioned to have her case dismissed on the grounds that under the Iowa Administrative Procedures Act (IAPA) a state employee was merely entitled to assurances that the employer followed its own rules on hearing complaints, and that complaints be heard on procedures, rather than on a case's substantive merit. The lower state district court agreed and thereupon dismissed Jew's case. Jew's attorney appealed. While awaiting the State Supreme Court's decision, Jew lobbied the state legislature to clarify the IAPA. In response, the legislature amended the state constitution to clarify that IAPA was not intended to deprive a person of his or her civil rights (Iowa Code, Section 216.16, Chapter 1245, Section 263, 1986). The State Supreme Court, in turn, acknowledged the legislature's opinion and struck down the lower court's ruling, which had interpreted IAPA in the narrow, procedural sense (*Jew v. University of Iowa*, 398 N.W. 2nd, 861, Iowa 1987).

CHAPTER 5

The Glass Ceiling at "XYZ Aerospace"

Employment discrimination is often subtle and difficult to prove. . . . Glass ceiling cases are even more difficult to prove because the decision to promote is very subjective and because courts are less likely to question internal business decisions in which the decision maker does not articulate blatant discriminatory reasons.

Paul Igasaki, Vice Chairman of the EEOC,
Discrimination in the Workplace

The standard conventional view of the glass ceiling is that there is active and conscious discrimination against Asian Americans. I believe that the glass ceiling is the outgrowth of a lot of subtle issues.

Engineer and chair
of the Asian American Employee Association at "XYZ Aerospace."

The statistical data cited in chapter 2 can be distilled to a single dominant and recurring fact—the disproportionate underrepresentation of Asian Americans in management. How is this to be explained? Their newly established high-profile professional status marks a turning point, especially if one recalls the pre-World War II status of Asian college graduates, relatively underemployed and typically confined to ethnic enclaves. Still, their failure to show up in the executive ranks is noteworthy, especially since the majority of Asian Americans (76.3%) work as wage and salary workers in the private sector of the economy, and only a small percentage (9.8%) are listed as self-employed (Gall and Gall 1993:278).

The demand for scientists and engineers has produced high entry salaries for those with bachelor's degrees alone. Asian American scientists and engineers with advanced degrees would ordinarily be expected to have a certain leverage. The United States attracts not only the largest number of international students from Asia but larger numbers of these immigrant professionals than many other nations (Ong, Cheng, and Evans 1992). Although entry-level salaries have undercut the incentive to pursue advanced degrees (Northrup and Malin 1985:33, 36), Asian ancestry students are much more likely than other students to be concentrated in engineering and the sciences at all levels: bachelors, masters, and doctoral.[1]

Yet these degrees do not translate into managerial jobs. As noted in chapter 2, accent discrimination, as well as deficiencies in language or communication skills, are possible barriers for this immigrant workforce.

There is, however, another consideration when it comes to the science and engineering workforce, which is the problematic implications of the "dual ladder" for mobility. While an erosion of internal job ladders typically characterized the restructuring of work around advanced technology in the post-World War II period (Burris 1993), industry executives frequently created a "professional" or "technical" ladder to retain engineers uninterested in the administrative duties of the "managerial" ladder.

> The dual ladder refers to the side-by-side existence of the usual ladder of hierarchical positions leading to authority over greater and greater numbers of employees and another ladder consisting of titles carrying successively higher salaries, higher status, and sometimes greater autonomy or more responsible assignments. (Goldner and Ritti 1967:489)

The professional ladder holds out the promise of privileges typically associated with being a professional—increased status, pay, and autonomy—all achievable within technical specialties rather than within company management. An ideology of individual freedom and responsibility may even be explicitly fostered by high-tech corporate cultures (Kunda 1992). But according to Goldner and Ritti (1967), the ladder fails in most regards, notably because it does not provide the control and autonomy that belonged to traditional professions, namely, control over the allocation of limited resources and autonomy to define alternative goals. One constraint is that work activities frequently require collaboration or coordination on projects, thereby thwarting independent or solo work. Second, while supervisory responsibility grants a certain control or influence over one's immediate work sphere, budgets and other resources are commanded by those in the management hierarchy. Managerial ambitions have thus been spurred by desire for greater involvement in decision-making processes that have consequences for one's work.

Concerns related to the dual ladder were evident in the present study as well, and similarly have to do with its ambiguous implications not only for mobility but for control over one's work situation. It is a "chicken-and-egg problem" whether engineers seek jobs in management because of dissatisfaction with status, pay, and autonomy in their specialties; or whether executives redirect mobility aspirations toward professionalism because of the shortage of either high-level positions or qualified applicants. Whatever the case, the professional ladder has become "synonymous with career immobility," even when created as a sincere attempt to "make alternative goals viable" and not just "to cool out those who have not made it into management" (Goldner and Ritti 1967:496–97).[2]

In the present study, a major glass ceiling barrier is the difficulty in crossing over from the technical to the managerial ladder. Moreover, just as the meaning of professionalism has changed, so too has the meaning of management—no longer narrowly defined in terms of supervisory functions. The latter will be taken up in the final chapter. The present chapter examines how such internal structural barriers are experienced in terms of racial, cultural (or gender) dynamics that make this crossing more possible for some groups than others. These issues were explored at a particular organizational site, a federal government research center.

THE ORGANIZATIONAL SITE

The image of Asian Americans as entrepreneurs and small businesses managers has obscured their employment in more large-scale or mainstream firms, the norm not only for the general population but also for this growing minority population. Of the three major spheres of employment (corporate, government, and academia), Asian American doctoral recipients are less likely to be employed in government than in the corporate sphere (45%) or academia (38.9%). They are similar to other groups, however, in terms of postgraduate commitments to the government sector: 9.6 percent of Asians, 10 percent of blacks, and 8.3 percent of Hispanics, or in general, 9.7 percent of *all* Ph.D.s in 1992 (Ries and Thurgood 1993:32).

There were four major reasons for selecting the particular study site in question: (1) it had a highly prestigious reputation in terms of research; (2) it had a large concentration of scientists and engineers, especially Asian Americans; (3) there existed long-term documented glass ceiling concerns of Asian Americans; and (4) it was a government operation that had developed a positive reputation in recent years for its public commitment to diversity.

The organization has about 2,000 full-time permanent and contract employees, and for purposes of anonymity, will be referred to as "XYZ Aerospace Technology" or simply "XYZ." The larger agency, of which XYZ is one of many centers, employs almost 20,000 employees nationwide, and will be referred to as "Super-Aviation Links" (SAL). The Asian American Employee Association (AAEA) and the Diversity Leadership Consortium (DLC) are also fictitious names.

The government context presented itself as an arena in which to view how diversity issues were pursued where profit is not a primary motivating factor, or where equity issues are incorporated into the "business rationale." Corporate efforts to diversify have been mostly voluntary, except where companies receiving federal contracts are bound by federal mandates to take more proactive steps to identify and remove institutional barriers (Reskin 1998:7–13). In contrast, public employers are officially committed to creating fair and equal access at all job levels. Yet an integrated workforce does not necessarily put minorities or women on a par with white males (Lewis and Nice 1994).[3] Promotional opportunities for Asian Americans in government have been far from ideal (Chinese for Affirmative Action 1986, 1989, 1992; Lan 1988; Asian Americans for Community Involvement, 1993:9, 15; Kim 1994; Kim and Lewis 1994). The strategies whereby XYZ had acquired its reputation for diversity were therefore of great interest.

Apart from XYZ Aerospace being a government organization with a prestigious reputation for research and an outward commitment to diversity, a major reason for choosing this facility was its large number of Asian scientists and engineers. Indeed, of all the centers in the loose consortium of allied centers nationwide, it had the largest percentage of Asian scientists and engineers. As pointed out in chapter 2, science and engineering are not only the occupational fields that Asian Americans are most likely to enter, but also the arenas in which they have been most vocal about their concerns regarding the glass ceiling. Scientists and engineers, 80 percent of whom are white, make up 58 percent of XYZ's workforce of 2,000. Thirteen percent of scientists and engineers are Asian Americans, who numbered 110 at the time of this study in 1997.

The organization's geographical location in California increases the likelihood of other converging characteristics. Since California has the largest concentration (40%) of Asian Americans in the United States (O'Hare and Felt, 1991:5), a larger concentration of Asian American scientists and engineers than in the country at large (U.S. Department of Commerce 1992),[4] as well as the largest proportion of aerospace and high technology companies of all states (Bureau of the Census 1995b, Saxenian 1998), there is a strong likelihood that Asian American scientists and engineers in general will be connected with aerospace and high technology research.[5] Despite recent downsizing, the federal government continues to be a key funder, employer, and customer of aerospace projects.[6] In 1994, pay inequity between whites and Asian/Pacific Islanders (APIs) at XYZ Aerospace was reflected in their differential representation in management. Whereas whites made up 81 percent of all GS (General Schedule) and related jobs, they were overrepresented—at 91 percent—at senior pay levels. In sharp contrast, while APIs were 4.3 percent of all GS and related jobs, they made up only 2.2 percent of those at senior pay levels (U.S. Office of Personnel Management 1994).[7]

The third section of this chapter (Managerial Underrepresentation) summarizes some of the statistical data compiled the by AAEA at XYZ. The qualitative interview data collected for the present study, on the other hand, sought to get a sense of individual career progress as well as an overview of how such individuals viewed the glass ceiling more generally.

Interview contacts were made through the AAEA, which had formally taken up glass ceiling issues in the past. Interviews included managers or senior executives, some of whom had served as chairs or co-chairs of this association. These individuals, and other active members of the Association, had a broad perspective on glass ceiling issues, and managers in particular were able to articulate their views on the possible impact that the association's activities had on their careers.

Formal and informal exchanges also occurred with two of Aerospace's Equal Employment Opportunity officers, two members of the EEO Council, two members of the DLC, and two human resources personnel. The goal here was to obtain a perspective of how diversity is officially managed in the organization. These views, however, are not necessarily representative of any official organizational position on the glass ceiling. Similarly, because the Asian Americans contacted were not derived from a random sample, the findings are not necessarily generalizable to other Asian American professionals at XYZ. The "snowball" method of referral, however, quickly identified key individuals with a direct interest or involvement with promotional concerns.

In total, nineteen individuals were interviewed, fifteen of whom were Asian American. Nine were chairs or co-chairs of the employee association and ten were managers, two of whom were senior executives. The majority of Asian interviewees were male (11 out of 15), though there was diversity here in terms of age (from 25 to 68) and length of employment at Aerospace (from 4 to 39 years), both of which influenced perceptions of the glass ceiling, as well as attitudes toward how aggressive the AAEA should be in advocating for social change.

Because the glass ceiling does not apply to those uninterested in managerial work, the focus of the study was on individuals who either had an express interest in managerial work or were actually on the managerial track. Identifying interviewees this way clearly risked overlooking those who may have once aspired to be a manager but had given up. One line manager thus indicated that this was particularly true of old timers, who were originally very interested in managerial work but eventually dropped out of the process after their applications were repeatedly denied. "I've heard the stories over and over again. People that have applied for jobs over and over again, and then they get sick and tired of it, and they don't apply any more, because they've been passed over." Many current concerns are identical with those raised in the earlier period in the agency's history.

The remainder of this chapter is organized into four sections: (1) an introduction to the agency and certain features of its organizational culture; (2) a detailed look at the objective profile of managerial underrepresentation for Asian Americans at XYZ Aerospace; (3) the contours of the glass ceiling as perceived by those interviewed for this study; and (4) a discussion of social change issues, including where these professionals saw the need for improvement, their conflicting orientations toward social change, and the kinds of remedies reflecting the organization's present efforts to address such mobility barriers.

THE ORGANIZATIONAL CULTURE

Super-Aviation Links (SAL), of which XYZ Aerospace is a subdivision, was founded in the 1950s. From its inception, the organizational culture that pervaded SAL was one of technical competence and an "ivory-tower" approach to research. Moreover, as a neutral, apolitical body, it was ideally suited to receive project assignments and activities that might otherwise have become a source of contention between rival organizational interests with more political agendas.

The agency derived its competitive spirit not from mere material incentives, but from the Cold War and the view of technical projects as having a larger historical significance for the nation and society at large. Insiders were motivated to take on long hours not simply to meet bureaucratic deadlines but because of the ideals associated with the mission of Super-Aviation Links. There was also an unusual degree of individual control over the work situation and opportunity for hands-on experience that made the work intrinsically satisfying. The projects themselves had a certain "glamour," and working in such an organizational enterprise bestowed the status of being affiliated with "the best and the brightest." Thus, although the salaries of scientists and engineers were not as competitive as in the private sector, recruitment of young talented scientists and engineers was not a problem.[8]

With risk inherent in every project venture, success has depended on technical skills. The organization was thus primed to deal with the risk. SAL's present efforts to encourage "controlled risk" is an issue we will return to in the next chapter. Historically, the XYZ workplace was unlike the conventional government-run bureaucracy we know today. Like SAL as a whole, it was largely decentralized in its operations, and like the other regional centers fairly insulated from politics at the epicenter. Decentralized work relations, specifically engineers controlling and managing most of their in-house affairs, were intended to optimize the conditions for exceptionally high standards of performance. According to Beverly Burris (1993), a flattened hierarchy is typical of work in "expert sectors," where diminished bureaucracy control goes hand-in-hand with increased skill levels and more democratic working conditions.

> At expert levels, much of the rigidity characteristic of bureaucratic rules and task specifications tends to be replaced by more flexible and collegial types of organization. . . . Tasks tend to be organized around ad hoc projects, with the formal structure of communication and chains of command routinely bypassed, leading to more decentralized authority among the expert sector, an emphasis on horizontal communication, and a sense of "adhocracy." (1993:146)

An interviewee with a history almost long as the organization thus reflected back nostalgically on the fact that work conditions for scientific and technical personnel within the agency as a whole had been highly desirable. "It's been positive. It's a good bunch of people here. In fact, early in my career, say, in the sixties and seventies, we had [the] cream of the crop. . . . Everybody wanted to get into the act. And we had our choice of many [of] the graduates from good universities." A younger and relatively more recent recruit observed that XYZ's overall reputation was still positive and that being associated with a small community of respected colleagues made for ideal collegial relations. That, combined with a flexible work situation, brought a great deal of work satisfaction.

> I can set my own hours as long as it's within reason. . . . I'm pretty much my own boss in terms of getting the work done. Somebody will give me an assignment and then it's up to me to determine how that's done. . . . I'd say the people I work with are tremendous. They're very easy to get along with, very easy to work with—and they're all good people, too. They're people I respect, and I think are kind, honest people, which . . . is very important to me. . . . Being associated with XYZ is still positive. I feel tied in with a lot of the people here. . . . I've gotten to know people over my eight years here so that it's like being in a little small town.

This generally positive attitude toward the organizational workplace was widely shared among Asian Americans at XYZ Aerospace. A 1991 survey by the AAEA indicated that many expressed a high level of satisfaction with the "work environment," "working at XYZ," and the opportunity to use one's "talents and expertise" to reach one's "maximum potential."

Despite such intrinsic job satisfaction, the agency is no longer the attractive workplace it once was. Thus, a manager who had been actively involved in recruiting at career fairs said she was quite frank about this to potential recruits: "I have to really tell it like it is now. It's not . . . the same glamorous thing to get into and know that you're there forever. . . . The organization as a whole is almost moving toward. . . . less than an outstanding performance in terms of how it's rewarding people." The once high-performing technological culture had moved in the direction of a traditional large-scale corporation—greater centralization, bureaucracy, and rigidity—a pattern that affected both the original élan of the Agency and its enterprise, as well as the way in which managerial work itself gets done. Thus another interviewee explained,

> I'm not too happy about the direction the whole agency is going. . . . Our budgets are being cut. . . . There just doesn't seem to be enough public interest whereas in [previous] days there was a tremendous amount of excitement, public excitement, public support for the . . . program. But it's become an old hat, and the agency is suffering somewhat from administrative burdens, whereas in the beginning, I think, the agency had a "can-do" attitude, and they were able to do a lot of things. [There] seems to be just ever-increasing administrative burden—more reports, generating more reports. And it's difficult to understand why these reports are

needed. . . . And when you have reports and response to headquarters [it] takes the time away from your real management job.

Downsizing, outsourcing, and uncertain job security have created real barriers to entering management. Still, managerial underrepresentation also suggests artificial barriers. In the area of technical competence, Asian American scientists and engineers are unquestioned as professionals. Yet, two longtime veterans in the organization commented on research and management:

1. As researchers we can do as well as others. There's no disparity in grades. Only when you look at managers.

2. The research job itself, it's very rewarding, don't get me wrong. And I have over 120 papers published with my name as author or coauthor, so it's a source of satisfaction. And that part, I'm pleased with it. And when they give grants, fund different projects and [choose] the best proposal [there is no] glass ceiling or racial discrimination in that form.

Moreover, the long-standing emphasis on technical over "people-oriented" skills points to a major organizational weakness responsible for glass ceilings, employee job dissatisfaction, and retention problems. Although "communications skills" have been cited as a major stumbling block for Asian Americans, a former manager noted a covert bias against Asians who spoke English with an accent, while those with European accents were more favorably judged. Whatever might be thought of their verbal skills, their organizational leadership became apparent as they began to mobilize around these issues early on.

The absence of minorities in high-level managerial positions was a concern for other employee groups as well. In an organization where scientists and engineers are its heartbeat, Asian Americans form a critical mass at 13 percent of the science and engineering workforce, compared with 4 percent for Hispanics, 2 percent for blacks, and 1 percent for Native Americans. To a greater extent than any other employee group, Asian Americans have documented their managerial underrepresentation for more than twenty years. Even so, only slowly did high-level administrators respond by becoming actively involved—by vocalizing the need for greater representation of women and minorities in management, and by supporting diversity efforts through a variety of means, including consultations with the various employee groups, improved ties with Equal Opportunity Office (EEO) and human resource personnel, funding for training courses, development workshops and speaker events, a formal mentoring program, and official approval for the creation of informal groups to facilitate dialogue and mutual understanding across different groups. The overall culture and politics of the workplace generally reflects a "liberal" atmosphere of leadership support for diversity. Indeed, this government agency was described as a "leader in the government service," for having "created some things that were touted as models within the federal government sector, let alone private industry."

Some workers at XYZ Aerospace, however, see recent diversification efforts as simply another bureaucratic layer, having little to do with the essential mission of the organization and one imposed by "political" considerations such as affirmative action hiring. For others, affirmative action and other diversification efforts have in small ways helped promote the recruitment and integration of minorities, though minorities remain excluded from key organizational networks. For others still, the mere fact that diversity issues are now part of upper management consciousness represents an overall change in the orientation of the organizational culture.

> I think the situation is different now than what it was 20 years ago. Yeah, when [other Asian Americans] had to elevate these issues up center management. Because back then, you had to really get as loud as you can, and bring in as many external forces as you can to get management here to pay attention to these issues.

Most, however, agree that numerous barriers remain, and when compared with other organizational concerns, diversity remains low in upper management's priorities.

Downsizing has dampened and compromised the organization's effectiveness in implementing certain diversity measures. After 1965, a peak budget year (as much as $5 billion a year), SAL began to cut back on spending. This trend reversed in the 1980s with the budget doubling between 1983 to 1992. Beginning in 1993, however, SAL entered a period of voluntary downsizing, corresponding with an overall reduction of 272,900 federal employees legislated for the year 1999. An XYZ employee thus pointed out that not only has there been a "freeze" on promotions but that an overall uncertainty hovers over the mission of the organization, with some evidence this, too, is changing:

> When the freeze started there was a long list of people who were ready and qualified to [be promoted]. There is mobility (in terms of transferring to jobs at the same level), but there're very few opportunities upward.

> I think on the negative side there are just "question marks" over the overall future of the center, whether XYZ will even be here in a few years, and then presuming it's here, what will XYZ look like. XYZ is shifting itself from Aeronautics . . . to information systems research. And I don't have a background in computer science, so one of the things I'm looking at is trying to sharpen and update my technical skills.

The next section offers a statistical overview of how Asian Americans at XYZ Aerospace have fared over the last twenty years with respect to managerial advancement.

Managerial Underrepresentation

Since 1973, the AAEA has represented the career development concerns of the more than 200 Asian American employees at the research center, approximately half of whom are scientists and engineers. Its major undertaking has been the study of Asian American representation at the managerial levels.

The original impetus behind such studies is unclear. According to an engineer who witnessed these early beginnings, they were initiated in 1971 at the request of the center director, whose explicit aim was to show that Asian professionals at the center were a "model" for other minorities who were more vocal and aggressive about the problems then existing at XYZ Aerospace. According to another scientist, they were launched only after the center faced a race discrimination suit from Asian professionals themselves. Whatever the case, the statistical findings proved surprising. Instead of being a model of mobility, Asian American employees were one grade lower than expected, and the critical comparison group was not the other minorities but white males. Although the term "glass ceiling" would not be coined for at least a decade, these early findings were clear evidence of a ceiling on mobility, which the center director himself reputedly acknowledged to be an indicator of "subtle discrimination."

Despite such documentation, nothing would be done about the problem for almost fifteen years. Refusal to even *admit* there were these barriers thereby became the single major barrier to change. Between 1971 and 1984 there were *no* high-ranking Asian American managers. When this information was brought to the attention of appropriate organizational bodies and officials during the 1980s, the atmosphere at meetings with the DLC was highly charged, so "tense" and "intimidating" that there was apparently a constant turnover in the chairs of other employee associations. When confronted with the allegation that Asian Americans were bypassed for promotion as a result of "subtle discrimination," an EEO officer allegedly reacted by asserting that everything was "fine as far as numbers."

Only when external pressure was applied did the center begin to respond. The assistance of Congressman Norm Mineta was enlisted, his inquiries spurring the promotion of two Asian Americans to higher ranking administrative levels (GS-15). The first Asian American senior executive was appointed in 1986. The major breakthrough in these negotiations came after the EEO officer from SAL's headquarters wrote a letter formally indicating that Asian Americans at XYZ faced a glass ceiling. As a chair of the AAEA stated: "This was the first time the agency admitted a problem. Only when they acknowledged a problem, could we begin working on a solution."

As a result of such intervention, the center undertook a number of initiatives recommended by the employee association. These included programs that could facilitate entry into management, such as temporary duty assignments, which lower level (GS-13 or GS-14) employees could apply for. They also included active outreach to Asian American candidates, including greater emphasis on recruiting Asian American applicants for Sloan Fellowships. In general, it appears that without the combination of affirmative action goals (i.e., the use of numerical goals as a gauge) and the "heat" of external, political pressure, the center's response would have been a bureaucratically insensitive one.

Despite such positive steps, Asian American scientists and engineers have been absent from these high-level administrative positions for most of XYZ Aerospace's history. In 1999 XYZ had no Asian Americans at the senior executive level. This was true in 1973 as well, because 4 out of the 198 Asian American employees who were managers were at the lower managerial levels. A comparison based on degree achieved (i.e., technical, B.S., M.A., Ph.D. degrees) found Asian American males in lower pay grades than their white male counterparts despite having the same or higher educational levels and more work experience. As stated in the summary report for 1973: "American Asians are approximately one grade lower than the white male in each category. Moreover, American Asians with M.S. and Ph.D. degrees are at a lower grade than whites with B.S. degrees. . . . Except at the B.S. level, the American Asians have more work experience."

Subsequent reports underscored not only continuing underrepresentation but growing dissatisfaction. In 1975, not only were Asian Americans "not paid equally for equal work," but seniority did not offer any advantage: "many of the promotions were given to the more recent and younger employees, while promotions to Asian-Americans with longevity service . . . were nominal. It is in this area that upgrading should be seriously considered."

By 1977, barriers began to be attributed to "racial discrimination" at the top. A glass ceiling was reflected in the concentration of scientists and engineers at the GS-13 level, the pay grade level just below management and senior technical staff. Two-thirds of these GS-

13 employees felt they were in "dead-end" jobs, while almost half of GS-14 employees felt that way. Not surprisingly, two-thirds of all Asian American employees said they were willing to transfer laterally within the organization if it would ultimately lead to a promotion. The 1997 report not only underscored the longstanding nature of the problem but now pointed to Asian Americans being an average of *two* grades below their white counterparts.

In 1980, the AAEA issued yet another report. While applicants for managerial positions had increased since 1977, so apparently had the barriers. The facts included extremely long delays in promotion, along with perceptions that Asians had to "work harder for advancements." Even new employees were dissatisfied and considered changing jobs. Perceptions of racial discrimination were prevalent.

- Nearly unanimous belief by all respondents that individuals are preselected.
- Over half the respondents believe that discrimination is practiced. . . . 60% of the respondents believe that management is responsible and 45% believe that discrimination is practiced on the basis of race. Eighteen of 19 employees with over 15 years service believe that discrimination exists.
- 64% of the responses indicate that Asians have to work harder for advancements than others. Same as 1974 survey.
- Half of the new employees, those with under 5 years service, want to advance . . . within the system but contemplate moving elsewhere if they feel that they can't advance.
- 30% of those respondents with over 15 years of experience have *not* been promoted at all and one individual with more than 24 years of service . . . is still a GS-4. (AAEA Report 1988)

The promotional disparity with whites was matched by persistent failure of agency heads to acknowledge or deal with this inequity. In separate letters to the Director of the Center and to the then Assistant Administrator in the EEO office, the AAEA pointed not only to this disparity in appointments at the highest levels but to the absence of leadership in addressing this situation:

> One out of ten from the nonminority group . . . is a chief of an office, branch, division, or directorate. This contrasts sharply with only 1 out of 44 Asian Americans, (2 branch and 2 office chiefs). No Asian American has ever held a division chief or director's position at XYZ Aerospace.

> The disparity is even greater in terms of GS ratings at higher levels. For example, 1 out of 14 nonminority [sic] has a GM or GS-15 rating. There are 33 SES [senior executive service] positions at XYZ Aerospace; not one of these positions . . . is held by a member of the minority group. Based on a fair and equal apportionment of the Asian American staff population one would expect at least three Asian American SES positions rather than zero. (Furthermore, there are no SES Asian Americans in the entire SAL organization.)

> The most significant fact of all is that the same trends were reported repeatedly to XYZ Aerospace management and the EEO by the Asian American Employee group over the past decade. In the interim no substantial reforms have been realized.

Although Asian Americans were promoted over the next three years into the managerial ranks, these promotions were at lower levels. Like other minority employees, they plateaued at the GM-13 level. The pipeline thereafter became extremely constricted. In 1987, 12 percent of Asian Americans were located at the GM-13 level. Only 7.6 percent of those at the GM-14 level were Asian American Pacific Islanders (AAPI). The GM-15 level saw even fewer Asian Americans in management, 4.9 percent, and their representation at the SES level was the worst, a mere 2.9 percent. As summarized by the 1988 AAEA report, "AAPI representation at all managerial levels except the GM-13 level is disproportionately lower than its share of the . . . workforce. The AAPI representation becomes progressively worse as the managerial position becomes higher." The report cited relatively infrequent promotions and longer "average time spent in a grade before promotion" as objective reasons for the disparity, while also acknowledging the subjective bias that some Asian Americans saw as deriving from management's view of them as "technical coolies."

In 1991, Asian Americans had grown to 10.7 percent of the workforce, yet their managerial representation remained only 5.3 percent. A survey of 250 of these employees that same year ruled out a lack of managerial interest as a reason for this disparity: Of the 105 who responded, 53 expressed interest in management positions. Regarding the job selection process, there were variable opinions, not mutually exclusive: 53 percent believed selections to be based on "merit & qualifications," another 53 percent thought candidates had already been "preselected," and 36 percent felt there was also "subtle racial or cultural bias." As in 1973, age continued to be a factor, with those under 30 years of age expressing more satisfaction with promotion rates than those over 50. Even so, Asian Americans at upper management levels were decidedly absent. Fifty-nine percent of respondents indicated that they must work harder and produce more than their peers to receive recognition.

By 1993, Asian Americans grew to 13.6 percent of the workforce while the numbers in management increased to 9.2 percent. The underrepresentation continued to be greater at the higher pay grade levels, with only 7 percent of those at the GS/GM-15 grade level (and above) being Asian American.

Finally, as late as 1997, few Asian Americans could be found at the senior executive level. There were at most only three such individuals, fewer than 1 percent of all Asian American scientists and engineers. With the later departure of these individuals, the current situation for Asian Americans is worse than it was in 1987, when their representation at the SES level was 2.9 percent.

THE CONTOURS OF THE GLASS CEILING

This section reports on those barriers that emerged as major themes in the interview data. Employees were asked to talk about their individual career progress and their perceptions of the glass ceiling at the center as well as to comment on the effectiveness of various strategies XYZ or the employee association had used to promote diversity.

In terms of everyday interaction, race or ethnicity were not a salient part of consciousness, and work relations were seldom said to be characterized by racial prejudice, either overt or covert. An instance several years ago involved rumors of an internal spy ring triggering the targeting of Asian American employees for special security searches. In the end, such suspicions were unfounded. The incident, however, sparked outrage on behalf of those who had been singled out, prompting an apology from the facility's head.

More typical of the biases that Asian Americans experienced were those that inhered in the corporate culture and the "old boy network." According to one executive, it was not uncommon for white male colleagues to make clumsy efforts at racial-ethnic humor (e.g., references to "the inscrutable one"). These were experienced as "subtle racial barriers," which one learned to "ignore" by developing "a fairly thick skin." Prevalent throughout the executive ranks, they are indicative of the ignorance of insensitivity that comes with racial homogeneity in these ranks.

There were also unstated norms or routines that affected participation, especially the implicit requirement for "conspicuous expertise." The dominance of a distinct managerial style intimidated subordinates, inhibited full participation, and represented a negative model for Asian Americans aspiring to be managers.

The following pages describe of corporate culture as it stands against "Asian" cultural values. These corporate cultural barriers are exacerbated by internal structural barriers: factors related to outreach and recruitment, the particular ladder on which an employee is positioned (e.g., technical or administrative), the availability of mentoring or of critical assignments with visibility, and finally, special or different standards for performance evaluation. Although corporate culture and internal structural opportunities can thus be seen as analytically distinct, they are nevertheless closely related. An employee's comfort level with respect to the organization's values, beliefs, and behavioral norms will affect his or her ability to advance within the organizational structure. Conversely, if an employee is poorly positioned structurally, this could mean less access to key networks and slower progress through the pipeline.

Corporate Culture and Asian Cultural Values

The culture of corporate America has been identified as "the most serious type of impediment by far to upward mobility and advancement" (Cabezas et al. 1989:96). Although racial stratification is the most visible manifestation of mobility barriers, the glass ceiling at XYZ in many ways was experienced not so much as a "racial issue" but expressly as a "cultural issue." Specifically, the aggressive behavioral style of white males not only permeated the workplace culture but was distinctly incongruent with those styles and values embodied by minorities and women. As an Asian male explained:

> The glass ceiling occurs because we're still operating under the cultural values of white males. . . . not all that compatible with Asian American culture or [the] culture represented by women. . . . If you're not aggressive, self-promoting, direct and articulate and . . . viewed as a risk-taker—if you don't have those traits—it's hard to climb the ladder of management, unless, of course, the whole culture of the organization changes. And that's very slow in coming. I mean, it's extremely slow. I talked about old boys' network. . . . It's not a racial issue; it's just a cultural issue.

Interviewees spoke at length about how such individualistic behavior stifled opinion and exchange as well as created an atmosphere of intimidation. Some of the organizational expectations for top managers— public speaking, assuming a controversial stance, or entering directly into volatile situations of imminent conflict—were at odds with their own cultural norms. Not surprisingly, routine performance requirements created undue "speech anxiety" among Asian Americans or others with a collective orientation, problems which extend to relations these employees have with supervisors and other authority figures (Cox 1994:114–15, 122–23, 125–26).

Contrasting conventional white male and Asian styles of participation, one person stated, "The Asian personality tends to be low-key, quiet. We'll talk when there is a requirement to talk. White males will pound the table." Interview after interview echoed the observation that Asian Americans were characterized as less "aggressive," "self-promoting," or "outspoken," and thereby less likely to be perceived as having the necessary "communication skills" or "leadership qualities." Thus, another person observed how the routine manner in which meetings are conducted works to the disadvantage of certain groups.

> I think if you sit in on several meetings at XYZ Aerospace, you'll see that there's a general style of communication, of how a decision is made. . . . The most vocal people will just get their opinions out . . . and try to drive them forward. That will be a small subset of the people represented there, and typically the Asians. . . . aren't going to be the first ones to get their opinions out there, and sometimes they won't get their opinions voiced at all because they don't want to vocalize what they're thinking for many different reasons . . . people who are more assertive will get their voices heard, will get perceived to be the more active-thinking, more involved people, and then so there's kind of a mindset set up by the superiors, the higher-level managers—"Well, Jim, he speaks up at all the meetings. He's got leadership, whereas Ted . . . he's not voicing his opinions. He's a good engineer, but I don't see him as management material."

Although "communication skills" or "leadership skills" are ostensibly neutral criteria or standards, the corporate culture favors those who aggressively advance their views at the expense of others: One has "to be willing to step on other people's toes," "think of only yourself, and not for the collective group; to beat other people down for their ideas, because your ideas are better." According to another, such behavior was interpersonally offensive, approaching "bullying."

A veteran employee pointed out how leadership ought to include qualities of deference and respect toward one's charges. Prior to being employed as an engineer by XYZ, he himself had worked in many menial jobs—as dishwasher, houseboy, and lemon picker. As a U.S. military officer in both the navy and air force, he earned respect because of the empathy and respect he bestowed upon his subordinates, whatever their job title or social class. Managerial leadership, however, would elude him at XYZ Aerospace, where he confronted a glass ceiling throughout his entire career.

For many, the implicit bias in XYZ Aerospace's organizational culture transformed deeply held values into negative attributes.

> I was brought up by my grandparents who were very devout Buddhists, and in Japan you don't promote yourself. That's a real "no-no," you know. . . . I was brought up with that, so it's very difficult for me, for example, in an interview process to say a lot of good things about [myself] . . . that's a detriment. . . . I think it's more ingrained than people realize, that trait.

Cultural values, such as modesty and self-effacement, not only fail to earn one recognition at XYZ Aerospace but also become a serious liability. As a young, aspiring manager pointed out, one is less likely to find bluffing or expressions of bravado among Asian Americans: "Most of them . . . do not know how to boast. But you gotta know how so your supervisors will know you did a good job not just above-average job." Even where Asian American employees are not actively self-disparaging (one way in which cultural modesty gets manifested), they may still unwittingly undercut evaluations of their own job performance by failing to "toot their own horn" and by assuming the objective merits of their work are obvious.

However, as the rank authority of the traditional bureaucracy has been replaced by technical expertise, the requirement has been for "conspicuous" and overt demonstrations of one's expertise, a criterion favoring men in general, but as the present study argues, a select stratum of males.

> In the expert sector, with its majority of men and minority of women, one of the most salient aspects of the workplace culture is the emphasis on expertise and the need to prove oneself and one's expertise; "conspicuous expertise," a constant fear of "not being the expert," and the common practice of doing a "snow job" to impress others have been found to be characteristic of expert-sector micropolitics. . . . Masculinity has traditionally been associated with proving one's expertise, particularly in technical matters. (Burris 1993:100)

The following middle manager did not find the selection process culturally biased for this reason, underscoring the importance of one's ability to "demonstrate" one's expertise:

> I don't see a glass ceiling into management. I don't think there are artificial barriers if you are (1) politically savvy, (2) have excellent communication skills, and (3) demonstrated expertise. Even if you're a *techie*, you acquire leadership skills by taking on the leadership of a research group or one formed by the center to develop a better method for a better administration. . . . If you're going to be a successful manager, you *have* to be aggressive. If an Asian American is articulate—he either is or isn't. I'm not going to hire an Asian American who isn't. . . . He's got to have those skills already.

> (DW: *What about different managerial styles?*)

> There are different managerial styles, but you have to somehow demonstrate that style.

Cultural factors emerge as artificial barriers for mobility; XYZ is unable to recognize managerial styles that depart from the "white male leadership" model.

The special qualities Asians possess by virtue of their cultural socialization are most likely to be displayed at the lower or middle management levels, especially in project management. When asked to identify some of these managerial traits, interviewees mentioned the following: (1) listening and consensus building skills, (2) "thoroughness and follow-through," (3) an ability to effectively coordinate a team, and (4) skill in assessing the *individual* rather than seeing the individual simply as part of a group.

These attributes capture some of those qualities frequently associated with a collective orientation. Listening skills were seen as lending themselves to organizational goals in different ways. Apart from being a formal courtesy extended to others and a sign of patience, the ability to listen attentively was associated with greater efficiency, especially in light of the competition for "air time" that frequently takes place in compressed and hurried meetings. As one manager observed, a "quiet" person is likely to "make a very thoughtful decision, and you don't have to hear a whole long, drawn out dissertation before they reach that decision." Similarly, another person noted that the same quality might facilitate a quick consensus through the ability to hear and absorb different viewpoints. Though she initially described it in terms of the etiquette involved in being "considerate," when asked to elaborate, she indicated this meant paying attention to the individual needs of everyone in the group, being "considerate in the sense that you consider everybody's needs and what they're really saying or asking, with some thought about what they need." In this way, good listeners were transformed into "consensus builders," managers who are "not autocratic, not dictatorial typically," departing markedly from the "real cut-throat kind of style."

A cultural concern about efficiency not only attends how things get communicated but how things actually get done. Thus, one person underscored "thoroughness and follow-through" as a trait Asian Americans are likely to bring to administrative tasks. Some of the negative experiences with existing managers lay in their very inability to see projects through to completion: "I've seen a lot of other managers who jump from project to project and never finish their work, and it's frustrating working with them." The following middle manager made a similar observation, noting that Asian Americans displayed a "get-it-done attitude," whereas non-Asian managers had difficulties in "expressing their stand" or "making decisions." When asked about artificial barriers, she responded:

> Some of what I perceive to be the barriers are just the differences in management styles. I've noticed a lot of non-Asian managers having a difficult time making decisions or at least expressing their stand on a subject area. Whereas, most of the Asian American managers I've seen want to discuss a subject and come to a conclusion at the same meeting ("get-it-done" attitude) and it becomes frustrating always waiting for things to happen.

The above observation is ironic in that the problems that Asian Americans encounter at the upper management levels will test their own abilities to take a stand and see a job through, though the context is a decidedly different one.

Given stereotypical views of their collective orientation, it may seem odd that Asian Americans are perceived as bringing a special ability or sensitivity when it comes to assessing the *individual*. Yet when asked to reflect upon the special qualities that they might bring to management, an administrative manager in human resources said they would "trust and believe in individual abilities," "look at what a person can do"; elaborating, "They don't look at a person as part of a group but as an individual." A recently retired employee repeatedly returned to the idea that individual performance and merit were the deciding criteria for advancement in China's bureaucracy. Objective assessments of an individual's abilities or potential fall far short of the ideal because of poor supervising and poor mentoring, issues to which I shall return.

Whatever special qualities one might identify with "Asian managerial skills," a very different management style dominates XYZ, one brought center stage through conspicuous displays of self-assertion. As an Asian American female moving up the ranks pointed out, the act of transforming one's self to fit this mold is experienced as "a very artificial and very uncomfortable choice." Adjustment to senior management, moreover, seemed to pivot around whether they possessed the "killer instinct." One executive traced his own abilities to having attended a Jesuit high school, where students were socialized to develop this instinct, to see themselves as among "the best" and to display their talents so that they were positioned "to lead." Other Asian senior executives were observed to have difficulty in these jobs by virtue of their inability to take a "controversial stand" or to "do battle" when the heat of conflict required direct confrontation rather than negotiation on the side.

At present, the appeal of middle and upper managerial work is linked with the desire to achieve visible results and to have a direct influence on organizational decisions or policy. A senior manager described himself as "very satisfied" with his job in this regard.

> I was very satisfied, even though it had nothing to do with my training. Maybe because I was in a position to influence things—not that I'm a power-hungry person, you know. But it was kind of interesting to be in a position to influence decisions. . . . [As] a close advisor to the organizational director [who] is usually very busy. . . . You exert a fair amount of influence in terms of what goes on, and I really enjoyed that. Made a lot of decisions in the name of the director.

The opportunity to influence the direction of the organization through the grooming of successors was in no small way a significant factor underlying another senior executive's own interest in managerial work. Explaining the appeal of managerial work, he said:

> It allows you to define, create, and implement a vision of where you want to go and where you want the organization to go, and how it fits within the overall Super-Aviation Links' vision. And second is, it helps you groom and train your successors or your "fast track" people.

A middle manager similarly noted that the ability to achieve "visible" results was an inherent attraction of the managerial role. The managerial title, and even autonomy, were specifically not important for this person. She expressed little desire to leave her present managerial work for greater responsibilities at the upper levels, though certain frustrations in her present managerial position were attributed to the inability of upper management to make the decisions to expedite her work.

> I prefer a position where results can be visible, rather than the research positions that seem to last forever. . . . Managerial was not important, simply a position where I can get things done [in the background] was sufficient. . . . I have quite a bit of autonomy which does not really matter to me. I can support someone who has clear directions as much as making up my own decisions.
>
> My disappointment is mainly in the lack of decision making at the upper levels. A lot of managers never really just make a simple decision. This hinders what I can do in support of the division staff and even for the managers themselves.

Recent changes in SES requirements in government place even greater demands upon managers in the executive ranks, requiring broad strategic vision, planning, and coordination with the "big picture" in mind. These and other requirements of the job may possibly dampen the ambitions of managerial aspirants, especially since upper managers already experience overwhelming responsibilities and questionable efficiency given the sheer volume of work. As one moves up the managerial hierarchy, moreover, conditions become more unstructured, heterogeneous, and dynamic. Common goals cannot be assumed. It is, as the former Jesuit-trained SESer, explained, a "killer type of environment," one that Asian Americans may find difficult to navigate:

> They [Asian Americans] have great personal skills, generally when it comes to a nonconfrontational audience. When you start working in a dynamic environment that is really diverse, then they start falling back, because they're generally uncomfortable working in an unstructured environment like that. . . . No protocol. It's a killer type of environment. . . . In projects, where there is a more homogeneous environment, they have the people skills, because it's more of a structured environment. You have the same goal. . . . So they can work fairly effectively in that type of environment.

(DW: *Are there managerial jobs like that?*)

Mostly in small projects. . . . When you move outside of the projects, then you start moving into more of an unstructured environment . . . higher up, like division chief, directorate head, and so forth. . . . That's when they start experiencing a lot of difficulty.

While the corporate culture in general is experienced as an artificial barrier for Asian American employees, it may already be apparent in this closing statement that there are many parts to this organizational "elephant." The upper reaches of management have their own subculture as well as an operating environment with far-flung boundaries. Trying to be in full control can actually cripple one's capacity to lead, which increasingly requires leading by example, by persuasion, and by willingness to delegate. Highly specialized scientists were perceived as lacking such leadership and communicative abilities.

One executive confessed that one of the major lessons he himself had to learn upon becoming an SESer was to delegate. Compared with other scientists and engineers, Asian Americans were seen as having even greater difficulty with this given their tendencies toward "perfectionism." With wry self-humor, he stated: "They've acquired a reputation of being 'control freaks.'"

They want everything to be perfect. That would work against them. Because when you're in the management ranks, you're going to see a lot of imperfection. That's part of the learning process. If you don't have people making mistakes, you're not going to learn, and that's how you learn the fastest by making mistakes. Controlled mistakes. If your manager doesn't allow you to make controlled mistakes, you're not going to learn. . . . How many Asians are willing to delegate and let somebody else carry out the responsibility, which in turn could impact their performance? You'll find that there are very few. . . . And that's *disaster* for them because when you get to be a division head, there's no way you're going to be able to control all this stuff.

As we shall see in the final chapter, some of the anxiety associated with delegation may be addressed by agencywide changes encouraging greater risk-taking. For the moment, however, we will examine obstacles related to moving up the structural ladder.

Internal Structural Barriers

Among the artificial barriers that the Federal Glass Ceiling Commission (1995:8, 32–36) identified as "within the direct control of business" were those having to do with outreach and recruitment practices as well as factors affecting advancement through the pipeline. I revisit these barriers, previously discussed in chapter 2, because they were independently raised as salient issues for Asian Americans at XYZ Aerospace.

The Dual Ladder

The career track to top management is to a large extent determined by structural considerations as well as by "who you know" at the top. One's initial placement within the organization or on a particular ladder, and the ability to get "on" or "off" it, are important considerations. Artificial barriers include placement in staff or administrative support jobs or in highly technical and professional jobs that are not on the career track to the top. The former includes those working in human resources, accounting, procurement, while the latter is largely made up of scientists and engineers.

At the XYZ facility, there is both an administrative and a technical ladder, and senior executive positions are *theoretically* available to employees on either ladder. In practice, it is much harder to rise into the executive ranks from the administrative side unless one's responsibilities also include larger business, cost-cutting functions. According to an EEO officer who was previously situated at SAL headquarters, those climbing the administrative ladder were more likely to attain SES positions at the *agencywide* level than at the facility level.

A large number of Asian American employees at XYZ Aerospace, however, are in administrative support positions that do not lead into upper management, though many of their work functions might be partly managerial in nature.[9] Thus, one person explained how her job involved "staffing and recruiting for positions, . . . handling employee relations problems, assessing organizational development needs, and recommending training for people." Such positions are officially "staff" not "line management" jobs, offering little or "no chance" of moving into the upper managerial ranks. As the same EEO officer attested, one's job title can thereby limit one from advancing in grade or salary: "Some are stuck at the GS-13 level for a lifetime."

It is as *scientists* or *engineers* that Asian Americans are significantly underrepresented at the SES level compared to other racial groups, even though, historically, XYZ Aerospace has recruited its managers from the *technical* side. Technical proficiency continues to be a necessary requirement. At issue is the *additional* cultural capital required.

Scientists and engineers in general are believed to experience greater difficulty because their highly specialized training shortchanges them on broad-based organizational and communication skills necessary for professional activities engaging a wider range of publics, organizational units, or domains.

The absence of conspicuous expertise is more specific to Asian Americans. Although concentration on the technical ladder might conceivably be also due to their interest in research careers, both survey and interview data pointed to significant managerial interest as well. The material rewards are significantly higher in the management ranks, with the top of this SES curve paying $30–35,000 above what one would receive at the same GS level as a researcher, with the opportunity, moreover, for a $20,000 a year bonus. One busy senior executive also enjoyed the greater managerial flexibility he could exercise.

> I had the luxury of selecting key members of the team. Each time I was put in an organization, I was able to bring along a trusted corps set of people. Then I made sure that those people advanced in their own career . . . got rewarded in terms of getting their promotions early.

As a middle manager explained, the "value" of a middle management position could be considered "half" that of an upper management position like that of director of an organizational unit:

> [The top two Asians] are assistant directors and deputy directors. They're not directors . . . if you weight the value of these jobs, the value of being a deputy director is only like being 50 percent of being a director, and the job of assistant director is almost like being like an office clerk. It's like a third of the value of being a director. So they'll give you these jobs, and they'll say, "Look what we did for you. But. . . . It's not like being a director. . . . I've seen more Asians promoted to middle manager jobs . . . not upper management, but middle manager jobs. It tends to make the statistics look good. But again, they're in the secondary position like the assistant or . . . they're support jobs.

A pivotal issue of debate again, of course, is whether the barriers are indeed artificial— or real, that is, because of lack of qualifications. Though it is generally at the point of midcareer that managerial aspirations are likely to develop, if this move is otherwise unplanned for, a candidate is likely to be ill-prepared.[10] Yet as subsequent sections of this chapter will point out, there are several artificial barriers that lie in the way of this very career development, with Asians less likely than white males to receive the mentoring, sponsorship, critical assignments, or overall career planning that systematically includes these considerations.

The window of opportunity for making this transition, moreover, was seen as exceedingly narrow. As one respondent explained, there might only be "two or three chances" in the course of one's entire career. Upon reflection, he noted he was given few such opportunities in his formative years. Insofar as scientists and engineers exercised some individual choice in the matter, they took advantage of every opportunity to apply for available openings. It was against this backdrop that a glass ceiling was concretely experienced.

> My complaint in the past was if you were not given an opportunity to manage . . . when you are in the 30s and early 40s, as a first line manager, you would never reach a middle manager by the time you are 50. And then you will never reach the top manager. And one person, any person, can have only two or three chances in his or her career to move from one area to the other . . . and if they don't let you to do it, you will forever be bounded in terms of the lower management, which is the most difficult part of the management. In the earlier part of my career, when I was in the 40s and I aspired to choose a managerial career because I thought it will be a faster way of promotions, and whenever the chances arrived, I applied [on] a number of occasions. It was just a dead end.

Similarly, the following respondent also reported encountering a glass ceiling as his applications were repeatedly turned down.

> I encountered quite a bit of discrimination through various job applications. I applied for low level jobs like group leader, branch chief. I'm a division leader now. And the first job I got was at the division but I applied for many jobs at the lowest level. I applied nine times, and I was turned down. I failed nine times in succession.

As we shall see later, disparate treatment—despite equivalent educational credentials– was a dominant perception, one further magnified by recruitment practices that bypassed the traditional way of training managers by bringing them up through the ranks. In recent years, managers have been recruited from *outside* the organization, thereby raising concern that this method of recruitment has "hardened" the glass ceiling for those on the inside. As one middle manager observed, there was little effort to diversify these recruitments: "they're white males, and they're at GS-13 and above levels. That's what's incredible." Such lateral promotions typified high-tech firms in general, where accumulated knowledge about a particular organization was no longer critical for managerial succession (Burris 1993:104- 110). Such flexibility, however, clouds the issue of career development within, which at XYZ lagged behind this larger bureaucratic restructuring.

Lack of Mentoring

In general, systematic individual career planning was more the exception than the rule at XYZ. The following SESer was atypical in this regard, as he explained:

That's because I'm process oriented. I set a goal, and then I pursue that goal. I say these are the steps that I have to take to achieve that goal, and I review those steps every so often. I say, "Where am I at now?" And when I fall back, I say, "Why am I falling back?"

(DW: *Do you think you're different that way from other Asians?*)

That may have been due to two factors. One is that my dad was like that. Second, the six years I spent with the Navy was geared toward that. I was with the submarine department in the navy. So everything was specifically target oriented.

Such planning enabled him to monitor his own career progress, but the mentoring was critical and indispensable for launching his career.

According to traditional Asian assumptions about guidance, one would expect to be mentored by supervisors, who would assume a more active, paternalistic role in monitoring and looking after one's career interests. One earned this attention by concentrating on performing assigned tasks. In the typical American workplace, on the other hand, the dominant operative norm is more individualistic, with each person responsible for his or her own career. As the following respondent explained, this individualistic norm is reinforced by managers who have little spare time to provide their subordinates with individual career guidance, at least not without the employee first taking the initiative.

It's easy to come into an organization, especially a large government organization, and say, "They're going to take care of me. As long as I do my work, I'll get recognized. I'll get my promotions." That would be fine, but that's not always the case, and things aren't going to work as smoothly as that at times. . . . I think that this is a cultural value that Asians have.

But American culture focuses on the individual, and so you really need to take care of yourself, and XYZ is pretty clear in career development. They say career development is the individual employee's responsibility, so even though there are certain mechanisms to help the employee—there's the performance plan, and career development plans—your manager may not have the time to come to you and say, "I'd like to sit down with you . . . and work out where you'll be in the next few years, so you'll get what you need to get your job done, and get to your fifteen- or twenty-year career goal." If the individual doesn't take the initiative to go to his or her manager and say, "I want to sit down and spend some time with you and talk about the work I'm doing and the areas I need to improve," that type of discussion isn't going to happen, and they're going to fall behind on their career. Or at least not advance as fast as they would like, and it's easy to . . . keep your head down and work for a few years, and then realize that after those three or four years, you haven't been able to make it to the next level, and someone else passes you by. The chances are that other person has taken some initiative, and maybe built some networks, and maybe positioned himself in some choice assignments to get to that promotion, whereas you've been more passive in your own career.

Given these individualistic norms governing mentoring, advice from superiors was highly valued. Women more than men reported finding mentors or advisors, and these were outside Asian American circles. A key ingredient in one woman's career progress was the formal and informal role played by her boss, who was attentive to her development and, at certain junctures, prepared her for the next stage by asking her about her readiness. In this way, she came to see the larger picture for her career unfolding: "My supervisor saw the next step before I saw it. She created the next step." For another, this mentoring was more diffuse, never formal, and one only achieved by her own active efforts to reach out to different people for advice. These exchanges were nevertheless rewarding ones.

> Nobody was really an active mentor, or to this day is an active mentor, of mine, which I would have loved . . . But nobody ever . . . fit that bill, or ever came up and said, "You want me to be your mentor, or how about if I be your mentor?" No, either they would come pat me on the shoulder. . . . Or I would tap them on the shoulder and say, "Hey, I'm thinking about something. Can I come and talk to you about it?" And so it was a two-way thing, and maybe that was a mentoring of sorts, and it really is. But it wasn't in the formal sense.

A male executive emphasized that a lack of mentoring was "absolutely" a major glass ceiling barrier for Asian Americans trying to climb the ladder. His own mentoring, in fact, had come from two former directors at XYZ Aerospace, both white males. "They mentored me all the way up."

> Mentors are extremely important. Without a mentor, you're going to fall into a lot of traps that a mentor can help you avoid . . . especially a mentor that has been around for a while and understands all the pitfalls. That mentor can really accelerate your progress, plus advance your case at the higher levels.

After they left, however, any further progress came through great struggle.

Apart from protection and sponsorship, a mentor provides critical feedback usually unobtainable from formal supervisors, who were commonly observed to fall short of pinpointing areas for improving one's performance. By contrast, a good mentor was seen as someone who "challenged" the individual in his or her thinking and, in turn, was willing to have his or her own ideas challenged or questioned.

> I had a lot of informal feedback from my mentors. The formal feedback that I got from people who may have been my supervisors but not necessarily my mentors were—well, they contained all the nice things. But they didn't contain areas where you should really improve or areas that you should perhaps tone down.

> (DW: *Isn't that ironic?*)

> Yeah. They're always saying positive [things], and they're afraid of saying the negative. . . . The mentors I had weren't afraid to whack me in the side of my head if I was doing something wrong. And by the same token, they gave me the opportunity to challenge them. And not risk being penalized if I thought they were doing something stupid.

At present, there are no Asian Americans—male or female—in the upper management ranks at XYZ Aerospace who can serve as role models or mentors. During the period in which this study was conducted, all three of the highest-level Asian American managers at XYZ left the organization, two because of retirement, one because of "burn-out." A subordinate commented on the void this left in her own career.

> This [mentoring] has been very important to me. Dr. _____ was the supervisor that hired me and I've been very appreciated and spoiled at the same time. While under his supervision, I didn't realize the importance but now that the agency has been losing a lot of people lately, it seems that role models and mentors are harder to find and that many of the newer managers don't really know how to be a role model or mentor. Many are more concerned with their personal advancement or

> overwhelmed with the number of areas they must cover that things like employee satisfaction, career advancement are lost or dropped.

Despite the preponderance of Asian American males in the science and engineering workforce, they have lost ground in terms of long-range planning that would pave the way for their steady progress up the ladder. As a member of the DLC pointed out:

> We don't even have enough Asian males in our pipeline. And that's a problem with how I think we handled the hiring aspects five to ten years ago. We now see impacts. Who would have ever known that, because they weren't looking at this in a real strategic way?

Ironically, the center's efforts to implement a formal mentoring strategy seems to have foundered from a lack of participants on both sides. According to a former EEO officer, more employees need to actively seek out mentors, including making use of this formal system designed to match up individuals with one another. Yet as she simultaneously acknowledged, this formal mentoring arrangement did not seem to be working because it was too much like trying to structure and formalize friendships. A member of the DLC likewise concurred that too much energy and time had been devoted not only to theorizing about the process but to "regimenting" it.

> We've tried mentoring programs just recently, although again, what we have done, I believe, is we have intellectually and almost in a research mentality mode, studied what a mentoring program should look like. We've torn it apart, we've dissected it, we've talked about theory, we've talked about academics, but we haven't gone and done it. And then . . . it was very regimented. . . . They didn't get a lot of sign-ups.

Whether formal or informal, any mentoring system at XYZ faces the challenge of ensuring that a wide range of mentoring needs are met for employees at different stages of their career, desiring different kinds of managerial experiences. The need for "serious mentorship" was underscored by a senior executive, who described how the quality of mentoring could be improved. Two chief recommendations were for greater involvement of senior-level executives in the individual mentoring process and for informal group workshops where employees could tackle the details relevant to their own career objectives.

> I think first . . . you have to get some serious mentorship program. Someone who is at the directorate level or higher who is willing to commit to guiding these Asians. Because we're not there, and everybody knows it. . . . The second is, having them understand, first of all that there are two ways in which you can get promoted, and that if you want to get into the management ranks, then there are the attributes and characteristics you need to have—communications, the interpersonal relationships, and so forth, and exactly what does that mean? What do you have to give up in order to acquire that? I think that best can be done in the informal workshop where you can present results of your survey: "Now let's discuss some of these points and what they mean to you."

While some organizational opportunities for training have been developed, less apparent are structural supports that will carry individuals over the longer stretch of their career. As a co-chair of the DLC summed up the training situation:

> We have training for the entry level that allows you to stay technical and allows you to get your Ph.D. And we have training if you choose project management. . . . But what we haven't done is tie a lot of these things together . . . to let you know . . . how maybe you can move and excel, up to and beyond the glass

ceiling. . . . We do it within very small, safe tiers, and those are very easy to define, and that's what we have done well . . . and we've done that agencywide.

Lack of Management Training or Access to Critical Developmental Assignments

Apart from mentoring, management training and access to critical developmental assignments were both seen as important stepping stones to management. Their value lies not only in the intrinsic learning that takes place but in the networking that occurs and the visibility one achieves. This point was underscored by the following senior executive as he talked about the importance of participating in management training and career development programs.

> I think that is extremely important in the sense [of]—how you build up your network. And then I met a lot of people from different Super-Aviation Link centers and different government organizations and within industry. . . . The formal programs like the career development program is where you start building up formal networking with different managers that you may not normally meet had you not gone to that type of program. So that activity does help in the sense that they get to know your name, if not know you personally.

For several reasons, however, management training was actually seen as less valuable than certain critical development assignments. For one, the door to management training is generally only open to individuals once they have already been accepted into the managerial track (e.g., promoted to the GS-15 level). Second, much of what is learned about management occurs on the job. Important committee assignments, on the other hand, were an exception in that they offered some experience in exercising some of the skills one would need to hone in upper management, such as learning to delegate.

> It [management training] gave you some of the tools to do the job, but it didn't necessarily help you. You had to want to do that, and if you wanted to do that, and you had some tools, then you could try. But if you are able to lead key committees that have a specific assignment that has to be done in a short period of time, then that assignment has key visibility to center management, and that's a good way you can acquire the experience of delegating and feel comfortable with it.

While there was little question about the value of participating on committees that offer high visibility, this attitude apparently is not widely shared among Asian employees at XYZ Aerospace. It was, in fact, the strong opinion of a former EEO officer that scientists and engineers needed to take the initiative of getting out of their labs to gain greater exposure, either by sitting on the employee association committee or on various other ad hoc committees at the center. A number of such assignments could only improve the appearance of their résumés, as a chair of the DLC also pointed out.

> If you want to get into upper management, there are a lot of different experiences you need to have along the way. Maybe some time working at headquarters. Maybe some time on a project team. Maybe some time in the "ad" [administration] building. There are things you can do to . . . make your resumé look good—as opposed to [your résumé simply indicating] you've been the last fifteen years as a line engineer on this program. You can also say, "I did this and this and this and this. And I went to school for a while.". . . things that make you look more like managerial timber.

Those interviewed were cognizant of how critical these assignments were through their involvement with the employee association, the DLC, the mentoring they had received, or their own experiences on the managerial track. As one person said, "In order for you to be recognized, you have to be appointed to certain committees and certain positions where your achievement can be highlighted. So even having your name be recognized [on] a certain . . . centerwide or agencywide committee is important." Another noted the downside of *not* seeking out these assignments: "You could be working in the trenches day to day, and be doing a good job, but no one would notice what you're doing. But working the special assignments and those tasks that are out of the ordinary is when you have an opportunity to prove yourself."

Lack of access to critical assignments as training grounds was thus an obstacle to further managerial advancement. It was, moreover, seen as an artificial barrier, and a subtle one at that: "You cannot say it's discrimination because you are not being named to one of the prestigious committees . . . Rather than appointing you, they'll say, 'I'll spare you the time of volunteering service.'" Agencywide assignments were considered prime assignments. As one senior executive explained: "High visibility assignments, I think, help. But you need to make sure that those assignments are agencywide. And when you work a year at headquarters, you generally get those agencywide assignments. . . ." In addition to visibility, this Washington experience broadened his network of associates and, upon his return to the center, helped launched his career given the support he now had of key people at headquarters:

> I not only got to meet a lot of the Congressional people, and I gave testimony, but I also got to know firsthand a lot of key SAL managers that I had to interact with, after I returned to XYZ Aerospace. . . . That's probably the reason that I was the first and only SESer for a long time. Because I had a lot of people back at headquarters backing my selection as an SES person.

While the agencywide assignment is ideal, an engineer who has successfully moved up the managerial ladder also credits her progress to assignments she was given at the center, involving a series of moves into different positions that increasingly brought her greater exposure at each juncture. Although she was hired "fairly low on the totem pole," the organization was not only flexible in enabling her to undertake these different assignments but "willing and able to put me into project management jobs fairly early, fairly quickly. . . . [I] got most all of my promotions on a pretty aggressive schedule, and so it's probably been on par with some of the white males and others."

The "spiral model" that characterized her career path took her out of the niches in which scientists and engineers generally get pigeonholed.

> I've done what I guess people say is a spiral model. . . . I've gone outside that box, went into something a little bit different, but complimentary. Then after that I applied for another job announcement that got me into another position, but it wasn't in my same home organization. . . . I stayed there for maybe three or four years. And then I spiraled out of that and went into another PDP [Professional Development Program], which was actually a line management position, for about a year . . . each time I was kind of spiraling up a little bit further in the chain.

Apart from the leveraging potential that each job experience had for subsequent career moves, what is equally striking is her openness—indeed, eagerness—to undertake jobs that stretched her in new directions, and the active role she played in maximizing her own opportunities at each stage. Given a certain reluctance for scientists and engineers, and Asian Americans in particular, to venture outside of certain "comfort zones," the ability to branch out into unfamiliar territory may have to do with a combination of psychological readiness as well as structural opportunity.

The career path of a senior executive also exemplified this spiral model, and a similar venturesome attitude was behind the multiple job changes that characterized his ascent.

> Job satisfaction is *extremely* important. That's why I moved around so much, because I got restless after a period of years. Because once I understood the job, knew everything there was, met all the challenges with that job, I had no interest. I had to move on. That sort of carried me throughout my navy career and throughout my Super Aviation Links career. After three or four years, I knew everything I had to know about that job, so I had to move on to another job and start over again.

> (DW: *Did you ever think of leaving the organization at all?*)

> Several times . . . because I just kind of got disenchanted with the way things were going. And each time I got ready to leave, the XYZ management came back and offered me a different position, which kind of stirred up my interest in staying again . . . each time they gave me a new job to keep me here. . . . They understood my "weaknesses."

Although the importance of management training and appointments to key job or committee assignments is undeniable, it would be a mistake to leave the impression that these are the sole routes to enhancing one's visibility. Such visibility may come from activities closely connected to one's career as a scientist and researcher. Technical expertise, as noted earlier, continues to be essential for managerial jobs. There is fairly consistent evidence that those who were seen as promising managerial candidates were also those who fully utilized the opportunities they had as researchers to acquire greater visibility. The following manager was extremely committed to his profession as a researcher and had turned down an opportunity to move into upper management for this very reason. When I asked if there might be a bias against promoting Asians because they were too technically oriented, he was emphatic in pointing out how his own visibility outside the agency came from invitations to speak publicly about his work or his involvement with professional associations. If organizational biases against technical work existed, they were dismissed as an illegitimate reason for exclusion.

> In my field . . . that's not a legitimate reason. Absolutely not. Nonsense! . . . To be good at what they're doing technically is the most important factor to counter the biases and prejudices of supervisors. My visibility came from technical competence. If asked to speak on a technical panel, I'd go. Working the outside lane is just as important as the inside lane. . . . My research area provides a lot of opportunities for the outside world to indicate you're technically competent. . . . The whole notion of working outside your organization can be exploited more. There are ways to gain recognition that have to do with technical and organizational competence. Sometimes I sense people are waiting around. The individual has to have that initiative. Everyone responds to a squeaky wheel. The squeaky wheel can be your competence through outside involvement and asking for such assignments. Any organization worth its salt should be encouraging this.

Similarly, the following senior executive also underscored the important role that public presentations played in his own career. Professional conferences provided opportunities to not only network and acquire visibility among one's peers but to be externally legitimated by sources outside the agency. In his case, these external activities also engaged him in review activities that had a crucial bearing upon the organization's own budgetary interests and future.

> [Networking] started off when I was a researcher, by giving talks at different peer-review conferences. I also met a lot of my peers who were doing work in similar areas. We exchanged notes. You build up the network. They may call you and collaborate with you on different projects, so that you build up your credibility and recognition as a researcher. . . . Giving talks is really important. Giving talks at major peer review conferences both national and international . . . sponsored by various professional societies. If you have an opportunity to talk before committees that are reviewing XYZ or committees that are determining XYZ's or SAL's budgets, those are extremely important. . . . That reinforces your own credibility and recognition externally, and makes a big difference, especially when you're going for an SES certification, because you need to be certified by people outside of the agency.

Performance Evaluation and the Preselection Process

At the outset of this chapter, it was noted that the central organizational norms and expectations about "who" would make a good leader were implicitly skewed toward favoring behavioral styles associated with white males. The preceding section, moreover, suggested that lack of management training or access to critical developmental assignments could also become barriers, though ones perhaps circumventable through visibility and exposure gained from one's own research and professional activities. While one might take various individual initiatives to position oneself for management, there was also the strong perception that these opportunities are generally restricted to those who had already been informally chosen or preselected for management. By virtue of their absence from senior executive positions, Asian Americans were not directly privy to such preselection processes. Upper management, moreover, would likely deny the existence of an informal list of pre-chosen candidates. If there was discrimination, it was subtle.

Cynical interpretations point to the operation of an old boy network. What this underscores in practice is how indispensable mentorship is for long-term visibility. A good mentor will not only provide critical feedback on one's performance but offer a certain protection through his or her sponsorship. As the following person explained, his mentor ensured that he received not only high visibility assignments but substantively meaningful ones in terms of networking and furthering his own knowledge.

> The mentor will keep the person's name in the spotlight. . . . If you have a mentor in a high enough position, your mentor can get you into that type of assignment. . . . He's going to be largely responsible for making sure you get the right assignment at headquarters. You can get an assignment at headquarters, but it can be a "nothing type" of assignment. But if your mentor is really on the ball, that mentor can get you a key assignment that will provide a lot of learning opportunities. So when I went to headquarters, the assignment I got was that I actually took over a division there while that person was away on a sabbatical. That gave me a lot of learning opportunities that I would not have gotten otherwise.

A major artificial barrier for Asian Americans lay in the fact that they were rarely identified for such "fast-tracking," and are thereby taken out of the running early on.

> Management does not identify Asians for fast-tracking for . . . key management positions at the directorate level or higher . . . personally grooming them along the way. That's where you have this artificial barrier. Because until you're on that list, your chances or probability of becoming director or higher is extremely low. . . . An informal list of people . . . get selected to give presentations at key events. So . . . they acquire a lot of visibility to the outside world. You're deciding you're going to promote this like a PR [public relations] agent—like an actor or actress.

Ironically, though Asian Americans are disinclined toward self-promotion, the very fact that they are not part of the old boy network forces them to exercise even greater initiative on their own behalf. Thus, the following GS-15 level manager described how his progress up the ladder had been an arduous one, the result of sheer perseverance and aggressiveness in applying for vacancies. He did not have the endorsement or sponsorship of his immediate supervisor, who resented these individual career moves and worked against him at every turn. The following account illustrates that the support and sanction of superiors is critical, if not everything. Without a mentor, this employee was left relying on his own self-promotional efforts.

> The training office does say that "these positions are open and anybody can apply, and please come and take at look at what is applicable for you." But if you're not chosen by somebody or sponsored by somebody, it's tough to get in. . . . I wasn't appointed to high visibility assignments. I actually went for them and aggressively asked for them. There were no role mentors. I had no individual career plan written. I had a goal and I didn't have any worthwhile feedback from the supervisors.

Reflecting on his history with the organization over the past several decades, another manager singled out the "buddy system" as the major reason for the glass ceiling.

> Promotion is not on merit but through social circles. . . . The criterion is not ability but friendship. I don't think people are out to "get" Asians. I just think that Asians aren't in these social circles. You can quote me on that. . . . It's my perception that what had happened in the old days was that the old white boy network reserved the managerial jobs for themselves. That was their preserve, they didn't want to let any minorities in.

In the context of his immediate work sphere, he had observed his supervisor promoting only a small coterie of individuals: "all his white male friends . . . got to be deputy directors, directors, branch chiefs, division chiefs, despite some of them being very, very poor administrators and very poor researchers." That these individuals turned out to be "inferior" or mediocre is perhaps the most objective evidence that the standards were either unreliable or vulnerable to inappropriate subjective biases. The detour into administration may have been welcomed by those faring poorly in research but such appointments did not bode well for the organization as a whole, according to those who had worked under such administrators. The widespread organizational crisis in administration during the 1970s prompted a center director to undertake a survey of all employees, leading to the finding that one divisional head had garnered more than 200 complaints.

Others who observed this pattern of suboptimal performance among white male administrators noted, ironically, that it rarely evoked criticism. In the above instance, the division head was not fired but moved "upstairs." In contrast, minorities and women who experienced difficulties as administrators became lightning rods for backlash. Their performance reflected badly upon minorities, women, and all those labeled "affirmative action" hires. In the case of white males, on the other hand, poor leadership was more likely to be seen as an *individual* problem rather than as a problem generalizable to other white males.

> I am appalled by the quality of individual that gets promoted here very often, who gets put at the level of responsibility that I think they have no qualification for or no right to be there. I think very often I'm amazed by the incompetence that's rewarded and promoted here. . . . There's a tolerance for white males to get promoted even though they're totally incompetent whereas there's not tolerance for an Asian, or other type of minority, or woman to get promoted, if they're incompetent. So, I think in one way that the glass ceiling is manifested in the lower tolerance that people feel towards Asians specifically and minorities in general. . . . Poor leadership has been a problem since the late 1970s and "X" [Asian administrator] was merely the lightning rod for people to focus their dissatisfactions with the center and the future onto him. The same thing with other Asians who get promoted. . . . So in a nutshell, I think women and minorities are scrutinized much more closely than white men.

A line manager who has actively worked to educate the workforce on diversity issues gave an example of the white backlash that occurred with the promotion of an Asian female. The account not only captures the harassment this candidate received after being selected for a particular managerial position but the tremendous amount of self-doubt and psychological turmoil she went through despite being unquestionably qualified.

> There was a young Asian female who was selected for [a certain managerial level] position. She got great pressure . . . from other applicants who were white males, who said, "You just got it because of Affirmative Action. And you didn't get it because you could do the job . . . [but] because of some quota." And so she was in tears. She was in tears! She called me, and, you know, I was livid. . . . This person had great experience, or else she never would have been selected. I had to tell her all these things in a pep-talk way. "You would never have been selected [for those reasons], you know. The criteria aren't such that they would let just anybody apply and select them just out of . . . frivolity. You had the credentials, you had the capability, you had the qualifying merit. You hold your head up high and you go do that job well. And you show them that was *the* right selection, and maybe *the only* selection that they could have made."

A double standard was clearly evident to those Asian professionals already in the management ranks. Several pointed to the fact that lack of managerial training was used as a pretext for exclusion when much of the formal and informal training is acquired later. As one person explained, it was a "Catch-22" situation to require management training beforehand, when eligibility for certain training tended to be available only *after* promotion to certain grade levels. Managers themselves indicated that much of their work was learned "on the job," not as a result of prior training. Reflecting on her own experience, a 36-year-old middle manager stated:

> I believe a lot of these skills (communication skills, interpersonal skills, supervisory, and leadership skills) must be *developed while in a management position* and cannot be learned and possessed before being in a management position. . . . I've had opportunities to take some management training but don't find that I learn anything from those classes.

Other Asian American managers also minimized the value of in-house training. A 45-year-old contracting officer with an MBA acknowledged that his own real managerial training came from "the school of hard knocks."

> The courses are designed to familiarize the specialist with the regulations, the processes, but it doesn't teach him how to make a decision. So that kind of comes from the school of hard knocks. You make some good decisions and some bad, and hopefully you learn from the bad decisions, and the good decisions.

A 68-year-old engineer with thirty-nine year history at XYZ similarly stated that managerial experience was primarily acquired on the job, noting with humor that in the past there was no pretense to the promotional process being fairly informal and casual.

> They give you a two- or three-week course at the training facility back east, but they don't really teach you how to be a manager. I think you really have to learn it on the job. What they used to do is they used to pick the best researchers. . . . They'd say, "Hey, we're promoting you to a manager."

A 57-year-old administrator with a Ph.D. in electrical engineering commented that on-the-job training was more important than the degree he had in hand.

> I have a Ph.D. in electrical engineering, and that background helps me to understand the research environment of our organization, R&D activities that go on in my organization. But I don't use that training per se. I don't have to have a Ph.D. to do my job. So it's sort of like on-the-job training along the way, so to speak, which got me here. I think I'm a good manager, and I've learned various skills on the job and also through training. You just acquire lots of experience when you're in management over the years, and you're using all those experiences, background to manage this organization. So it's pretty broad. . . . I use those to manage the organization.

Apart from the questionable value of managerial training, it was galling to Asian Americans to repeatedly see *other* standards ignored as well, specifically, the emphasis that government gave to educational and work experience as formal promotional criteria. Because Asian Americans were strong candidates by these standards, their resentment at being bypassed by those who were comparatively weaker in this regard was the source of many anecdotal accounts that called attention to preferences given to those in the old boy network.

A senior scientist with a Ph.D. thus recounted how upper management repeatedly ignored his objectively superior degree qualifications, leaving the indelible impression that allegations about his being unqualified were merely a smokescreen for special preferences. Although eventually promoted into the managerial ranks, he was initially denied the opportunity on the grounds that he lacked management training, and later denied the opportunity for training on the grounds that he was not management material. Refused the privilege of receiving training at the XYZ's own facilities, he relied on his own resources to pursue an MBA.

> So finally I said, "If I have to do it, I have to do it myself." And to go to evening school . . . is one of the least desirable avenues for any XYZ employee because usually you get paid full-time . . . for training in the XYZ facilities. . . . Working full-time and holding an evening job is not desirable for most of the XYZ employees. [I wanted] to prove the point that management is not that difficult, or that it should be limited to a particular race or particular age group. That's why I went for the MBA training.

Although getting an MBA on his own was a way of proving himself, it is the irrelevance of the degree —except as a screening device—that is significant. As a chair of the DLC frankly stated: "I'd be surprised if there were two MBAs at XYZ in managerial positions."

Eventually appointed as branch chief at the GS-15 level, he was again bypassed on two subsequent occasions when he sought to move to the level of Assistant Division Chief. In the first instance, the center hired someone from outside the division, who lacked his experience and who did not have superior degree qualifications. When confronted with these contradictions, management offered a new rationale for their decision—alleged concern that his own technical project might suffer if he were to be promoted.

> I was told, "He [the other candidate] is an excellent candidate. He has excellent qualifications." So I asked what was his qualification. They said, "Oh, he has a Master's degree in Electrical Engineering from [name of University]." "Oh," I said "I have a Master's and a Ph.D. degree from the same university." Then I was told he has an MBA degree from [name of University], which is a correspondence course. I said, "I have an MBA from [name of University], which is a much better university. Besides I've been in the division and know the things, and I've been at headquarters for a year." But then the argument was, "You are so valuable as a member of the technical staff. We cannot afford to lose you. If you move up the managerial ladder, your technical project will flounder." I didn't buy that argument at all. I could have trained and nurtured the project half-time, and carried the managerial duties [as well] . . . that's the first time I began to realize there is a subconscious— I'm not saying there is conscious discrimination—they prefer white males over Asian Americans.

Later on, when the position of Assistant Division Chief again became open, he once again applied and once again was passed over, this time by someone with even lower qualifications.

> I was encouraged to apply and I did. I was not even considered, and the whole process was totally ludicrous to me because I was told they selected somebody who has better scientific qualifications. But in the end it's somebody who has only a bachelor's degree with no publications or records. . . . The rating is very subjective.

Despite the organization's professed concern for objective qualifications, the outcome of decisions on managerial promotions was seen as heavily favoring those recruited through the old boy network that operated not only locally but agencywide. Personal experiences and anecdotes further reinforced the perception that these decisions were consistent only in the sense that they consistently removed certain candidates from managerial consideration, while continually adjusting the rationale for exclusion. As one person succinctly stated, "If they want to promote you, they don't need a reason. If they don't want to hire you, they'll come up with a thousand reasons why not."

The rationales ran the gamut, from one's lacking management training or certain degree requirements, to the appropriateness of one's age (one was "too young" or "too old"). Getting access to key assignments or developmental training helped to get one noticed by upper management. Yet Asian Americans saw upper management as instrumental in creating the perception that Asian Americans were "not interested" in management as; for example, by soliciting applications from those already committed to research activities. As one person explained, "The game is being played that they don't ask those, except those they know aren't interested. They never had an Asian appointment to the Sloan Fellowship. It's a way to keep the pipeline dried up and empty."

Whatever the reality behind this perception, some Asian American managers admitted they had assumed these positions by accident—or at least not out of strong personal choice or preference. Thus, a branch chief indicated that he preferred *not* to be doing this kind of work but that "'somebody has to do it.' I never sought management. I didn't look for it because I was already at the GS-15 level. . . . Being a manager was a necessary evil."

A major part of the managerial work he was engaged in involved "protecting the researchers from administrative burdens," and making sure researchers have a role and input into program development. Specifically, this meant providing "added value" so that this work does not slip away to competing institutions, such as universities. Offers to enter upper management were similarly unattractive for the very reason that this work would remove him even further from basic research and program development. "People have asked me if I would work at higher levels of management. But I have no interest in upper management because it would make no substantive contribution to the kind of program I am interested in, which is basic research programs." Upper management was described as "good at implementation but not good at the development of programs." At worst, it entailed risking a "loss of scientific credibility."

A second manager similarly noted his detour into management came despite his having been "intent on doing research." It was only because his research position had been abolished that he started to seriously consider management and explicitly requested a headquarters assignment so as to prepare himself for such work.

> That was fairly early on in my career here. . . . So at that time I thought I'd try management, and I made my desires known. I know that to get into management you have to experience various things, so I asked for headquarters assignment because I know that to get into any sort of significant management position, you should have spent some years, some time at headquarters in Washington, D.C. . . . understand their environment, because . . . we interact with headquarters quite a bit. So they sent me to headquarters for a while. . . . Washington is another place I lived for a year. . . . Waited my time and there was an opportunity to move into one of the technical assistant positions here [at XYZ Aerospace].

Another manager was appointed to the administrative ranks not as a result of any innate desire or personal interest in this line of work but as the unwitting outcome of his political efforts to break through some of the glass ceiling barriers for Asian Americans. His political advocacy work gained him a certain visibility, which eventually led to his appointment as chief engineer. "It was the challenge. It was pitting yourself against the system that drove me to do this. It wasn't the extra pay. The extra pay wasn't important."

If the circuitous route by which the above individuals entered management indicates how managerial careers are routinely launched at XYZ Aerospace, then the current way in which upper management fills such positions is less than satisfactory. More importantly, despite the fact that more than half of the 105 individuals who responded to the 1991 survey had expressed an interest in managerial work, the perception persists that Asian Americans are neither interested nor qualified to assume these positions. A head of the Diversity Leadership Council called attention to the pervasiveness of this stereotype as follows:

> I think the perception at XYZ and maybe a lot of organizations is that Asians don't want to be in charge. . . . They're good workers, they're good analysts, they're good engineers, they're good accountants, because they really get in and learn it and do well, but they're not meant to be in charge.

(DW: *Of a project?*)

Or an organization. Not just the people part, but the whole thing. Setting the tone, being accountable, being the one whom everybody comes to when something goes wrong. . . . I've heard that Asian friends of mine, that they see that perception coming back at them. That they're not good business managers. Meaning actually managing the business of the organization.

Despite fears on the part of white males regarding diversification of the managerial pool, bad appointments through the old boy network hindered those working under such administrators.

I know I'm a very good manager. I've been told by my subordinates as well as my superiors that I was very a good manager, in terms of administrative ability as well as personnel judgment. . . . The disappointment was that the people who were chosen above me were not as competent. . . . I mean, it's not only one occasion, there are a couple of occasions. Their lack of performance [indicates] that the system is not choosing the best person available.

Perfunctory reviews of minority and women candidates, however, reinforce the view that these candidates are not taken as seriously as those who come through the old boy network. One person thus recalled his own interview by a white manager.

I remember one time there was an opening for this technical assistant, and I applied for the job. And then he invited me in for an interview. And I remember sitting upstairs in his office, and he had a set of questions that he had prepared. So he'd read off a question, and I'd start to expand—you know, give him my answers. And I looked at him, and he was kind of looking out the window. . . . He wasn't really paying attention. All he was doing was going through the motions, so he could say, "I interviewed an Asian."

In sum, while the popular mindset is accustomed to thinking of preferential treatment in terms of "unfair" advantages given to minorities and women, the strong opinion among Asian American professionals was that the preferences have instead gone disproportionately to white males. Some, though not all, of those denied the opportunity to prove themselves have held out the hope that the overall corporate environment may have changed in the last few years, and that this will at least open the door to a younger generation of Asian Americans to enter management..

Age

Increasing seniority has been associated with increasing perceptions of a glass ceiling (Asian Americans for Community Involvement 1993:2, 18-19). Jayjia Hsia thus observed: "Across all fields, Asian Americans with less than fifteen years of experience earned comparatively higher salaries than those with more experience. Overall, Asian Americans with fifteen years or more of experience earned up to 4 percent less than whites with similar experience" (Hsia 1988:199).

At XYZ Aerospace, this pattern was also found to be true: Older employers were more likely to perceive artificial barriers than younger recruits. To the extent that age affects career mobility, three theories are particularly relevant: One is cultural, the second relates to competitiveness on the market, and the third relates to location on the ladder.

The first explanation suggests that older and less acculturated Asian Americans will have greater language problems and experience other social and cultural constraints that prevent them from venturing outside certain networks or niches. The other side of this cultural hypothesis is that younger, more assimilated Asian Americans will likely be less reserved, less culturally conservative, and more outspoken, "savvy," or venturesome than their older counterparts. While they may lack the experience that comes with age and longevity in a career, they are manifestly more skilled in making themselves visible.

A second possible reason for the greater barriers experienced by more senior scientists and engineers relates to institutional efforts to retain "young, promising" recruits who are competitively sought after by other employers. According to one senior scientist, this practice occurs at the expense of "older, productive" members. As an engineer who had been repeatedly bypassed for promotion attested, the organization felt confident that they would not lose him because of his age. It is in this context that a close colleague jokingly remarked: "You'll never get a promotion because you're old. You'll never change jobs. We've got you!"

Finally, a third theory for why perceptions of a glass ceiling may vary by age has mainly to do with one's location on the ladder. At XYZ Aerospace, opportunities to apply for managerial jobs with important decision-making responsibilities do not arise until one has already passed through certain grade levels. GS-13 is, strictly speaking, a "nonmanagerial" position and was considered the cut-off point or dividing line between nonmanagerial and managerial jobs. Younger Asian Americans, those below GS-13, were said to be more optimistic about their career prospects. The following 25-year-old male thus stated he was "highly satisfied" and felt that his own hard work was paying off thus far.

> I think I am on track. So at 27, you should be [at grade level] 13. At thirty, you should be at 14. If by thirty I am not on 14, that means I am slow. . . . There is "no unequal opportunity. . . . " I haven't encountered any problems with promotion. . . . If you work hard, well, and are reliable, you will get promoted. You might have [a] problem communicating with your supervisors. I do know interpersonal barriers exist, but I have not experienced it personally. If you are good, sooner or later you will get promoted.

While acknowledging that language and interpersonal barriers may exist for certain individuals, he is generally confident that unless downsizing and budget cuts exacerbate matters, his career trajectory will unfold as he imagines it will. His supervisor and superiors have already given him a certain amount of "exposure" with visible job assignments and, more informally, he has even played on the same softball team.

Younger recruits are also optimistic because the organization has granted them certain career development opportunities. But as several senior Asian Americans pointed out, it is only with increasing seniority that one presses against the upper levels of the corporate structure. A chief engineer thus predicted: "the younger [Asian Americans] . . . don't feel that strongly about the glass ceiling. And that's because they haven't bumped up against it yet. They're not old enough, but it's going to hit them sooner or later." Another engineer, close to retirement, confirmed this, stating that his younger colleagues were now coming around to his view: "Some of the younger . . . Asian Americans didn't see it [the problem of a glass ceiling] because they were in their twenties. Now they're in their thirties. They recognize that I spoke with a voice of experience instead of a voice of dissatisfaction only."

In short, it is ironic that while younger recruits may be better equipped in terms of being more outspoken, articulate, acculturated, and comfortable with dominant norms, they are also more likely to be complacent. Despite certain differences in their perceptions of a glass ceiling, interviewees—regardless of age—shared the view that preparation for managerial work was necessary, that it required time, training, mentoring, exposure, and upper management support. Only longitudinal follow-up of these younger professionals will determine whether their careers unfold at the pace they expect.

SOCIAL CHANGE ISSUES

While a majority of those interviewed felt there was a glass ceiling for Asian Americans at XYZ Aerospace, there were differences of opinion regarding how change might be brought about, the kinds of issues to press forward with, as well as how vocal, strident, or aggressive Asian Americans should be in bringing pressures to bear upon upper management.

Commitment on the Part of Upper Management

Upper management's awareness of glass ceiling issues was seen as a partial one, depending on how familiar or connected administrators were with the human resources office, the DLC, or the various employee associations. More important, the commitment to diversity issues has centered on whether there were external pressures upon the organization to change.

During the 1980s when Congressman Norman Mineta was still in office, Asian Americans had strong support from these quarters, and political pressure resulted in tangible appointments. Similarly, when President Clinton and an EEO officer from SAL headquarters, respectively, visited XYZ Aerospace, their support for diversity set the tone and direction for the center director and the local EEO office, helping to forge and cement commitments to diversity. Unfortunately, these same commitments were weakened when this backing from high-ranking officials was no longer available. Thus, an Asian American manager indicated how Clinton's concerns about reelection led to a waning of his support, with consequences for the center's own commitment to diversity.

> For a while it looked like it [diversity] was doing pretty well because there was a big shakeup here with Clinton first coming in, pushing diversity, and of course, "X", the administrator of XYZ was following Clinton's lead. So there was a big "to-do" here about upper management, and how many people at the round table upstairs were people of color. . . . And there was a big concern that in the phone book all of the pictures of upper managers were all white male, so they had to remove the pictures and take the pictures down off the wall. . . . Then the EEO agency headquarters' person came out, and was expressing quite a concern here about diversity also, so for a while there was a push, and as I said, in the last three or four years, maybe the last couple of years, there's been a reversal on diversity issues. And so even though the EEO office still feels that there is a diversity problem. . . . it's changing and being reversed.

Downsizing and Retreat from Diversity

While the bottom line to diversifying the workforce at the upper ranks of administration is upper management's own commitment to identify, hire, and promote minorities, downsizing has compromised the government's ability to address such issues. A freeze on promotions at the GS-13 and GS-14 levels constituted a real barrier, releasing upper management from whatever control or responsibility it had on such appointments. An Asian American manager who had been highly critical of the artificial barriers created by the old boy network stated: "We've had budget cuts. Morale at the center is extremely poor. . . . Nothing to do with the glass ceiling. . . . "

One consequence of downsizing was that many employees ceased focusing on their individual careers. Others apparently left the organization for greener pastures. Attrition at the senior executive level was particularly noted. Reflecting on this loss of talent, the following managerial aspirant indicated that the organizational imperative to downsize outweighed any concern about what the loss of such talent might mean for productivity.

> An organization that isn't valuing all its employees will lose its key individuals. That's especially true when it comes down to women and minorities. A person like "X". . . . Let's say, he's not feeling valued here. He's going to take his skills and go to the university, and [the center] will be losing out on this. We're losing his experience and we're also sending a signal out to all Asians here that, "Boy, you know, Asians aren't really valued, and if you want to get ahead you might as well go elsewhere." Their most important goal is to downsize. So whoever's leaving helps them out. They don't care who it is. But beyond just losing people, it's also a loss of productivity, and not even a loss of productivity but more of not being able to get as much productivity out your people as you can.

The Asian American administrator, referred to above as "X," was one of the few high-level senior executives. His collegues saw his departure within a year of this interview as a major loss. The 1991 survey conducted at XYZ Aerospace indicated that among the career development questions that evoked the most uncertainty was whether career opportunities for Asians and Pacifics had improved over that which existed "five years ago": 57 percent said they were "not sure" in this regard. Even more telling, however, was the fact that 55 percent were unsure if they would continue to work at the organization until their retirement.

In addition to the freeze on promotions, certain managerial positions were eliminated. With fewer positions, many internal plans to institutionalize or promote diversity, such as mentoring and management training programs, were, in turn, canceled or shelved. With budget cuts, the financial incentives that formerly motivated employees were no longer available. Apart from the organization's retreat from diversity, a new appraisal system for employees reduced the ability of managers to encourage and reward productivity. In the past, performance evaluations rated employees on a five-point scale from "fair" to "highly successful." The new system, on the other hand, was a two-tier "pass-fail" evaluation, a shift seen by one line manager as disempowering managers and lowering employee performance.

> We used to, as government service, probably up to two to three years ago, follow up with very specific award money, depending on where you fell in your performance rating. That wasn't bad, you know, and we actually gave, not promotions, but what we called "quality increases." Within your GS level you could get a step increase, which was a major thing. Sometimes it's $2,000–$3,000 per year that was right in your

pocket, and it was something that you could put down for a mortgage application—that you had gotten this next mini-promotion. That's gone by the wayside, and what [the agency] has accepted is now a two tier pass-fail performance appraisal system. And it's sad. What does that look like to people? It looks like, "Well gee, I just can be a mediocre employee, and we'll all get a "pass." I won't get a "fail" at least . . . it's a big demotivator.

Asian American Employee Association:
Networking, Career Development, and Advocacy

The AAEA has had a long history at the center, having originated some twenty-five years ago as a result of orders from SAL headquarters. Its statistical reports on managerial underrepresentation were referred to earlier in this chapter. Although it has no official decision-making powers, the twelve-member advisory board has sought to represent the approximately 200–plus Asian Americans at XYZ on matters related to professional mobility.

Throughout the association's history, its role has shifted. In the early years, advocacy for greater representation dominated. Subsequently, its role expanded to include career development activities that promoted mentoring relationships, networking among employees, educational forums, and expansion of the career development aspect of the human resources office. Most recently, sponsorship of social and cultural events has assumed a much larger position. Overall, the AAEA has achieved a certain respect and credibility for advancing employee concerns at XYZ Aerospace, and in this regard has been "very effective," as the following participant pointed out:

> I think it's been the leader of the groups. It's had some real politically-wise and very savvy people as leaders of that employee association. This group was the first to form at the center back in 1972. The group has been able over the years to make very cogent issues come forward, and they've "walked the walk" of just working through management chains of command. And they have also gone to the outside and used congress people to add pressure. And that's been effective when they've needed to do that. They've had very good, very professional, very savvy, very "together" people in that group. I think other employee groups have looked to that group as a model too. And so I'm very proud of the heritage of that group.

While attitudes toward the employee group's present effectiveness are mixed, this may be related to the diversity of opinion over its role. The 1991 survey asked Asian American employees to rate on a scale from "1 to 5" (where 1 = strongly disagree, 3 = not sure, and 5 = strongly agree) the role that they thought the association should play to: (1) organize social events, (2) settle personal grievances, (3) get an individual promoted, (4) get more Asians and Pacific Islanders hired, (5) get more Asians and Pacific Islanders into management positions, (6) promote multicultural awareness, and (7) promote networking and career development. Out of 250 employees canvassed, 105 (or 42%) responded, 65 of whom were scientists and engineers. The strongest support went to promoting multicultural awareness (59 - strongly agreed, 33 - agreed) and networking and career development (53 - strongly agreed, 36 - agreed). There was also fairly strong support for getting more Asians and Pacific Islanders into management positions (36 - strongly agreed, 41 - agreed) or getting more such individuals hired (21 - strongly agreed, 33 - agreed). The hiring issue also evoked the most uncertainty (34 - not sure). The strongest disagreement as well as uncertainty, however, was expressed towards individual job concerns, specifically to the idea of the association involving itself in getting an individual promoted (25 - strongly disagreed, 20 - disagreed, 33 - not sure) or settling personal grievances (23 - strongly disagreed, 16 - disagreed, 33 - not sure). With respect to organizing social events, there was far more agreement (17 - strongly agreed, 48 - agreed) than disagreement (7 - strongly disagreed, 7 - disagreed).

My interviews, on the other hand, focused specifically on perceptions of the employee group's effectiveness. Despite general agreement that glass ceiling barriers existed, there were different perspectives on the kind of networking that should be emphasized. The differences capture a source of tension and disagreement over issues of cooperation and confrontation. At one end was the view that the employee group was a "constructive" force that deemphasized blame tactics in favor of working cooperatively with management toward addressing the glass ceiling, even if seen by some as having developed into a "clique" or "old boy network" of its own. As a previous chair noted,

> I think we're seen more as a constructive force than as a destructive force. We're seen as one that's solution-oriented. We've gone away from beating up the managers and saying, "You guys are doing a bad job," to saying, "these are some of the things you could do to help Asians out." So I think generally we're perceived well. Sometimes we may be perceived as a clique in its own, or some easy network that's grown up and formed its own old boys' network.

The second view was more critical of the employee group's advocacy role, contending that the organizational separateness of the employee groups themselves created the appearance of being "confrontational," of creating occasions for "pointing fingers at management for not doing enough." The association was, in this context, seen as *not collaborative enough*, as having set itself apart from the administration rather than seeking to become an integral part of the larger organizational structure. While the avenues for this collaboration or integration were not spelled out, the guiding sentiment was that these boundaries and differences should be transcended, either individually or collectively.

> The groups like the Asian American Employee group . . . they could—how do I want to put this? They could try to become part of the group, so to speak, part of the organizational structure rather than being on the outside. It's almost always confrontational. I wouldn't say, it's not confrontational but . . . here's the Asian American organization, the Asian American Employee group, and here's the management. I mean, it's not a team, you know. These people are outside and they're pointing fingers at the management for not doing enough, etc. I'd like to see more collaboration. Maybe when you have an organization like this, it's natural that it happens. But maybe individually . . . we have to somehow encourage becoming part of the group, part of the inner . . . part of the old boys' network.

The third view of the employee group is the most critical. In contrast to the collaborative stance favored above, others remarked that the employee group had retreated from the activist, advocacy role salient in its early years. The dominant opinion here was that it needed to regain some of that posture by being much *more* aggressive and vocal where upper management is concerned. Networking among Asian Americans was seen as insufficiently political or strategic, with the majority of activities less directed toward substantively addressing glass ceiling issues than creating occasions for events whose functions appeared purely "social or celebratory" in nature. Even where the advisory committee participated in job search efforts, its activities appeared to these critics to be limited to e-mail communications that encouraged Asian Americans to apply for vacancies in the managerial track. Thus, a formerly active participant of the employee group pointed out that certain concrete advocacy positions had been rejected by newer members who found these approaches "too aggressive, adversarial."

> We need to be "nice" people. We shouldn't make any waves. We should try to fit in." I disagree with that. When we lost Mineta, we should have kept some pressure going, asking the administration, "why aren't we getting any more "SESers?" We've given up on that. When we were in a group, we were pushing an Asian American book of resumes for possible vacancies here at XYZ Aerospace, and were giving them supposedly to all of the directorates, and that died very quickly. The new group felt it wasn't something we should be doing.

While even casual, social networking can potentially serve political ends, critics complained about the absence of any long-range vision or goal. Even a firm believer in the constructive role played by the employee group acknowledged that networking suffered from a lack of any clear, concrete goals.

> This network of senior people and junior people. . . . It's really taken a lot of conscious and focused effort on our side to keep this process going. [With respect to the barriers to mentoring, he responded] I think lack of a clear focus. If you're just there to network, how do you propagate the goal of networking? That's more of a thing that just happens. That's something you strive for.

A lack of vision and clear objectives was reiterated by another. In addition, the point was made that the advisory group also needed to think more strategically in terms of who would advocate their position to upper management and how they would coordinate their efforts with other employee groups.

> Maybe average in effectiveness in change. I wouldn't say they've been extremely successful. I think with [the former DLC head] gone now, I don't know who's championing their cause, but . . . they really need a champion.

> (DW: *What do they need to do as an employee group?*)

> First of all, they need to really sharpen up their vision, and then lay out some objectives that they want to accomplish to reach their goal. And then they need to go over these objectives with whoever is going to be advocating their position with upper management. It used to be the head of DLC. . . . They also need to make sure that they have some coordination or interaction with some of the other advisory groups because once or twice that I know of, they came up with something that they had not coordinated with another advisory group. And that got that advisory group really upset. . . . It nullified what they were trying to do.

> (DW: *Do you know what they did that nullified their own work?*)

> They came up with a set of goals—including the percentage of people they wanted in certain grade levels, at management ranks—but they didn't look at the other races, and that got surfaced through upper management, and the rest of the advisory groups. That created a real ruckus.

> (DW: *Is it like fighting over the same small piece of pie?*)

> Right. . . . They've established a meeting now between the heads of all the advisory groups to meet with the DLC head chair, and I don't know if that's still going on or

not. If it isn't, I would recommend that it be restarted, and if it is then that's the right forum to use.

The above three views not only reflected different postures with respect to what the employee group's political style or objectives but also different views regarding the relative importance of certain artificial barriers. Differences in analyses here seem to be at the root of their overall differences in orientation toward change. The patterns described below are, again, general ones, and are not intended to pigeonhole individuals whose positions and perspectives may actually overlap or straddle these analytical typologies.

Those who saw the employee association as taking a constructive or problem-solving approach to the glass ceiling tended to see as key barriers the absence of mentoring relationships and the lack of exposure to career development opportunities. Artificial barriers posed by corporate culture and the old boys' network were acknowledged, but the focus and emphasis were on human resource strategies.

In contrast, the two other perspectives on the employee group's role gave greater emphasis to the fact that the old boy network was a major artificial barrier. The difference between these two views revolved around how open or closed this network was perceived. Those who labeled the employee group overly "confrontational" were of the opinion that the old boy network was not as closed as it appeared and were optimistic about the ability of outsiders to penetrate such networks. Minimizing confrontation, therefore, was seen as the necessary first step toward bridging differences. The inevitability of inner circles was taken as a given, so the task of outsiders was to find ways to become part of the team, rather than setting themselves apart from this group.

> The key to moving up [is] to become part of the old boys' network because you want to move ahead. Old boys' network—no matter who's up there—the old boys' network would exist, whether Asian, women or whatever. If you want to move up, then you should become part of the old boys' network. That's the positive side. If you don't do that, I think, maybe it's difficult to move up, unless you're a really, really, extremely talented individual who shines no matter where you are. Then that's a different story. But if you're not that super, superhuman individual, then it's good to become part of the team, so to speak, you know, part of the old boys' network.

Those who viewed Asian Americans as "insufficiently aggressive," on the one hand, were pessimistic about the openness of the old boys' network. Thus, even critics who advocated aggressive actions on the part of the employee association did not motion for aggressive overtures to become part of this inner network. Part of the reason was the perception that there were few ways to practically cultivate such ties. Another reason was the belief that discrimination constricted the pipeline and that conflicts of interest were more salient than points of commonality.

In this way, opinions about the nature of artificial barriers strongly influenced political orientation and style. Conflicting orientations toward social change are not unique to XYZ Aerospace. Linda Trinh Vo thus noted, "With increasing numbers of Asians entering the professional ranks, the glass ceiling is one issue that can unite the native-born and foreign-born populations, yet organizers disagree over how stridently Asians should approach these matters" (1996:97).

At XYZ, Asian American unity seemed to break down more along age or generational lines rather than nativity status. Surprisingly, it is the older generation that has been cast as too political or "militant" by their younger counterparts. The latter, in turn, have been perceived as naïve and overly optimistic about their own careers. One major reason for these differences is that the older generation has lived through that part of the agency's history where the issue of diversity at upper levels of management was not even part of the consciousness of the organization. Their own efforts to call attention to the problem and to implement change exposed them firsthand to how unresponsive the organizational culture and structure could be. A chair of the employee group during this period reported that several center directors had privately admitted to him that there was discrimination at XYZ Aerospace, though his efforts to inform various division chiefs of the problem brought a "cold reception." After former congressman Norman Mineta's intervention, the administration left the strong message that it was not going to reward those who criticized. "That was all we got and it changed the stats a little," said one person. "Asians put their jobs on the line. Yet the two who got promoted were those who didn't participate in the protest." Those who were politically active, on the other hand, found themselves branded "troublemakers."

Perhaps because junior professionals joined the XYZ workforce after certain organizational changes had already been implemented or were underway, they are less critical. Yet what is striking is that most Asians who saw biases in the selection process did not alter their view even after "breaking through" the glass ceiling. Instead, their experience merely reinforced their belief that despite equal or superior training or qualifications, Asian Americans had to work that much harder to achieve the same goal. This attitude is consistent with that reflected in the survey responses of Asian American employees at XYZ Aerospace, where 59 percent believed they had to "work harder to gain recognition." Thus, a manager of 17 years stated that for change to occur at this point, what was needed could be summed up quite simply: "Just the willingness of the people in power to let you get up there," "to actively seek these minorities."

The very status of the employee associations as bodies with no formal decision-making power may also explain why Asian Americans were divided over whether they should pursue a more active role in demanding reform. Thus, while a certain formal relationship has developed between the AAEA and the EEO office and upper management, advisory status still means that upper management can be responsive or not—can take their advice or, as one person put it, "trash it." An aggressive stance on an already sensitive issue could mean losing any influence that might otherwise be exerted, especially if upper management appears otherwise receptive. On the other hand, where there is little formal accountability on the part of upper management, the role of a pressure group may be perceived as the only viable one, especially when faith in top management's commitment to diversity is problematic or simply distracted by other priorities. As one person pointed out, a close working relationship with such employee associations was not taken seriously at XYZ Aerospace. In fact, at one time a center director had specifically instructed an EEO officer to "shield him from all the advisory committees."

However divided Asian Americans may be in their opinion of the employee group, there is significant consensus that glass ceiling problems are not solely the responsibility of employee groups and that broader-based efforts toward organizational change are also necessary. This includes involving key actors—for example, the center director, other upper level managers, and representatives from the training or personnel office. Ideally, procedures would be institutionalized to offset existing biases. For example, at one time, the employee group had proposed to counter tendencies toward preselection by setting up a board of two or three people who would participate in the final selection of a candidate. While this suggestion died soon thereafter because supervisors wanted to retain as much control as possible over the hiring process, it is illustrative of the difference between token promotions and changes that might be made in the corporate culture or structure.

Token Promotions vs. Transformation of the Corporate Culture or Structure

"I want you to know I'm against affirmative action." This was the first response to my telephone inquiry about the glass ceiling at XYZ Aerospace. "That's okay," I responded, "affirmative action is one of the issues I'm interested in exploring, and whatever your position, I want to be able to understand your perspective." Apart from noting that Asian Americans had in the past been bypassed repeatedly by white males, he saw a new "pecking order" placing Asians behind other minorities as well. Whether upper management *intended* to play its employees off of one another, the effect was the same. He also suggested that stereotypes about Asian American success contributed to deliberate decisions to redirect managerial jobs elsewhere. Specifically, he said that supervisors believed Asians not only are hard workers but can make do with less.

> Some in management see Asians as "technical coolies." That's all. "Y" was so competent, he was asked to work on twenty projects simultaneously. Yet the branch chief didn't think he needed a promotion, saying, "He has a house in Tahoe." Most perceive Asians as being able to live on less. This is another reason they are not readily given promotions.

In practice, affirmative action means many things, and there is no consensus on even some elementary meanings and definitions of the term. One can think of affirmative action strategy in terms of broadening outreach efforts to include underrepresented groups. Another affirmative action strategy involves ensuring sufficient minority or female representation on hiring or promotional review panels. The most problematic and controversial form of affirmative action has involved the hiring or promotion of candidates who are allegedly less qualified than others in the applicant pool.

Those critical about the ability of affirmative action to address the glass ceiling noted the following, that: (1) an emphasis on "numbers" implied a quota, which meant that there was an implicit "limit" on the number of qualified Asian Americans who could be promoted; (2) affirmative action did not deal with the conditions producing underrepresentation; or (3) affirmative action could mean that the candidate was somehow "less qualified," inviting white backlash.

Two examples of the last point are significant because they involved *Asian Americans* who were hired or promoted. In one instance, an Asian American security chief was hired over the objections of the Asian American who indicated he had overseen the job search and thoroughly interviewed as many as fifteen of the applicants. In his view, there were more highly qualified candidates. Against his advice, his boss hired the Asian candidate because he wanted someone "Asian," an appointment that turned out to be an embarrassment. An even more problematic appointment was that of an Asian to the position of center director. The following human resources person stated that this appointment was a "disaster" for the organization, attracting criticisms that threatened all of their affirmative action programs:

> I don't think preferences work because it creates resentment. When affirmative action is misapplied, it causes resentment, and people who are not well qualified are picked. . . . They are symbols. Almost lost all our programs. . . . He couldn't represent us.

Recall, however, that there is a double standard here—that white male administrators found incompetent did not generate a backlash against whites.

Although affirmative action is commonly understood as a narrow, legal concern with statistical parity, its critics (including the above person) saw numbers as essential for benchmarking or monitoring the progress of various groups. In general, those supportive of affirmative action were more likely to feel that (1) "numbers" were an important gauge as to what one should strive for, and that this did not necessitate a limit on the numbers who could be promoted; (2) affirmative action also includes a wide range of strategies dealing with the conditions contributing to underrepresentation; and (3) backlash overlooks the artificial barriers that confront even qualified applicants, given that there is not yet a level playing field.

As a government organization formally committed to monitoring and following equal opportunity guidelines, XYZ Aerospace has been in the past conservative in its understandings of affirmative action, with its responsibilities as an EEO employer focused on keeping statistics. Several respondents pointed out that former EEO officers had been expressly hired because they would not "make waves" or really go beyond reporting the problem to "coming up with solutions." While those interviewed had different opinions of affirmative action, or what they thought it meant, they shared an interest in moving beyond the numbers toward directly addressing problematic aspects of the corporate culture or structure.

A former chair of the employee group thus underscored the need to get at what he called the "grass-roots issue" behind the glass ceiling.

> What I've been hoping to accomplish through my efforts is to communicate a deeper understanding of these issues going beyond the numbers. You can look at the numbers and show that there is underrepresentation, and I think there's a knee-jerk reaction that management will take: "Oh, there's underrepresentation. We'll pick three Vietnamese and throw them into the job. We'll promote them and take care of the problem there," and that's not really solving the problem . . .
>
> It's going down to the lower level, and getting to the grassroots issue. Not looking at the surface, looking at the numbers. You've got to look at why you're having the problem, why you're not, you know—why we're not considering enough Asians for this position? why not enough Asians are applying for this position? Looking at grassroots fundamental causes as to why the numbers are the way they are, instead of just focusing on the numbers, and saying, "It has to be fixed". . . . That just sets up this whole numbers game, where tokenism goes on. . . . And it invites a lot of backlash.

Precisely because glass ceiling issues are specifically about the "organizational bias," "token" promotions are shortsighted. Even given good intentions on the part of upper management, poor appointments can occur for at least three reasons: (1) an inability to accurately assess the merits of a candidate, perhaps because he or she is from a different cultural background; (2) perception of legal pressures to meet numerical goals; or (3) failure to create the necessary cultural and structural supports for such an individual on the job.

Since ignorance was seen as a reason for backlash and resistance to change, including structural reform itself, transforming the culture of the organization in this way was an important first step in this undertaking. The DLC, an umbrella group that had been formed as an advisory group to the center director, had orchestrated several events toward this end. Although some activities were said to have also generated "a lot of lip service" about the value of diversity, they were nevertheless concrete, "action-oriented" to convey a more in-depth or "experiential" understanding about diversity. One of the cochairs noted among the DLC's accomplishments its role in orchestrating a street fair that attracted more than 2,500 people, launching a year-long dialogue project involving at least 300 employees and organizing a one-day conference that touched on topics such as the glass ceiling, media stereotypes, and managing a diverse workforce.

Another example of a grassroots solution aimed at consciousness-raising was a centerwide project that systematically drew upon the knowledge base of the center's employee associations. The goal was to extend official affirmative action efforts, thereby fostering organizational relationships that could lead to mutual understanding and great collaboration. A rotational job in the center director's office was also created to enhance individual opportunities for greater managerial experience, exposure, and visibility in functions critical to the facility's operations.

Perhaps the most important reason for such consciousness-raising activities is the desire to enlist voluntary engagement—to have diversity viewed more as a "moral imperative" rather than a "mandatory," legal, or "top-down" requirement. The following person perceived the organization's overall concern for diversity as one largely propelled by a fear of lawsuits.

> [The official line seems to be] Well, we gotta have EEO or else we gonna have lawsuits. We can't discriminate against people or else we're going to get sued. . . . we're going to be sensitive to minority issues as a federal mandate, from a legal perspective, because we don't want to get sued. And I never hear any talk about the real costs in terms of loss of employees or suffering morale.

His own thoughts about diversity, on the other hand, were guided by the belief that addressing the artificial barriers would enhance the overall productivity of the organization because an organization perceived as fair and equitable would operate under conditions of high morale. The mundane issues that affect day-to-day participation would would also likely be addressed.

Others who were officially involved in diversity efforts behind the scenes felt race, ethnicity, and gender issues were already part of the organization's daily consciousness. Referring to his own involvement as chair of the AAEA and as participant on Equal Opportunity Council meetings, the following person reiterated how diversity was taken quite seriously.

It is every day in everyone's consciousness. It is. EEO/Affirmative action is . . . a big issue here. Affirmative Action, we always talk about that. We always want to find ways to improve the tolerance level of people with different backgrounds. We always talk about programs where you can recruit students from different backgrounds. We always talk about how you can improve everyday environment. We talk about disabled and gays and lesbians as part of that. . . . we talk about building an elevator and stairs for the disabled. . . . We have a big program for women and we have one for "federally employed" and "federally employed women."

A senior manager similarly emphasized how issues of diversity, fairness, and the glass ceiling were matters uppermost in the minds of senior management. While consciousness-raising efforts sometimes convey the impression that more is talked about rather than acted upon, the same executive insisted that many things are implemented:

No, things *are* implemented. . . . I personally don't carry out all these things in my social discussions, what you're referring to, you know. . . . Those are not the only formal meetings. We have promotion boards and things where we very consciously try to promote and make sure that minorities are considered. We don't try to put them ahead of other, better qualified people, but at least we go around to make sure that everybody's considered, all the minorities and female folks around here are considered. Not only that, we make sure that awards—whenever there's a consideration for those items, awards, cash awards, recognition, whatever—we make it a point . . . to make sure that we consider minorities and women, at least take a look again. . . . I think we do a lot. We try, at least.

Implementation, moreover, is an ongoing process. As the vice-chair of the DLC pointed out, top-down monitoring of the hiring process requires a number of "checkpoints" along the way, beginning with outreach and extending to the actual point of hire. All of this is intended to offset the bias created by the lack of diversity among those recruiting.

Who are the selecting officials? Typically they're white males. They will pick who is comfortable to them. There have been specific examples just recently where we are trying to call people on the decisions they make, where we know in a vacancy announcement that there were people of color who applied and weren't chosen for the job. We are asking officials why these people of color not chosen. They need to justify that [their decisions], and we're going up to higher ranks of management to have that discussion. . . . "X" [the chair] and I are trying to get to processes so that we can put in incentives, checkpoints, management oversight checkpoints, and ask questions early on. And so maybe we won't get outcome like. . . . "Hey, I'm picking this other person because that's the only person I'm really comfortable with." That's not how they word it, but that's really what it boils down to.

Work relations also require more accountability from supervisors in terms of their performance evaluations of subordinates. Feedback is especially important if applicants are not selected. When asked about "artificial barriers," a human resource manager pointed to "insufficient supervising" as an issue that placed Asian employees at a disadvantage compared with white males. Although critical feedback was acknowledged to be "hard to do," it was necessary if employees were to receive a realistic review of their strengths and weaknesses and, therefore, how they might improve. Such evaluations were thwarted by the "chaotic management structure" said to characterize XYZ Aerospace as a whole. As a chair of the employee association explained,

The organizational culture at XYZ Aerospace is an extension of the larger agency culture. It's a rather chaotic management structure where there are no clear levels of responsibility. It opens up opportunities to those who are aggressive. This is a cultural environment which is contrary to the traditional Asian preference for clear lines of authority. For example, I have two different bosses—a supervisor who is responsible for my performance evaluation and appraisal and a project manager who determines my assignments. They may not speak to one another, and I would have to get the project manager, who knows my work better, to lobby on my behalf. This kind of structure repeats itself all the way, with each person having two or three bosses.

Another employee added that ongoing organizational change frustrated any long-term career planning.

I've been fortunate to be in the right place at the right time and personally have not had to think about career planning much. However, as new people are hired, or for those that are not very satisfied, I can see that this is important. The problem here, though, is that many times, you plan to go through a course of events to achieve a goal, but the management and the system changes while you are in that course and when you are done, you cannot get what you were shooting for. Managers can say that if you had this experience or that class, you could be qualified for "whatever" position. By the time you get the experience or the class, that manager could be gone or the infrastructure changed. That lack of consistency is very damaging.

The human resource office's efforts to assist employees in monitoring their own career were all the more appreciated for this reason. As a chair of the employee group explained:

The human resources group has been really committed to helping us out. They've just been pulled in many different directions because they have lots of other obligations as well. But, we said, "What is a typical career path, so that someone who is starting out can kind of see what they need to do to get to their end goal of becoming a manager? It took some negotiation . . . to commit to something like that on paper because you can't guarantee that if a person does step "A, B, and C" they'll get to their goal. It's not that straightforward. So there was a reluctance to do that, and also it's hard to define what a typical path is just because everyone's career takes their own unique path. But ultimately, they did commit to something on paper, and set that down and put it out [inaudible] in a [printed] guide . . . it was sent out. That was helpful.

Although there is agreement that downsizing has led to the suspension of certain diversity measures, social change efforts are nevertheless sustained in certain quarters. The vice-chair of the DLC stated that the any further falling away from equity issues would prompt her own departure. The ability—or inability—of government to compete with companies on this very issue of diversity would be the deciding issue.

You asked me what would make me leave—if I don't see some action. Because another angle I bring to this is as vice-chair. What I've been doing is kind of bench-marking on the outside: what are some companies doing in the diversity arena? Don't tell me what you talk about; tell me what you're doing. How do you then nurture your folks, look at them from a career development standpoint? How do you hire aggressively for color and women? How do you retain them? And some companies [come] in with some very, very neat ideas. And I'm going, "Gee, why don't I join those companies?" They're not perfect either. I certainly know that. But the fact that they're doing things is wonderful. We used to be the leader in the government service.

These examples suggest that despite downsizing, social change efforts continue to occur. The bottom line is whether consciousness-raising along with the institutionalization of structural supports on behalf of diversity significantly improve the rate of promotions for minorities and women. On an agencywide level, new qualifications for SES positions were instituted January 1, 1998. Some possible implications for Asian Americans will be discussed in the following chapter.

NOTES

1. The top three areas in which Asians are most likely to receive their doctorates are the physical sciences, engineering, and life sciences (Ries and Thurgood 1993:54).

2. According to Goldner and Ritti, entry-level, preladder engineers see promotional opportunities on the technical and managerial ladders as similar. They also see those on the professional ladder as having greater latitude and opportunities than themselves to make importnat technical decisions. Engineers already on the professional ladder, on the other hand, saw managers as having greater influence in this regard. In one large electronics equipment manufacturing company, the lower status of engineering professionals became transparent when the two ladders were merged, placing engineers below their "equivalents" on the managerial ladder. Thus these newly subordinated professionals felt their interests were better served by this change to a single hierarchy since they were at least positioned on a career track to positions of greater authority (Goldner and Ritti 1967:495–96).

3. Although the authors suggest that Asian males have an *advantage* over white males where their occupational distribution is most different from that of white males, these pay disparities seem to have been inflated by the use of *national* data rather than data that adjusts for the concentration of Asians in high-income states.

4. For example, whereas Asian/Pacific Islander males were 7% (or 107,391) of all engineers and 6% (14,593) of all natural scientists in the U.S., their proportional concentration in California was more than double these respective national percentages, with API males making up 17% (or 40,810) of all engineers and 12% (3,454) of all natural scientists, that is, physicists, chemists (except biochemists), atmospheric and space scientists, geologists and geodesists, physical scientists, n.e.c. (not elsewhere classified), and biological and life scientists.

5. For example, while Asian Pacific Islander males were 8% (or 10,249) of all aerospace engineers in the nation (131,786), in California they were 14% (or 6,473) of all aerospace engineers (47,827) (U.S. Department of Commerce 1992). Between 1972 and 1996, the aerospace industry in California employed 165,000 wage and salary workers, making up 33% of all high technology jobs (State of California 1997).

6. Northrup and Malin noted more than a decade ago how the federal government's interest and involvement in aerospace research and development affected engineers and scientists and the companies employing them.

> The federal government is a major underwriter of research and development, supporting thousands of E/S [engineers/scientists] working on government-funded projects. The federal government is the biggest customer of the aerospace industry, which employs about 20% of all research and development E/S, and is also a sizable customer of many large companies in other industries. It, therefore, follows that not only do policies and actions of the federal government affect large numbers of E/S, but also these policies will have a strong influence on the companies employing E/S. (Northrup and Malin 1985:39)

7. Federal government positions have been designated by wage grades referred to as GS (general schedule) or GM (general management) levels. At XYZ Aerospace, the GS levels ranged from GS-4 to GS-16, and the GM levels ranged from GM-13 to GM-15. (The GM category is in the process of being phased out, a response to downsizing efforts.) GS-14 is the minimum pay rate for senior engineers, scientists, and managers. The highest grade is SES (senior executive service), while the glass ceiling is seen as resting at around the GS-12 or GS-13 levels.

8. Part of this institutional flexibility derived from the availability of "excepted" positions for attracting highly qualified personnel. These positions were exempted from the restrictions imposed by federal pay regulations, and thus were the means by which government salaries could compete with industry standards.

9. For example, 1997 statistical data on Asian Americans at XYZ indicated that at 13% of the workforce, they made up 12% of "administrative professionals." While the percent of Asians in the "administrative" pool approximates that in the "professional" pool, suggesting they are moving up the ladder, the category of "administrative professionals" includes not only high-level administrators but personnel performing administrator support functions, for example, clerks, secretaries, and human resources personnel.

10. In their book *Striking the Mother Lode in Science* (1992), Paula Stephan and Sharon Levin offer several theories about the relevance of age for researchers in scientific fields. Specifically, the scientists they studied were academic scientists, primarily Ph.D.s in the physical, earth, and life sciences (as opposed to mathematics or engineering). In a chapter titled, "Why Age May Matter," the authors discuss how age is related to "the will to do science," or the willingness to continue along this career path. Even though the authors do not directly explore age in relationship to managerial aspirations or rewards, what they *do* indicate that is of relevance to the glass ceiling is that it is at the midcareer point that researchers begin to personally review and assess their career accomplishments and weigh these against other life goals. This is also the point at which complaints of the glass ceiling also appear. How Asian Americans respond to career obstacles at midlife will likely be highly variable, depending on the degree to which they value the "puzzle, ribbon, or gold."

Three motivating forces behind "the will to do science"—the "puzzle, ribbon, and gold"—undergo a reassessment or reevaluation as one approaches one's middle years (around 40) or midcareer (associate or full professorship). In other words, age or stage of one's career affect a researcher's *attitude* or orientation toward these original goals. From this developmental point of view, scientists are like other human beings who begin to recognize their own mortality. They begin to weigh their work aspirations against other sources of rewards in their lives as well as against the possibility of their achieving or satisfying the goals that originally motivated them in their early years. For scientists, this means "taking stock" of their present status in the scientific community, their productivity or contributions (ability to solve "the puzzle"), and the degree to which this has won them social recognition among their colleagues or peers ("the ribbon"). The "gold" factor takes the form of determining whether there is sufficient material incentive for placing work issues above nonwork issues. Increasing age makes it increasingly apparent that financial rewards will decline with each additional year simply because there are fewer years left in one's career to collect. As a result, one may make rational calculations as to whether the costs of doing research, and the further investments in time required, are worth the effort. Since the remaining years in which one can "cash in" on one's investments are limited, the kind of financial rewards a scientist is receiving from publications, royalties, consulting fees, and speaking engagements may be important factors determining whether he or she continues along this path. In this accounting process, material factors can also affect whether the "puzzle" aspect of science continues to be intrinsically satisfying. If funding pressures for doing this work become onerous, what was once "fun" or "play" becomes a "chore." Alternative professional opportunities, moreover, may present themselves as viable, competing alternatives to research at this time, including a detour into administration.

CHAPTER 6

The Bigger Picture

In light of glass ceiling barriers identified in the previous chapter, a natural question arises as to whether the idea of a diverse leadership is sufficiently compelling to motivate change. Since the glass ceiling was first identified at XYZ Aerospace in the 1970s, recruiting and training senior managers has become an even greater challenge in the context of a global business environment. Like their corporate counterparts, government organizations over the last decade have been forced to reconsider how to increase their own organizational flexibility and responsiveness to changing circumstances. Part of the response has been the development of new core executive requirements by the U.S. Office of Personnel Management, calling for a broad range of skills. Another has been greater receptivity to diversity in the management ranks and to a range of affirmative action strategies that would address artificial barriers. The intersection of these distinct strategies has significance for Asian American scientists and engineers at XYZ Aerospace.

The sweeping challenges facing senior managers will have implications for managerial aspirations themselves. In this context, the tendency for Asian Americans at XYZ to be clustered in lower and middle management positions might clearly be an issue of choice as opposed to either lack of qualifications or artificial barriers. The following factors, discussed at length in the preceding chapter, were indicative of artificial barriers:

- The objectively slower advancement of Asian Americans compared with white males despite similar levels of education or work experience;
- An organizational culture that is incongruent with the behavioral habits or interactional styles of minorities and women;
- The dual ladder and the absence of career development plans that would facilitate transition from the technical to the managerial ladder; and
- The absence of mentoring, especially in an organizational context which otherwise lacks a good succession plan.

While there is increasing recognition in Fortune 500 companies that organizational factors are responsible in important ways for the *differential preparedness* of its workers as well as for whether talent is recognized, the business rationale for diversity has been insufficiently persuasive at XYZ. During the 1970s and 1980s, there was active resistance to the very idea of diversifying leadership at the facility. According to an early chair of the employee group, a climate of intimidation served to suppress glass ceiling complaints:

> My group was getting tremendous pressure from management. Once I decided as chairperson to proceed along a certain line, I was going to go all the way, come hell or high water. . . . Others were tired of the problem and agreed, "We should get this problem corrected." They shared the same idea, same thought—to better the situation of Asian Americans as a group, whom we all felt were being discriminated against. . . . The younger ones were visibly shaken by the pressure they were receiving from their management.

Anecdotal evidence suggests that backlash continues where managerial appointments have involved minorities and women. Diversity workshops involving managers, in turn, have not always been greeted with enthusiasm from those who have "heard it all before." Whether these are isolated instances or symptoms of deeper organizational resistance, the commitment to diversity is still largely the function of the EEO/human resources units rather than one where equal opportunity principles have been internalized throughout the organization. Recommendations put forth in a 1995 EEO agencywide study of the glass ceiling at SAL underscored the very need for greater commitment on the part of senior managers and accountability on the part of supervisors in this regard. Also emphasized was the need for practices or procedures that would facilitate identifying and training high potential individuals at all levels of the pipeline and that would more clearly define and widely publicize eligibility and promotional criteria.

A major goal of this concluding chapter is to look at aspects of the broader context that bear upon artificial barriers and underrepresentation at the upper managerial levels. This includes examining first how the assumption of a level playing field has contributed to the invisibility of glass ceiling barriers. Second, the meaning of artificial barriers as defined by the U.S. Department of Labor will be revisited for the purpose of demonstrating the flexibility that organizations theoretically have at their disposal for cultivating the kind of employees that will contribute to overall performance.

Third, a broad analytical distinction will be drawn between "new" diversity strategies and "old" affirmative action strategies to illustrate how corporate cultural change involves a balancing act between various kinds of diversity considerations. In the case of government agencies, the EEO and OFCCP[1] have advocated measures that have helped level the playing field through the formalization of personnel procedures, an undervalued hallmark of affirmative action approaches.

Fourth, the new core executive requirements that have been instituted governmentwide to address global uncertainty and to broaden the skills of its senior managers may perhaps lend themselves to promoting greater diversity as well. Specifically, the core qualification related to "leading people" is of particular relevance here. Organizational inertia at XYZ and SAL in general was attributed by many to the agency's commitment to technological excellence and superiority at the expense of managerial skills that would simultaneously cultivate the "social or cultural capital" of its workforce. Retention problems and the costs of untapped employee potential must therefore be factored into the "business equation."[2]

Fifth, because the clustering of Asian Americans at lower and middle management levels echoes a pattern found in other workplaces, this issue will be taken up in the context of "middleman minority theory." Although some aspects of the theory do *not* seem to apply to XYZ's employees, the discussion is intended to catalyze further reflection on these and other issues that may help to explain their underpresentation in upper management.

The closing remarks in this chapter outline some remedies XYZ Aerospace might pursue to address the barriers scientists and engineers face as well as to better gauge the extent of the glass ceiling in general.

THE ILLUSION OF A LEVEL PLAYING FIELD

As noted in chapters 1 and 2, the existence of the glass ceiling for Asian Americans might come as a surprise for several reasons: the general lack of research on the topic, the ideological claims of the American Dream, the dominant stereotype of Asian Americans as a highly mobile group, and the elusiveness of corporate culture. Together, they have contributed to the assumption of a level playing field.

Asian Americans have majored in science and engineering for a variety of reasons, including parental and teacher influences, strong quantitative abilities, job market opportunities, and perceived discrimination in other fields (Kwoh 1947:102–10; Hsia 1988:128–32). It is thus ironic that the science and engineering fields are associated with glass ceilings for Asian Americans. As the following engineer at XYZ Aerospace explained, his father had tried to discourage both his brother and him from becoming mechanical engineers because of his own experiences of discrimination in this line of work.

> My father did not want me or my brother to go into mechanical engineering, ironically, even though that's his area. He wanted us to go into medicine or law or become a professor, and that wasn't really my interest or my brother's interest. . . . He ran into problems with his own career. . . . He was working for a big utility company and they were very set in their ways, and I think he always felt like he was bypassed for promotions for political reasons or because he was Chinese. And he didn't want us to go through that.

A point that cannot be overemphasized is that glass ceilings can be set in place by practices that are seemingly neutral. Active prejudice is not required for racially undesirable outcomes. Unlike blacks in the Texaco suit *(Roberts v. Texaco, Inc.)* and, more recently, the suit against Freddie Mac *(Morgan v. Federal Home Loan Mortgage Corp.)*, Asian Americans at XYZ did not encounter racial epithets.[3] Even those privy to insensitive or ethnic humor imputed ignorance rather than malice. Some even see the operation of the old boy network as "natural" since most people prefer working with those whom they know or share interests with.

While overt prejudice was absent, discrimination was not ruled out. Rather it was subtle, subjective, and cloaked in the language of merit and universalistic criteria. Thus, Asian Americans experienced management's dismissal of their objective qualifications as a series of mere pretexts for exclusion. Like the shifting rationales invoked to exclude Jewish college applicants in the early part of the twentieth century,[4] the only constant was a selection process that tapped into the old boy network and standards congruent with the behavior of certain "white males." Like white women, whose "interactive" leadership style deviated from the "command-and-control" model that white males exhibited, Asian American professionals were uncomfortable with this "one best model." The head of the DLC, a white male and strong advocate of minority and women employees, illustrated how bias can stem from seemingly innocuous forms of subjectivity, cultural interests, and experiences.

> Sometimes it's real subjective. . . . If I interview five people—and one of them is real family-oriented, loves to play golf, is a big 49ers fan, he and I are going to hit it off. . . . I'm going to be more drawn to that person than someone who's quiet and shy and retiring, who likes to read and go to the opera. . . . I'll be more inclined to say, "I *think* I'll work better [with that person]."

Citing a range of social science evidence, Barbara Reskin (1998) emphasizes how employer evaluations are typically highly subjective:

> For example, according to a 1994 survey of 3,347 private firms with at least 20 employees, employers attached the greatest importance to characteristics that are hardest to assess objectively such as applicants' attitudes, and the least importance to more objective measures such as years of schooling, tests administered during the interviews, and teachers' recommendations. . . . Evaluation criteria are most subject to bias when the evaluation criteria are vague, ambiguous, or subjective . . . and in work settings in which majority-group members predominate. . . . Although explicit criteria and objective measures of performance reduce the likelihood of evaluation bias and thus of employment discrimination . . . subjective evaluation and vague criteria appear to be the norm. (Reskin 1998:33–34)

The glass ceiling barriers identified in the previous chapter suggest that the playing field is far from level. Artificial barriers were both formal and informal. Among the former structural barriers is that posed by the dual ladders, which is "neutral" and "universal" in the sense that it is a hurdle that must be crossed by *all* scientists and engineers who seek to reinvent themselves as managers. Yet it is likely to be a major stumbling block to Asian Americans for two reasons: (1) their tendency to rely on the formal, bureaucratic rules as a guide; and (2) the overall absence of mentoring that would demystify some of the formal rules and make explicit some of the informal rules to getting ahead.

Notwithstanding systematic efforts to formalize procedures and promotional criteria, the unwritten, informal rules themselves have become stumbling blocks. At present, neutral procedures produce racially biased outcomes because mentoring continues to be largely informal, occurring largely within the old boy network. Such biases are "subtle and difficult to expose," including corporate management's "unspoken preference for certain employees"(Gordon 1995:4, 17). Personal connections, in fact, have been among those neutral procedures found to be *most* closely associated with racially-biased outcomes. As Gertrude Ezorsky writes: "The neutral procedures that have had the greatest racist impact within employment are selection by (1) personal connections, (2) qualification standards, and (3) seniority status . . . although these policies may be administered by racially impartial persons, they are linked to overt racism, past, present, and future. Indeed, in some situations they serve as instruments of *overt* racism" (1991:14).[5]

In sum, while a level playing field is frequently *assumed* because of a variety of neutral procedures, these procedures themselves are vulnerable to artificial bias. What is particularly significant about glass ceiling research is the renewed focus on *institutional* forms of discrimination, whereby organizations premised on universalistic standards nevertheless permit biases which tilt the playing field.[6]

ARTIFICIAL VS. REAL BARRIERS

"Artificial" barriers have been defined and treated as those barriers impeding qualified individuals. "Real" barriers by extension imply the absence of necessary qualifications. Although the Federal Glass Ceiling Commission did not explicitly draw this contrast, the distinction was implicit and deserves closer examination because of the fine line that exists here. Importantly, it has implications for the degree of responsibility to be borne, respectively, by the employer and employee.[7]

Even if one takes the bottom-line view that all hiring and promotion decisions should be based simply and solely on "qualifications," the dividing line between real and artificial barriers is a blurry one. The Commission explicitly designated lack of mentoring and lack of management training as artificial barriers. Yet these artificial barriers have a direct bearing on real barriers, on preparedness, and the very issue of who is—or is not—qualified. If women are unprepared to enter managerial work because they have been poorly mentored compared with men, or provided with fewer developmental opportunities, what is to be done? If their *lack of* required skills is the main consideration, then they are being held back by a "real" barriers. If, on the other hand, it is recognized that mentoring and management opportunities have gone disproportionately to white males, then employers are better positioned to remove such artificial constraints.

Qualifications for management encompass not only certain educational or formal kinds of work experience but also certain ineffable qualities—a certain "presence," leadership style, or some other kind of "cultural capital" (Bourdieu 1977)—qualities that inhere not simply in the individual but in a set of relationships. As corporations have moved toward more diffuse or decentralized forms of governance and, in turn, away from "command-and-control" models of management (Rosener 1995:26–44), there has been growing appreciation for leadership style qualities commonly associated with women. Yet as Rosener observed, this shift will not necessarily translate into mobility for women, since some organizations have simply turned to training men in these skills, no longer seeing them as distinctly female.

> As doubts about the effectiveness of the command-and-control model made their way into the executive suite, these same behaviors began to appear in a positive light and were no longer considered female. They were now simply good leadership traits. It is revealing, for example, that in defending the role of intuition and emotion in management decisions, Herbert Simon [author of a much discussed article on the topic] made no mention of the prevailing view of these qualities as "female" and therefore irrational and unreliable. Similarly, when the attributes associated with the interactive leadership style are considered organizationally effective, they are often presented as gender-neutral. Ironically, in some organizations men are now being trained to be interactive leaders while women are still hitting the glass ceiling because they *are* interactive leaders. (Rosener 1995:12–13)

Whatever footing on the ladder Asian Americans many gain because of their special "cultural skills," these qualities, too, may well be co-opted in the same way, as they too are bypassed in favor of those candidates for whom there is an "unspoken preference."

In short, despite commonly held assumptions of a level playing field, the issue of where one draws the line between "artificial" and "real" barriers is ultimately a political decision, one that has less to do with the capabilities of the candidates in question than with the biases of decision makers.

CORPORATE CULTURAL CHANGE: CONSIDERATIONS FOR DIVERSITY MANAGEMENT

While there are work contexts that still rely upon paternalistic, command-and-control forms of management, the dynamic environment in which corporations presently operate encourages flexible, nonhierarchical relations that give employees greater initiative and discretion in problem-solving and other tasks (Cox 1994; Saxenian 1998; Thomas 1996:57–78). The litany is by now familiar: Employee commitment is mobilized through trust and respect for individual creativity, initiative, and judgment; in-house competition is replaced by team spirit and flexible work rules which free talent to assume risks rather than blindly conform; and the corporate culture functions to create those cultural forms which enable employees to realign themselves to this new order.

Corporations have also latched onto the idea of diversity management for the marketing advantages it promised. Beginning in the 1970s and throughout the 1980s, "diversity management" came to be seen as offering a strategic, competitive edge that increased productivity or sales (Fernandez with Barr 1993). All presumably have a stake in this progressive order, which is reflected in a multicultural leadership that cuts across race, class, and gender lines. As diversity management has come into vogue, it has reinvigorated notions of meritocracy that suggest there is "cultural capital" to be exploited by managing diversity well. Diversity is viewed as something that has positive value, that might be appreciated for its own sake, or for the diversity of perspectives that might be brought to problem solving. Such ideas are appealing to those who would like to approach diversity as something other than a formal legislated mandate, associated with backlash and resentment on the part of those left out.[8]

An example of such a diversity strategy at XYZ was the formation of voluntary discussion groups that sought to break down stereotypes. These discussion groups made up of diverse employees and guided by facilitators have been ongoing since 1995, and have given the agency a reputation for being a "trend-setter" or model for other organizations. The experiment was unprecedented not only because the organization allowed employees (at least 300 of whom have participated) to meet on company time, but because it reflected a sustained commitment toward breaking down some of the barriers individuals face when interacting with others from different backgrounds. These barriers may take the form of psychological and social discomfort that is inadvertently triggered as employees experience subconscious biases about other groups, or that they believe others hold toward them. A former head of the DLC described the process as follows:

> The thing we've done in the last three or four years is called the [name of the small group sessions]. That made national news. It's been a big deal, even at the White House. . . . It's in its third or fourth year now. . . . We get reps from various cultures on a team—it's all voluntary—to meet with a facilitator. . . . Once a month or every two weeks for one or two hours to just *talk* about diversity. What was it like to grow up

Asian American, and what's it like now, and what are your fears, hot buttons? It's pretty heavy stuff. As far as I can tell, in that sense we're "trend-setting," because that's not something companies do. But it's all on the diversity as opposed to the affirmative action side. Understanding diversity, appreciating it. I know where you're coming from. I know a little bit more about what it's like for you.

These discussion groups represent a stepping-stone to corporate cultural change. Despite the enthusiasm with which they have been met, they have also been subject to criticism that often attaches itself to brown-bag lunches or short-term exchanges, that is, that the direct implications for structural mobility are not transparent. Whether such internal discussions alter the power structure depends on many things, including the degree to which upper management and other key decision makers are actively involved.

The larger critique directed against diversity strategies in general is that this new frame has in some quarters also marked a turn or retreat away from conventional affirmative action approaches. According to Avery Gordon, diversity management has compared itself positively and in contradistinction to affirmative action on several points:

> Diversity management is highly invested in distinguishing itself from affirmative action. Affirmative action is seen as rule-bound while diversity is seen as culture-bound, or boundless. Affirmative action is viewed as social engineering while diversity is viewed as social representation. Affirmative action is racialized and gendered, diversity is individualized, custom-made. While affirmative action is juridically enforced, a source of obligation and responsibility, diversity is positive, a source of communal pleasure. . . . Affirmative action confers property rights on supposedly culturally unassimilable groups, but diversity confers cultural rights on individuals possessing valuable properties. In short, affirmative action puts the corporation in the business of "helping people who are disadvantaged," but diversity puts "people from diverse backgrounds" to work "helping companies to succeed." (1995:9)

As a template of somewhat different assumptions, diversity strategies encompass but also transcend race and gender and are purportedly more inclusive.[9] In the ideal scenario, a long-term process of mutual adjustment is anticipated, until a diverse leadership emerges "naturally" as corporations assume some of the burden for being responsive to a diverse workforce (ibid:12).

For several reasons, Gordon has suggested that diversity management, thus pursued, is problematic. While organizational change need not preclude and, in fact, may encourage attending to race and gender issues as part of this "diversity mixture," the bottom line is productivity and profitability. Race and gender considerations that are not clearly tied in with this goal or relevant to a consumer market could be treated as "arbitrary" considerations. For example, where teams of diverse work groups have been organized for the very purpose of enhancing creative problem-solving, innovation has derived from bringing together people with different functions or areas of work specialization (Cox and Finley 1995:67–68), rather than with certain ascribed characteristics, such as race and gender. Second, such colorblind procedures ignore other organizational or informal practices that have racial and gendered consequences—the very conditions that led to presidential executive orders and court injunctions mandating affirmative action (Reskin 1998:23–37).

Gordon's fear is that without clear incentives, fewer companies may find it in their interests to pursue affirmative action strategies voluntarily. At present, approximately one-fifth of all employees are estimated to work for companies that have voluntary plans, while more than half of all firms do not use any kind of affirmative action. Profit-oriented firms as a whole have been less likely than public and nonprofit organizations to use affirmative action procedures (Reskin 1998:16–17). Fortune companies, however, have been more committed to such programs.[10] Thirdly, even if a diverse managerial leadership is achieved, Gordon reminds us that this achievement can be shortsighted if a business agenda is pursued without regard to how such policy affects society at large and, specifically, if it is not guided by values related to civil rights, moral responsibility, and social justice issues.

While affirmative action is often misconceived of as "quotas," it actually involves an array of policies and practices directed not only toward historical forms of discrimination but toward proactively preventing further discrimination. Thus, Reskin (ibid.:3) notes, through the "formalization of personnel practices, affirmative action has helped replace cronyism with more objective procedures and policies that benefit most workers," adding "as practiced in the United States today is much closer to Americans' values than the rhetoric would have us believe."

> Although the executive orders and the 1972 EEO Act did not use the term "affirmative action," they required the kinds of proactive efforts to prevent discrimination that are the essence of affirmative action. In the 1990s, approximately three million people worked in Federal agencies covered by these regulations (ibid.:13).

The criticisms that Asian Americans at XYZ had of affirmative action need to be seen in the context of what they saw as major barriers: (1) corporate cultural biases, (2) lack of mentoring, (3) and the operation of an old boy network. Attempts to promote from underrepresented groups matter little, for example, if there is an implicit organizational preference, say, for a narrow range of leadership skills. Similarly, even aggressive recruitment may not be sufficient to counter the organizational inertia that has stood in the way of addressing many implicit organizational biases, from how positions are filled to how work is organized, managed, or executed. For these reasons, affirmative action, pursued without attention to such organizational biases, was seen as shortsighted, undermining long-term retention and possibly the organization's meritocratic goals.

As a government organization, XYZ Aerospace continues to display a commitment to "older" diversity strategies first introduced in the 1970s. In practice, these affirmative action strategies have included hiring goals and career development issues, for example, "targeting recruitment efforts at minorities and women," "facilitating the assimilation of minorities and women," "developing role models by recruiting minorities and women for high-level positions," and "fostering mentoring relationships where white males mentor minorities" (Thomas 1996:81–82). Moreover, despite certain ideological attacks on affirmative action in recent years, the federal government's EEO programs have been shown to be effective in improving the managerial representation (albeit at the lower levels) not only of women and other minorities (Reskin 1998:49–50) but also of Asian Americans (Asian Americans for Community Involvement 1993:21–23).[11]

Without the existence of hiring goals, it is doubtful that the present holding pattern could even be maintained, especially when other types of organizational changes are not imminent. For this reason, even a chair of the employee association who insisted on the need to move beyond "numbers" expressed concern that the agency had shifted to a new methodology for calculating underrepresentation, namely, national statistics as the baseline for measuring parity.[12] In response to my inquiries regarding the current situation, he wrote that this would effectively lower the number of Asian Americans who might be targeted for hire:

> Unfortunately, AAPIs have taken a huge loss recently when [the agency] decided each center has to use national, not local demographics, in determining our parity levels. So since Asian Americans are less populous in the nation, XYZ Aerospace is now *overrepresented* in AAPIs. . . . How all this works out is still not clear.

Whatever the outcome for Asian Americans seeking to enter the pipeline, these new hiring goals would not necessarily make it any easier to recruit other minorities either. Insofar as the availability pool is based on national statistics, the expectation is that one would recruit proportionally. A former head of the DLC explained that national statistics posed certain difficulties for recruitment because of the geographical concentration of certain racial populations. African American scientists and engineers are more likely to live outside California. The high cost of living in California, along with the absence of a large African American community, would be major obstacles to attracting these potential hires.

> It bothered me when I first saw it [the document establishing new guidelines for recruitment]. They claim that we recruit nationally, and to a certain extent we do recruit nationally, but most of hiring isn't, because someone who lives in North Carolina isn't going to move out here. They can't afford to move out here. So a lot of our hiring is here. And if we're going to be forced to meet the kind of comparisons we have for, say, African Americans in particular, they aren't here. And they're not moving here. This is not a big African American community. So that puts a different kind of burden on management—the white males trying to fine-tune this. "Okay, let's see, we've got women, men, we've got five different kinds of minorities. . . ." We're looking at all these lists and cross-matches of things we've got to do. Very difficult, when you get so caught up in these numbers. By the time we've gotten to looking at these numbers, our hour is up, and we've got to go back to work.

While certain problems are thus attributed to the number crunching associated with hiring, the more serious constraint seems to be the low priority which affirmative action goals have against other hiring goals. As the same person went on to explain, upper management's justification for *not* making special outreach efforts to minorities and women in its most recent recruitment efforts had to do with cost effectiveness. Since the center hires only about fifty people in the course of a year, the resources needed to mount a more diverse recruitment were seen as unjustifiable. The availability of *other* qualified candidates, moreover, diminished this prospect even further. It is via such neutral recruitment procedures, and the better tie-ins that others have with this employment stream—by virtue of numbers, geographical availability, or informal networks—that minorities and women do not even get to the door.

> There was a process that we designed for [upper management] to implement, but there always seems to be a reason why this had not occurred. "We couldn't do that this month. We had these candidates and they were good candidates and we need to hire them now, and so we didn't have time to go out and find an Asian American, or an African American or some candidate like that. . . ." It's hard to put a big recruiting program in place if you're only hiring fifty people. If you're hiring 200 to 300, you go and send recruiting teams out. It's really hard when it's only fifty.

It is in this larger context of such competing economic or business priorities that this section has sought to discuss certain broad analytical distinctions between diversity strategies and affirmative action strategies. *Empirically*, there is a certain overlap or complementarity in actual practices and ideals, including that which occurs when affirmative action strategies are loosely referred to as practices that would enhance "diversity." Both are concerned with the full use of human resources, including diversity throughout the ranks. Whereas affirmative action originated out of a concern for addressing racial inequalities in the workplace and continues to be committed to rectifying these and other forms of historical under-representation, the new rhetoric surrounding diversity emphasizes the stake that employers have in this venture, either because a multitalented workforce will bring leverage in a volatile market or at the very least relief from the costs of employee attrition and retraining.

Despite the DLC recommendation that SAL's upper management demonstrate the *business* rationale for racial or gender diversity, this idea has yet to "trickle down" or be heard in ways that would constitute a compelling basis for more broad-based commitment and for the kinds of organizational steps necessary for addressing the glass ceiling. Among those interviewed at XYZ, the rationale for more fully utilizing one's work force came from observations of problems that occurred from *not* attending to issues of diversity—namely, a glass ceiling for certain segments of the workforce, a past history of incompetent administrators, low morale and defection of highly trained personnel from the organization. The same DLC chair thus noted that the glass ceiling created retention problems that undercut XYZ's efforts at hiring women and minorities at XYZ.

> One of the reasons we've lost as many as we've hired is the glass ceiling, career development. . . . They get in, they spend a little while, and then they say, "Wait a minute. I can see what's going on here. That building is all white guys. I'm not ever going to get to that building. I'm going to work somewhere else." And so a lot of the good ones leave. They get fed up trying to beat their head against this glass ceiling.

Whether the failure to fully capitalize upon the potential of those facing glass ceiling barriers is better articulated in the language of business rationales, on the one hand, or traditional EEO concerns for historical underrepresentation and equity issues, on the other hand, there is a pressing need for upper managers to respond to these concerns as the task of "leading people" enters the realm of executive management rather than merely being the responsibility of human resources managers.

THE GLOBAL CONTEXT AND NEW EXECUTIVE CORE REQUIREMENTS

In the 1990s, skill qualifications have increasingly come to be seen not merely as an autonomous individual performance issue but rather as contingent on a broader, organic vision of employee relations. The deindustrialization of the 1970s led to downsizing, mergers, costcutting, fragmentation, and high unemployment (Bluestone and Harrison 1982). This development coincided with a move toward flattened hierarchies and decentralized authority structures and had direct implications for diversity management (Gordon 1995; Rosener 1995; Saxenian 1998; Thomas 1996). In such a corporate environment, senior management has moved away from bureaucratic control in terms of "face-time" spent with subordinates, instead chosing a strategy of addressing larger publics, both within and outside the organization.

In this context, Rosabeth Moss Kanter has emphasized that *persuasion* has become an indispensable managerial skill, especially in newer and innovative forms of organization:

> In the new environment . . . the unquestioned authority of managers in the corporation of the past has been replaced by the need for negotiations and relationships outside the immediate managerial domain, by the need for managers to *persuade* rather than *order*, and by the need to acknowledge the expertise of those below. (Kanter 1983:48)

Elsewhere, she notes that the skills of persuasion are one of "three new sets of skills" that managers must acquire in "integrative" environments where a team orientation derives from seeing problems in terms of a larger "whole."

> First are "power skills"—skills in persuading others to invest information, support, and resources in new initiatives driven by an "entrepreneur." Second is being able to manage the problems associated with the greater use of teams and employee participation. And third is understanding how change is designed and constructed in an organization—how the microchanges introduced by individual innovators relate to macrochanges or strategic reorientations. (ibid.:35–36)

Managerial expectations can thus be seen as tied to the demands of the current global economy, the reorganization of work relations, and issues related to increasing or decreasing centralization. Whether the barriers experienced by Asian Americans attempting to enter management are best understood in these terms, their perceived lack of communication skills is a recurring theme, with differing views as to whether this alleged handicap is a "real" or "artificial" barrier.

Large-scale changes have brought about revisions in the formal criteria by which candidates for senior executive positions in government are evaluated in the 1990s. As of January 1, 1998, the newest set of executive core qualifications was implemented across the federal government by the U.S. Office of Personnel Management (see table 6.1). An agencywide announcement by SAL made clear that this change involved an explicit shift from simply seeing management narrowly in terms of "managing the workplace" toward embracing a much larger, global environment and an ability to assess this larger context. This change in senior executive service qualifications is reflected in the following table, which shows how leadership requirements have evolved from the time SES positions were first created in 1979 until they were revised in 1997.

Historically, the *Qualifications Standards* for federal employment has held that education and work experience are the two most important criteria for both hiring and promotion (U.S. Office of Personnel Management 1993). In fact, the major source of inequity identified by Asian American scientists or engineers with a long history at XYZ Aerospace was preferences for white male applicants with lower degree qualifications and fewer years of work experience. A glass ceiling was thus documented for many years. Significantly, it is only at the very highest degree levels that education gives Asian Americans (males at least) an advantage over their white male counterparts.[13]

Since the 1970s, upper managerial work has radically changed. A Ph.D. is still important given that many of the organizations at XYZ are research organizations. However, it is no longer required and is itself insufficient. It may even be a handicap insofar as it

Table 6.1. Foundation for Development, Selection, and Management of Executives.

1979–1984 Six Activity Areas	1994–1997 Five Executive Core Qualifications	Revised in 1997 Five Executive Core Qualifications
Integration of internal and external program/policy issues	Strategic Vision	Leading Change
	Human Resources Management	Leading People
Organizational representation and liaison		Results Driven
	Program Development and Evaluation	
Direction and guidance of programs, projects, or development		Business Acumen
	Resources Planning and Management	Building Coalitions/ Communications
Acquisition and administration of financial and material resources	Organizational Representation and Liaison	
Utilization of human resources		
Review of implementation and results		

Source: U.S. Office of Personnel Management, *OPM Message to the Senior Executive*, SES-98-02, Winter 1998

reinforces a candidate's technical skills without enlarging his or her organizational vision. As the following senior executive explained:

> Ph.D.s are the worst in that their emphasis is on the technical objectives without enough attention paid to the people skills required to create esprit de corps among the workers. This is particularly important in today's environment if one wants to retain critical employees as an effective and integrated part of the workforce.

New core criteria for senior management were arrived at as a result of long-term research conducted by the U.S. Office of Personnel Management. By law, an independent Qualifications Review Board administered by the OPM must certify SES appointees (U.S. Office of Personnel Management 1998b). This research by the OPM involved federal representatives from seventeen agencies, data from the private sector (including competency models used by Fortune 100 companies), and focus group participation.[14] These changes in government criteria mirror some of the conditions in the private sector, where uncertainty and turbulent conditions have become the norm, aptly referred to as "permanent white water" (Thomas 1998:42). SAL has had its share of downsizing, some of this involving an about-face in managerial appointments of personnel who no longer fit into the organization's new priorities. (One Asian American thus reported being demoted when his managerial post was eliminated after only a short tenure.)

Five core qualifications have emerged as interdependent criteria required of all senior executives—leading change, leading people, results-driven, having business acumen, and building coalitions/communications.[15] These values are explicitly intended to reinforce the idea of an "SES corporate culture," where senior executives provide a strategic leadership that "transcends their commitment to a specific agency mission or an individual profession" (U.S. Office of Personnel Management 1997:1). As government agencies begin to reorient themselves in response to these new guidelines, there has been a fundamental shift toward valuing entrepreneurship, a customer service orientation, partnerships, traits such as resilience and political savvy, and innovation based on encouraging employee feedback, creativity, and continued learning. A key characteristic to "leading change" is the very ability to respond deftly to uncertainty: "Being open to change and new information; tolerating ambiguity; adapting behavior and work methods in response to new information, changing conditions, or unexpected obstacles; adjusting rapidly to new situations warranting attention and resolution." Qualities an executive is expected to demonstrate in "leading people" include "empowering people by sharing power and authority," "fostering commitment, team spirit, pride, trust, and group identity," and "resolving conflicts in a positive and constructive manner [and] attending to morale and organizational climate issues" (U.S. Office of Personnel Management 1998a:2).

With downsizing and greater decentralization, the authority structure and managerial relations have undergone certain changes. Specifically, an integrated team with greater trust, responsibility, and accountability is being encouraged among the professional workers in the science and engineering workforce. Part of this change is motivated by the impossibility of monitoring or supervising every aspect of an operation or project in its detail, something that may have been possible in the organization's earlier years. While this downward shift likely relieves upper managers of the burdens of excessive oversight or micro-management, at the same time senior executive positions have become more challenging because of new requirements for an even broader vision, long-term perspective, a more encompassing scope of responsibilities, and more demanding communication skills than was the case in the past. For example, a core executive requirement—"building coalitions/communication"—calls for a senior executive to move fluidly between any number of internal and external contexts: It involves "the ability to explain, advocate and express facts and ideas in a convincing manner, and negotiate with individuals and groups internally and externally. It also involves the ability to develop an expansive professional network with other organizations, and to identify the internal and external politics that impact the work of the organization" (U.S. Office of Personnel Management 1998b:3–4).

A senior executive described how demanding such jobs can be, characterizing his own job as "overwhelming," "very difficult," and "high stress," a sharp contrast to the nostalgic memories he had of times when he was involved entirely in research. According to a contracting officer, the sheer number of regulatory requirements and statutes at SAL is so restrictive that managerial work lacks a great deal of autonomy in decision making. The huge amounts of data that inundate upper managers are due to the transformation of managerial work by technological systems (Burris 1993:104–10).

Entering the senior executive ranks, by definition, also means a loss of stability in two respects. For one, such jobs often require a great deal of travel or geographical mobility simply because of the tasks associated with managing and coordinating various branches of the organization. Moreover, even though one may be given responsibility and allotted a certain amount of resources, both financial and personnel, for managing an organization within the facility, there may be insufficient flexibility when it comes to the tasks involved, selecting personnel, or reallocating the budget to objectives. For this reason, an executive officer stated, "You are encouraged to take assignments they give you," implying there were a number of task assignments that were not within his control. Second, there is a loss of job security. The security which government employees enjoy is formally lost upon becoming a senior executive. As the same officer explained:

> After you have worked for SAL for three years, it would be hard for the organization to terminate you without showing cause. When you join the SES ranks, however, you have to give up your tenure rights. You actually sign a form stating this. What this means is that you do not have any retention rights. You can be terminated any time. In addition, you can be reassigned to any location, once given 30 days notice. If, in turn, you give up your SES position, you are on your own to find another non-SES position. At that point, you will need to start all over again in terms of regaining your tenure rights. The pay at the SES level is not significantly higher, especially when compared to industry for the same level of responsibilities.

Although his own reasons for pursuing management had more to do with the "challenge" and helping his particular division to survive through his highly successful fund-raising efforts, this source of job satisfaction ultimately could not compensate for the toll taken by all the traveling required.

Management by engineers or scientists has been the norm in the past, and there is no question that the broader mandates facing senior managers continue to emphasize technical competence. A key characteristic of another executive core requirement—"results driven," where the following technical abilities are underscored—reflects this view: "Understanding and appropriately applying procedures, requirements, regulations, and policies related to specialized expertise; understanding linkages between administrative competencies and mission needs; keeping current on issues, practices, and procedures in technical areas" (U.S. Office of Personnel Management 1998a:4). The technical mandate is formidable and perhaps daunting to those unaccustomed to dealing with sweeping agendas. In earlier years, when SAL was a much smaller organization, each project could be attended to with meticulous oversight, and the agency could still trailblaze because of a certain agility due to its size. As the organization grew, however, it operated more conservatively, weighted down not only by bureaucratic paperwork and increasing regulations, but also by the very task of supervision, which essentially granted individual members of a research team little latitude to make mistakes. Increasingly, the agency faces tremendous competition from numerous organizations involved in aerospace research—universities, private companies, as well as other government agencies. As a result, SAL actively encourages greater "risk-taking" as an essential step for quickening the pace of innovation and thereby avoiding mediocrity. An executive at XYZ thus commented:

> It's a definite change. SAL had an aversion to risk before and as a result, started diminishing as a premier organization because they [managers and engineers alike] didn't want to take a lot of chances, whereas when they first started, they undertook a lot of programs which had large risks. But they were able to overcome that and

had several successful missions. So they kept growing and got recognized as a premier organization, because with each mission you learn something. And this is what you call "lessons learned." You make a mistake. As a result, you're probably not going to make that mistake again. . . . . This is what SAL, I think, is trying to get back into again.

The process of moving into the senior corps and this new workplace culture included personal lessons for this same executive. Importantly, he had to learn to be comfortable with delegating responsibility. This meant not only carefully selecting and properly training one's subordinates but ultimately having confidence in one's own assessments and abilities.

It took me a long while to say, "I can really trust this individual. . . ." It started when I was flying experiments, because I found out I couldn't really control everything. We were flying *big* flight experiments where my experiment team was 15–20 people, and I couldn't track everything that was going on, so I had to trust that my key leaders were doing their job to keep me informed. . . . In the first experiment, we learned a *lot*. We did a lot more efficiently. . . . What saved me was that first experiment was a fairly small experiment with a fairly small team. So it was easier for me to delegate and develop a sense of confidence with that. The next experiment they gave me was far bigger, so if I had not learned how to delegate with the first one, I would have been in real trouble with the second.

Displaying confidence in one's subordinates meant retreating from oversight: "When you delegate something, you don't keep riding that person to see what that person is doing." This was, in turn, possible because team members learned to communicate openly about any problems or concerns. Explaining how he approached training, he said:

We worked together. All my task leaders and I had informal meetings where we would just discuss where we were, and that's how we established a communication dialogue and developed trust in each other, so that if they ran into a problem, then everybody else on the team knew that right away. They weren't afraid to say, "Hey, we may have a problem." And everyone bent over backwards to help them out, and so we all benefited from the open dialogue.

SAL has been explicit about distinguishing new leadership skills from the technical or managerial skills valued in the past. While leadership and technical skills are not mutually exclusive, the proper balance still has yet to be articulated, much less achieved. Diversity management aside, XYZ was criticized for its exclusive concern with technical qualifications to the neglect of people-oriented skills. In commenting on the objectivity of the review process, a DLC head noted the process to be fair and without bias at this level but faulted the very criteria used for choosing managers. Specifically, failure to give greater emphasis to people-management skills was seen as having ramifications for all employees.

I'll see a two-page write-up on a person—"ought to be promoted to a GS-15 branch chief". . . . And everything that's in there is all about their technical quality. What a great engineer they are. How great all their projects look. There's nothing in there about how good *a manager* they are. Do they empower people? Do they train them? Do they have good career development? Do they give their people good experiences? There's nothing in there about that. . . . I think that's because XYZ does not necessarily want . . . people in manager positions who are in fact good managers. They want them to be strong technically—good procurement people, good accountants, good engineers, good project managers—but not good supervisors. So what you end up with is a lot of branch and division chiefs headed

> by strong technical people, who are not people-oriented. They're not sensitive to, maybe, the needs of their young employees—not all of them but most of them—who need some mentoring and development to get them ready to move up. And so you end up with people—not simply minorities not getting good supervisors—but white males, too.

Because management generally does not make its employees feel "valued" in the process of engaging them to "get the job done," retention has been a major problem.

> I think if they paid more attention to people, people wouldn't leave. They'd feel as though somebody cared about them, and was helping their careers. I think a lot of the reason they leave is that they think nobody cares about them. . . . Is it important to get the job done? Absolutely. But what about the next job? Do you want those people still there for the next job? Because when they get tired of working for you, after they get this job done, they're going to *leave*. What are you going to do the next time you have a job to get done? They won't be there. Because you didn't *treat* them right. You didn't make them feel *valued*. You didn't train them, educate them. It's easy to say the only important thing is to get the job done. But then you get the job done and everybody dies. . . . You should care.

Reflecting this concern for the human resources side of career development, the DLC at XYZ apparently played a key role in seeing that the core requirement having to do with "leading people" was given due attention in the new OPM leadership guidelines.

In sum, senior management has become more demanding than ever before. Only at the *agencywide* level and on the *administrative professional* ladder (i.e., as nonscientists and non-engineers) were Asian Americans *better* represented at the SES level than all other groups, including white males.[16] As scientists and engineers, however, they are rarely found in upper management, and the stereotypical explanations suggest that they are "too highly specialized," "too narrowly trained," "lacking in communication skills" or a "broad enough vision." While such stereotypes apply to scientists and engineers in general, Asian Americans have acquired the additional stereotype of being seen as "simply technicians," who "do not want to be in charge." Their concentration at the lower and middle management levels has contributed to this view.[17] A cynical theory is that they function as "middleman minorities."

MIDDLEMAN MINORITY THEORY

Whereas the model minority thesis *symbolically* pits Asian Americans against other groups, middleman minority theory suggests that they are *structurally* situated in ways that leave the "middleman" (in this case, Asian Americans) open to certain forms of intergroup hostility. As the name implies, middleman minority theory positions certain ethnic, racial, cultural, or religious minorities at the center or middle of a very hierarchical social order or set of relationships. In the classic form of the theory, Asians were the *petit bourgeois* class that monopolized sectors of the economy shunned by large-scale corporate capitalists. As small-scale business entrepreneurs in trades and services, they transmitted goods and services that would not otherwise be available in urban ghettoes. In doing so, they thereby came to occupy a "middle" position between "elites and masses" or between "producers and consumers" (Bonacich and Modell 1980; Wong 1985). Korean Americans are a prime example of a "middleman minority," which was blocked from pursuing professional or white-collar work in the mainstream because of language or citizenship requirements but which found opportunity structures in poor inner-city neighborhoods bypassed by large retail outlets and chain stores (Ong, Park, and Tong 1994; Min 1996). According to Barringer et al. (1995:202), "the 'middleman' hypothesis might apply best to Koreans, Asian Indians, Chinese, and Vietnamese, in that order."

Even historically prior to their appearance as urban ethnic retailers, Asian immigrants have found themselves "caught in the middle" when employers have played them against each other or against white workers, exploiting existing patterns of parochial conflict or mutual suspicion for social control purposes. This was true in agriculture, construction (Takaki 1990b:25–30; Chan 1991:25–61), and manufacturing (Brown and Philips 1986). White workers were themselves manipulated by this divide-and-control strategy. When not pitted against strikebreakers, they were co-opted into existing structures of authority by being made foremen or supervisors of ethnic minority labor (Smith 1961; Roediger 1991).

Where Asian Americans have entered mainstream bureaucracies as professionals and encountered a glass ceiling, they have found themselves stuck at "mid-level positions" between white executives in upper management and lower echelon workers, which include significant numbers of blacks, Latinos, and other minorities ("Asian Americans' Awkward," 22 August 1995). As lower or middle managers, they have less power and authority than high-level executives and traditionally face more undesirable responsibilities, such as allocating already scarce resources, serving termination notices to employees, managing conflict, and the like. One theory is that they function as a kind of "racial wedge" or "shock absorber"— as buffers for antagonism that might otherwise be directed toward "higher-ups," whose decisions actually shape policies and social relations at large.

At XYZ Aerospace most Asian American managers did not see their role or function *in these terms*. One saw his managerial duties as a part of his fundamental commitment to protect basic research programs, and thus the relation with his immediate colleagues was a *protective* one of garnering resources for projects of vital mutual interest. Others, however, did perceive lower or middle management positions as onerous, negatively characterizing them as "secondary" positions—assistants with no decision-making power—jobs crudely characterized as "dog work." One person remarked that this work involved the "dirty work" of sometimes "totally impossible" tasks, reserved for "technical coolies."

> Some jobs are very easy to do, and once done, you will be recognized. Other jobs are totally impossible to do, and Asians are always known to be the persons to do the dirty work . . . technical coolies. . . . It seems that the "easy-to-please" jobs are not coming to the Asian Americans as easily as they should be.

The one respondent who came closest to characterizing his own position as one of social control noted that when the center faced a possible race discrimination suit, he was urged in his managerial role to contain and mute glass ceiling complaints. This occurred in the agency's early history when Asian American professionals were individually and collectively mobilizing to make their concerns public.

In their competition for SES positions, Asian Americans have felt squeezed between the old boy network and "traditional" affirmative action candidates. Yet, given the increasingly challenging tasks and expectations confronting senior executives, one can only wonder if the door to the executive suite will be eventually wedged open when they have lost their overall attractiveness. To fully address the middleman minority thesis, one would need descriptive detail about concrete managerial tasks and functions, especially as this bears on relationship with subordinates. Although it was not within the purview of this study to explore the nature of managerial jobs themselves, what we already know about the task requirements of senior executives suggests that the financial returns of upper management may not be sufficient to compensate for the demands of the job, the loss of tenure rights, a certain loss of autonomy with job assignments that place one at the center's disposal, and the extraordinary family sacrifices involved. An Asian American male, reflecting on his approximately seventeen years of service in this capacity, said it was impossible to balance his work responsibilities with family life.

> I was on the road 50 percent of the time. It was important that I had a wife that was supportive. Not spending time with my kids was a major trade-off. . . it does mean some kind of sacrifice on your family time, because a lot of these programs take you away from your family, "X" number of weeks or months. You need to be prepared to do that.

Whatever one thinks of middleman minority theory, these and other considerations may discourage many Asian Americans from seeking senior management positions. *Some* of the managers interviewed for this study would have preferred remaining researchers. If this were uniformly true for all Asian American professionals at XYZ Aerospace, then it would make little sense to speak of a glass ceiling. Where doubts have surfaced about the existence of the glass ceiling, one or more of the following patterns were noted:

- Asian Americans have made notable progress in lower and middle management positions, precisely because of their educational achievements;

- Asian American scientists and engineers are *not* applying for upper management positions, and their absence from SES ranks seems to be at least partly an outcome of individual choice (e.g., lack of managerial interest); and

- Asian Americans face "real" (not artificial) barriers in terms of qualifying for upper managerial positions, which require even broader communication skills than what is required of lower or middle managers.

As noted at the outset of this chapter, there is also a range of factors identified with a glass ceiling. The coexistence of these apparently discrepant perceptions in no way implies an inherent conflict. Indeed, *all* these patterns are a part of a spectrum marking different aggregate profiles presently available on this professional workforce.

CONCLUDING REMARKS

Like any other group, Asian Americans will likely manifest a range of coping strategies or individual responses to the glass ceiling (Chow 1994). Typical responses to blocked mobility have been "overachievement" or further investments in education (Chun 1980; Hirschman and Wong 1984; Sue and Okazaki 1990). Other personal strategies include individual efforts to developing an image, set of behaviors, or "corporate manners" consistent with the organizational culture (Wu 1997:195–228). As noted in chapter 2, reactions have also included lateral transfers to other companies or decisions to pursue self-employment. According to J. D. Hokoyama, President and Executive Director of LEAP (Leadership Education for American Pacifics), when the aerospace industry was at its height, lateral transfers to other companies was quite common, and one could easily move, say, from TRW to Hughes Aircraft or to McDonnell Douglass (personal communication, 1993). Such transfers are now harder to come by. More important than the "glass ceiling" during periods of economic restructuring has been the "floor," or job security. At XYZ, the security of government employment is an attraction that wards off defections to the private sector. According to one interviewee, at an early point in the agency's history the possibility of lateral transfers *within* the center was specifically introduced in response to Asian American complaints of a glass ceiling.[18]

Litigation in general has been a last resort to workplace barriers. Compared to other groups, Asian Americans have been less likely to litigate than other groups. Reporting on the 1991-1995 period, EEO Vice Chair Paul Igasaki stated that Asian Americans "file less than 1 percent of the total number of charges per year":

> Employment discrimination of all kinds is occurring presently at a level as high or higher than that at any time in history, despite the fact that some forms of discrimination have become less overt. Over the five-year period between 1991 and 1995, the number of discrimination charges filed with the EEOC increased from 63, 899 in 1991 to 87,580 in 1995, an increase of 27 percent. During the same time span, the number of charges filed by Asian Pacific Islanders did not increase significantly. Asian Americans file less than 1 percent of the total number of charges per year. The number of charges filed by Asian Americans as they relate to specific issues such as discharge, hiring, and promotion in the workplace has not changed significantly over the last five years. Despite evidence suggesting that the numbers should be higher, the number of charges filed by Asian Americans is low. (1996:16)

Rather than indicating a positive employment situation, the low percentage of discrimination suits filed by Asian Americans probably underestimates the workplace problems experienced and in no way suggests that they would not be skillful litigants if compelled (McClain, 1994).[19]

Apart from these individual strategies for dealing with the glass ceiling, there are also broad-based remedies that companies themselves have adopted. These have included "job enrichment and enlargement programs" that have had the effect of notably improving the overall effectiveness of all employees. How diversity management is approached at XYZ— its successes, problems, and remedies-in-place—is thus consequential. Indeed, many of the organizational challenges faced by XYZ will be shared by other places of employment. These include workplaces where a diverse workforce is publicly spotlighted as an important organizational goal and where there is concern about how this commitment can be practically sustained or systematically pursued in light of competing priorities.

Because glass ceiling barriers are largely subtle, affirmative action guided by numerical goals has been as important as uncovering the artificial barriers themselves. Given, moreover, that neutral standards are vulnerable to subjective biases, EEO and Affirmative Action officers play an active and important role in recruitment, on promotion boards, and on various awards panels. Such oversight, however, is only a partial, "band-aid" remedy precisely because many barriers are systemic, not transparently discriminatory, and not easily traceable to the specific individuals or specific procedures.

In the context of a culturally diverse workforce, concepts of unstated norms and everyday agendas may not be equally shared. One reason for perceptions of bias is that employee notions of what is required to advance need to be better realigned with the realities in the workplace.[20] A formal mentoring process is already in place, and it is expected that further efforts will be made to fine-tune and facilitate the matching process so that formality itself is not a barrier to potential users. Workshops have been organized in the past to surface some of the unwritten or unspoken rules which lie "beneath the ripple," as one person put it.

To the extent that employees have not assumed an active role in monitoring their own career progress, informal workshops might also be specifically geared toward grappling with the concrete specifics related to self-critical examination of individual career plans. There is a certain precedence for this kind of "group mentoring" activity at XYZ Aerospace. During the early 1990s, the Asian American Employee Association organized small group discussions led by Asian American managers or senior persons on different topics, such as engineering, technical work, administrative work, or project management. One participant, now a project manager, indicated that the emphasis was on mentoring related to career mobility or career change. (One might be in administrative work but interested in moving into technical work or project management, or alternatively, one might be in technical work seeking advancement into management, and so on.) These mini-conferences provided more of a general overview of career development issues related to management than they did a context for comparing formal and informal expectations.

From the point of view of those interviewed at both the upper and lower ends of the managerial ladder, the move into management is nowhere near as predictable or straightforward as it might be. However small XYZ might be compared with other government organizations, its organizational structure has been described by insiders as "chaotic" and "overwhelming." Systematic mentoring, a whole range of career monitoring procedures, and exit interviews are elements in the scope of things which upper management might undertake to gain a better hold over glass ceiling barriers.

Despite the ongoing perception of a glass ceiling among scientists and engineers, XYZ Aerospace has not conducted any facility-wide studies of its own that would enable it to evaluate either employee progress or job satisfaction. Although a primary responsibility of the EEO office is to keep statistics on who is underrepresented, objective data on employee mobility have not been subjected to *controlled* comparisons, at least not within the recent period. (Agencywide statistics were thus more useful in this regard.[21]) The most recent centerwide studies in this vein were initiated by the Asian American employee group but are quite dated. At the time of this writing, no statistical study has been conducted since 1988 that would indicate whether Asian American advancement has been disproportionately slower than that of white males. Similarly, no survey of Asian American employees has been conducted since 1991 that would indicate their level of managerial interest. Attitudes toward upper managerial jobs and their desirability, in fact, may have changed, especially since there have been major changes in what is required of senior executives over the last few years.

The present EEO officer was aware of the need for surveys focusing on job satisfaction, managerial interest, and employee adjustment to the organizational culture. SAL as a whole, she indicated, intended to conduct "cultural climate" surveys at each of its centers as a way of canvassing employees for their perceptions of diversity and the glass ceiling. Whether or not there is truth to the stereotypical perception that scientists and engineers "do not have a broad enough vision" or that Asian Americans in particular dislike being "in charge" of things, a carefully designed survey might possibly explore such perceptions.

Other proactive steps that the EEO office is considering are aimed at "steering" the employee groups in ways that would better enable them to accomplish their own goals. Since the Asian American Employee Association presently lacks a clear vision of its mission, guidance from the EEO office would most likely be welcomed. One possible arena for collaboration might revolve around the convening of focus groups for the purpose of surfacing the range of experiences on given topics that might then be systematically explored through centerwide surveys. Apart from focus groups serving as a preliminary or exploratory tool, they might also be the *preferred* mode for other endeavors where the goal is specification rather generalization, as in better understanding the success or failure of particular programs (Morgan 1993). At a broader level, the success of focus groups is already apparent in the small "multicultural" discussion groups that continue to be XYZ's centerpiece as a diversity strategy. The employee interest here was said to be even greater than that shown for other workshops, which have variously focused on diversity awareness training, disability training, or the prevention of sexual harassment. That it was something employees "really want to do, because they get something out of it" spoke loudly for its continuance.

While XYZ Aerospace has been a "trend-setter" in certain regards, more proactive measures are still called for in terms of career development, mentoring, and a rational succession plan. Statistics and survey data can assist with monitoring the progress of employees as an *aggregate*, but individual career progress is another matter. To ensure that XYZ has the managers it needs further up the line, career development plans have already been developed by the DLC with the assistance of the EEO Office and human resources office. However, they have not received the high priority attention they need from upper management in order to be implemented. Moreover, there are no managerial succession plans to really speak of, according to one senior executive: "XYZ has not had a good succession plan. They never groom successors, and that has been the *biggest* problem. They're reaction-oriented, rather than really planning for the future."

In general, the underlying goal behind any coherent career development or managerial succession plan is that employees will be systematically exposed to a range of experiences that are mutually reinforcing, cumulative, and consistent with their own career goals as well as those of the organization. Ideally, this should include quality mentoring from high-level managers, constructive and critical feedback from supervisors, and individual career development plans leading to high visibility assignments.

These concluding remarks do not by any means exhaust the possibilities in terms of actions which might be taken. According to a narrow, legal definition of equal opportunity, the government's role should be restricted to protecting *individuals* from actions, especially intentional acts to discriminate (Praeger 1982). Many of the artificial barriers discussed in this book, however, were not of this nature, but rather features of the organizational structure or culture. Key units, personnel, or individuals at XYZ have already begun to tackle some of these. The challenge is to integrate these various activities so that they are internally coherent ones mirroring management's ownership of these practices. Government remains the single largest employer. Though XYZ Aerospace employs but a fraction of government workers, how it achieves diversity is singularly important, not only for the legal obligations attached to federally funded projects but because federal policy is a significant marker for all employment policies.

NOTES

1. The Department of Labor's Office of Federal Contract Compliance Programs (OFCCP) is primarily responsible for monitoring corporations which have contracts with the federal government. In addition to awarding and recognizing exemplary corporate performance, the OFCCP conducts corporate management reviews as part of its enforcement strategy. During the 1993-1994 period, 53 such reviews were conducted, involving 29 industries, employing about 1.4 million people nationwide.

2. The organizational priorities at SAL have emphasized scientific research and technological development. In sharp contrast, employers marketing directly to a diverse consumer base may more readily see the value of having some of their key decision-makers reflect the diversity of this consumer population. Other companies still, whose products require no particular cultural sensitivity at the marketing level, e.g., oil companies, may be less attuned not only to customer needs but to the need for diversity in their leadership ranks.

3. In a 14 August 1998 letter from EEOC Director Tulio L. Diaz, Jr., it was disclosed that racial epithets and jokes continued to be sent through the company's e-mail system despite a federal judge's ruling that the company had taken sufficient remedial action to address a hostile work environment. As a federally chartered mortgage underwriting company, Freddie Mac was also shown to have blacks underrepresented in professional, managerial, and office positions.

4. See Duster (1976) for a discussion of how the discourse around merit and universalistic criteria has been permeated with arbitrary rationalizations for exclusion, which serve mainly to perpetuate the existing structure of privilege.

5. Ezorsky explains how informal recruitment through "word of mouth" and reliance on personal contacts is a common way in which jobs get filled yet unfairly disadvantages those previously excluded from certain work arenas through job discrimination or social segregation. Qualification standards, in turn, can be exclusionary, especially if employers insist on educational credentials and work experience requirements that may be irrelevant or not reliably linked to ability to do the job. Finally, seniority, while offering workers undeniably important protections and benefits against arbitrary treatment, disproportionately benefits whites because of the legacy left by discriminatory hiring practices in the past.

6. Major sources of racial inequality have been legislative acts which are neutral on the surface. The right to vote in some Southern states, for example, was once premised on the prerequisite that one's grandfather had voted. Since slaves had been never been given voting rights in the first place, this "grandfather's clause" was inherently discriminatory (Duster, 1976: 73, fn 1).

7. Given a certain discursive slippage in the English language, I am by no means suggesting that "artificial" barriers (e.g., discrimination) are not "real" in the sense that they do not have an objective reality or existence. What I mean is simply that "real barriers" are those having to do with the individual prerequisites for promotion. To be consistent with this distinction, discrimination would be better described as an "artificial" barrier, although this is not to deny that it certainly has real, substantive consequences

8. This backlash and resentment is not necessarily rooted in realistic assumptions. According to research reviewed by Barbara Reskin (1998: 71-84), affirmative action rarely entails reverse discrimination. Moreover, not only did it not hamper business productivity, or increase the costs of doing business, but it was shown to actually improve productivity by encouraging employment practices that fully utilized employees' skills.

9. Roosevelt Thomas, Jr., founder of the American Institute for Managing Diversity, has shown how complex and multidimensional diversity can be. His principle thesis, in fact, is that it goes beyond persons *per se* to the ideas they may embody: "Diversity in its broadest sense applies not merely to a collection of people who are alike in some ways and different in others, but also to intangibles—ideas, procedures, ways of looking at things" (Thomas, 1996: 46). According to Thomas, race and gender issues are only one of many possible "diversity mixtures," which include workforce diversity, (along a number of dimensions, including age, tenure, lifestyle, sexual orientation, education, experience, geographic origin), globalism, acquisitions and mergers, work/family issues, and cross-functional coordination. Among the multiple responses management can take toward diversity, Thomas identifies a series of eight "action options" (include/exclude, deny, assimilate, suppress, isolate, tolerate, build relationships, foster mutual adaptation). Depending on the context, each might be a reasonable option: "None of the options is inherently good or bad in itself. It all depends on the context" (Thomas, 1996: 30). Under some circumstances, it may even make rational business sense to limit certain forms of diversity. The majority of corporations, he says, tend to do exactly that, with very few entertaining option 8 ("fostering mutual adaptation"), which essentially moves beyond assimilation toward endorsing and accommodating diversity.

10. According to Anne Fisher (1994: 270), many of the CEOs at Fortune 100 companies had affirmative action programs in place to meet corporate objectives that were unrelated to government regulations. Similarly, Diane Wu (1997: 240) has noted elsewhere, "more than half of Fortune 1000 companies have some sort of program aimed at advancing minority personnel. Most of these programs are related to marketing strategies and intended to increase corporate profits; any humanitarian benefits are essentially 'positive spillover.'"

11. A comparison was made of employers who had EEO policies for the managerial level and those employers who did not. Based on employee perceptions of Asian American representation at lower, middle-, and upper-management, employers without EEO policies elicited somewhat more responses pointing to underrepresentation.

12. XYZ Aerospace presently has the highest concentration of API scientists and engineers of all SAL centers. Since Asian Americans make up 3.6% of the total U.S. population, the fact that already 13% of XYZ's scientists and engineers are Asian and Pacific Islanders means a lower threshold for hiring in the future. The national baseline thus has very different implications than if one were to base recruitment on local demographics, such as the percentage of Asians in the state population (10%). In various regions of Northern California, the figures for Asian American population were much larger than their national average: "Asian populations comprise more than 15% of San Francisco, San Mateo, and Santa Clara counties, more than 10% of Alameda and Solano counties, and slightly over 9% of Contra Costa county, all in the San Francisco Bay Area, as well as between 5% and 10% of the cluster of counties extending north and inland from the Bay Area" (Oliver et al., 1995:1–2).

13. Where the bachelor's degree was the highest degree, API males were more than a half a grade lower (and API females almost 2 grades lower) than the average grade of nonminority males. At the master's level, API males and females were both about a grade lower than

nonminority males. Only at the doctorate level were API males at a relative advantage, where their average grade (15.0) was a grade higher than nonminority males (13.7). No information was available for API female doctorates.

14. The task of actually selecting senior managers, however, is a joint responsibility assumed by Qualifications Review Boards (QRB: independent peer review boards administered by the OPM) and by the employing agency. Their tasks complement rather than overlap one another. A QRB team assesses "executive experience and potential—not technical expertise," whereas the employer determines "whether they are the most superior candidate for a particular position" (U.S. Office of Personnel Management, 1998b:3).

15. For a fuller description of these qualifications, their key characteristics, and the leadership competencies entailed, see the U.S. Office of Personnel Management (1998b).

16. Specifically, 12.5% of API males were in these positions, compared to 4.5% of nonminority males. In terms of average years of federal service, Asian males also spent considerably less time at each grade level *above* the GS-13 level than nonminority males similarly situated (four years less, on the average).

17. As of September 1995, 44.7% of API males and 49.6% of API females were at the GS-13 level.

18. During the early 1970s, the glass ceiling was such that the center director instituted a policy that permitted lateral transfers within the organizations, especially for Asian Americans who wanted to advance themselves. They would, in other words, be allowed to change their jobs from one organizational line to the another, provided they got the approval of both organizations.

19. Since 1993, 805 promotion charges were filed by Asian Americans before the U.S. Equal Employment Opportunity Commission. James H. Goldweber, Director, Office of Research Information and Planning, personal communication 25 July 1997.

20. Phenomenologist Alfred Schutz (1976: 93) saw the underlying rules of social life as made up of "recipes for action" which are in actuality "incoherent," "only partially clear," and "not at all free from contradictions." These formulas for daily living might have been clear when adopted at "time 1" when their rationality and practicality were fully understood, but at "time 2" they become "habits," practices that are only "partially clear" to the person using these ideas. So long as we live in a fairly stable or homogeneous environment, we seldom question the premises of everyday routine or "common-sense" knowledge, as long as they are sufficient for the purposes at hand. What is unfamiliar or strange is so because "thinking as usual" no longer applies; there are no longer any "recipes" for action.

21. A 1995 agency-wide study by the EEO acknowledged the continued existence of a glass ceiling for minorities at SAL. Asian American scientists and engineers are unquestionably underrepresented in senior management, with evidence that those on this ladder are advancing at a slower rate than might be expected. The average grade of API males and females tended to fall below that of other groups after controlling for educational level, time in grade (4 or more years), and current performance (looking only at those with "highly successful" or "outstanding" ratings).

REFERENCES

Books, Journal Articles, and Interviews

Abelman, Nancy, and John Lie. 1995. *Blue Dreams: Korean Americans and the Los Angeles Riots.* Cambridge, MA: Harvard University Press.

Alvesson, Mats. 1995. *Cultural Perspectives on Organizations.* New York: Cambridge University Press.

American Council on Education Fact Sheet. 1997. From *Current Population Survey, U.S. Bureau of the Census.* Washington, DC: U.S. Government Printing Office.

Ancheta, Angelo N. 1998. *Race, Rights, and the Asian American Experience.* New Brunswick, New Jersey: Rutgers University Press.

Asian American Report. 1982. An Occasional Publication of the Asian American Studies Program, University of California, Berkeley.

Asian Americans for Community Involvement (AACI). 1993. *Qualified But . . . A Report on Glass Ceiling Issues Facing Asian Americans in Silicon Valley.* San Jose: Asian Americans for Community Involvement of Santa Clara County, Inc.

Asian Pacific American Institute for Congressional Studies. 1998. *Newsletter.* Washington, DC: Asian Pacific American Institute for Congressional Studies (summer).

Azores, Tania. 1986–1987. Educational Attainment and Upward Mobility: Prospects for Filipino Americans. *Amerasia Journal* 13, no. 1:39–52.

Barringer, Herbert, Robert W. Gardner, and Michael J. Levin, eds. 1995. *Asians and Pacific Islanders in the United States.* New York: Russell Sage Publications. Foundation, for the National Committee for Research on the 1980 Census.

Beach, W. G. 1932. *Oriental Crime in California.* Palo Alto, CA: Stanford University Press.

Bonacich, Edna. 1988. The Social Costs of Immigrant Entrepreneurship. *Amerasia Journal* 14, no. 1:119–28.

———. 1989. The Role of the Petite Bourgeoisie within Capitalism: A Response to Pyong Gap Min. *Amerasia* 15 (2):195–203.

———, and John Modell, 1980. *The Economic Basis of Ethnic Solidarity: Small Business in the Japanese American Community.* Berkeley: University of California Press.

Boswell, Terry E. 1986. A Split Labor Market Analysis of Discrimination Against Chinese Immigrants, 1850–1882. *American Sociological Review* 51 (3):352–71.

Bourdieu, Pierre. 1977. Cultural Reproduction and Social Reproduction. In *Power and Ideology in Education.* Eds. Jerome Karabel and A. H. Halsey. New York: Oxford University Press.

Bowen, William G., and Derek Bok. 1998. *The Shape of the River: Long-term Consequences of Considering Race in College and University Admissions.* Princeton, NJ: Princeton University Press.

Brown, Shirley V. 1988. *Increasing Minority Faculty: An Elusive Goal.* Princeton, NJ: Educational Testing Service.

Burris, Beverly H. 1993. *Technocracy at Work.* Albany: State University of New York Press.

Cabezas, Amado Y., and Gary Kawaguchi. 1988. Empirical Evidence for Continuing Asian American Income Inequality: The Human Capital Model and Labor Market Segmentation. In *Reflections on Shattered Windows: Promises and Prospects for Asian American Studies.* Eds. Gary Y. Okihiro, Shirley Hune, Arthur A. Hansen, and John M. Liu. Pullman: Washington State University Press.

———. 1990. Industrial Sectorization in California in 1980: The Continuing Significance of Race/Ethnicity, Gender, and Nativity," In *Income and Status Differences Between White and Minority Americans: A Persistent Inequality.* Ed. Sucheng Chan. Lewiston, NY: Edwin Mellen Press. pp. 57–99.

Cabezas, Amado, Larry Shinagawa, and Gary Kawaguchi. 1987. New Inquiries into the Socioeconomic Status of Pilipino Americans in California in 1980," *Amerasia Journal* 13:1–21, 1986–87.

Cabezas, Amado, Tse Ming Tam, Brenda M. Lowe, Anna Wong, and Kathy Owyang Turner. 1989. Empirical Study of Barriers to Upward Mobility of Asian Americans in the San Francisco Bay Area. In *Frontiers of Asian American Studies: Writing, Research, and Commentary.* Eds. Gail M. Nomura, Russell Endo, Stephen H. Sumida, and Russell C. Leong Pullman: Washington State University Press.

Cabezas, Amado Y., and Harold T. Yee. 1977. *Discriminatory Employment of Asian Americans: Private Industry in the San Francisco—Oakland SMSA.* San Francisco: Asian American Service Institute for Assistance to Neighborhoods.

Caplan, Nathan. 1985. Study Shows Boat Refugees' Children Achieve Academic Success. *Refugee Reports* 6, no. 10:1–6.

———, Marcella H. Choy, and John K. Whitmore. 1992. Indochinese Refugee Families and Academic Achievement. *Scientific American* 266, no. 2:36–42.

———. 1994. *Children of the Boat People: A Study of Educational Success.* Ann Arbor: University of Michigan Press.

Caplan, Nathan, John K. Whitmore, and Marcella H. Choy. 1990. *The Boat People and Achievement in America: A Study of Family Life, Hard Work, and Cultural Values,* 1989. *American Journal of Sociology* 96 (1):251–52.

Carnevale, Anthony Patrick, and Susan Carol Stone. 1995. *The American Mosaic: An In-depth Report on the Future of Diversity at Work.* New York: McGraw-Hill.

Carnoy, Martin. 1995. *Faded Dreams: The Politics and Economics of Race in America.* New York: Cambridge University Press.

Carter, Deborah J., and Reginald Wilson. 1997. *Minorities in Higher Education Fifteenth Annual Status Report, 1996–1997.* Washington, DC: American Council on Education, April.

Catalyst, *Women of Color in Corporate Management: Opportunities and Barriers,* Executive Summary (New York: Catalyst), 1999

Caudill, William, and George Devos. 1956. Achievement, Culture, and Personality: The Case of Japanese Americans. *American Anthropologist* 58:1,102–126.

Chamallas, Martha. 1994. Jean Jew's Case: Resisting Sexual Harassment in the Academy. *Law and Feminism* 6, no. 1:71–90.

Chan, Sucheng. 1982. Training T.A.s to Deal with Asian Immigrant Undergraduates with Poor Verbal Skills. Application for an Instructional Improvement Grant, Council for Educational Development.

———. 1986. *This Bittersweet Soil.* Berkeley: University of California Press.

———. 1989. Beyond Affirmative Action: Empowering Asian American Faculty. *Change* 21, no. 6:48–51.

———. 1991a. *Asian Americans: An Interpretive History.* Boston: Twayne Publishers.

———. 1991b. Current Socioeconomic Status, Politics, Education, and Culture. In *Asian Americans: An Interpretive History.* Boston: Twayne Publishers.

———. 1991c. The Exclusion of Chinese Women, 1870–1943. In *Entry Denied: Exclusion and the Chinese Community in America, 1882–1943.* Ed. Sucheng Chan. Philadelphia: Temple University Press.

Chan, Sucheng, n.d. "They Shall Write! Anthropological Observations on Teaching Verbal Skills to Asian-ancestry Students," Unpublished paper, 29 pps.

Chen, Joanne. 1993. The Asian American Dream? *A. Magazine* 2, no. 3.

Chen, Edward. 1994. Speak-English-Only Rules and the Demise of Workplace Pluralism. *Asian Law Journal* 1, no. 2:155–188.

Cheng Hirata, Lucie. 1980, October. Social Mobility of Asian Women in America: A Critical Review. In *Conference on the Educational and Occupational Needs of Asian-Pacific-American Women.* Ed. U.S. Department of Education. Washington, DC: U.S. Government Printing Office.

Cherian, Joy. 1993. Asian Americans: An Emerging Force to Break the Glass Ceiling. Remarks at the 1993 Annual Program of the Chinese-American Librarians Association, New Orleans, Louisiana, 28 June.

Chin, Ronald. 1989. Asian Americans in Corporate Organizations. In *A Look beyond the Model Minority Image: Critical Issues in Asian America.* Ed. Grace Yun. New York: Minority Rights Group.

Chinese for Affirmative Action. 1986. *The Broken Ladder: Asian Americans in City Government.* San Francisco: Chinese for Affirmative Action.

———. 1989. *The Broken Ladder '89: Asian Americans in City Government.* San Francisco: Chinese for Affirmative Action.

———. 1992. *The Broken Ladder '92: Asian Americans in City Government.* San Francisco: Chinese for Affirmative Action.

———. 1994. *Resource Guide for the Emerging and Established Employee Group.* San Francisco: Chinese for Affirmative Action.

———. 1995. *Asian American Civil Rights Symposium: Summary Report of Proceedings.* San Francisco: Chinese for Affirmative Action.

Chiu, Ping. 1963. *Chinese Labor in California, 1850–1880: An Economic Study.* Madison: State Historical Society of Wisconsin.

Cho, Sumi K. 1992. *The Struggle for Asian American Civil Rights: Race, Gender, and the Construction of Power in Academia.* Ph.D. diss., University of California, Berkeley.

————. 1997. Converging Stereotypes in Racialized Sexual Harassment: Where the Model Minority Meets Suzie Wong. In *Critical Race Feminism: A Reader.* Ed. Adrien Katherine Wing. New York: New York University Press.

Chow, Esther Ngan-Ling. 1994. Asian American Women at Work. In *Women of Color in U.S. Society.* Eds. Maxine Zinn and Bonnie Dill. Philadelphia: Temple University Press.

Chung, Joseph S. 1979. Small Ethnic Business as a Form of Disguised Unemployment and Cheap Laboring. In *Civil Rights Issues of Asian and Pacific Americans: Myths and Realities.* Ed. U.S. Commission on Civil Rights. Washington, DC: U.S. Government Printing Office.

Colcough, Glenna, and Charles M. Tolbert II. 1992. *Work in the Fast Lane: Flexibility, Divisions of Labor, and Inequality in High-tech Industries.* New York: State University of New York Press.

Cowan, Neil M., and Ruth Schwartz Cowan. 1989. *Our Parents' Lives: The Americanization of Eastern European Jews.* New York: Basic Books.

Cox, Taylor, Jr. 1994. *Cultural Diversity in Organizations: Theory, Research & Practice.* San Francisco: Berrett-Koehler Publishers, Inc.

Cox, Taylor H., Jr., and Joycelyn A. Finley. 1995. An Analysis of Work Specialization and Organization Level as Dimensions of Workforce Diversity. In *Diversity in Organizations: New Perspectives for a Changing Workplace.* Eds. Martin Chemers, Stuart Oskamp, and Mark A. Costanzo. Thousand Oaks, CA: Sage Publications, Inc.

Cregler, L. L., et al. (1994). Careers in Academic Medicine and Clinical Practice for Minorities: Opportunities and Barriers. *Journal of the Association for Academic Minority Physicians* 5, no. 2:68–73.

Cruse, Harold. 1987. *Plural But Equal.* New York: William Morrow.

Domhoff, William. 1998. *Who Rules America? Power and Politics in the Year 2000.* Mountain View, CA: Mayfield Publishing Company.

Duleep, Harriet Orcutt, and Seth Sanders. 1992. Discrimination at the Top: American-born Asian and White Men. *Industrial Relations* 31, no. 3:416–32.

Duster, Troy. 1976. The Structure of Privilege and Its Universe of Discourse. *The American Sociologist* 11, no. 2:73–78.

Duster, Troy, David Minkus, and Colin Samson. 1988. Bar Association of San Francisco Minority Employment Survey: Final Report. Department of Sociology, University of California, Berkeley, 18 April.

EEOC Factsheet, January 1992 FS/E–1. Facts about National Origin Discrimination.

Escueta, Eugenia, and Eileen O'Brien. 1991. Asian Americans in Higher Education: Trends and Issues. *Research Briefs*, 2, no. 4:1–11.

Espiritu, Yen Le. 1997. Stretching Gender, Family, and Community Boundaries, 1840s–1930s. In *Asian American Women and Men.* Thousand Oaks, CA: Sage Publications.

Excerpts From the Meeting of the Board of Regents of the University of California Presentation By and Discussion with Professor Franchot and Discussion with Professor Widaman, 14 May 1998.

Ezorsky, Gertrude. 1991. *Racism and Justice: The Case for Affirmative Action.* Ithaca, New York: Cornell University Press.

Federal Glass Ceiling Commission. 1995. *Good for Business: Making Full Use of the Nation's Human Capital.* Washington, DC: U.S. Government Printing Office.

Fernandez, John P., with Mary Barr. 1993. *The Diversity Advantage: How American Business Can Out-perform Japanese and European Companies in the Global Marketplace.* New York: Lexington Books.

Fischer, Claude S., Michael Hout, Martin Sanchez Jankowski, Samuel R. Lucas, Ann Swidler, and Kim Voss. 1996. *Inequality by Design: Cracking the Bell Curve Myth.* Princeton, New Jersey: Princeton University Press.

Fong, Pauline, and Amado Cabezas. 1980. Economic and Employment Status of Asian-Pacific Women. In *Conference on the Educational and Occupational Needs of Asian-Pacific-American Women August 24 and 25, 1976.* Washington, DC: U.S. Department of Education, Office of Educational Research and Improvement, National Institute of Education.

Freeman, Richard B. 1978. Discrimination in the Academic Marketplace. In *Essays and Data on American Ethnic Groups.* Ed. Thomas Sowell. Washington, DC: The Urban Institute.

Friday, Chris. 1994a. Asian American Labor and Historical Interpretation. *Labor History* 35, no. 4:524–26.

———. 1994b. *Organizing Asian American Labor: the Pacific Coast Canned-salmon Industry, 1870–1942.* Philadelphia: Temple University Press.

Fullerton, Howard N., Jr. 1989. New Labor Force Projections, Spanning 1988 to 2000. *Monthly Labor Review* (November):3–12.

Fullilove, Robert E., and Philip Uri Treisman. 1990. Mathematics Achievement Among African American Undergraduates at the University of California, Berkeley: An Evaluation of the M Mathematics Workshop Program. *Journal of Negro Education* 59, no. 3:463–78.

Gall, Susan B., and Timothy L. Gall. 1993. *Statistical Record of Asian Americans.* Detroit: Gale Research Inc.

Gaquin, Deidre A., and Mark S. Littman, eds. 1998. *1998 County and City Extra: Annual Metro, City, and County Data Book.* Lanham, MD: Bernan Press.

Gardner, Robert W., Bryant Robey, and Peter C. Smith. 1985. Asian Americans: Growth, Change, and Diversity, *Population Bulletin* 40, no. 4:1–44.

Glazer, Nathan, and Daniel Patrick Moynihan. 1963. *Beyond the Melting Pot: The Negroes, Puerto Ricans, Jews, Italians, and Irish of New York City.* Cambridge, MA: M.I.T. Press.

Golder, Fred H., and R. R. Ritti. 1967. Professionalization as Career Immobility. *American Journal of Sociology* 72:489–502.

Gordon, Avery. 1995. The Work of Corporate Culture Diversity Management. *Social Text* 44, 13, no. 3:3–30.

Gordon, Milton M. 1964. *Assimilation in American Life: The Role of Race, Religion, and National Origins.* New York: Oxford University Press.

Greenbaum, Marcia L. 1995. Arbitrator, "Dr. Terence H. Williams, M.B.Ch.B., Ph.D., D.Sc. and University of Iowa College of Medicine: Arbitration Opinion & Award, Terence H. Williams Discrimination Complaint and Other Claims." Award Date: Oct. 10, 1995, 162 pps.

Greenbaum, Marcia L. 1997. Arbitrator, "Dr. Terence H. Williams, M.B.Ch.B., Ph.D., D.Sc. and University of Iowa College of Medicine: Arbitration Remedy Award." Award Date: December 19, 1997, 6 pps.

Gwilliam, Ivary, Chiosso, Cavalli & Brewer, Plaintiff's Factual Summary to the Honorable Robert Bostick, *Wang V. Regents of the University of California et al.*, 14 November 1995.

Herrnstein, Richard J., and Charles Murray. 1994. *The Bell Curve: Intelligence and Class Structure in American Life*. New York: Free Press.

Hing, Bill Ong. 1993a. Making and Remaking Asian America: Immigration Policy. In *The State of Asian Pacific America: Policy Issues to the Year 2020*. Los Angeles: LEAP Asian Pacific American Public Policy Institute and UCLA Asian American Studies Center.

———. 1993b. *Making and Remaking Asian America through Immigration Policy*. Stanford, CA: Stanford University Press.

———. 1993c. Social Forces Unleashed after 1969, in *Making and Remaking Asian America through Immigration Policy* 1850–1990 Stanford, CA: Stanford University Press.

Hirschman, Charles, and Morrison Wong. 1981. Trends in Socioeconomic Achievement among Immigrant and Native-born Asian Americans, 1960–1976. *The Sociological Quarterly* 22:495–513.

———. 1984. Socioeconomic Gains of Asian Americans, Blacks, and Hispanics: 1960–1976. *American Journal of Sociology* 90:584–607.

———. 1986. The Extraordinary Educational Achievement of Asian-Americans: A Search for Historical Evidence and Explanations. *Social Forces* 65, no. 1:1–27.

Hossfeld, Karen J. 1990. "Their Logic Against them": Contradictions in Sex, Race, and Class in Silicon Valley. In *Women Workers and Global Restructuring*. Ed. Kathryn Ward. Philadelphia: Temple University Press.

———. 1994a. Hiring Immigrant Women: Silicon Valley's "Simple Formula." In *Women of Color in American Society*. Eds. D. Stanley Zinn and Maxine Eitzen. Philadelphia: Temple University Press.

———. 1994b. *Small, Foreign and Female: Profiles of Gender, Race and Nationality in Silicon Valley*. Berkeley: University of California Press.

Hsia, Jayjia. 1988. *Asian Americans in Higher Education and at Work*. Hillsdale, NJ: Lawrence Erlbaum Associates, Inc.

Hsia, Jayjia, and Marsha Hirano-Nakanishi. 1995. The Demographics of Diversity: Asian Americans and Higher Education. In *The Asian American Educational Experience*. Eds. Don T. Nakanishi and Tina Yamano Nishida. New York: Routledge.

Hsu, Ruth. 1966. Will the Model Minority Please Identify Itself? American Ethnic Identity and Its Discontents. *Diaspora* 5, no. 1:37–64.

Johnston, William B. 1987. *Workforce 2000: Work and Workers for the Twenty-first Century*. Indianapolis, IN: Hudson Institute.

Hune, Shirley. 1998. *Asian Pacific American Women in Higher Education: Clearing Visibility & Voice*. Washington, DC: Association of American Colleges and Universities.

Hune, Shirley, and Kenyon S. Chan. 1997. SPECIAL FOCUS: Asian Pacific American Demographic and Educational Trends. In *Minorities in Higher Education, Fifteenth Annual*

Status Report, 1996–1997. Eds. Deborah J. Carter and Reginald Wilson. Washington, DC: American Council on Education.

Huynh, Craig Trinh-Phat. 1996. Vietnamese-Owned Manicure Businesses in Los Angeles. In *Reforming the Immigration Debate: A Public Policy Report.* Eds. Bill Ong Hing and Ronald Lee. Los Angeles: LEAP Asian Pacific American Public Policy Institute.

Igasaki, Paul M. 1996. Discrimination in the Workplace: Asian Americans and the Debate over Affirmative Action. *Asian American Policy Review,* VI:15–24.

Jaco, Daniel E., and George L. Wilber. 1975. Asian Americans in the Labor Market. *Monthly Labor Review* (July):33–38.

Jew, Charles C. and Stuart A. Brody. 1967. Mental Illness among the Chinese: I. Hospitalization Rates over the Past Century, *Comprehensive Psychiatry* 9, no. 2:129–34.

Jew, Jean. Telephone interview by author. October, 22, November 1998.

Jiobu, Robert M. 1988. Ethnic Hegemony and the Japanese of California. *American Sociological Review* 53 (3):353–67.

Kamphoefner, Walter D. 1996. German Americans: Paradoxes of a Model Minority. In *Origins and Destinies: Immigration, Race, and Ethnicity in America.* Eds. Silvia Pedraza and Rubén Rumbaut. Belmont, CA: Wadsworth.

Kanter, Rosabeth Moss. 1983. *The Change Masters: Innovation & Entrepreneurship in the American Corporation.* New York: Touchstone.

Kawaguchi, Gary, and Amado Cabezas. 1989. *Errors of Commission: The U.S. Commission on Civil Rights Report on the Economic Status of Americans of Asian Descent.* Paper Presented at the Sixth National Conference of the Association of Asian American Studies, Hunter College, CUNY, June.

Kim, Bok Lim. 1973. Asian Americans: No Model Minority. *Social Work* 18:44–53.

Kim, Illsoo. 1981. *New Urban Immigrants: The Korean Community in New York.* Princeton, NJ: Princeton University Press.

Kim, Kwang Chung, and Won Moo Hurh. 1983. Korean Americans and the 'Success' Image: A Critique. *Amerasia* 10 (2): 3–21.

Kim, Pan S. 1994. A Status Report on Asian Americans in Government. *Asian American Policy Review* 4:93–104.

Kim, Pan Suk, and Gregory B. Lewis. 1994. Asian Americans in the Public Service: Success, Diversity, and Discrimination. *Public Administration Review* 54, no. 3:285–90.

Kim, Chung, and Won Moo Hurh. 1983. Korean Americans and the Success Image: A Critique. *Amerasia Journal* 10, no. 2:3–21.

Kingston, Paul William, and Lionel S. Lewis, eds. 1990. *The High-status Track: Studies of Elite Schools and Stratification.* Albany, NY: State University of New York Press Press.

Kitano, Harry. 1969. *Japanese Americans: The Evolution of A Subculture.* Englewood Cliffs, NJ: Prentice-Hall, Inc.

Kitano, Harry, and Stanley Sue. 1973. The Model Minorities. *The Journal of Social Issues* 29:1–9.

Knoll, Tricia. 1982. *Becoming Americans: Asian Sojourners, Immigrants, and Refugees in the Western United States.* Portland, OR: Coast to Coast Books.

Koyama, Janice, et al. 1989. *Asian Americans at Berkeley.* A Report to the Chancellor, May.

Kunda, Gideon. 1995. *Engineering Culture: Control and Commitment in a High-tech Corporation.* Philadelphia: Temple University Press.

Kwang, Chung Kim, and Won Moo Hurh. 1994. Korean Americans and the Model Minority Myth, 1970s–Present. In *Peoples of Color in the American West.* Eds. Sucheng Chan, Douglas Henry Daniels, Mario T. Garcia, and Terry P. Wilson. Lexington, MA: DC Heath and Company.

Kwoh, Beulah Ong. 1947. Occupational Status of the American-born Chinese College Graduates, Master's diss., University of Chicago.

Lan, Dean. 1988. *Informational Hearing on Asian, Filipino, Pacific Islander AFPI Demographics and Employment.* Official Report to the State Personnel Board, 7 September. Sacramento: State Printing Office.

Lau, Yvonne May. 1988. Alternative Career Strategies among Asian American Professionals: The Second Rice Bowl. Ph. D. diss., Northwestern University.

Leap, Terry L. 1993. *Tenure, Discrimination, and the Courts.* Ithaca, NY: Cornell University Press.

Lee, Gen Leigh. 1996. Cambodian-Owned Donut Shops. In *Reframing the Immigration Debate: A Public Policy Report.* Eds. Bill Ong Hing and Ronald Lee. Los Angeles: LEAP Asian Pacific American Public Policy Institute.

Lee, Stacy. 1996. *Unraveling the Model Minority Stereotype: Listening to Asian American Youth.* New York: Teachers' College Press.

Lieberson, Stanley. 1980. *A Piece of the Pie: Blacks and White Immigrants Since 1880.* Berkeley: University of California Press.

Leong, Anna. 1996. Multiethnic Literature in the Asian American Studies Composition Classroom. In *Affirmative Action and Discrimination: Asian and Pacific Americans in Higher Education.* Proceedings of the 9th Annual Conference of APAHE, Radisson/Miyako Hotel, San Francisco, 8–10 March.

Leong, Anna. Telephone interview by author, 30 October 1998.

Lesser, Jeff. 1985–1986. Always "Outsiders": Asians, Naturalization, and the Supreme Court. *Amerasia Journal* 1:83–100.

Levine, David O. 1986. *The American College and the Culture of Aspiration, 1915–1940.* Ithaca, NY: Cornell University Press.

Levine, Larry. 1996. *The Opening of the American Mind.* Boston: Beacon Press.

Lewis Gregory B., and David Nice. 1994. Race, Sex, and Occupational Segregation in State and Local Governments. *American Review of Public Administration* 24, no. 4:393–410.

Li, Peter. 1977. Ethnic Businesses among Chinese in the United States. *Journal of Ethnic Studies* 4:35–41.

Li, Wen Lang. 1987. Two Generations of Chinese Americans: Differentials in Education and Status Attainment Process. *Plural Societies* 17, no. 1:95–107.

Light, Ivan. 1987. Ethnic Enterprise in America: Japanese, Chinese, and Blacks. In *From Different Shores: Perspectives on Race and Ethnicity in America.* Ed. Ron Takaki. New York: Oxford University Press.

———. and Edna Bonacich. 1988. *Immigrant Entrepreneurs: Koreans in Los Angeles, 1965–1982.*Berkeley : University of California Press, 1988

Liu, John M. 1984. Race, Ethnicity, and the Sugar Plantation System: Asian Labor in Hawaii, 1850 to 1900. In *Labor Immigration Under Capitalism: Asian Workers in the United States.* Eds. Lucie Cheng and Edna Bonacich. Berkeley: University of California.

———. 1994. Pacific Rim Development and the Duality of Post-1965 Asian Immigration to the United States. In *The New Asian Immigration in Los Angeles and Global Restructuring.* Eds. Paul Ong, Edna Bonacich, and Lucie Cheng. Philadelphia: Temple University Press.

Loewen, James W. 1988. *The Mississippi Chinese: Between Black and White.* Prospect Heights, IL: Waveland Press.

Lopez, Ian F. Haney. 1996. *White by Law: The Legal Construction of Race.* New York: New York University Press.

Lott, Juanita T. 1991. Policy Implications of Population Changes in the Asian American Community. *Asian American Policy Review* II (spring):57–64.

Lydon, Sandy. 1985. *Chinese Gold: The Chinese in the Monterey Bay Region.* Capitola, CA: Capitola Book Company.

Lyman, Stanford Morris. 1966. The Race Relations Cycle of Robert E. Park. *Pacific Sociological Review* 2 (January):16–22.

———. 1973. Review of *The Story of the Chinese in America*, by Betty Lee Sung. *Journal of Ethnic Studies* 1, no. 1:71–72.

Mannheim, Karl. 1936. *Ideology and Utopia.* New York: Harcourt, Brace, & World, Inc.

Mark, Shirley. 1990. Asian American Engineers in the Massachusetts High Technology Industry: Are Glass Ceilings a Reality? Master's thesis, Massachusetts Institute of Technology.

Massey, Douglas S., and Nancy A. Denton. 1993. The Perpetuation of the Underclass. In *American Apartheid: Segregation and the Making of the Underclass.* Cambridge, MA: Harvard University Press.

Matsuda, Mari J. 1991. Voices of America: Accent, Antidiscrimination Law, and a Jurisprudence for the Last Reconstruction. *Yale Law Journal* 100:1329–407.

Mazumdar, Sucheta. 1984. Punjabi Agricultural Workers in California, 1905–1945. In *Labor Immigration Under Capitalism: Asian Workers in the United States.* Eds. Lucie Cheng and Edna Bonacich. Berkeley: University of California Press.

McClain, Charles J. 1994. *In Search of Equality: The Chinese Struggle Against Discrimination in Nineteenth-century America.* Berkeley: University of California Press.

———. 1995. Tortuous Path, Elusive Goal: The Asian Quest for American Citizenship. *Asian Law Journal* 2, no. 1:33–60.

McClain, Charles, and Laurene Wu McClain. 1991. The Chinese Contribution to the Development of American Law. In *Entry Denied: Exclusion and the Chinese Community in America, 1882–1943.* Ed. Sucheng Chan. Philadelphia: Temple University Press.

McCurdy, Howard E. 1993. *Inside NASA: High Technology and Organizational Change in the U.S. Space Program.* Baltimore: Johns Hopkins University Press.

McLeod, Beverly Marie. 1986. *The Social Psychological Adaptation of Immigrant Chinese Professionals in California's Silicon Valley.* Ph.D. diss., University of California at Santa Cruz.

Mears, Eliot Grinnell. 1928. *Resident Orientals on the American Pacific Coast: Their Legal and Economic Status*. Chicago: University of Chicago Press.

Mei, June. 1984. Socioeconomic Origins of Emigration: Guangdong to California, 1850 to 1882. In *Labor Immigration under Capitalism: Asian Workers in the United States*. Eds. Lucie Cheng and Edna Bonacich. Berkeley: University of California Press.

Miller, Susan Katz. 1992. Asian-Americans Bump against Glass Ceilings. *Science* 258, no 5085:1224–28.

Mills, C. Wright. 1959. *The Sociological Imagination*. New York: Oxford University Press.

———. 1986–1987. Filipino and Korean Immigrants in Small Business: A Comparative Analysis. *Amerasia Journal* 13, no. 1:53–71.

———. 1988. *Ethnic Business Enterprise: Korean Small Business in Atlanta*, New York :Center for Migration Studies.

———. 1989. The Social Costs of Immigrant Entrepreneurship: A Response to Edna Bonacich, *Amerasia* 15 (2) 187–194.

———. 1996a. The Entrepreneurial Adaptation of Korean Immigrants. In *Origins and Destinies: Immigration, Race, and Ethnicity in America*. Eds. Silvia Pedraza and Ruben Rumbaut. Belmont, CA: Wadsworth.

———. 1996b. *Caught in the Middle: Korean Communities in New York and Los Angeles: Korean Merchants in America's Multiethnic Cities*. Berkeley: University of California Press.

Min, Pyong Gap, and Charles Jaret. 1985. Ethnic Business Success: The Case of Korean Small Business in Atlanta. *Sociology and Social Research* 69, no. 3:412–35.

Minami, Dale. 1988. Office of the Attorney General, Asian and Pacific Islander Advisory Committee: Final Report, December.

———. 1990. Guerrilla War at UCLA: Political and Legal Dimensions of the Tenure Battle. *Amerasia Journal* 16, no. 1:81–107.

Montero, Darrel. 1983. *Vietnamese Americans: Patterns of Resettlement and Socioeconomic Adaptation in the U.S., 1979, Social Forces* 62 (1): 285–87, September.

Morgan, David L., ed. 1993. *Successful Focus Groups: Advancing the State of the Art*. Newbury Park, CA: Sage Publications, Inc.

Moynihan, Daniel Patrick. 1965. *The Negro Family: The Case for National Action*. Washington, DC: U.S. Department of Labor.

Nakanishi, Don. 1993a. Asian Pacific Americans in Higher Education: Faculty and Administrative Representation and Tenure. In *Building A Diverse Faculty*. Eds. Joanne Gainen and Robert Boice. San Francisco: Jossey-Bass Publishers.

———. 1993b. Asian Pacific Americans in Higher Education: Faculty and Administrators. *New Directions for Teaching and Learning* 53:51–59.

Nakano Glenn, Evelyn. 1984. The Dialectics of Wage Work: Japanese-American Women and Domestic Service, 1905–1940. In *Labor Immigration under Capitalism: Asian Workers in the United States*. Eds. Lucie Cheng and Edna Bonacich. Berkeley: University of California Press.

National Science Foundation. 1994. Characteristics of Doctoral Scientists and Engineers in the United States: 1991. Arlington, VA: National Science Foundation.

Nee, Victor G., and Brett de Bary Nee. 1974. *Longtime Californ'*. Boston: Houghton Mifflin Co.

Nee, Victor, and Jimmy Sanders. 1985. The Road to Parity: Determinants of the Socioeconomic Achievement of Asian Americans. *Ethnic and Racial Studies* 8:75–93.

New York Times, *The Downsizing of America* (New York: Times Books), 1996

Nguyen, Beatrice Bich-Dao. 1994. Accent Discrimination and the Test of Spoken English: A Call for an Objective Assessment of the Comprehensibility of Nonnative Speakers. *Asian Law Journal* 1, no. 1:117–53.

Northrup, Herbert R., and Margot E. Malin. 1985. *Personnel Policies for Engineers and Scientists: An Analysis of Major Corporate Practice, Manpower and Human Resources Studies*, no. 11, Industrial Research Unit, the Wharton School, University of Pennsylvania. Philadelphia: Trustees of the University of Pennsylvania.

Office of Student Research. 1998a. Berkeley's 1997 New Undergraduates: A Statistical Profile Report: OSR98–003, July. Berkeley: Office of Student Research.

———. 1998b. Undergraduate Statistics for the University of California, Berkeley, Fall 1997, Report: OSR97–004, 9 January. Berkeley: Office of Student Research.

O'Hare, William P., and Judy C. Felt. 1991. *Asian Americans: America's Fastest Growing Minority Group*. Washington, DC: Population Reference Bureau, no. 19 in A Series of Occasional Papers, Population Trends and Public Policy (February):1–16.

Oliver, J. Eric, Fredric C. Gey, Jon Stiles, and Henry Brady. 1995. *Pacific Rim Asian Demographic Data Book*. University of California: Office of the President, Research Report.

Ong, Paul. 1993. *Beyond Asian Americans and Poverty: Community Economic Development Policies and Strategies*. Los Angeles: LEAP Asian Pacific American Policy Institute.

Ong, Paul, and Tania Azores. 1994. Asian Immigrants in Los Angeles: Diversity and Divisions. In *The New Asian Immigration in Los Angeles and Global Restructuring*. Eds. Paul Ong, Edna Bonacich, and Lucie Cheng. Philadelphia: Temple University Press.

Ong, Paul, and Evelyn Blumenberg. 1994. Scientists and Engineers. In *The State of Asian Pacific America: Economic Diversity, Issues and Policies*. Ed. Paul Ong. Los Angeles: LEAP Asian Pacific American Policy Institute and UCLA Asian American Studies Center.

Ong, Paul, and Suzanne J. Hee. 1993a. Work Issues Facing Asian Pacific Americans. In *Asian Pacific America: Policy Issues to the Year 2020, Los Angeles: Leadership Education for Asian Pacifics*. Los Angeles: LEAP Asian Pacific American Policy Institute and UCLA Asian American Studies Center.

———. 1993b. Work Issues Facing Asian Pacific Americans: Labor Policy. In *The State of Asian Pacific America: Policy Issues to the Year 2020*. Los Angeles: LEAP Asian Pacific American Policy Institute and UCLA Asian American Studies Center.

———. 1994. Economic Diversity. In *The State of Asian Pacific America: Economic Diversity, Issues and Policies*. Ed. Paul Ong. Los Angeles: LEAP Asian Pacific American Policy Institute and UCLA Asian American Studies Center.

Ong, Paul, and John M. Liu. 1994. U.S. Immigration Policies and Asian Migration. In *The New Asian Immigration in Los Angeles and Global Restructuring*. Eds. Paul Ong, Edna Bonacich, and Lucie Cheng. Philadelphia: Temple University Press.

Ong, Paul, Lucie Cheng, and Leslie Evans. 1992. Migration of Highly Educated Asians and Global Dynamics. *Asian and Pacific Migration Journal* 1, nos. 3–4:543–67.

Ong, Paul, Kye Young Park, and Yasmin Tong. 1994. Korean-Black Conflict. In *The New Asian Immigration in Los Angeles and Global Restructuring*. Eds. Paul Ong, Edna Bonacich, and Lucie Cheng. Philadelphia: Temple University Press.

Oren, Dan A. 1985. *Joining the Club: A History of Jews at Yale*. New Haven: Yale University Press.

Organization of Chinese Americans. 1992. *Shattering the Glass Ceiling: Entering the Pipeline of Progress*. Pittsburgh, PA: Tiffany Publishing.

Osajima, Keith. 1988. Asian Americans as the Model Minority: An Analysis of the Popular Press Image in the 1960s and 1980s. In *Reflections on Shattered Windows*. Eds. Gary Y. Okihiro, Shirley Hune, Arthur A. Hansen, and John M. Liu. Pullman: Washington State University Press.

Ouchi, William G. 1981. *Theory Z: How American Business Can Meet the Japanese Challenge*. New York: Avon Books.

Park, Edward Jang-Woo. 1992. *Asian Americans in Silicon Valley: Race and Ethnicity in the Postindustrial Economy*. Ph.D. diss., University of California at Berkeley.

———. 1996. Asian American Entrepreneurs in the High Technology Industry in Silicon Valley. In *Reframing the Immigration Debate: A Public Policy Report*. Eds. Bill Ong Hing and Ronald Lee. Los Angeles: LEAP Asian Pacific American Public Policy Institute.

Park, Robert E. 1950. *Race and Culture*. Glencoe, IL: Free Press.

Pascale, Richard Tanner. 1981. *The Art of Japanese Management: Applications for American Executives*. New York: Warner Books.

Peters, Thomas J., and Robert H. Waterman, Jr. 1982. *In Search of Excellence: Lessons from America's Best-run Companies*. New York: Warner Books.

Petersen, William. 1971. *Japanese Americans*. New York: Random House.

Portes, Alejandro, and Ruben G. Rumbaut. 1990. *Immigrant America: A Portrait*. Berkeley: University of California Press.

Portes, Alejandro, and Min Zhou. 1996. Self-Employment and the Earnings of Immigrants. *American Sociological Review*, 61:219–30.

Praeger, Jeffrey. 1982. Equal Opportunity and Affirmative Action: the Rise of New Social Understandings. *Research in Law, Deviance and Social Control* 4:191–218.

Quadagno, Jill. 1994. *The Color of Welfare: How Racism Undermined the War on Poverty*. New York: Oxford University Press.

Rawls, Rebecca L. 1991. Minorities in Science, Special Report, *C & EN*, 15 April, 20–35.

Reskin, Barbara F. 1998. *The Realities of Affirmative Action in Employment*. Washington, DC: American Sociological Association.

Ries, Paula, and Delores H. Thurgood. *Summary Report 1992: Doctorate Recipients from United States Universities*. Washington, DC: National Academy Press, 1993.

Roediger, David R. 1991. *The Wages of Whiteness: Race and the Making of the American Working Class*. London: Verso.

Rose, Eric. 1998. Black Ghetto Formation in Oakland, 1852–1965: Social Closure and African American Community Development. *Research in Community Sociology* 8:255–74.

Rose, Peter I. (1985). Asian Americans: From Pariahs to Paragons. In *Clamor at the Gates*. Ed. Nathan Glazer. San Francisco: Institute for Contemporary Studies.

Rosener, Judy. 1991. *Valuing Diversity in Leading-edge Organizations, Workforce America: Managing Employee Diversity As A Vital Resource.* Homewood, IL: Business One Irwin.

————. 1995. *America's Competitive Secret.* New York: Oxford University Press.

Sanborn, Kenneth O. 1977. Intercultural Marriage in Hawaii. In *Adjustment in Intercultural Marriage.* Eds. Wen-Shing Tseng, John F. McDermott, and Thomas W. Maretzki. Honolulu: University of Hawai'i Press, 1977

Sanders, Jimmy M., and Victor Nee. 1996. The Immigrant Self-Employment: The Family as Social Capital and the Value of Human Capital. *American Sociological Review,* 61:231–49.

Sands, Roberta G., L. Alayne Parson, and Josann Duane. 1992. Faculty-Faculty Mentoring and Discrimination: Perceptions among Asian, Asian American, and Pacific Island Faculty. *Equity and Excellence* 25, nos. 2–4:124–29.

Saxenian, Annalee. 1998. *Regional Advantage: Culture and Competition in Silicon Valley and Route 128.* Cambridge, MA and London: Harvard University Press.

Schlesinger, Arthur M., Jr. 1992. *The Disuniting of America: Reflections on a Multicultural Society.* New York: W.W. Norton and Company.

Schutz, Alfred. 1976. The Stranger. In *Collected Papers II: Studies in Social Theory.* Ed. Arvid Brodersen. The Hague: Martinus Mijhoff.

Schwarz, Leo W., ed. 1956. *Great Ages and Ideas of the Jewish People.* New York: Random House.

Sharma, Miriam. 1984. Labor Migration and Class Formation among the Filipinos in Hawaii, 1906–1946. In *Labor Immigration under Capitalism: Asian Workers in the United States.* Eds. Lucie Cheng and Edna Bonacich. Berkeley: University of California.

Shimabukuro, Milton. 1980. Chinese in California State Prisons, 1870–1890. In *The Chinese American Experience: Papers from the Second National Conference on Chinese American Studies.* Ed. Genny Lim. San Francisco: The Chinese Historical Society of America and the Chinese Culture Foundation of San Francisco.

Shinigawa, Larry Hajime, and Gin Yong Pang. 1996. Asian American Panethnicity and Intermarriage. *Amerasia Journal* 22, no. 2:127–152.

Sibley, Elbridge. 1953. Some Demographic Clues to Stratification. In *Class, Status and Power: A Reader in Social Stratification.* Eds. Reinhard Bendix and Seymour Martin Lipset. Glencoe, IL: Free Press.

Siu, Paul. 1953. *The Chinese Laundryman: A Study of Social Isolation.* New York: New York University Press, 1987.

Smith, Lillian. 1961. Two Men and A Bargain. In *Killers of the Dream.* New York: Norton.

Smith, William Carlson. 1937. Population Factors and Race Relations. In *Americans in Process: A Study of Our Citizens of Oriental Ancestry.* Ann Arbor, MI: Edwards Brothers, Inc.

Sowell, Thomas. 1976. Affirmative Action Reconsidered. *The Public Interest* 41 (winter): 47–65.

Spindler, George, and Louise Spindler. 1990. *The American Cultural Dialogue and Its Transmission.* London: Falmer Press.

State of California. 1997. *California Statistical Abstract.* Sacramento, CA: State Printing Office.

Steinberg, Stephen. 1982. *The Ethnic Myth: Race, Ethnicity, and Class in America.* Boston: Beacon Press.

———. 1995. *Turning back: The Retreat from Racial Justice in American Thought and Policy.* Boston: Beacon.

Stephan, Paula E., and Sharon G. Levin. 1992. *Striking the Mother Lode in Science.* Oxford University Press, 1992.

Strong, Edward K. 1934. *The Second-Generation Japanese Problem.* Palo Alto, CA: Stanford University Press.

Sue, Stanley, and Sumie Okazaki. 1990, August. Asian American Educational Achievements: A Phenomenon in Search of an Explanation. *American Psychologist* 45 8:913–20.

Suzuki, Bob H. 1977. Education and Socialization of Asian Americans: A Revisionist Analysis of the Model Minority Thesis. *Amerasia Journal* 4:23–51.

———. 1989. Asian Americans As the "Model Minority": Outdoing Whites? Or Media Hype? *Change* (November/December):13–19.

Swidler, Ann. 1986. Culture in Action: Symbols and Strategies. *American Sociological Review* 51 (April):273–86.

Synnott, Marcia Graham. 1979. *The Half-opened Door: Discrimination and Admissions at Harvard, Yale, and Princeton, 1900–1970.* Westport, CT: Greenwood Press.

Takagi, Dana Y. 1990. From Discrimination to Affirmative Action: Facts in the Asian American Admissions Controversy. *Social Problems* 37, no. 4:578–92.

———. 1992. *The Retreat from Race: Asian-American Admissions and Racial Politics.* New Brunswick, New Jersey: Rutgers University Press.

Takaki, Ronald. 1990a. *Iron Cages: Race and Culture in 19th Century America.* New York: Oxford University Press.

———. 1990b. *Strangers from a Different Shore: A History of Asian Americans.* New York: Penguin Books.

Takagi, Paul, and Tony Platt. 1978. Behind the Gilded Ghetto: An Analysis of Race, Class and Crime in Chinatown. *Crime and Social Justice* (spring–summer):2–25.

Tamayo, Bill. 1991. Broadening the "Asian Interests" in United States Immigration Policy. *Asian American Policy Review* II (spring):65–80.

Tan, Alexis. 1990. *Why Asian Americans Journalists Leave Journalism and Why they Stay.* New York: Asian American Journalists Association.

Tang, Joyce. 1993a. The Career Attainment of Caucasian and Asian Engineers. *Sociological Quarterly* 34, no. 3:467–96.

———. 1993b. Caucasians and Asians in Engineering: A Study of Occupational Mobility and Departure. In *Research in the Sociology of Organizations.*

———. 1993c. Whites, Asians, and Blacks in Science and Engineering: A Reconsideration of their Economic Prospects in *Research in Social Stratification and Mobility* Vol. 12 JAI Press Inc.

Tienda, Marta, and Ding-Tzann Lii. 1987. Minority Concentration and Earnings Inequality; Blacks, Hispanics, and Asians Compared. *American Journal of Sociology* 93, no.1:141–65.

Thomas, Roosevelt, Jr. 1996. *Redefining Diversity.* New York: Amacom.

Thornton, Russell. 1987. *American Indian Holocaust and Survival: A Population History Since 1492.* Norman: University of Oklahoma Press.

Nash, J. Madeline. Tigers in the Lab. 1994. *TIME Domestic* 144, no. 21, 21 November.

Triesman, Uri. 1992. Studying Students Studying Calculus: A Look at the Lives of Minority Mathematics Students in College. *The College Mathematics Journal* 23, no. 5: 362–72.

———. 1988. Part I: A Study of the Mathematics Performance of Black Students at the University of California, Berkeley. In *Conference Board of the Mathematical Sciences: Issues in Mathematics*. Eds. Naomi Fisher, Harvey Keynes, and Philip Wagreich. Mathematicians and Education Reform, Proceedings of the 6–8 July 1988 Workshop.

Trueba, Henry T., Li Rong Lilly Cheng, and Kenji Ima. 1993. *Myth or Reality: Adaptive Strategies of Asian Americans in California*. London: Falmer Press, 1993.

Tsuang, Grace. 1989. Assuring Equal Access of Asian Americans to Highly Selective Universities. *The Yale Law Journal* 98, no. 3:659–87.

Tung, Rosalie. Telephone interview by author, 19 February 1996.

———. Interview by author, Vancouver, British Columbia, Canada, 20 September 1998.

University of California. 1998. Office of the President News, Systemwide Overview of Fall 1998 Unduplicated Freshman Admits. Oakland, CA: University of California, Office of the President.

U.S. Bureau of the Census. 1988. *We, the Asian and Pacific Islander Americans*. Washington, DC: U. S. Government Printing Office.

———. 1992a. The Asian and Pacific Islander Population in the United States: March 1991 and 1990. *Current Population Reports*. Washington, DC: U.S. Government Printing Office.

———. 1992b. *1990 Census of Population: Supplementary Reports, Detailed Occupation and Other Characteristics from the EEO File for the United States*. Washington, DC: U.S. Bureau of the Census.

———. 1993. *We, the American Asians*. Washington, DC: U.S. Government Printing Office, Population Reference Bureau.

———. 1995a. The Nation's Asian and Pacific Islander Population—1994 *Statistical Brief*. Washington, DC: U. S. Government Printing Office.

———. 1995b. *1992 Census of Manufactures: Industry Series*. Washington, DC: U.S. Government Printing Office.

———. 1997. *Statistical Abstract of the United States* 117th Edition, Washington, DC: Government Printing Office.

———. 1998. Current Population Reports P20–507, *The Foreign–Born Population in the United States: March 1997 Update*. U.S. Government Printing Office: Washington, DC, March.

U.S. Commission on Civil Rights. 1977. *Last Hired, First Fired: Layoffs and Civil Rights*. Washington, DC: U.S. Government Printing Office.

———. 1978. *Social Indicators of Equality for Minorities and Women*. Washington, DC: U.S. Government Printing Office.

———. 1979. *Civil Rights Issues of Asian and Pacific Americans: Myths and Realities*. Washington, DC: U.S. Government Printing Office.

———. 1980. *The Tarnished Golden Door: Civil Rights Issues in Immigration*. Washington, DC: U. S. Government Printing Office.

———. 1992. *Civil Rights Issues Facing Asian Americans in the 1990s*. Washington, DC: U.S. Government Printing Office.

————. 1998. *Economic Status of Americans of Asian Descent: An Exploratory Investigation.* Washington, DC: U.S. Government Printing Office.

U.S. Department of Commerce. 1992. *Technical Documentation.* Equal Employment Opportunity (EEO) File. Washington, DC: U.S. Government Printing Office.

U.S. Department of Labor. 1991. *A Report on the Glass Ceiling Initiative.* Washington, DC: U.S. Government Printing Office.

————. 1992. *Job Mobility Paths of Recent Immigrants to the U.S.* (Division of Immigration and Policy Research, Bureau of International Labor Affairs, September). By Howard Wial.

U.S. General Accounting Office. 1990. *Asian Americans: A Status Report.* GAO/HRD–90–36FS. Washington, DC: U.S. Government Printing Office.

U.S. Immigration and Naturalization Service. 1997. *Statistical Yearbook of the Immigration and Naturalization Service, 1996.* U.S. Government Printing Office: Washington, DC.

U.S. Office of Personnel Management. 1993. *Qualifications Standards Handbook: for General Schedule Positions.* Washington, DC: Government Printing Office.

————. 1994. *Demographic Profile of the Federal Workforce.* Washington, DC: Government Printing Office.

————. 1998a. *Executive Core Qualifications.* Washington, DC: Government Printing Office.

————. 1998b. *Guide to Senior Executive Service Qualifications.* Washington, DC: Government Printing Office.

Useem, Michael, and Jerome Karabel. 1990. Pathways to Top Corporate Management. In *The High–Status Track: Studies of Elite Schools and Stratification.* Eds. Paul William Kingston and Lionel S. Lewis. Albany: State University of New York Press.

Valentine, Charles A. *Culture and Poverty: Critique and Counter-proposals.* Chicago: University of Chicago Press, 1968.

Varon, Barbara F. 1967. The Japanese Americans: Comparative Occupational Status, 1960 and 1950. *Demography* 4: 809–19.

Vo, Linda Trinh. 1996. Asian Immigrants, Asian Americans, and the Politics of Economic Mobilization in San Diego. *Amerasia Journal* 22, no. 2:89–108.

Waldinger, Roger, Howard Aldrich, Robin Ward, and associates. 1990. *Ethnic Entrepreneurs: Immigrant Business in Industrial Societies.* Newbury Park: Sage Publications, Inc.

Walker-Moffat, Wendy. 1995. *The Other Side of the Asian American Success Story.* San Francisco: Jossey-Bass.

Walters, Dan. 1986. *The New California: Facing the 21st Century.* Sacramento: California J Press.

Wang, L. Ling–Chi. 1988. Meritocracy and Diversity in Higher Education: Discrimination against Asian Americans in the Post-Bakke Era. *The Urban Review* 20, no. 3:1–21.

————. 1990. A Critique of Strangers from A Different Shore, *Amerasia Journal* 16, no. 2: 71–80.

————. n. d. The Politics of Assimilation and Repression: The Chinese in the United States, 1940–1970. Unpublished Manuscript on File at the University of California, Asian American Studies Library.

Wang, Marcy. Interview by author Berkeley, CA, 17 February 1996.

————. Telephone interview by author, 29 October 1998, 23 November 1998.

Washington Association for Asian and Pacific American Education. *Asian/Pacific American Men and Women Administrators Co-existing in Educational Leadership*. Tumwater, WA: Superintendent of Public Instruction, 1980

Wechsler, Harold Stuart. 1977. *The Qualified Student: A History of Selective College Admissions in America*. New York: John Wiley.

Wey, Nancy. 1980. Asian Americans in Academia. In *Political Participation of Asian Americans: Problems and Strategies*. Ed. Yung-Hwan Jo. Chicago: Pacific/Asian American Mental Health Research Center.

Wilson, William Julius. 1987. *Declining Significance of Race*. Chicago: University of Chicago Press.

————. 1997. *When Work Disappears: The World of the New Urban Poor*. NY: Vintage.

Wong, Eugene F. 1985. Asian American Middleman Minority Theory: The Framework of an American Myth. *Journal of Ethnic Studies* 13, no. 1:51–88.

Wong, Paul, and Richard Nagasawa. 1991. Asian American Scientists and Engineers: Is There a Glass Ceiling for Career Advancement? *Chinese American Forum* 6, no 3:3–6.

Woo, Deborah. 1985. The Socioeconomic Status of Asian American Women in the Labor Market: An Alternative View. *Sociological Perspectives* 28, no. 3:307–38.

————. 1989. The Gap between Striving and Achieving: The Case of Asian American Women. In *Making Waves*. Ed. Asian Women United. Boston: Beacon Press.

————. 1990. The "Overrepresentation" of Asian Americans: Red Herrings and Yellow Perils. *Sage Publications Race Relations Abstracts* 15, no. 2:3–36.

Woo, Deborah. 1994. *The Glass Ceiling and Asian Americans*, research monograph for the Federal Glass Ceiling Commission, Washington, D.C., July. (http: www.ilr.cornell.edu)

————. 1995. *The Status of Minority Faculty: Recruitment and Retention*. Report for Acting Dean Susan Harding, Social Science Division, University of California, Santa Cruz, August.

————. 1996. Asian Americans in Higher Education: Issues of Diversity and Access. *Race, Gender & Class* 3, no. 3:11–37.

Woodrum, Eric. 1981. An Assessment of Japanese American Assimilation, Pluralism, and Subordination. *American Journal of Sociology* 87, no. 1:157–69.

Wu, Diana Ting Liu. 1997. *Asian Pacific Americans in the Workplace*. Walnut Creek, CA: AltaMira Press.

Wu, Frank, and May Nicholson. 1997. Spring. Facial Aspects of Media Coverage on the John Huang Matter. *Asian American Policy Review* 7:1–37.

Xiaoge, Xiong. 1990. Asian-American Entrepreneurs Enrich Silicon Valley Tradition. *Electronic Business*, 12 November, 80–81.

Yamashita, Robert C., and Peter Park. 1985. The Politics of Race: The Open Door, Ozawa and the Case of the Japanese in America. *Review of Radical Political Economics* 17, no. 3:135–46.

Yamato, Alexander. 1993. Who Am I? Second Generation Asian Americans. In *Asian Americans in the United States*. 2 vols. Eds. Alexander Yamato, Soo-Young Chin, Wendy L. Ng, and Joel Franks. Dubuque, IA: Kendall/Hunt Publishing Co.

Yang, Jeff, and Betty Wong, eds. 1993. Power Brokers: The 25 Most Influential People in Asian America. *A. Magazine* 2, no. 3:25–34.

Yim, Sun Bin. 1984. The Social Structure of Korean Communities in California, 1903–1920. In *Labor Immigration under Capitalism: Asian Workers in the United States.* Eds. Lucie Cheng and Edna Bonacich. Berkeley: University of California Press.

Yun, Grace. 1989. Status of Asian American University Faculty. In *A Look beyond the Model Minority Image: Critical Issues in Asian America.* Ed. Grace Yun. New York: Minority Rights Group.

Yung, Judy. 1995. *Unbound Feet: A Social History of Chinese Women in San Francisco.* Berkeley: University of California Press.

Zavella, Patricia. 1987. *Women's Work & Chicano Families: Cannery Workers of the Santa Clara Valley.* Ithaca, NY: Cornell University Press.

Zhou, Min, and John R. Logan. 1989. Returns on Human Capital in Ethnic Enclaves: New York City's Chinatown. *American Sociological Review* 54:809–20, October.

Zweigenhaft, Richard L., and William Domhoff. 1998. *Diversity in the Power Elite: Have Women and Minorities Reached the Top?* New Haven, CT: Yale University Press.

Newspaper Articles

"A Reverse Brain Drain" in Taiwan. *Oakland Tribune*, 19 July 1993.

Aerospace Careers in Low Orbit. *Los Angeles Times*, 16 November 1992.

America's Opportunity Gap. *New York Times*, 5 June 1995.

Architecture Grad Students Detail Charges Against Faculty. *Daily Californian*, 11 November 1992.

Arts Philanthropist. *AsianWeek*, 3 November 1995.

Asian Americans' Awkward Status. *San Francisco Chronicle*, 22 August 1995.

Asian Americans Finding Cracks in the Glass Ceiling. *Los Angeles Times*, 15 July 1998.

Asian Growth in the 1990s. *San Francisco Chronicle*, 5 December 1988.

Asians Fear Shortchange in '90 Census. *Oakland Tribune*, 20 December 1987.

Asians Living in Lap of Luxury? *AsianWeek*, 19 June 1995.

Bad News for Asian American Journalists. *AsianWeek*, 13 August 1998.

Battling the Bamboo Ceiling. *Houston Post*, 31 May 1993.

Cal Architectural Department Accused of Harassment and Blatant Favoritism. *Oakland Tribune*, 28 October 1992.

Chinese American Establishes Job Recruiting Firm in Asia. *AsianWeek*, 30 September 1994.

Chinese in A Global Economy. *Oakland Tribune.* 26 May 1982.

Chong–Moon Lee. *San Francisco Chronicle*, 5 November 1995.

Discord at UC Berkeley Architecture School. *San Francisco Chronicle*, 19 October 1992.

East, West Teaching Traditions Collide. *San Jose Mercury News*, 23 February 1993.

For Big Fees, Towers Perrin Gave Clients Similar Reports. *Wall Street Journal*, 11 March 1997.

For Immigrant, A Billion-Dollar High-Tech Deal: Maryland Entrepreneur to Sell Firm He Founded. *Washington Post*, 28 April 1998.

Growing into the 21st Century. *AsianWeek*, 19 January 1997.

High-Tech Firm Targets APA Entrepreneurs. *AsianWeek*, 30 June 1995.

It's Asians' Turn in Silicon Valley. *New York Times*, 14 January 1992.

Labor of Language: Translators Grease Skids in Diverse Communities. *San Francisco Chronicle*, 15 July 1998.

The Mainstream Press and the Asian American Communities (editorial). *East/West News*, 4 August 1988.

New Sense of Race Arises among Asian-Americans. *New York Times*, 30 May 1996.

$1 Million Deal in UC Bias Suit. *San Francisco Chronicle*, 9 January 1996.

Over Affirmative Action Reveals Ambiguities on the Issue. *Washington Post*, 20 June 1998.

Professors Blast Census Plans for Asians in 1990. *AsianWeek*, 11 December 1987.

Report Cites Lack of Asians at Executive Levels in State Agencies. *East West News*, 5 September 1988.

"Reverse Brain Drain" Draws Asian Americans to Work Overseas. *AsianWeek*, 8 July 1994.

Review Rocks UC Architecture Department. *Daily Californian*, 13 November 1992.

Silicon Valley Pioneer. *AsianWeek*, 8 March 1996.

Skilled Asians Leaving U.S. for High-tech Jobs at Home. *New York Times*, 21 February 1995

Special Report: Asians in America. *San Francisco Chronicle*, 25–26 July 1988.

Students Urge UC to Quash Sex Bias. *San Francisco Examiner*, 17 November 1992

Success Story, Japanese American Style. *New York Times*, 9 January 1966.

Success Story of one Minority in the U.S. *U.S. News and World Report*, 26 December 1966

Tales of Sex Harassment at UC. *Oakland Tribune*, 17 November 1992.

INDEX